BAHÁ'Í
WORLD FAITH

BAHÁ'Í WORLD FAITH

SELECTED WRITINGS OF
BAHÁ'U'LLÁH AND
'ABDU'L-BAHÁ

The Prophetic Cycle
hath, verily, ended.
The Eternal Truth is
now come. *Bahá'u'lláh*

BAHÁ'Í PUBLISHING TRUST
Wilmette, Illinois, U. S. A.

Approved by the Reviewing Committee of the
National Spiritual Assembly.

Library of Congress Catalog Card Number: 56-8259

Second Edition, 1956
Third Printing, 1966

PRINTED IN U.S.A.

INTRODUCTION

The purpose of this book is to offer the student of religion a compilation of Bahá'í Sacred Writings which, in one convenient volume, discloses their universal range of themes, their direct application to modern life and their incomparable spiritual power. Here is a World Bible revealed for men of all races and lands; a new creation which affirms and fulfils the highest assurance which, from age to age, the succession of Prophets have enkindled within the human soul. The past is not denied but extended through the present to establish a firm foundation for a new era of justice and peace. The illumination cast upon our own age, indeed, reveals the former religions and their Founders in a clearer light than they have ever been manifest before. The Bahá'í concept of the unity of the Prophets of God bans religion as creed and ceremony but resurrects faith in realization of one eternal divine Truth which now, for the first time, can be apprehended in its plan and purpose for the human race.

What is the meaning of the word *Bahá'í?*

This word derives from the title by which the Founder of the Faith is known: Bahá'u'lláh, meaning "Glory of God." It designates the individual follower or believer, as Christian or Buddhist identifies the follower of Christ or Buddha. Like those words, it is also the adjective form used to describe whatever is directly related to the Faith, as for example, in the term Bahá'í religion, Bahá'í meeting or Bahá'í community. A Bahá'í is one who accepts Bahá'u'lláh as his Lord, knows His teachings and obeys His precepts; the Bahá'í religion is the religion of Bahá. The name 'Abdu'l-Bahá means "Servant of Bahá" and identifies the rank and mission of Bahá'u'lláh's eldest Son, the One appointed by Him to be the Interpreter of His Word, the Exemplar of His new creation, and the Center of His Covenant with mankind.

The range of theme found in the Bahá'í Writings is indicated by the subjects chosen for the nine chapters. In Chapter One we find passages on Bahá'u'lláh's statement of His Mission, and the nature of this Day. Chapter Two reveals the station of the Prophets in the one eternal Faith of God and of Bahá'u'lláh the Promised One. Chapter Three expounds the nature of the soul and the relationship of man to God through His Manifestation. In Chapter Four, Bahá'u'lláh establishes laws and principles for the new era. Chapter Five presents passages appointing 'Abdu'l-Bahá and describing His Mission as Interpreter and Center of Bahá'u'lláh's Covenant.

The next four chapters contain excerpts from writings and public addresses of 'Abdu'l-Bahá, which disclose application of the Bahá'í Teachings to life in our age. Thus, Chapter Six presents the text of addresses delivered in America on universal peace, and Chapter Seven illumines the spiritual mystery of man's being. In Chapter Eight we find passages which offer us 'Abdu'l-Bahá's consummate wisdom and love. Chapter Nine contains excerpts from 'Abdu'l-Bahá's Will and Testament, together with passages which trace the development and function of Bahá'í institutions as embodiment of the spirit of unity.

Bahá'u'lláh, whose given name was Ḥusayn-ʻAlí, was born on November 12, 1817, in the ancient land of Persia. Like Buddha, He appeared in a family of wealth and high degree qualified to secure for Him an eminent appointment in the imperial government of the Sháh. The Persia of that time remained in a condition resembling the feudalism of Europe. Arbitrary authority, unchecked by a constitution, was vested in the person of the Sháh and exercised through a socially irresponsible aristocracy at court and in provincial palaces. The system was interpenetrated by the customs and laws of a traditional Islám supported by a vast army of priests, teachers and ecclesiastical lords. Theology determined the aim and content of education. The mass of the people lived under the exploitation of a medieval church-state.

Confined within its own culture and territory, divided theologically even from other Islamic peoples by the bitter schism between Shíʻih and Sunní, left far behind by a West swiftly changing through science and technology, Persia nevertheless was stirring with its own vision of righteousness and religious reform.

Within Islám itself, certain teachers had, in prophetic tradition, found conviction that the fulfilment of ancient assurances was at hand. They felt that God had willed an end to evil, ignorance, injustice and hypocrisy. They foresaw a new Dispensation superseding the decadence that had overtaken the Faith of Muḥammad. They awaited a time of judgment and sifting of the people of the entire world. In the darkness engulfing their society they were as men with lanterns looking for the place of dawn.

In such a land, ignored by the West, where spiritual enlightenment contrasted with official corruption, feudal pomp with helpless serfdom, memory of departed glories with betrayal of the trust committed to them by Muḥammad, the Seal of the Prophets, Providence found the theatre for the enactment of the most stupendous events in the long, dramatic history of revealed religion.

Respected and admired for His qualities, virtues and essential dignity, untempted by the prizes of a public career, Ḥusáyn-'Alí came to His spiritual Mission on the path of sacrifice laid down by 'Alí-Muḥammad, known to history as the Báb. From May 23, 1844 to July 9, 1850, the Báb (the term meaning "Door" or "Gate") proclaimed the birth of a new, world Faith. He abrogated laws of the Muḥammadan Dispensation no longer effective; called upon kings and rulers to heed the Call and govern with justice; identified true faith in God with moral purity and righteous deeds; gathered about Him a company of devoted, heroic believers; aroused the spirit of hope among the people; and caused the clergy and civil authorities to be fearful of losing their privilege and power.

By order of church and state, the Báb was denounced as heretic and instigator of rebellion, subjected to the bastinado, twice immured in isolated castle-dungeons, and in 1850 this Martyr-Prophet was publicly executed in the city of Tabríz.

The Báb accomplished a twofold Mission. His Dispensation brought to an end the cycle of prophecy. He revealed the oneness of the Prophets. He inaugurated a new cycle of reality when the ancient assurances of faith are to be fulfilled in the unity of mankind. He also described His religion as preparation for the appearance of Bahá'u'lláh and Himself as Precursor, or Herald, of the greater One to follow Him. Though the spirit of all former Prophets returned to earth in Him, the religions of East and West knew Him not.

After the martyrdom of the Báb, official rancor centered upon Ḥusayn-'Alí, who had become the outstanding leader of the Bábí community. He was immured in a dungeon of Ṭihrán. During the year 1853, while He was suffering this affliction, the Holy Spirit descended and revealed to Him His Mission as Bahá'u'lláh, the Promised One of all religions and nations. In a letter addressed in a later year to the Sháh of Persia, Bahá'u'lláh wrote: "O king! I was but a man like others, asleep upon My couch, when lo, the breezes of the All-Glorious were wafted over Me, and taught Me the knowledge of all that hath been. This thing is not from me, but from One Who is Almighty and All-Knowing, and He bade Me lift up My voice between earth and heaven. . . ." (p. 55)

Forty years of exile and imprisonment had begun. From Ṭihrán, Bahá'u'lláh, members of His family and a company of followers of the Báb were sent to Baghdád, in the expectation that His absence from Persia would further weaken the remnant of believers. From Baghdád Bahá'u'lláh was exiled to Constantinople, which transferred jurisdiction of the civil and ecclesiastical charges from Persia to the Sultan, head of Sunní Islám. Under the Sultan, the policy of repression and of refusal to give Bahá'u'lláh a hearing continued. From Constantinople the party was dispatched to Adrianople. In 1868 the Turkish regime committed Bahá'u'lláh and His party to the pestilential prison-fortress of 'Akká, in Syria, now Israel.

Before leaving Baghdád for Constantinople, Bahá'u'lláh declared His Mission (1863) to the company of Bábís, and from that time the believers have been Bahá'ís save for the few who rejected His claim and sought to perpetuate Bábism beyond its destined time. It was in that city also that He revealed the incomparable *Kitáb-i-Íqán* (Book of Assurance) which opened the Holy Books and interpreted their laws and precepts as formative stages in the evolution of one World Faith. *The Kitáb-i-Íqán* is unsurpassed in its exposition of the unique stations of the former Prophets. Followers of those Faiths may well ponder those passages in which their essential purposes and spiritual significances are extolled.

At Adrianople Bahá'u'lláh proclaimed His Mission in Tablets addressed to kings and rulers, summoning them to true faith in God as trustees of the welfare of their people.

The period of Bahá'u'lláh's exile and confinement in 'Akká witnessed the climax of His Ministry and the rich harvest of His voluminous Revelation. Both to kings and to the world's religious leaders He directed appeals, warnings and exhortations, foreseeing the tribulations which must overtake mankind through repudiation of the Prophet whose Mission alone can unite the peoples and establish peace. (Excerpts from these Tablets are identified in the index of the present volume.) "Never since the beginning of the world hath the Message," He has stated, "been so openly proclaimed."

What have been termed "mighty and final effusions of His indefatigable pen"—Tablets revealing ordinances and truths—together with the Holy Book, characterize this fateful time. (Some of these Tablets appear in Chapter Four.)

Bahá'u'lláh's works include the mysticism of *Seven Valleys,* the succinct and vital wisdom of *Hidden Words,* the approach to God in prayer and meditation, proclamation to kings, appeal and warning to sacerdotal heads of religion, the interpretation of Sacred Scriptures, the establishment of institutions, the formulation of laws and the appointment of a Center of His Covenant effective after His own Ascension. No prior Revelation has so fully provided for the preservation and spread of its teachings in their essential purity, nor created the Order in which the religious community is to function and evolve.

Bahá'u'lláh ascended in 'Akká in 1892, His Revelation completed, His Mission fulfilled. His arrival in the Holy Land under decree of the Sultan brought to consummation the prophecy of Jewish and Christian scriptures. The land made holy by all the Prophets had received its Lord. His incarceration could not prevent Bahá'u'lláh from His expression of the divine Will.

The appointment by Bahá'u'lláh of 'Abdu'l-Bahá to be the Interpreter of His Word, Exemplar of His Faith and Center of His Covenant has no historic parallel. It means that divine authority and guidance continued after Bahá'u'lláh's Ascension. Revelation ceased, but the form, the mode, the pattern and the criterion were set up to assure the creation of a religious society unconditioned by the racial, creedal and nationalistic attitudes of the believers themselves. It means that the qualities requisite for such a task were available. The Bahá'ís have more than a Book; they have a continuing leadership raised above their human control. From 1892 'Abdu'l-Bahá's Mission unfolded until His death in 1921—thirty years, the life of a generation, expressed through countless actions, letters, discussions and public discourses which proclaimed the Faith to the world and gave it application to the mental and social life of our time.

Unlike former Prophets, Bahá'u'lláh likewise could create a social institution, the House of Justice, its members to be chosen by the Bahá'ís and its deliberations promised His inspiration.

By His appointment of 'Abdu'l-Bahá, and His establishment of a new social order, Bahá'u'lláh has provided for the uninterrupted continuance of the providential element in religion and supplied the means by which humanity can direct its powers into the channels of progress and peace.

'Abdu'l-Bahá fulfilled His Mission by providing a Will and Testament to take effect after His departure. In this document He described the social institutions of the Faith and established a hereditary Guardianship within the family of Bahá'u'lláh qualified to interpret the sacred writings and preside at deliberations of the International House of Justice.

The Bahá'í community has survived and been tested and purified at successive stages by bitter persecution, by the Ascension of Bahá'u'lláh and by the death of 'Abdu'l-Bahá. Their faith is not only reverence for Bahá'u'lláh but unity of action in a worldwide order. The whole man, and the wholeness of his relationship to society, now has a spiritual meaning and sanction. The division of religion into lay and clerical elements has come to an end.

HORACE HOLLEY

CONTENTS

I

WRITINGS OF BAHÁ'U'LLÁH

II

WRITINGS OF 'ABDU'L-BAHÁ

I
WORDS OF BAHÁ'U'LLÁH

BAHÁ'Í World Faith

CHAPTER ONE

THE GREAT ANNOUNCEMENT

The Purpose of the Prophets

The Revelation which, from time immemorial, hath been acclaimed as the Purpose and Promise of all the Prophets of God, and the most cherished Desire of His Messengers, hath now, by virtue of the pervasive Will of the Almighty and at His irresistible bidding, been revealed unto men. The advent of such a Revelation hath been heralded in all the sacred Scriptures. Behold how, notwithstanding such an announcement, mankind hath strayed from its path and shut out itself from its glory.

Say: O ye lovers of the One true God! Strive, that ye may truly recognize and know Him, and observe befittingly His precepts. This is a Revelation, under which, if a man shed for its sake one drop of blood, myriads of oceans will be his recompense. Take heed, O friends, that ye forfeit not so inestimable a benefit, or disregard its transcendent station. Consider the multitude of lives that have been, and are still being, sacrificed in a world deluded by a mere phantom which the vain imaginations of its peoples have conceived. Render thanks unto God, inasmuch as ye have attained unto your heart's Desire, and been united to Him Who is the Promise of all nations. Guard ye, with the aid of the one true God—exalted be His glory—the integrity of the station which ye have attained, and cleave to that which shall promote His Cause. He, verily, enjoineth on you what is right and conducive to the exaltation of man's station. Glorified be the All-Merciful, the Revealer of this wondrous Tablet.

The True Believer

Behold, how the divers peoples and kindreds of the earth have been waiting for the coming of the Promised One. No sooner had He, Who is the Sun of Truth, been made manifest, than, lo, all turned away from Him, except them whom God was pleased to guide. We dare not, in this Day, lift the veil that concealeth the exalted station which every true believer can attain, for the joy which such a revelation must provoke might well cause a few to faint away and die.

He Who is the Heart and Center of the Bayán hath written: "The germ that holdeth within itself the potentialities of the Revelation that is to come is endowed with a potency superior to the combined forces of all those who follow Me." And, again, He saith: "Of all the tributes I have paid to Him Who is to come after Me, the greatest is this, My written confession, that no words of Mine can adequately describe Him, nor can any reference to Him in My Book, the Bayán, do justice to His Cause."

Whoso hath searched the depths of the oceans that lie hid within these exalted words, and fathomed their import, can be said to have discovered a glimmer of the unspeakable glory with which this mighty, this sublime, and most holy Revelation hath been endowed. From the excellence of so great a Revelation the honor with which its faithful followers must needs be invested can be well imagined. By the righteousness of the one true God! The very breath of these souls is in itself richer than all the treasures of the earth. Happy is the man that hath attained thereunto, and woe betide the heedless.

This Wondrous Day

Verily I say, this is the Day in which mankind can behold the Face, and hear the Voice, of the Promised One. The Call of God hath been raised, and the light of His countenance hath been lifted up upon men. It behoveth every man to blot out the trace of every idle word from the tablet of his heart, and to gaze, with an open and unbiased mind, on the signs of His Revelation, the proofs of His Mission, and the tokens of His glory.

Great indeed is this day! The allusions made to it in all the sacred Scriptures as the Day of God attest its greatness. The soul of every Prophet of God, of every Divine Messenger, hath thirsted for this wondrous Day. All the divers kindreds of the earth have, likewise, yearned to attain it. No sooner, however, had the Day Star of His Revelation manifested itself in the heaven of God's Will, than all, except those whom the Almighty was pleased to guide, were found dumbfounded and heedless.

O thou that hast remembered Me! The most grievous veil hath shut out the peoples of the earth from His glory, and hindered them from hearkening to His call. God grant that the light of unity may envelop the whole earth, and that the seal, "the Kingdom is God's," may be stamped upon the brow of all its peoples.

How Severe the Tests

By the righteousness of God! These are the days in which God hath proved the hearts of the entire company of His Messengers and Prophets, and beyond them those that stand guard over His sacred and inviolable Sanctuary, the inmates of the celestial Pavilion and dwellers of the Tabernacle of Glory. How severe, therefore, the test to which they who join partners with God must needs be subjected!

The Time Fore-Ordained

The time fore-ordained unto the peoples and kindreds of the earth is now come. The promises of God, as recorded in the holy Scriptures, have all been fulfilled. Out of Zion hath gone forth the Law of God, and Jerusalem, and the hills and land thereof, are filled with the glory of His Revelation. Happy is the man that pondereth in his heart that which hath been revealed in the Books of God, the Help in Peril, the Self-Subsisting. Meditate upon this, O ye beloved of God, and let your ears be attentive unto His Word, so that ye may, by His grace and mercy, drink your fill from the crystal waters of constancy, and become as steadfast and immovable as the mountain in His Cause.

In the Book of Isaiah it is written: "Enter into the rock, and hide thee in the dust, for fear of the Lord, and for the glory of His majesty." No man that meditateth upon this verse can fail to recognize the greatness of this Cause, or doubt the exalted character of this Day—the Day of God Himself. This same verse is followed by these words: "And the Lord alone shall be exalted in that Day." This is the Day which the Pen of the Most High hath glorified in all the holy Scriptures. There is no verse in them that doth not declare the glory of His holy Name, and no Book that doth not testify unto the loftiness of this most exalted theme. Were We to make mention of all that hath been revealed in these heavenly Books and holy Scriptures concerning this Revelation, this Tablet would assume impossible dimensions. It is incumbent, in this Day, upon every man to place his whole trust in the manifold bounties of God, and arise to disseminate, with the utmost wisdom, the verities of His Cause. Then, and only then, will the whole earth be enveloped with the morning light of His Revelation.

Beware Lest Ye Fail

Bestir yourselves, O people, in anticipation of the days of Divine justice, for the promised hour is now come. Beware lest ye fail to apprehend its import and be accounted among the erring.

Why the People Have Denied God

Consider the past. How many, both high and low, have, at all times, yearningly awaited the advent of the Manifestations of God in the sanctified persons of His chosen Ones. How often have they expected His coming, how frequently have they prayed that the breeze of Divine mercy might blow, and the promised Beauty step forth from behind the veil of concealment, and be made manifest to all the world. And whensoever the portals of grace did open, and the clouds of divine bounty did rain upon mankind, and the light of the Unseen did shine above the horizon of celestial might, they all denied Him, and turned away from His face—the face of God Himself. . . .

Reflect, what could have been the motive for such deeds? What could have prompted such behavior towards the Revealers of the beauty of the All-Glorious? Whatever in days gone by hath been the cause of the denial and opposition of those people hath now led to the perversity of the people of this age. To maintain that the testimony of Providence was incomplete, that it hath therefore been the cause of the denial of the people, is but open blasphemy. How far from the grace of the All-Bountiful and from His loving providence and tender mercies it is to single out a soul from amongst all men for the guidance of His creatures, and, on one hand, to withhold from Him the full measure of His divine testimony, and, on the other, inflict severe retribution on His people for having turned away from His chosen One! Nay, the manifold bounties of the Lord of all beings have, at all times, through the Manifestations of His Divine Essence, encompassed the earth and all that dwell therein. Not for a moment hath His grace been withheld, nor have the showers of His loving-kindness ceased to rain upon mankind. Consequently, such behavior can be attributed to naught save the petty-mindedness of such souls as tread the valley of arrogance and pride, are lost in the wilds of remoteness, walk in the ways of their idle fancy, and follow the dictates of the leaders of their faith. Their chief concern is mere opposition; their sole desire is to ignore the truth. Unto every discerning observer it is evident and manifest that had these people in the days of each of the Manifestations of the Sun of Truth sanctified their eyes, their ears, and their hearts from whatever they had seen, heard, and felt, they surely would not have been deprived of beholding the beauty of God, nor strayed far from the habitations of glory. But having weighed the testimony of God by the standard of their own knowledge, gleaned from the teachings of the leaders of their faith, and found it at variance with their limited understanding, they arose to perpetrate such unseemly acts. . . .

Consider Moses! Armed with the rod of celestial dominion, adorned with the white hand of Divine knowledge, and proceeding from the Párán of the love of God, and wielding the serpent of power and everlasting majesty, He shone forth from the Sinai of light upon the world. He summoned all the peoples and kindreds of the earth to the kingdom of eternity, and invited them to partake of the fruit of the tree of faithfulness. Surely you are aware of the fierce opposition of Pharaoh and his people, and of the stones of idle fancy which the hands of infidels cast upon that blessed Tree. So much so that Pharaoh and his people finally arose and exerted their utmost endeavor to extinguish with the waters of falsehood and denial the fire of that sacred Tree, oblivious of the truth that no earthly water can quench the flames of Divine wisdom, nor mortal blasts extinguish the lamp of everlasting dominion. Nay, rather, such water cannot but intensify the burning of the flame, and such blasts cannot but insure the preservation of the lamp, were ye to observe with the eye of discernment, and walk in the way of God's holy will and pleasure. . . .

And when the days of Moses were ended, and the light of Jesus, shining forth from the Day Spring of the Spirit, encompassed the world, all the people of Israel arose in protest against Him. They clamored that He Whose advent the Bible had foretold must needs promulgate and fulfil the laws of Moses, whereas this youthful Nazarene, who laid claim to the station of the divine Messiah, had annulled the laws of divorce and of the sabbath day—the most weighty of all the laws of Moses. Moreover, what of the signs of the Manifestation yet to come? These people of Israel are even unto the present day still expecting that Manifestation which the Bible hath foretold! How many Manifestations of Holiness, how many Revealers of the light everlasting, have appeared since the time of Moses, and yet Israel, wrapt in the densest veils of satanic fancy and false imaginings, is still expectant that the idol of her own handiwork will appear with such signs as she herself hath conceived! Thus hath God laid hold of them for their sins, hath extinguished in them the spirit of faith, and tormented them with the flames of the nethermost fire. And this for no other reason except that Israel refused to apprehend the meaning of such words as have been revealed in the Bible concerning the signs of the coming Revelation. As she never grasped their true significance, and, to outward seeming, such events never came to pass, she, therefore, remained deprived of recognizing the beauty of Jesus and of beholding the Face of God. And they still await His coming! From time immemorial even unto this day, all the kindreds and peoples of the earth have clung to such fanciful and unseemly thoughts, and thus have deprived themselves of the clear waters streaming from the springs of purity and holiness. . . .

To them that are endowed with understanding, it is clear and manifest that, when the fire of the love of Jesus consumed the veils of Jewish limitations, and His authority was made apparent and partially enforced, He, the Revealer of the unseen Beauty, addressing one day His disciples, referred unto His passing, and, kindling in their hearts the fire of bereavement, said unto them: "I go away and come again unto you." And in another place He said: "I go and another will come, Who will tell you all that I have not told you, and will fulfil all that I have said." Both these sayings have but one meaning, were ye to ponder upon the Manifestations of the Unity of God with Divine insight.

Every discerning observer will recognize in the Dispensation of the Qur'án both the Book and the Cause of Jesus were confirmed. As to the matter of names, Muḥammad, Himself, declared: "I am Jesus." He recognized the truth of the signs, prophecies, and words of Jesus, and testified that they were all of God. In this sense, neither the person of Jesus nor His writings hath differed from that of Muḥammad and of His holy Book, inasmuch as both have championed the Cause of God, uttered His praise, and revealed His commandments. Thus it is that Jesus, Himself, declared: "I go away and come again unto you." Consider the sun. Were it to say now, "I am the sun of yesterday," it would speak the truth. And should it, bearing the sequence of time in mind, claim to be other than that sun, it still would speak the truth. In like manner, if it be said that all the days are but one and the same, it is correct and true. And if it be said, with respect to their particular names and designations, that they differ, that again is true. For though they are the same, yet one doth recognize in each a separate designation, a specific attribute, a particular character. Conceive accordingly the distinction, variation, and unity characteristic of the various Manifestations of holiness, that thou mayest comprehend the allusions made by the Creator of all names and attributes to the mysteries of distinction and unity, and discover the answer to thy question as to why that everlasting

Beauty should have, at sundry times, called Himself by different names and titles. . . .

When the Unseen, the Eternal, the Divine Essence, caused the Day Star of Muḥammad to rise above the horizon of knowledge, among the cavils which the Jewish divines raised against Him was that after Moses no Prophet should be sent of God. Yea, mention hath been made in the Scriptures of a Soul Who must needs be made manifest and Who will advance the Faith, and promote the interests of the people of Moses, so that the Law of the Mosaic Dispensation may encompass the whole earth. Thus hath the King of eternal glory referred in His Book to the words uttered by those wanderers in the vale of remoteness and error: " 'The hand of God,' say the Jews, 'is chained up.' Chained up be their own hands; and for that which they have said, they were accursed. Nay, outstretched are both His hands!" "The hand of God is above their hands." Although the commentators of the Qur'án have related in divers manners the circumstances attending the revelation of this verse, yet thou shouldst endeavor to apprehend the purpose thereof. He saith: How false is that which the Jews have imagined! How can the hand of Him Who is the King in truth, Who caused the countenance of Moses to be made manifest, and conferred upon Him the robe of Prophethood—how can the hand of such a One be chained and fettered? How can He be conceived as powerless to raise up yet another Messenger after Moses? Behold the absurdity of their saying; how far it hath strayed from the path of knowledge and understanding! Observe how in this Day also, all these people have occupied themselves with such foolish absurdities. For over a thousand years they have been reciting this verse, and unwittingly pronouncing their censure against the Jews, utterly unaware, that they themselves, openly and privily, are voicing the sentiments and belief of the Jewish people! Thou art surely aware of their idle contention, that all Revelation is ended, that the portals of Divine mercy are closed, that from the day springs of eternal holiness no Sun shall rise again, that the Ocean of everlasting bounty is forever stilled, and that out of the Tabernacle of ancient glory the Messengers of God have ceased to be made manifest. Such is the measure of the understanding of these small-minded, contemptible people. These people have imagined that the flow of God's all-encompassing grace and plenteous mercies, the cessation of which no mind can contemplate, has been halted. From every side they have risen and girded up the loins of tyranny, and exerted the utmost endeavor to quench with the bitter waters of their vain fancy the flame of God's Burning Bush, oblivious that the globe of power shall, within its own mighty stronghold, protect the Lamp of God. . . .

Behold how the sovereignty of Muḥammad, the Messenger of God, is today apparent and manifest amongst the people. You are well aware of what befell His Faith in the early days of His Dispensation. What woeful sufferings did the hand of the infidel and erring, the divines of that age and their associates, inflict upon that spiritual Essence, that most pure and holy Being! How abundant the thorns and briars which they have strewn over His path! It is evident that that wretched generation, in their wicked and satanic fancy, regarded every injury to that immortal Being as a means to the attainment of an abiding felicity; inasmuch as the recognized divines of that age, such as 'Abdu'lláh-i-Ubayy, Abú Amír, the hermit, Ka'b-ibn-i-Ashraf, and Naḍr-ibn-i-iḤariṯẖ, all treated Him as an impostor, and pronounced Him a lunatic and a calumniator. Such sore accusations they brought against Him that in recounting them God forbiddeth the ink to flow, Our pen to move, or the page to bear them. These malicious imputations provoked the people to arise and torment Him. And how fierce that torment, if the divines of the age be its chief instigators, if they denounce Him to their followers, cast Him out from their midst, and declare Him a miscreant! Hath not the same befallen this Servant, and been witnessed by all?

For this reason did Muḥammad cry out: "No Prophet of God hath suffered such harm as I have suffered." And in the Qur'án are recorded all the calumnies and reproaches uttered against Him, as well as all the afflictions which He suffered. Refer ye thereunto, that haply ye may be informed of that which hath befallen His Revelation. So grievous was His plight, that for a time all ceased to hold intercourse with Him and His companions. Whoever associated with Him fell a victim to the relentless cruelty of His enemies. . . .

Consider, how great is the change today! Behold, how many are the Sovereigns who bow the knee before His name! How numerous the nations and kingdoms who have sought the shelter of His shadow, who bear allegiance to His Faith, and pride themselves therein! From the pulpit-top there ascendeth today the words of praise which, in utter lowliness, glorify His blessed name; and from the heights of minarets there resoundeth the call that summoneth the concourse of His people to adore Him. Even those Kings of the earth who have refused to embrace His Faith and to put off the garment of unbelief, none-the-less confess and acknowledge the greatness and overpowering majesty of that Day Star of loving-kindness. Such is His earthly sovereignty, the evidences of which thou dost on every side behold. This sovereignty must needs be revealed and established either in the lifetime of every Manifestation of God or after His ascension unto His true habitation in the realms above. . . .

It is evident that the changes brought about in every Dispensation constitute the dark clouds that intervene between the eye of man's understanding and the Divine Luminary which shineth forth from the day spring of the Divine Essence. Consider how men for generations have been blindly imitating their fathers, and have been trained according to such ways and manners as have been laid down by the dictates of their Faith. Were these men, therefore, to discover suddenly that a Man, Who hath been living in their midst, Who, with respect to every human limitation, hath been their equal, had risen to abolish every established principle imposed by their Faith—principles by which for centuries they have been disciplined, and every opposer and denier of which they have come to regard as infidel, profligate and wicked,—they would of a certainty be veiled and hindered from acknowledging His truth. Such things are as "clouds" that veil the eyes of those whose inner being hath not tasted the Salsibil of detachment, nor drunk from the Kawthar of the knowledge of God. Such men, when acquainted with those circumstances, become so veiled that, without the least question, they pronounce the Manifestation of God as infidel, and sentence Him to death. You must have heard of such things taking place all down the ages, and are now observing them in these days.

It behoveth us, therefore, to make the utmost endeavor, that, by God's invisible assistance, these dark veils, these clouds of Heaven-sent trials, may not hinder us from beholding the beauty of His shining Countenance, and that we may recognize Him only by His own Self.

Manifestations of God

To every discerning and illuminated heart it is evident that God, the unknowable Essence, the Divine Being, is immensely exalted beyond every human attribute, such as corporeal existence, ascent and descent, egress and regress. Far be it from His glory that human tongue should adequately recount His praise, or that human heart comprehend His fathomless mystery. He is, and hath ever been, veiled in the ancient eternity of His Essence, and will remain in His Reality everlastingly hidden from the sight of men. "No vision taketh in Him, but He taketh in all vision; He is the Subtile, the All-Perceiving." . . .

The door of the knowledge of the Ancient of Days being thus closed in the face of all beings, the Source of infinite grace, according to His saying, "His grace hath transcended all things; My grace hath encompassed them all," hath caused those luminous Gems of Holiness to appear out of the realm of the spirit, in the noble form of the human temple, and be made manifest unto all men, that they may impart unto the world the mysteries of the unchangeable Being, and tell of the subtleties of His imperishable Essence.

These sanctified Mirrors, these Day Springs of ancient glory, are, one and all, the Exponents on earth of Him Who is the central Orb of the universe, its Essence and ultimate Purpose. From Him proceed their knowledge and power; from Him is derived their sovereignty. The beauty of their countenance is but a reflection of His image, and their revelation a sign of His deathless glory.

They are the Treasuries of Divine knowledge, and the Repositories of celestial wisdom. Through them is transmitted a grace that is infinite, and by them is revealed the Light that can never fade. . . . These Tabernacles of Holiness, these Primal Mirrors which reflect the light of unfading glory, are but expressions of Him Who is the Invisible of the Invisibles. By the revelation of these Gems of Divine virtue all the names and attributes of God, such as knowledge and power, sovereignty and dominion, mercy and wisdom, glory, bounty, and grace, are made manifest.

These attributes of God are not, and have never been, vouchsafed specially unto certain Prophets, and withheld from others. Nay, all the Prophets of God, His well-favored, His holy and chosen Messengers are, without exception, the bearers of His names, and the embodiment of His attributes. They only differ in the intensity of their revelation, and the comparative potency of their light. Even as He hath revealed: "Some of the Apostles We have caused to excel the others."

It hath, therefore, become manifest and evident that within the tabernacles of these Prophets and chosen Ones of God the light of His infinite names and exalted attributes hath been reflected, even though the light of some of these attributes may or may not be outwardly revealed from these luminous Temples to the eyes of men. That a certain attribute of God hath not been outwardly manifested by these Essences of Detachment doth in no wise imply that they who are the Day Springs of God's attributes and the Treasuries of His holy names did not actually possess it. Therefore, these illuminated souls, these beauteous Countenances have, each and every one of them, been endowed with all the attributes of God, such as sovereignty, dominion, and the like, even though to outward seeming they be shorn of all earthly majesty. . . .

The Truth of His Mission

Know thou of a certainty that the Unseen can in no wise incarnate His Essence and reveal it unto men. He is, and hath ever been, immensely exalted beyond all that can either be recounted or perceived. From His retreat of glory His voice is ever proclaiming: "Verily, I am God; there is none other God besides Me, the All-Knowing, the All-Wise. I have manifested Myself unto men, and have sent down Him Who is the Day Spring of the signs of My Revelation. Through Him I have caused all creation to testify that there is none other God except Him, the Incomparable, the All-Informed, the All-Wise." He Who is everlastingly hidden from the eyes of men can never be known except through His Manifestation, and His Manifestation can adduce no greater proof of the truth of His Mission than the proof of His own Person.

The Standard of His Truth

O Salmán! The door of the knowledge of the Ancient Being hath ever been, and will continue for ever to be, closed in the face of men. No man's understanding shall ever gain access unto His holy court. As a token of His mercy, however, and as a proof of His loving-kindness, He hath manifested unto men the Day Stars of His divine guidance, the Symbols of His divine unity, and hath ordained the knowledge of these sanctified Beings to be identical with the knowledge of His own Self. Whoso recognizeth them hath recognized God. Whoso hearkeneth to their call, hath hearkened to the Voice of God, and whoso testifieth to the truth of their Revelation, hath testified to the truth of God Himself. Whoso turneth away from them, hath turned away from God, and whoso disbelieveth in them, hath disbelieved in God. Every one of them is the Way of God that connecteth this world with the realms above, and the Standard of His Truth unto every one in the kingdoms of earth and heaven. They are the Manifestations of God amidst men, the evidences of His Truth, and the signs of His glory.

Oneness of the Prophets

The Bearers of the Trust of God are made manifest unto the peoples of the earth as the Exponents of a new Cause and the Revealers of a new Message. Inasmuch as these Birds of the celestial Throne are all sent down from the heaven of the Will of God, and as they all arise to proclaim His irresistible Faith, they, therefore, are regarded as one soul and the same person. For they all drink from the one Cup of the love of God, and all partake of the fruit of the same Tree of Oneness.

These Manifestations of God have each a twofold station. One is the station of pure abstraction and essential unity. In this respect, if thou callest them all by one name, and dost ascribe to them the same attributes, thou hast not erred from the truth. Even as He hath revealed: "No distinction do We make between any of His Messengers." For they, one and all, summon the people of the earth to acknowledge the unity of God, and herald unto them the Kawthar of an infinite grace and bounty. They are all invested with the robe of prophethood, and are honored with the mantle of glory. Thus hath Muḥammad, the Point of the Qur'án, revealed: "I am all the Prophets." Likewise, He saith: "I am the first Adam, Noah, Moses, and Jesus." Similar statements have been made by Imám 'Alí. Sayings such as these, which indicate the essential unity of those Exponents of Oneness, have also emanated from the Channels of God's immortal utterance, and the Treasuries of the gems of Divine knowledge, and have been recorded in the Scriptures. These Countenances are the recipients of the Divine Command, and the Day Springs of His Revelation. This Revelation is exalted above the veils of plurality and the exigencies of number. Thus He saith: "Our Cause is but One." Inasmuch as the Cause is one and the same, the Exponents thereof also must needs be one and the same. Likewise, the Imáms of the Muḥammadan Faith, those lamps of certitude, have said: "Muḥammad is our first, Muḥammad is our last, Muḥammad our all."

It is clear and evident to thee that all the Prophets are the Temples of the Cause of God, Who have appeared clothed in divers attire. If thou wilt observe with discriminating eyes, thou wilt behold them all abiding in the same tabernacle, soaring in the same heaven, seated upon the same throne, uttering the same speech, and proclaiming the same Faith. Such is the unity of those Essences of Being, those Luminaries of infinite and immeasurable splendor! Wherefore, should one of these Manifestations of Holiness proclaim saying: "I am the return of all the Prophets," He, verily, speaketh the truth. In like manner, in every subsequent Revelation, the return of the former Revelation is a fact, the truth of which is firmly established. . . .

The other station is the station of distinction, and pertaineth to the world of creation, and to the limitations thereof. In this respect, each Manifestation of God hath a distinct individuality, a definitely prescribed mission, a predestined revelation, and specially designated limitations. Each one of them is known by a different name, is characterized by a special attribute, fulfils a definite mission, and is entrusted with a particular Revelation. Even as He saith: "Some of the Apostles We have caused to excel the others. To some God hath spoken, some He hath raised and exalted. And to Jesus, Son of Mary, We gave manifest signs, and We strengthened Him with the Holy Spirit."

It is because of this difference in their station and mission that the words and utterances flowing from these Well Springs of Divine knowledge appear to diverge and differ. Otherwise, in the eyes of them that are initiated into the mysteries of Divine wisdom, all their utterances are, in reality, but the expressions of one Truth. As most of the people have failed to appreciate those stations to which We have referred, they, therefore, feel perplexed and dismayed at the varying utterances pronounced by Manifestations that are essentially one and the same.

It hath ever been evident that all these divergencies of utterance are attributable to differences of station. Thus, viewed from the standpoint of their oneness and sublime detachment, the attributes of Godhead, Divinity, Supreme Singleness, and Inmost Essence, have been, and are applicable to those Essences of Being, inasmuch as they all abide on the throne of Divine Revelation, and are established upon the seat of Divine Concealment. Through their appearance the Revelation of God is made manifest, and by their countenance the Beauty of God is revealed. Thus it is that the accents of God Himself have been heard uttered by these Manifestations of the Divine Being.

Viewed in the light of their second station — the station of distinction, differentiation, temporal limitations, characteristics and standards—they manifest absolute servitude, utter destitution, and complete self-effacement. Even as He saith: "I am the servant of God. I am but a man like you." . . .

Were any of the all-embracing Manifestations of God to declare: "I am God," He, verily, speaketh the truth, and no doubt attacheth thereto. For it hath been repeatedly demonstrated that through their Revelation, their attributes and names, the Revelation of God, His names and His attributes, are made manifest in the world. Thus, He hath revealed: "Those shafts were God's, not Thine." And also He saith: "In truth, they who plighted fealty unto Thee, really plighted that fealty unto God." And were any of them to voice the utterance, "I am the Messenger of God," He also speaketh the truth, the indubitable truth. Even as He saith: "Muḥammad is not the father of any man among you, but He is the Messenger of God." Viewed in this light, they are all but Messengers of that ideal King, that unchangeable Essence. And were they all to proclaim, "I am the Seal of the Prophets," they, verily, utter but the truth, beyond the faintest shadow of doubt. For they are all but one person, one soul, one spirit, one being, one revelation. They are all the manifestation of the "Beginning" and the "End," the "First" and the "Last," the "Seen" and "Hidden"—all of which pertain to Him Who is the Innermost Spirit of Spirits and Eternal Essence of Essences. And were they to say, "We are the Servants of God," this also is a manifest and indisputable fact. For they have been made manifest in the uttermost state of servitude, a servitude the like of which no man can possibly attain. Thus in moments in which these Essences of Being were deep immersed beneath the oceans of ancient and everlasting holiness, or when they soared to the loftiest summits of Divine mysteries, they claimed their utterances to be the Voice of Divinity, the Call of God Himself.

Were the eye of discernment to be opened, it would recognize that in this very state, they have considered themselves utterly effaced and non-existent in the face of Him Who is the All-Pervading, the Incorruptible. Methinks, they have regarded themselves as utter nothingness, and deemed their mention in that

Court an act of blasphemy. For the slightest whisperings of self within such a Court is an evidence of self-assertion and independent existence. In the eyes of them that have attained unto that Court, such a suggestion is itself a grievous transgression. How much more grievous would it be, were aught else to be mentioned in that Presence, were man's heart, his tongue, his mind, or his soul, to be busied with any one but the Well-Beloved, were his eyes to behold any countenance other than His beauty, were his ear to be inclined to any melody but His Voice, and were his feet to tread any way but His way. . . .

By virtue of this station they have claimed for themselves the Voice of Divinity and the like, whilst by virtue of their station of Messengership, they have declared themselves the Messengers of God. In every instance they have voiced an utterance that would conform to the requirements of the occasion, and have ascribed all these declarations to Themselves, declarations ranging from the realm of Divine Revelation to the realm of creation, and from the domain of Divinity even unto the domain of earthly existence. Thus it is that whatsoever be their utterance, whether it pertain to the realm of Divinity, Lordship, Prophethood, Messengership, Guardianship, Apostleship, or Servitude, all is true, beyond the shadow of a doubt. Therefore these sayings which We have quoted in support of Our argument must be attentively considered, that the divergent utterances of the Manifestations of the Unseen and Day Springs of Holiness may cease to agitate the soul and perplex the mind.

Breakers of the Covenant

Consider the former generations. Witness how every time the Day Star of Divine bounty hath shed the light of His Revelation upon the world, the people of His Day have arisen against Him, and repudiated His truth. They who were regarded as the leaders of men have invariably striven to hinder their followers from turning unto Him Who is the Ocean of God's limitless bounty.

Behold how the people, as a result of the verdict pronounced by the divines of His age, have cast Abraham, the Friend of God, into fire; how Moses, He Who held converse with the Almighty, was denounced as liar and slanderer. Reflect how Jesus, the Spirit of God, was, notwithstanding His extreme meekness and perfect tender-heartedness, treated by His enemies. So fierce was the opposition which He, the Essence of Being and Lord of the visible and invisible, had to face, that He had nowhere to lay His head. He wandered continually from place to place, deprived of a permanent abode. Ponder that which befell Muḥammad, the Seal of the Prophets, may the life of all else be a sacrifice unto Him. How severe the afflictions which the leaders of the Jewish people and of the idol-worshipers caused to rain upon Him, Who is the sovereign Lord of all, in consequence of His proclamation of the unity of God and of the truth of His Message! By the righteousness of My Cause! My Pen groaneth, and all created things weep with a great weeping, as a result of the woes He suffered at the hands of them that have broken the Covenant of God, violated His Testament, rejected His proofs, and disputed His signs. Thus recount We unto thee the tale of that which happened in days past, haply thou mayest comprehend.

Thou hast known how grievously the Prophets of God, His Messengers and Chosen Ones, have been afflicted. Meditate a while on the motive and reason which have been responsible for such a persecution. At no time, in no Dispensation, have the Prophets of God escaped the blasphemy of their enemies, the cruelty of their oppressors, the denunciation of the learned of their age, who appeared in the guise of uprightness and piety. Day and night they passed through such agonies as none can ever measure, except the knowledge of the one true God, exalted be His glory.

Consider this wronged One. Though the clearest proofs attest the truth of His Cause; though the prophecies He, in an unmistakable language, hath made have been fulfilled; though, in spite of His not being accounted among the learned, His being unschooled and inexperienced in the disputations current among the divines, He hath rained upon men the showers of His manifold and Divinely-inspired knowledge; yet, behold how this generation hath rejected His authority, and rebelled against Him! He hath, during the greater part of His life, been sore-tried in the clutches of His enemies. His sufferings have now reached their culmination in this afflictive Prison, into which His oppressors have so unjustly thrown Him. God grant that, with a penetrating vision and radiant heart, thou mayest observe the things that have come to pass and are now happening, and, pondering them in thine heart, mayest recognize that which most men have, in this Day, failed to perceive. Please God, He may enable thee to inhale the sweet fragrance of His Day, to partake of the limitless effusions of His grace, to quaff thy fill, through His gracious favor, from the most great Ocean that surgeth in this Day in the name of the Ancient King, and to remain firm and immovable as the mountain in His Cause.

Say: Glory be to Thee Who hast caused all the holy Ones to confess their helplessness before the manifold revelations of Thy might, and every Prophet to acknowledge His nothingness at the effulgence of Thy abiding glory. I beseech Thee, by Thy name that hath unlocked the gates of Heaven and filled with ecstacy the Concourse on high, to enable me to serve Thee, in this Day, and to strengthen me to observe that which Thou didst prescribe in Thy Book. Thou knowest, O my Lord, what is in me; but I know not what is in Thee. Thou art the All-Knowing, the All-Informed.

The Meaning of True Unity

Beware, O believers in the Unity of God, lest ye be tempted to make any distinction between any of the Manifestations of His Cause, or to discriminate against the signs that have accompanied and proclaimed their Revelation. This indeed is the true meaning of Divine Unity, if ye be of them that apprehend and believe this truth. Be ye assured, moreover, that the works and acts of each and every one of these Manifestations of God, nay whatever pertaineth unto them, and whatsoever they may manifest in the future, are all ordained by God, and are a reflection of His Will and Purpose. Whoso maketh the slightest possible difference between their persons, their words, their messages, their acts and manners, hath indeed disbelieved in God, hath repudiated His signs, and betrayed the Cause of His Messengers.

The Prophetic Cycle Hath Ended

It is evident that every age in which a Manifestation of God hath lived is divinely ordained, and may, in a sense, be characterized as God's appointed Day. This Day, however, is unique, and is to be distinguished from those that have preceded it. The designation "Seal of the Prophets" fully revealeth its high station. The Prophetic Cycle hath, verily, ended. The Eternal Truth is now come. He hath lifted up the Ensign of Power, and is now shedding upon the world the unclouded splendor of His Revelation.

He Hath Recreated All Things

Praise be to God, the All-Possessing, the King of incomparable glory, a praise which is immeasurably above the understanding of all created things, and is exalted beyond the grasp of the minds of men. None else besides Him hath ever been able to sing adequately His praise, nor will any man succeed at any time in describing the full measure of His glory. Who is it that can claim to have attained the heights of His exalted Essence, and what mind can measure the depths of His unfathomable mystery? From each and every revelation emanating from the Source of His glory, holy and never-ending evidences of unimaginable splendor have appeared, and out of every manifestation of His invincible power oceans of eternal light have outpoured. How immensely exalted are the wondrous testimonies of His almighty sovereignty, a glimmer of which, if it but touched them, would utterly consume all that are in the heavens and in the earth! How indescribably lofty are the tokens of His consummate power, a single sign of which, however inconsiderable, must transcend the comprehension of whatsoever hath, from the beginning that hath no beginning, been brought into being, or will be created in the future till the end that hath no end. All the Embodiments of His Names wander in the wilderness of search, athirst and eager to discover His Essence, and all the Manifestations of His Attributes implore Him, from the Sinai of Holiness, to unravel His mystery.

A drop of the billowing ocean of His endless mercy hath adorned all creation with the ornament of existence, and a breath wafted from His peerless Paradise hath invested all beings with the robe of His sanctity and glory. A sprinkling from the unfathomed deep of His sovereign and all-pervasive Will hath, out of utter nothingness, called into being a creation which is infinite in its range and deathless in its duration. The wonders of His bounty can never cease, and the stream of His merciful grace can never be arrested. The process of His creation hath had no beginning, and can have no end.

In every age and cycle He hath, through the splendorous light shed by the Manifestations of His wondrous Essence, recreated all things, so that whatsoever reflecteth in the heavens and on the earth the signs of His glory may not be deprived of the outpourings of His mercy, nor despair of the showers of His favors. How all-compassing are the wonders of His boundless grace! Behold how they have pervaded the whole of creation. Such is their virtue that not a single atom in the entire universe can be found which doth not declare the evidences of His might, which doth not glorify His holy Name, or is not expressive of the effulgent light of His unity. So perfect and comprehensive is His creation that no mind nor heart, however keen or pure, can ever grasp the nature of the most insignificant of His creatures; much less fathom the mystery of Him Who is the Day Star of Truth, Who is the invisible and unknowable Essence. The conceptions of the devoutest of mystics, the attainments of the most accomplished amongst men, the highest praise which human tongue or pen can render are all the product of man's finite mind and are conditioned by its limitations. Ten thousand Prophets, each a Moses, are thunderstruck upon the Sinai of their search at His forbidding voice, "Thou shalt never behold Me!"; whilst a myriad Messengers, each as great as Jesus, stand dismayed upon their heavenly thrones by the interdiction, "Mine Essence thou shalt never apprehend!" From time immemorial He hath been veiled in the ineffable sanctity of His exalted Self, and will everlastingly continue to be wrapt in the impenetrable mystery of His unknowable Essence. Every attempt to attain to an understanding of His inaccessible Reality hath ended in complete bewilderment, and every effort to approach His exalted Self and envisage His Essence hath resulted in hopelessness and failure.

How bewildering to me, insignificant as I am, is the attempt to fathom the sacred depths of Thy knowledge! How futile my efforts to visualize the magnitude of the power inherent in Thine handiwork—the revelation of Thy creative power! How can mine eye, which hath no faculty to perceive itself, claim to have discerned Thine Essence, and how can mine heart, already powerless to apprehend the significance of its own potentialities, pretend to have comprehended Thy nature? How can I claim to have known Thee, when the entire creation is bewildered by Thy mystery, and how can I confess not to have known Thee, when, lo, the whole universe proclaimeth Thy Presence and testifieth to Thy truth? The portals of Thy grace have throughout eternity been open, and the means of access unto Thy Presence made available, unto all created things, and the revelations of Thy matchless Beauty have at all times been imprinted upon the realities of all beings, visible and invisible. Yet, notwithstanding this most gracious favor, this perfect and consummate bestowal, I am moved to testify that Thy court of holiness and glory is immeasurably exalted above the knowledge of all else besides Thee, and the mystery of Thy Presence is inscrutable to every mind except Thine own. No one except Thyself can unravel the secret of Thy nature, and naught else but Thy transcendental Essence can grasp the reality of Thy unsearchable being. How vast the number of those heavenly and all-glorious Beings Who, in the wilderness of their separation from Thee, have wandered all the days of their life, and failed in the end to find Thee! How great the multitude of the sanctified and immortal Souls Who were lost and bewildered while seeking in the desert of search to behold Thy face! Myriad are Thy ardent Lovers Whom the consuming flame of remoteness from Thee hath caused to sink and perish, and numberless are the faithful Souls Who have willingly laid down their lives in the hope of gazing on the light of Thy countenance. The sighs and moans of these longing hearts that pant after Thee can never reach Thy holy court, neither can the lamentations of the Wayfarers that thirst to appear before Thy face attain Thy seat of glory.

Manifold Woes and Trials

Praise be to Thee, O Lord My God, for the wondrous revelations of Thy inscrutable decree and the manifold woes and trials Thou hast destined for Myself. At one time Thou didst deliver Me into the hands of Nimrod; at another Thou hast allowed Pharaoh's rod to persecute Me. Thou, alone, canst estimate, through Thine all-encompassing knowledge and the operation of Thy Will, the incalculable afflictions I have suffered at their hands. Again Thou didst cast Me into the prison-cell of the ungodly, for no reason except that I was moved to whisper into the ears of the well-favored denizens of Thy Kingdom an intimation of the vision with which Thou hadst, through Thy knowledge, inspired Me, and revealed to Me its meaning through the potency of Thy might. And again Thou didst decree that I be beheaded by the sword of the infidel. Again I was crucified for having unveiled to men's eyes the hidden gems of Thy glorious unity, for having revealed to them the wondrous signs of Thy sovereign and everlasting power. How bitter the humiliations heaped upon Me, in a subsequent age, on the plain of Karbilá! How lonely did I feel amidst Thy people! To what a state of helplessness I was reduced in that land! Unsatisfied with such indignities, My persecutors decapitated Me, and, carrying aloft My head from land to land paraded it before the gaze of the unbelieving multitude, and deposited it on the seats of the perverse and faithless. In a later age, I was suspended, and My breast was made a target to the darts of the malicious cruelty of My foes. My limbs were riddled with bullets, and My body was torn asunder. Finally, behold now, in this Day, My treacherous enemies have leagued themselves against Me, and are continually plotting to instill the venom of hate and malice into the souls of Thy servants. With all their might they are scheming to accomplish their purpose. . . . Grievous as is My plight, O God, My Well-Beloved, I render thanks unto Thee, and

My Spirit is grateful for whatsoever hath befallen Me in the path of Thy good-pleasure. I am well pleased with that which Thou didst ordain for Me, and welcome, however calamitous, the pains and sorrows I am made to suffer.

The Divine Spirit Awoke Him

Lay not aside the fear of God, O ye the learned of the world, and judge fairly the Cause of this unlettered One to Whom all the Books of God, the Protector, the Self-Subsisting, have testified. . . . Will not the dread of Divine displeasure, the fear of Him Who hath no peer or equal, arouse you? He Whom the world hath wronged hath, at no time, associated with you, hath never studied your writings, nor participated in any of your disputations. The garb He weareth, His flowing locks, His headdress, attest the truth of His words. How long will ye persist in your injustice? Witness the habitation in which He, Who is the incarnation of justice, hath been forced to dwell. Open your eyes, and beholding His plight, meditate diligently upon that which your hands have wrought, that haply ye may not be deprived of the light of His Divine utterance, nor remain bereft of your share of the ocean of His knowledge.

Certain ones among both commoners and nobles have objected that this wronged One is neither a member of the ecclesiastical order nor a descendent of the Prophet. Say: O ye that claim to be just! Reflect a little while, and ye shall recognize how infinitely exalted is His present state above the station ye claim He should possess. The Will of the Almighty hath decreed that out of a house wholly devoid of all that the divines, the doctors, the sages, and scholars commonly possess His Cause should proceed and be made manifest.

The Breathings of the Divine Spirit awoke Him, and bade Him arise and proclaim His Revelation. No sooner was He roused from His slumber than He lifted up His voice and summoned the whole of mankind unto God, the Lord of all worlds. We have been moved to reveal these words in consideration of the weakness and frailty of men; otherwise, the Cause We have proclaimed is such as no pen can ever describe, nor any mind conceive its greatness. To this beareth witness He with Whom is the Mother Book.

To Build Anew the World

The Ancient Beauty hath consented to be bound with chains that mankind may be released from its bondage, and hath accepted to be made a prisoner within this most mighty Stronghold that the whole world may attain unto true liberty. He hath drained to its dregs the cup of sorrow, that all the peoples of the earth may attain unto abiding joy, and be filled with gladness. This is of the mercy of your Lord, the Compassionate, the Most Merciful. We have accepted to be abased, O believers in the Unity of God, that ye may be exalted, and have suffered manifold afflictions, that ye might prosper and flourish. He Who hath come to build anew the whole world, behold, how they that have joined partners with God have forced Him to dwell within the most desolate of cities!

Every Soul Endowed

Say: O people! Withhold not from yourselves the grace of God and His mercy. Whoso withholdeth himself therefrom is indeed in grievous loss. What, O people! Do ye worship the dust, and turn away from your Lord, the Gracious, the All-Bountiful? Fear ye God, and be not of those who perish. Say: The Book of God hath been sent down in the form of this Youth. Hallowed, therefore, be God, the most excellent of makers! Take ye good heed, O peoples of the world, lest ye flee from His face. Nay, make haste to attain His presence, and be of them that have returned unto Him. Pray to be forgiven, O people, for having failed in your duty towards God, and for having trespassed against His Cause, and be not of the foolish. He it is Who hath created you; He it is Who hath nourished your souls through His Cause, and enabled you to recognize Him Who is the Almighty, the Most Exalted, the All-Knowing. He it is Who hath unveiled to your eyes the treasures of His knowledge, and caused you to ascend unto the heaven of certitude—the certitude of His resistless, His irrefutable, and most exalted Faith. Beware that ye do not deprive yourselves of the grace of God, that ye do not bring to naught your works, and do not repudiate the truth of this most manifest, this lofty, this shining, and glorious Revelation. Judge ye fairly the Cause of God, your Creator, and behold that which hath been sent down from the Throne on high, and meditate thereon with innocent and sanctified hearts. Then will the truth of this Cause appear unto you as manifest as the sun in its noon-tide glory. Then will ye be of them that have believed in Him.

Say: The first and foremost testimony establishing His truth is His own Self. Next to this testimony is His Revelation. For whoso faileth to recognize either the one or the other He hath established the words He hath revealed as proof of His reality and truth. This is, verily, an evidence of His tender mercy unto men. He hath endowed every soul with the capacity to recognize the signs of God. How could He, otherwise, have fulfilled His testimony unto men, if ye be of them that ponder His Cause in their hearts. He will never deal unjustly with any one, neither will He task a soul beyond its power. He, verily, is the Compassionate, the All-Merciful.

Say: So great is the glory of the Cause of God that even the blind can perceive it, how much more they whose sight is sharp, whose vision is pure. The blind, though unable to perceive the light of the sun, are, nevertheless, capable of experiencing its continual heat. The blind in heart, however, among the people of the Bayán—and to this God is My witness—are impotent, no matter how long the Sun may shine upon them, either to perceive the radiance of its glory, or to appreciate the warmth of its rays.

Say: O people of the Bayán! We have chosen you out of the world to know and recognize Our Self. We have caused you to draw nigh unto the right side of Paradise—the Spot out of which the undying Fire crieth in manifold accents: "There is none other God besides Me, the All-Powerful, the Most High!" Take heed lest ye allow yourselves to be shut out as by a veil from this Day Star that shineth above the day-spring of the Will of your Lord, the All-Merciful, and whose light hath encompassed both the small and the great. Purge your sight, that ye may perceive its glory with your own eyes, and depend not on the sight of any one except your Self, for God hath never burdened any soul beyond its power. Thus hath it been sent down unto the Prophets and Messengers of old, and been recorded in all the Scriptures.

Strive, O people, to gain admittance into this vast Immensity for which God ordained neither beginning nor end, in which His voice hath been raised, and over which have been wafted the sweet savors of holiness and glory. Divest not yourselves of the Robe of grandeur, neither suffer your hearts to be deprived of remembering your Lord, nor your ears of hearkening unto the sweet melodies of His wondrous, His sublime, His all-compelling, His clear, and most eloquent voice.

This New World Order

The world's equilibrium hath been upset through the vibrating influence of this most great, this new World Order. Mankind's ordered life hath been revolutionized through the agency of this unique, this wondrous System—the like of which mortal eyes have never witnessed.

Immerse yourselves in the ocean of My words, that ye may unravel its secrets, and discover all the pearls of wisdom that lie hid in its depths. Take heed that ye do not vacillate in your determination to embrace the truth of this Cause—a Cause through which the potentialities of the might of God have been revealed, and His sovereignty established. With faces beaming with joy, hasten ye unto Him. This is the changeless Faith of God, eternal in the past, eternal in the future. Let him that seeketh, attain it; and as to him that hath refused to seek it—verily, God is Self-Sufficient, above any need of His creatures.

Say: This is the infallible Balance which the Hand of God is holding, in which all who are in the heavens and all who are on the earth are weighed, and their fate determined, if ye be of them that believe and recognize this truth. Say: Through it the poor have been enriched, the learned enlightened, and the seekers enabled to ascend unto the presence of God. Beware, lest ye make it a cause of dissension amongst you. Be ye as firmly settled as the immovable mountain in the Cause of your Lord, the Mighty, the Loving.

The Remedy the World Needeth

The All-Knowing Physician hath His finger on the pulse of mankind. He perceiveth the disease, and prescribeth, in His unerring wisdom, the remedy. Every age hath its own problem, and every soul its particular aspiration. The remedy the world needeth in its present-day afflictions can never be the same as that which a subsequent age may require. Be anxiously concerned with the needs of the age ye live in, and center your deliberations on its exigencies and requirements.

We can well perceive how the whole human race is encompassed with great, with incalculable afflictions. We see it languishing on its bed of sickness, sore-tried and disillusioned. They that are intoxicated by self-conceit have interposed themselves between it and the Divine and Infallible Physician. Witness how they have entangled all men, themselves included, in the mesh of their devices. They can neither discover the cause of the disease, nor have they any knowledge of the remedy. They have conceived the straight to be crooked, and have imagined their friend an enemy.

Incline your ears to the sweet melody of this Prisoner. Arise, and lift up your voices, that haply they that are fast asleep may be awakened. Say: O ye who are as dead! The Hand of Divine bounty proffereth unto you the Water of Life. Hasten and drink your fill. Whoso hath been re-born in this Day, shall never die; whoso remaineth dead, shall never live.

Tablets to the Kings

O kings of the earth! He Who is the sovereign Lord of all is come. The Kingdom is God's, the omnipotent Protector, the Self-Subsisting. Worship none but God, and, with radiant hearts, lift up your faces unto your Lord, the Lord of all names. This is a Revelation to which whatever ye possess can never be compared, could ye but know it.

We see you rejoicing in that which ye have amassed from others and shutting out yourselves from the worlds which naught except My guarded Tablet can reckon. The treasures ye have laid up have drawn you far away from your ultimate objective. This ill beseemeth you, could ye but understand it. Wash from your hearts all earthly defilements, and hasten to enter the Kingdom of your Lord, the Creator of earth and heaven, Who caused the world to tremble and all its peoples to wail, except them that have renounced all things and clung to that which the Hidden Tablet hath ordained.

This is the Day in which He Who held converse with God hath attained the light of the Ancient of Days, and quaffed the pure waters of reunion from this Cup that hath caused the seas to swell. Say: By the one true God! Sinai is circling round the Day Spring of Revelation, while from the heights of the Kingdom the Voice of the Spirit of God is heard proclaiming: "Bestir yourselves, ye proud ones of the earth, and hasten ye unto Him." Carmel hath, in this Day, hastened in longing adoration to attain His court, whilst from the heart of Zion there cometh the cry: "The promise is fulfilled. That which had been announced in the holy Writ of God, the most Exalted, the Almighty, the Best-Beloved, is made manifest."

O kings of the earth! The Most Great Law hath been revealed in this Spot, this scene of transcendent splendor. Every hidden thing hath been brought to light, by virtue of the Will of the Supreme Ordainer, He Who hath ushered in the Last Hour, through Whom the Moon hath been cleft, and every irrevocable decree expounded.

Ye are but vassals, O kings of the earth! He Who is the King of Kings hath appeared, arrayed in His most wondrous glory, and is summoning you unto Himself, the Help in Peril, the Self-Subsisting. Take heed lest pride deter you from recognizing the Source of Revelation, lest the things of this world shut you out as by a veil from Him Who is the Creator of heaven. Arise, and serve Him Who is the Desire of all nations, Who hath created you through a word from Him, and ordained you to be, for all time, the emblems of His sovereignty.

By the righteousness of God! It is not Our wish to lay hands on your kingdoms. Our mission is to seize and possess the hearts of men. Upon them the eyes of Bahá are fastened. To this testifieth the Kingdom of Names, could ye but comprehend it. Whoso followeth his Lord, will renounce the world and all that is therein; how much greater, then, must be the detachment of Him Who holdeth so august a station! Forsake your palaces, and haste ye to gain admittance into His Kingdom. This, indeed, will profit you both in this world and in the next. To this testifieth the Lord of the realm on high, did ye but know it.

How great the blessedness that awaiteth the king who will arise to aid My Cause in My Kingdom, who will detach himself from all else but Me! Such a king is numbered with the companions of the Crimson Ark—the Ark which God hath prepared for the people of Bahá. All must glorify his name, must reverence his station, and aid him to unlock the cities with the keys of My Name, the omnipotent Protector of all that inhabit the visible and invisible kingdoms. Such a king is the very eye of mankind, the luminous ornament on the brow of creation, the fountain-head of blessings unto the whole world. Offer up, O people of Bahá, your substance, nay your very lives, for his assistance.

O kings of Christendom! Heard ye not the saying of Jesus, the Spirit of God, "I go away, and come again unto you"? Wherefore, then, did ye fail, when He did come again unto you in the clouds of heaven, to draw nigh unto Him, that ye might behold His face, and be of them that attained His Presence? In another passage He saith: "When He, the Spirit of Truth, is come, He will guide you into all truth." And yet, behold how, when He did bring the truth, ye refused to turn your faces towards Him, and persisted in disporting yourselves with your pastimes and fancies. Ye welcomed Him not, neither did ye seek His Presence, that ye might hear the verses of God from His own mouth, and partake of the manifold wisdom of the Almighty, the All-Glorious, the All-Wise. Ye have, by reason of your failure, hindered the breath of God from being wafted over you, and have withheld from your souls the sweetness of its fragrance. Ye continue roving with delight in the valley of your corrupt desires. Ye, and all ye possess, shall pass away. Ye shall, most certainly, return to God, and shall be called to account for your doings in the presence of Him Who shall gather together the entire creation . . .

Twenty years have passed, O kings, during which We have, each day, tasted the agony of a fresh tribulation. No one of them that were before Us hath endured the things We have endured. Would that ye could perceive it! They that rose up against Us have put us to death, have shed our blood, have plundered our property, and violated our honor. Though aware of most of our afflictions, ye, nevertheless, have failed to stay the hand of the aggressor. For is it not your clear duty to restrain the tyranny of the oppressor, and to deal equitably with your subjects, that your high sense of justice may be fully demonstrated to all mankind?

God hath committed into your hands the reins of the government of the people, that ye may rule with justice over them, safeguard the rights of the downtrodden, and punish the wrong-doers. If ye neglect the duty prescribed unto you by God in His Book, your names shall be numbered with those of the unjust in His sight. Grievous, indeed, will be your error. Cleave ye to that which your imaginations have devised, and cast behind your backs the commandments of God, the Most Exalted, the Inaccessible, the All-Compelling, the Almighty? Cast away the things ye possess, and cling to that which God hath bidden you observe. Seek ye His grace, for he that seeketh it treadeth His straight Path.

Consider the state in which We are, and behold ye the ills and troubles that have tried Us. Neglect Us not, though it be for a moment, and judge ye between Us and Our enemies with equity. This will, surely, be a manifest advantage unto you. Thus do We relate to you Our tale, and recount the things that have befallen Us, that ye might take off Our ills and ease Our burden. Let him who will, relieve Us from Our trouble; and as to him that willeth not, My Lord is assuredly the best of helpers.

Warn and acquaint the people, O Servant, with the things We have sent down unto Thee, and let the fear of no one dismay Thee, and be Thou not of them that waver. The day is approaching when God will have exalted His Cause and magnified His testimony in the eyes of all who are in the heavens and all who are on the earth. Place, in all circumstances, Thy whole trust in Thy Lord, and fix Thy gaze upon Him, and turn away from all them that repudiate His truth. Let God, Thy Lord, be Thy sufficing succorer and helper. We have pledged Ourselves to secure Thy triumph upon earth and to exalt Our Cause above all men, though no king be found who would turn his face towards Thee.

Lay not aside the fear of God, O kings of the earth, and beware that ye transgress not the bounds which the Almighty hath fixed. Observe the injunctions laid upon you in His Book, and take good heed not to overstep their limits. Be vigilant, that ye may not do injustice to anyone, be it to the extent of a grain of mustard seed. Tread ye the path of justice, for this, verily, is the straight path.

Compose your differences, and reduce your armaments, that the burden of your expenditures may be lightened, and that your minds and hearts may be tranquillized. Heal the dissensions that divide you, and ye will no longer be in need of any armaments except what the protection of your cities and territories demandeth. Fear ye God, and take heed not to outstrip the bounds of moderation, and be numbered among the extravagant.

We have learned that you are increasing your outlay every year, and are laying the burden thereof on your subjects. This, verily, is more than they can bear, and is a grievous injustice. Decide justly between men, and be ye the emblems of justice amongst them. This, if ye judge fairly, is the thing that behoveth you, and beseemeth your station.

Beware not to deal unjustly with any one that appealeth to you, and entereth beneath your shadow. Walk ye in the fear of God, and be ye of them that lead a godly life. Rest not on your power, your armies, and treasures. Put your whole trust and confidence in God, Who hath created you, and seek ye His help in all your affairs. Succor cometh from Him alone. He succoreth whom He will with the hosts of the heavens and of the earth.

Know ye that the poor are the trust of God in your midst. Watch that ye betray not his trust, that ye deal not unjustly with them and that ye walk not in the ways of the treacherous. Ye will most certainly be called upon to answer for His trust on the day when the Balance of Justice shall be set, the day when unto every one shall be rendered his due, when the doings of all men, be they rich or poor, shall be weighed.

If ye pay no heed unto the counsels which, in peerless and unequivocal language, We have revealed in this Tablet, Divine chastisement shall assail you from every direction, and the sentence of His justice shall be pronounced against you. On that day ye shall have no power to resist Him, and shall recognize your own impotence. Have mercy on yourselves and on those beneath you. Judge ye between them according to the precepts prescribed by God in His most holy and exalted Tablet, a Tablet wherein He hath assigned to each and every thing its settled measure, in which He hath given, with distinctness, an explanation of all things, and which is in itself a monition unto them that believe in Him.

Examine Our Cause, inquire into the things that have befallen Us, and decide justly between Us and Our enemies, and be ye of them that act equitably towards their neighbor. If ye stay not the hand of the oppressor, if ye fail to safeguard the rights of the down-trodden, what right have ye then to vaunt yourselves among men? What is it of which ye can rightly boast? Is it on your food and your drink that ye pride yourselves, on the riches ye lay up in your treasures, on the diversity and the cost of the ornaments with which ye deck yourselves? If true glory were to consist in the possession of such perishable things, then the earth on which ye walk must needs vaunt itself over you, because it supplieth you, and bestoweth upon you these very things, by the decree of the Almighty. In its bowels are contained, according to what God hath ordained, all that ye possess. From it, as a sign of His mercy, ye derive your riches. Behold then your state, the thing in which ye glory! Would that ye could perceive it!

Nay! By Him Who holdeth in His grasp the kingdom of the entire creation! Nowhere doth your true and abiding glory reside except in your firm adherence unto the precepts of God, your wholehearted observance of His laws, your resolution to see that they do not remain unenforced, and to pursue steadfastly the right course.

O Kings of the earth! Give ear unto the Voice of God, calling from this sublime, this fruit-laden Tree, that hath sprung out of the Crimson Hill, upon the holy Plain, intoning the words: "There is none other God but He, the Mighty, the All-Powerful, the All-Wise." . . . Fear God, O concourse of kings, and suffer not yourselves to be deprived of this most sublime grace. Fling away, then, the things ye possess, and take fast hold on the Handle of God, the Exalted, the Great. Set your hearts towards the Face of God, and abandon that which your desires have bidden you to follow, and be not of those who perish. Relate unto them, O servant, the story of 'Alí (the Báb), when He came unto them with truth, bearing His glorious and weighty Book, and holding in His hands a testimony and proof from God, and holy and blessed tokens from Him. Ye, however, O kings, have failed to heed the Remembrance of God in His days and to be guided by the lights which arose and shone forth above the horizon of a resplendent Heaven. Ye examined not His Cause when so to do would have been better for you than all that the sun shineth upon, could ye but perceive it. Ye remained careless until the divines of Persia—those cruel ones —pronounced judgment against Him, and unjustly slew Him. His spirit ascended unto God, and the eyes of the inmates of Paradise and the angels that are nigh unto Him wept sore by reason of this cruelty. Beware that ye be not careless henceforth as ye have been careless aforetime. Return, then, unto God, your Maker, and be not of the heedless . . . My face hath come forth from the veils, and shed its radiance upon all that is in heaven and on earth; and yet, ye turned not towards Him, notwithstanding that ye were created for Him, O concourse of kings! Follow, therefore, that which I speak unto you, and hearken unto it with your hearts, and be not of such as have turned aside. For your glory consisteth not in your sovereignty, but rather in your nearness unto God and your observance of His command as sent down in His holy and preserved Tablets. Should any one of you rule over the whole earth, and over all that lieth within it and upon it, its seas, its lands, its mountains, and its plains, and yet be not remembered by God, all these would profit him not, could ye but know it . . . Arise, then, and make steadfast your feet, and make ye amends for that which hath escaped you, and set then yourselves towards His holy Court, on the shore of His mighty Ocean, so that the pearls of knowledge and wisdom, which God hath stored up within the shell of His radiant heart, may be revealed unto you . . . Beware lest ye hinder the breeze of God from blowing over your hearts, the breeze through which the hearts of such as have turned unto Him can be quickened . . .

Hearken, O King (Sultán 'Abdu'l-'Azíz), to the speech of Him that speaketh the truth, Him that doth not ask thee to recompense Him with the things God hath chosen to bestow upon thee, Him Who unerringly treadeth the straight Path. He it is Who summoneth thee unto God, thy Lord, Who showeth thee the right course, the way that leadeth to true felicity, that haply thou mayest be of them with whom it shall be well.

Beware, O King, that thou gather not around thee such ministers as follow the desires of a corrupt inclination, as have cast behind their backs that which hath been committed into their hands and manifestly betrayed their trust. Be bounteous to others as God hath been bounteous to thee, and abandon not the interests of thy people to the mercy of such ministers as these. Lay not aside the fear of God, and be thou of them that act uprightly. Gather around thee those ministers from whom thou canst perceive the fragrance of faith and of justice, and take thou counsel with them, and choose whatever is best in thy sight, and be of them that act generously.

Know thou for a certainty that whoso disbelieveth in God is neither trustworthy nor truthful. This, indeed, is the truth, the undoubted truth. He that acteth treacherously towards God will, also, act treacherously towards his king. Nothing whatever can deter such a man from evil, nothing can hinder him from betraying his neighbor, nothing can induce him to walk uprightly.

Take heed that thou resign not the reins of the affairs of thy state into the hands of others, and repose not thy confidence in ministers unworthy of thy trust, and be not of them that live in heedlessness. Shun them whose hearts are turned away from thee, and place not thy confidence in them, and entrust them not with thine affairs and the affairs of such as profess thy faith. Beware that thou allow not the wolf to become the shepherd of God's flock, and surrender not the fate of His loved ones to the mercy of the malicious. Expect not that they who violate the ordinances of God will be trustworthy or sincere in the faith they profess. Avoid them, and preserve strict guard over thyself, lest their devices and mischief hurt thee. Turn away from them, and fix thy gaze upon God, thy Lord, the All-Glorious, the Most Bountiful. He that giveth up himself wholly to God, God shall, assuredly, be with him; and he that placeth his complete trust in God, God shall, verily, protect him from whatsoever may harm him, and shield him from the wickedness of every evil plotter.

Wert thou to incline thine ear unto My speech and observe My counsel, God would exalt thee to so eminent a position that the designs of no man on the whole earth can ever touch or hurt thee. Observe, O King, with thine inmost heart and with thy whole being, the precepts of God, and walk not in the paths of the oppressor. Seize thou, and hold firmly within thy grasp, the reins of the affairs of thy people, and examine in person whatever pertaineth unto them. Let nothing escape thee, for therein lieth the highest good.

Render thanks unto God for having chosen thee out of the whole world, and made thee king over them that profess thy faith. It well beseemeth thee to appreciate the wondrous favors with which God hath favored thee, and to magnify continually His name. Thou canst best praise Him if thou lovest His loved ones, and dost safeguard and protect His servants from the mischief of the treacherous, that none may any longer oppress them. Thou shouldst, moreover, arise to enforce the law of God amongst them, that thou mayest be of those who are firmly established in His law.

Shouldst thou cause rivers of justice to spread their waters amongst thy subjects, God would surely aid thee with the hosts of the unseen and of the seen, and would strengthen thee in thine affairs. No God is there but Him. All creation and its empire are His. Unto Him return the works of the faithful.

Place not thy reliance on thy treasures. Put thy whole confidence in the grace of God, thy Lord. Let Him be thy trust in whatever thou doest, and be of them that have submitted themselves to His Will. Let Him be thy helper and enrich thyself with His treasures, for with Him are the treasuries of the heavens and of the earth. He bestoweth them upon whom He will, and from whom He will He withholdeth them. There is none other God but Him, the All-Possessing, the All-Praised. All are but paupers at the door of His mercy; all are helpless before the revelation of His sovereignty, and beseech His favors.

Overstep not the bounds of moderation, and deal justly with them that serve thee. Bestow upon them according to their needs, and not to the extent that will enable them to lay up riches for themselves, to deck their persons, to embellish their homes, to acquire the things that are of no benefit unto them, and to be numbered with the extravagant. Deal with them with undeviating justice, so that none among them may either suffer want, or be pampered with luxuries. This is but manifest justice.

Allow not the abject to rule over and dominate them who are noble and worthy of honor, and suffer not the high-minded to be at the mercy of the contemptible and worthless, for this is what We observed upon Our arrival in the City (Constantinople), and to it we bear witness. We found among its inhabitants some who were possessed of an affluent fortune and lived in the midst of excessive riches, while others were in dire want and abject poverty. This ill beseemeth thy sovereignty, and is unworthy of thy rank.

Let My counsel be acceptable to thee, and strive thou to rule with equity among men, that God may exalt thy name and spread abroad the fame of thy justice in all the world. Beware lest thou aggrandize thy ministers at the expense of thy subjects. Fear the sighs of the poor and of the upright in heart who, at every break of day, bewail their plight, and be unto them a benignant sovereign. They, verily, are thy treasures on earth. It behoveth thee, therefore, to safeguard thy treasures from the assaults of them who wish to rob thee. Inquire into their affairs, and ascertain, every year, nay every month, their condition, and be not of them that are careless of their duty.

Set before thine eyes God's unerring Balance and, as one standing in His Presence, weigh in that Balance thine actions every day, every moment of thy life. Bring thyself to account ere thou art summoned to a reckoning, on the Day when no man shall have strength to stand for fear of God, the Day when the hearts of the heedless ones shall be made to tremble.

It behoveth every king to be as bountiful as the sun, which fostereth the growth of all beings, and giveth to each its due, whose benefits are not inherent in itself, but are ordained by Him Who is the Most Powerful, the Almighty. The King should be as generous, as liberal in his mercy as the clouds, the outpourings of whose bounty are showered upon every land, by the behest of Him Who is the Supreme Ordainer, the All-Knowing.

Have a care not to entrust thine affairs of state entirely into another's hands. None can discharge thy functions better than thine own self. Thus do We make clear unto thee Our words of wisdom, and send down upon thee that which can enable thee to pass over from the left hand of oppression to the right hand of justice, and approach the resplendent ocean of His favors. Such is the path which the kings that were before thee have trodden, they that acted equitably towards their subjects, and walked in the ways of undeviating justice.

Thou art God's shadow on earth. Strive, therefore, to act in such a manner as befitteth so eminent, so august a station. If thou dost depart from following the things We have caused to descend upon thee and taught thee, thou wilt, assuredly, be derogating from that great and priceless honor. Return, then, and cleave wholly unto God, and cleanse thine heart from the world and all its vanities, and suffer not the love of any stranger to enter and dwell therein. Not until thou dost purify thine heart from every trace of such love can the brightness of the light of God shed its radiance upon it, for to none hath God given more than one heart. This, verily, hath been decreed and written down in His ancient Book. And as the human heart, as fashioned by God, is one and undivided, it behoveth thee to take heed that its affections be, also, one and undivided. Cleave thou, therefore, with the whole affection of thine heart, unto His love, and withdraw it from the love of any one besides Him, that He may aid thee to immerse thyself in the ocean of His unity, and enable thee to become a true upholder of His oneness. God is my witness. My sole purpose in revealing to thee these words is to sanctify thee from the transitory things of the earth, and aid thee to enter the realm of everlasting glory, that thou mayest, by the leave of God, be of them that abide and rule therein. . . .

I swear by God, O King! It is not my wish to make My plaint to thee against them that persecute Me. I only plead my grief and My sorrow to God, Who hath created Me and them, Who well knoweth our state and Who watcheth over all things. My wish is to warn them of the consequences of their actions, if perchance they might desist from treating others as they have treated Me, and be of them that heed My warning.

The tribulations that have touched Us, the destitution from which We suffer, the various troubles with which We are encompassed, shall all pass away, as shall pass away the pleasures in which they delight and the affluence they enjoy. This is the truth which no man can reject. The days in which We have been compelled to dwell in the dust will soon be ended, as will the days in which they occupied the seats of honor. God shall, assuredly, judge with truth between Us and them, and He, verily, is the best of judges.

We render thanks unto God for whatsoever hath befallen Us, and We patiently endure the things He hath ordained in the past or will ordain in the future. In Him have I placed My trust; and into His hands have I committed My cause. He will, certainly, repay all them that endure with patience and put their confidence in Him. His is the creation and its empire. He exalteth whom He will, and whom He will He doth abase. He shall not be asked of His doings. He, verily, is the All-Glorious, the Almighty.

Let thine ear be attentive, O King, to the words We have addressed to thee. Let the oppressor desist from his tyranny, and cut off the perpetrators of injustice from among them that profess thy faith. By the righteousness of God! The tribulations We have sustained are such that any pen that recounteth them cannot but be overwhelmed with anguish. No one of them that truly believe and uphold the unity of God can bear the burden of their recital. So great have been Our sufferings that even the eyes of Our enemies have wept over Us, and beyond them those of every discerning person. And to all these trials have We been subjected, in spite of Our action in approaching thee, and in bidding the people to enter beneath thy shadow, that thou mightest be a stronghold unto them that believe in and uphold the unity of God.

Have I, O King, ever disobeyed thee? Have I, at any time, transgressed any of thy laws? Can any of thy ministers that represented thee in 'Iráq produce any proof that can establish my disloyalty to thee? No, by Him Who is the Lord of all worlds! Not for one short moment did We rebel against thee, or against any of thy ministers. Never, God willing, shall We revolt against thee, though We be exposed to trials more severe than any We suffered in the past.

In the day time and in the night season, at even and at morn, We pray to God on thy behalf, that He may graciously aid thee to be obedient unto Him and to observe His commandment, that He may shield thee from the hosts of the evil ones. Do, therefore, as it pleaseth thee, and treat Us as befitteth thy station and beseemeth thy sovereignty. Be not forgetful of the law of God in whatever thou desirest to achieve, now or in the days to come. Say: Praise be to God, the Lord of all worlds!

O King of Paris! Tell the priest to ring the bells no longer. By God, the True One! The Most Mighty Bell hath appeared in the form of Him Who is the Most Great Name, and the fingers of the will of thy Lord, the Most Exalted, the Most High, toll it out in the heaven of Immortality, in His Name, the All-Glorious. Thus have the mighty verses of thy Lord been again sent down unto thee, that thou mayest arise to remember God, the Creator of earth and heaven, in these days when all the tribes of the earth have mourned, and the foundations of the cities have trembled, and the dust of irreligion hath enwrapped all men, except such as thy Lord, the All-Knowing, the All-Wise, was pleased to spare. . . . Give ear, O King, unto the Voice that calleth from the Fire which burneth in this Verdant Tree, upon this Sinai which hath been raised above the hallowed and snow-white Spot, beyond the Everlasting City: "Verily, there is none other God but Me, the Ever-Forgiving, the

Most Merciful!" We, in truth, have sent Him Whom We aided with the Holy Spirit (Jesus), that He may announce unto you this Light that hath shone forth from the horizon of the will of your Lord, the Most Exalted, the All Glorious, and Whose signs have been revealed in the West, that ye may set your faces towards Him (Bahá'u'lláh), on this Day which God hath exalted above all other days, and whereon the All-Merciful hath shed the splendor of His effulgent glory upon all who are in heaven and all who are on earth. Arise thou to serve God and help His Cause. He, verily, will assist thee with the hosts of the seen and unseen, and will set thee king over all that whereon the sun riseth. Thy Lord, in truth, is the All-Powerful, the Almighty. . . . Attire thy temple with the ornament of My Name, and thy tongue with remembrance of Me, and thine heart with love for Me, the Almighty, the Most High. We have desired for thee naught except that which is better for thee than what thou dost possess and all the treasures of the earth. Thy Lord, verily, is knowing, informed of all. . . .

O King! We heard the words thou didst utter in answer to the Czar of Russia, concerning the decision made regarding the war. Thy Lord, verily, knoweth, is informed of all Thou didst say: "I lay asleep upon my couch, when the cry of the oppressed, who were drowned in the Black Sea, awakened me." This is what we heard thee say, and, verily, thy Lord is witness unto what I say. We testify that that which wakened thee was not their cry, but the promptings of thine own passions, for We tested thee, and found thee wanting. Comprehend the meaning of My words, and be thou of the discerning . . . Hadst thou been sincere in thy words, thou wouldst have not cast behind thy back the Book of God, when it was sent unto thee by Him Who is the Almighty, the All-Wise. We have proved thee through it, and found thee other than that which thou didst profess. Arise, and make amends for that which escaped thee. Ere long the world and all that thou possessest will perish, and the kingdom will remain unto God, thy Lord and the Lord of thy fathers of old. It behoveth thee not to conduct thine affairs according to the dictates of thy desires. Fear the sighs of this Wronged One, and shield Him from the darts of such as act unjustly. For what thou hast done, thy kingdom shall be thrown into confusion, and thine empire shall pass from thine hands, as a punishment for that which thou hast wrought. Then wilt thou know how thou hast plainly erred. Commotions shall seize all the people in that land, unless thou arisest to help this Cause, and followest Him Who is the Spirit of God (Jesus) in this, the straight Path. Hath thy pomp made thee proud? By my Life! It shall not endure; nay, it shall soon pass away, unless thou holdest fast by this firm Cord. We see abasement hastening after thee, while thou art of the heedless . . . Abandon thy palaces to the people of the graves, and thine empire to whosoever desireth it, and turn, then, unto the Kingdom. This, verily, is what God hath chosen for thee, wert thou of them that turn unto Him . . . Shouldst thou desire to bear the weight of thy dominion, bear it then to aid the Cause of thy Lord. Glorified be this station which whoever attaineth thereunto hath attained unto all good that proceedeth from Him Who is the All-Knowing, the All-Wise . . . Exultest thou over the treasures thou dost possess, knowing they shall perish? Rejoicest thou in that thou rulest a span of earth, when the whole world, in the estimation of the people of Bahá, is worth as much as the black in the eye of a dead ant? Abandon it unto such as have set their affections upon it, and turn thou unto Him Who is the Desire of the world. Whither are gone the proud and their palaces? Gaze thou into their tombs, that thou mayest profit by this example, inasmuch as We made it a lesson unto every beholder. Were the breezes of Revelation to seize thee, thou wouldst flee the world, and turn unto the Kingdom, and wouldst expend all thou possessest, that thou mayest draw nigh unto this sublime Vision.

O Czar of Russia! Incline thine ear unto the voice of God, the King, the Holy, and turn thou unto Paradise, the Spot wherein abideth He Who, among the Concourse on high, beareth the most excellent titles, and Who, in the kingdom of creation, is called by the name of God, the Effulgent, the All-Glorious. Beware lest thy desire deter thee from turning towards the face of thy Lord, the Compassionate, the Most Merciful. We, verily, have heard the thing for which thou didst supplicate thy Lord, whilst secretly communing with Him. Wherefore, the breeze of My loving-kindness wafted forth, and the sea of My mercy surged, and We answered thee in truth. Thy Lord, verily, is the All-Knowing, the All-Wise. Whilst I lay chained and fettered in the prison, one of thy ministers extended Me his aid. Wherefore hath God ordained for thee a station which the knowledge of none can comprehend except His knowledge. Beware lest thou barter away this sublime station . . . Beware lest thy sovereignty withhold thee from Him Who is the Supreme Sovereign. He, verily, is come with His Kingdom, and all the atoms cry aloud: "Lo! The Lord is come in His great majesty!" He Who is the Father is come, and the Son (Jesus), in the holy vale, crieth out: "Here am I, here am I, O Lord, My God!", whilst Sinai circleth round the House, and the Burning Bush calleth aloud: "The All-Bounteous is come mounted upon the clouds! Blessed is he that draweth nigh unto Him, and woe betide them that are far away."

Arise thou amongst men in the name of this all-compelling Cause, and summon, then, the nations unto God, the Exalted, the Great. Be thou not of them who called upon God by one of His names, but who, when He Who is the Object of all names appeared, denied Him and turned aside from Him, and, in the end, pronounced sentence against Him with manifest injustice. Consider and call thou to mind the days whereon the Spirit of God (Jesus) appeared, and Herod gave judgment against Him. God, however, aided Him with the hosts of the unseen, and protected Him with truth, and sent Him down unto another land, according to His promise. He, verily, ordaineth what He pleaseth. Thy Lord truly preserveth whom He willeth, be he in the midst of the seas, or in the maw of the serpent, or beneath the sword of the oppressor . . .

Again I say: Hearken unto My Voice that calleth from My prison, that it may acquaint thee with the things that have befallen My Beauty, at the hands of them that are the manifestations of My glory, and that thou mayest perceive how great hath been My patience, notwithstanding My might, and how immense My forebearance, notwithstanding My power. By My Life! Couldst thou but know the things sent down by My Pen, and discover the treasures of My Cause, and the pearls of My mysteries which lie hid in the seas of My names and in the goblets of My words, thou wouldst, in thy love for My name, and in thy longing for My glorious and sublime Kingdom, lay down thy life in My path. Know thou that though My body be beneath the swords of My foes, and My limbs be beset with incalculable afflictions, yet My spirit is filled with a gladness with which all the joys of the earth can never compare.

Set thine heart towards Him Who is the Point of adoration for the world, and say: O peoples of the earth! Have ye denied the One in Whose path He Who came with the truth, bearing the announcement of your Lord, the Exalted, the Great, suffered martyrdom? Say: This is an Announcement whereat the hearts of the Prophets and Messengers have rejoiced. This is the One Whom the heart of the world remembereth and is promised in the Books of God, the Mighty, the All-Wise. The hands of the Messengers were, in their desire to meet Me, upraised towards God, the Mighty, the Glorified. . . . Some lamented in their separation from Me, others endured hardships in My path, and still others laid down their lives for the sake of My Beauty, could ye but know it. Say: I, verily, have not sought to extol Mine Own Self, but rather God Himself were ye to judge fairly. Naught can be seen in Me except God and His Cause, could ye but perceive it. I am the One Whom the tongue of Isaiah hath extolled, the One with Whose name both the Torah and the Evangel were adorned. . . . Blessed be the king whose sovereignty hath withheld him not from his Sovereign, and who hath turned unto God with his heart. He, verily, is accounted of those that have attained unto that which God, the Mighty, the All-Wise, hath willed. Ere long will such a one find himself numbered with the monarchs of the realms of the Kingdom. Thy Lord is, in truth, potent over all things. He giveth what He willeth to whomsoever He willeth, and withholdeth what He pleaseth from whomsoever He willeth. He, verily, is the All-Powerful, the Almighty.

O Queen in London! Incline thine ear unto the voice of thy Lord, the Lord of all mankind, calling from the Divine Lote-Tree: Verily, no God is there but Me, the Almighty, the All-Wise!

Cast away all that is on earth, and attire the head of thy kingdom with the crown of the remembrance of thy Lord, the All-Glorious. He, in truth, hath come unto the world in His most great glory, and all that hath been mentioned in the Gospel hath been fulfilled. The land of Syria hath been honored by the footsteps of its Lord, the Lord of all men, and north and south are both inebriated with the wine of His presence. Blessed is the man that inhaled the fragrance of the Most Merciful, and turned unto the Dawning-Place of His Beauty, in this resplendent Dawn. The Mosque of Aqsá vibrated through the breezes of its Lord, the All-Glorious whilst Bathá (Mecca) trembleth at the voice of God, the Exalted, the Most High. Whereupon every single stone of them celebrateth the praise of the Lord, through this Great Name.

Lay aside thy desire, and set then thine heart towards thy Lord, the Ancient of Days. We make mention of thee for the sake of God, and desire that thy name may be exalted through thy remembrance of God, the Creator of earth and heaven. He, verily, is witness unto that which I say. We have been informed that thou hast forbidden the trading in slaves, both men and women. This, verily, is what God hath enjoined in this wondrous Revelation. God hath, truly, destined a reward for thee, because of this. He, verily, will pay the doer of good his due recompense, wert thou to follow what hath been sent unto thee by Him Who is the All-Knowing, the All-Informed. As to him who turneth aside, and swelleth with pride, after that the clear tokens have come unto him, from the Revealer of signs, his work shall God bring to naught. He, in truth, hath power over all things. Man's actions are acceptable after his having recognized (the Manifestation). He that turneth aside from the True One is indeed the most veiled amongst His creatures. Thus hath it been decreed by Him Who is the Almighty, the Most Powerful.

We have also heard that thou hast entrusted the reins of counsel into the hands of the representatives of the people. Thou, indeed, hast done well, for thereby the foundations of the edifice of thine affairs will be strengthened, and the hearts of all that are beneath thy shadow, whether high or low, will be tranquillized. It behoveth them, however, to be trustworthy among His servants, and to regard themselves as the representatives of all that dwell on earth. This is what counselleth them, in this Tablet, He Who is the Ruler, the All-Wise. . . . Blessed is he that entereth the assembly for the sake of God, and judgeth between men with pure justice. He, indeed, is of the blissful. . . .

Turn thou unto God and say: O my Sovereign Lord! I am but a vassal of Thine, and Thou art, in truth, the King of Kings. I have lifted my suppliant hands unto the heaven of Thy grace and Thy bounties. Send down, then, upon me from the clouds of Thy generosity that which will rid me of all save Thee, and draw me nigh unto Thyself. I beseech Thee, O my Lord, by Thy name, which Thou hast made the king of names, and the manifestation of Thyself to all who are in heaven and on earth, to rend asunder the veils that have intervened between me and my recognition of the Dawning-Place of Thy signs and the Day Spring of Thy Revelation. Thou art, verily, the Almighty, the All-Powerful, the All-Bounteous. Deprive me not, O my Lord, of the fragrances of the Robe of Thy mercy in Thy days, and write down for me that which Thou hast written down for Thy handmaidens who have believed in Thee and in Thy signs, and have recognized Thee, and set their hearts towards the horizon of Thy Cause. Thou art truly the Lord of the worlds and of those who show mercy the Most Merciful. Assist me, then, O my God, to remember Thee amongst Thy handmaidens, and to aid Thy Cause in Thy lands. Accept, then, that which hath escaped me when the light of Thy countenance shone forth. Thou, indeed, hast power over all things. Glory be to Thee, O Thou in Whose hand is the kingdom of the heavens and of the earth.

Say: O King of Berlin! Give ear unto the Voice calling from this manifest Temple: Verily, there is none other God but Me, the Everlasting, the Peerless, the Ancient of Days. Take heed lest pride debar thee from recognizing the Dayspring of Divine Revelation, lest earthly desires shut thee out, as by a veil, from the Lord of the Throne above and of the earth below. Thus counselleth thee the Pen of the Most High. He, verily, is the Most Gracious, the All-Bountiful. Do thou remember the one whose power transcended thy power (Napoleon III), and whose station excelled thy station. Where is he? Whither are gone the things he possessed? Take warning, and be not of them that are fast asleep. He it was who cast the Tablet of God behind him, when We made known unto him what the hosts of tyranny had caused Us to suffer. Wherefore, disgrace assailed him from all sides, and he went down to dust in great loss. Think deeply, O King, concerning him, and concerning them who, like unto thee, have conquered cities and ruled over men. The All-Merciful brought them down from their palaces to their graves. Be warned, be of them who reflect . . . O banks of the Rhine! We have seen you covered with gore, inasmuch as the swords of retribution were drawn against you; and you shall have another turn. And We hear the lamentations of Berlin, though she be today in conspicuous glory.

O king! I was but a man like others, asleep upon My couch, when lo, the breezes of the All-Glorious were wafted over Me, and taught Me the knowledge of all that hath been. This thing is not from Me, but from One Who is Almighty and All-Knowing. And He bade Me lift up My voice between earth and heaven, and for this there befell Me what hath caused the tears of every man of understanding to flow. The learning current amongst men I studied not; their schools I entered not. Ask of the city wherein I dwelt, that thou mayest be well assured that I am not of them who speak falsely. This is but a leaf which the winds of the will of thy Lord, the Almighty, the All-Praised, have stirred. Can it be still when the tempestuous winds are blowing? Nay, by Him Who is the Lord of all Names and Attributes! They move it as they list. The evanescent is as nothing before Him Who is the Ever-Abiding. His all-compelling summons hath reached Me, and caused Me to speak His praise amidst all people. I was indeed as one dead when His behest was uttered. The hand of the will of thy Lord, the Compassionate, the Merciful, transformed Me. Can any one speak forth of his own accord that for which all men, both high and low, will protest against him? Nay, by Him Who taught the Pen the eternal mysteries, save him whom the grace of the Almighty, the All-Powerful, hath strengthened. The Pen of the Most High addresseth Me saying: Fear not. Relate unto His Majesty the Sháh that which befell thee. His heart, verily, is between the fingers of thy Lord, the God of Mercy, that haply the sun of justice and bounty may shine forth above the horizon of his heart. Thus hath the decree been irrevocably fixed by Him Who is the All-Wise.

Look upon this Youth, O King, with the eyes of justice; judge thou, then, with truth concerning what hath befallen Him. Of a verity, God hath made thee His shadow amongst men, and the sign of His power unto all that dwell on earth. Judge thou between Us and them that have wronged Us without proof and without an enlightening Book. They that surround thee love thee for their own sakes, whereas this Youth loveth thee for thine own sake, and hath had no desire except to draw thee nigh unto the seat of grace, and to turn thee toward the right-hand of justice. Thy Lord beareth witness unto that which I declare.

O King! Wert thou to incline thine ear unto the shrill of the Pen of Glory and the cooing of the Dove of Eternity which, on the branches of the Lote-Tree beyond which there is no passing, uttereth praises to God, the Maker of all names and Creator of earth and heaven, thou wouldst attain unto a station from which thou wouldst behold in the world of being naught save the effulgence of the Adored One, and wouldst regard thy sovereignty as the most contemptible of thy possessions, abandoning it to whosoever might desire it, and setting thy face toward the Horizon aglow with the light of His countenance. Neither wouldst thou ever be willing to bear the burden of dominion save for the purpose of helping thy Lord, the Exalted, the Most High. Then would the Concourse on high bless thee. O how excellent is this most sublime station, couldst thou ascend thereunto through the power of a sovereignty recognized as derived from the Name of God! . . . .

O King of the age! The eyes of these refugees are turned towards and fixed upon the mercy of the Most Merciful. No doubt is there whatever that these tribulations will be followed by the outpourings of a supreme mercy, and these dire adversities be succeeded by an over-flowing prosperity. We fain would hope, however, that His Majesty the Sháh will himself examine these matters, and bring hope to the hearts. That which We have submitted to thy Majesty is indeed for thine highest good. And God, verily, is a sufficient witness unto Me. . . .

O would that thou wouldst permit Me, O Sháh, to send unto thee that which would cheer the eyes, and tranquillize the souls, and persuade every fair-minded person that with Him is the knowledge of the Book. . . . But for the repudiation of the foolish and the connivance of the divines, I would have uttered a discourse that would have thrilled and carried away the hearts unto a realm from the murmur of whose winds can be heard: "No God is there but He!" . . .

I have seen, O Sháh, in the path of God what eye hath not seen nor ear heard. . . . How numerous the tribulations which have rained, and will soon rain, upon Me! I advance with My face set towards Him Who is the Almighty, the All-Bounteous, whilst behind Me glideth the serpent. Mine eyes have rained down tears until My bed is drenched. I sorrow not for Myself, however. By God! Mine head yearneth for the spear out of love for its Lord. I never passed a tree, but Mine heart addressed it saying: "O would that thou wert cut down in My name, and My body crucified upon thee, in the path of My Lord!" . . . By God! Though weariness lay Me low, and hunger consume Me, and the bare rock be My bed, and My fellows the beasts of the field, I will not complain, but will endure patiently as those endued with constancy and firmness have endured patiently, through the power of God, the Eternal King and Creator of the nations, and will render thanks unto God under all conditions. We pray that, out of His bounty—exalted be He—He may release, through this imprisonment, the necks of men from chains and fetters, and cause them to turn, with sincere faces, towards His Face, Who is the Mighty, the Bounteous. Ready is He to answer whosoever calleth upon Him, and nigh is He unto such as commune with Him.

O ye the elected representatives of the people in every land! Take ye counsel together, and let your concern be only for that which profiteth mankind, and bettereth the condition thereof, if ye be of them that scan heedfully. Regard the world as the human body which, though at its creation whole and perfect, hath been afflicted, through various causes, with grave disorders and maladies. Not for one day did it gain ease, nay its sickness waxed more severe, as it fell under the treatment of ignorant physicians, who gave full rein to their personal desires, and have erred grievously. And if, at one time, through the care of an able physician, a member of that body was healed, the rest remained afflicted as before. Thus informeth you the All-Knowing, the All-Wise.

We behold it, in this day, at the mercy of rulers so drunk with pride that they cannot discern clearly their own best advantage, much less recognize a Revelation so bewildering and challenging as this. And whenever any one of them hath striven to improve its condition, his motive hath been his own gain, whether confessedly so or not; and the unworthiness of this motive hath limited his power to heal or cure.

That which the Lord hath ordained as the sovereign remedy and mightiest instrument for the healing of all the world is the union of all its peoples in one universal Cause, one common Faith. This can in no wise be achieved except through the power of a skilled, an all-powerful and inspired Physician. This, verily, is the truth, and all else naught but error.

Tablets to the Leaders of Religion

Say: O leaders of religion! Weigh not the Book of God with such standards and sciences as are current amongst you, for the Book itself is the unerring balance established amongst men. In this most perfect balance whatsoever the peoples and kindreds of the earth possess must be weighed, while the measure of its weight should be tested according to its own standard, did ye but know it.

The eye of My loving-kindness weepeth sore over you, inasmuch as ye have failed to recognize the One upon Whom ye have been calling in the daytime and in the night season, at even and at morn. Advance, O people, with snow-white faces and radiant hearts, unto the blest and crimson Spot, wherein the Sadratu'l-Muntahá is calling: "Verily, there is none other God beside Me, the Omnipotent Protector, the Self-Subsisting!"

O ye leaders of religion! Who is the man amongst you that can rival Me in vision or insight? Where is he to be found that dareth to claim to be My equal in utterance or wisdom? No, by My Lord, the All-Merciful! All on the earth shall pass away; and this is the face of your Lord, the Almighty, the Well-Beloved.

We have decreed, O people, that the highest and last end of all learning be the recognition of Him Who is the Object of all knowledge; and yet, behold how ye have allowed your learning to shut you out, as by a veil, from Him Who is the Day Spring of this Light, through Whom every hidden thing hath been revealed. Could ye but discover the source whence the splendor of this utterance is diffused, ye would cast away the peoples of the world and all that they possess, and would draw nigh unto this most blessed seat of glory.

Say: This, verily, is the heaven in which the Mother Book is treasured, could ye but comprehend it. He it is Who hath caused the Rock to shout, and the Burning Bush to lift up its voice, upon the Mount rising above the Holy Land, and proclaim: "The Kingdom is God's, the sovereign Lord of all, the All-Powerful, the Loving!"

We have not entered any school, nor read any of your dissertations. Incline your ears to the words of this unlettered One, wherewith He summoneth you unto God, the Ever-Abiding. Better is this for you than all the treasures of the earth, could ye but comprehend it.

Say: O concourse of patriarchs! He Whom ye were promised in the Tablets is come. Fear God, and follow not the vain imaginings of the superstitious. Lay aside the things ye possess, and take fast hold of the Tablet of God by His sovereign power. Better is this for you than all your possessions. Unto this testifieth every understanding heart, and every man of insight. Pride ye yourselves on My Name, and yet shut yourselves out as by a veil from Me? This indeed is a strange thing! . . .

Say: O concourse of archbishops! He Who is the Lord of all men hath appeared. In the plain of guidance He calleth mankind, whilst ye are numbered with the dead! Great is the blessedness of him who is stirred by the Breeze of God, and hath arisen from amongst the dead in this perspicuous Name. . . .

Say: O concourse of bishops! Trembling hath seized all the kindreds of the earth, and He Who is the Everlasting Father calleth aloud between earth and heaven. Blessed the ear that hath heard, and the eye that hath seen, and the heart that hath turned unto Him Who is the Point of Adoration of all who are in the heavens and all who are on earth. . . . O concourse of bishops! Ye are the stars of the heaven of My knowledge. My mercy desireth not that ye should fall upon the earth. My justice, however, declareth: "This is that which the Son (Jesus) hath decreed." And whatsoever hath proceeded out of His blameless, His truth-speaking, trustworthy mouth, can never be altered. The bells, verily, peal out My Name, and lament over Me, but My spirit rejoiceth with evident gladness. The body of the Loved One yearneth for the cross, and His head is eager for the spear, in the path of the All-Merciful. The ascendancy of the oppressor can in no wise deter Him from His purpose. . . . The stars of the heaven of knowledge have fallen, they that adduce the proofs they possess in order to demonstrate the truth of My Cause, and who make mention of God in My name. When I came unto them, in My majesty, however, they turned aside from Me. They, verily, are of the fallen. That is what the Spirit (Jesus) prophesied when He came with the truth, and the Jewish doctors cavilled at Him, until they committed what made the Holy Spirit to lament, and the eyes of such as enjoy near access to God to weep.

Say: O concourse of priests! Leave the bells, and come forth, then, from your churches. It behoveth you, in this day, to proclaim aloud the Most Great Name among the nations. Prefer ye to be silent, whilst every stone and every tree shouteth aloud: "The Lord is come in His great glory!" . . . He that summoneth men in My name is, verily, of Me, and he will show forth that which is beyond the power of all that are on earth. . . . Let the Breeze of God awaken you. Verily, it hath wafted over the world. Well is it with him that hath discovered the fragrance thereof and been accounted among the well-assured. . . . O concourse of priests! The Day of Reckoning hath appeared, the Day whereon He Who was in heaven hath come. He, verily, is the One Whom ye were promised in the Books of God, the Holy, the Almighty, the All-

Praised. How long will ye wander in the wilderness of heedlessness and superstition? Turn with your hearts in the direction of your Lord, the Forgiving, the Generous.

O Pope! Rend the veils asunder. He Who is the Lord of Lords is come overshadowed with clouds, and the decree hath been fulfilled by God, the Almighty, the Unrestrained. . . . He, verily, hath again come down from Heaven even as He came down from it the first time. Beware that thou dispute not with Him even as the Pharisees disputed with Him (Jesus) without a clear token or proof. On His right hand flow the living waters of grace, and on His left the choice Wine of justice, whilst before Him march the angels of Paradise, bearing the banners of His signs. Beware lest any name debar thee from God, the Creator of earth and heaven. Leave thou the world behind thee, and turn towards thy Lord, through Whom the whole earth hath been illumined. . . . Dwellest thou in palaces whilst He Who is the King of Revelation liveth in the most desolate of abodes? Leave them unto such as desire them, and set thy face with joy and delight towards the Kingdom. . . . Arise in the name of thy Lord, the God of Mercy, amidst the peoples of the earth, and seize thou the Cup of Life with the hands of confidence, and first drink thou therefrom, and proffer it then to such as turn towards it amongst the peoples of all faiths. . . .

Call thou to remembrance Him Who was the Spirit (Jesus), Who, when He came, the most learned of His age pronounced judgment against Him in His own country, whilst he who was only a fisherman believed in Him. Take heed, then, ye men of understanding heart! Thou, in truth, art one of the suns of the heaven of His names. Guard thyself, lest darkness spread its veil over thee, and fold thee away from His light. . . . Consider those who opposed the Son (Jesus), when He came unto them with sovereignty and power. How many the Pharisees who were waiting to behold Him, and were lamenting over their separation from Him! And yet, when the fragrance of His coming was wafted over them, and His beauty was unveiled, they turned aside from Him and disputed with Him. . . . None save a very few, who were destitute of any power amongst men, turned towards His face. And yet, today, every man endowed with power and invested with sovereignty prideth himself on His Name! In like manner, consider how numerous, in these days, are the monks who, in My Name, have secluded themselves in their churches, and who, when the appointed time was fulfilled, and We unveiled Our beauty, knew Us not, though they call upon Me at eventide and at dawn. . . .

The Word which the Son concealed is made manifest. It hath been sent down in the form of the human temple in this day. Blessed be the Lord Who is the Father! He, verily, is come unto the nations in His most great majesty. Turn your faces towards Him, O concourse of the righteous! . . . This is the day whereon the Rock (Peter) crieth out and shouteth, and celebrateth the praise of its Lord, the All-Possessing, the Most High, saying: "Lo! The Father is come, and that which ye were promised in the Kingdom is fulfilled! . . ." My body longeth for the cross, and Mine head waiteth the thrust of the spear, in the path of the All-Merciful, that the world may be purged from its transgressions. . . .

O Supreme Pontiff! Incline thine ear unto that which the Fashioner of moldering bones counselleth thee, as voiced by Him Who is His Most Great Name. Sell all the embellished ornaments thou dost possess, and expend them in the path of God, Who causeth the night to return upon the day, and the day to return upon the night. Abandon thy kingdom unto the kings, and emerge from thy habitation, with thy face set towards the Kingdom, and, detached from the world, then speak forth the praises of thy Lord betwixt earth and heaven. Thus hath bidden thee He Who is the Possessor of Names, on the part of thy Lord, the Almighty, the All-Knowing. Exhort thou the kings and say: "Deal equably with men. Beware lest ye transgress the bounds fixed in the Book." This indeed becometh thee. Beware lest thou appropriate unto thyself the things of the world and the riches thereof. Leave them unto such as desire them, and cleave unto that which hath been enjoined upon thee by Him Who is the Lord of creation. Should any one offer thee all the treasures of the earth, refuse to even glance upon them. Be as thy Lord hath been. Thus hath the Tongue of Revelation spoken that which God hath made the ornament of the book of creation. . . . Should the inebriation of the wine of My verses seize thee, and thou determinest to present thyself before the throne of thy Lord, the Creator of earth and heaven, make My love thy vesture, and thy shield remembrance of Me, and thy provision reliance upon God, the Revealer of all power. . . . Verily, the day of ingathering is come, and all things have been separated from each other. He hath stored away that which He chose in the vessels of justice, and cast into fire that which befitteth it. Thus hath it been decreed by your Lord, the Mighty, the Loving, in this promised Day. He, verily, ordaineth what He pleaseth. There is none other God save He, the Almighty, the All-Compelling.

Leaders of religion in every age have hindered their people from attaining the shores of eternal salvation, inasmuch as they held the reins of authority in their mighty grasp. Some for the lust of leadership, others through want of knowledge and understanding, have been the cause of the deprivation of the people. By their sanction and authority, every Prophet of God hath drunk from the chalice of sacrifice, and winged His flight unto the heights of glory. What unspeakable cruelties they that have occupied the seats of authority and learning have inflicted upon the true Monarchs of the world, those Gems of Divine virtue! Content with a transitory dominion, they have deprived themselves of an everlasting sovereignty. . . . Among these "veils of glory" are the divines and doctors living in the days of the Manifestation of God, who, because of their want of discernment and their love and eagerness for leadership, have failed to submit to the Cause of God, nay, have even refused to incline their ears unto the Divine Melody. "They have thrust their fingers into their ears." And the people also, utterly ignoring God and taking them for their masters, have placed themselves unreservedly under the authority of these pompous and hypocritical leaders, for they have no sight, no hearing, no heart, of their own to distinguish truth from falsehood. Notwithstanding the divinely-inspired admonitions of all the Prophets, the Saints, and Chosen Ones of God, enjoining the people to see with their own eyes and hear with their own ears, they have disdainfully rejected their counsels and have blindly followed, and will continue to follow, the leaders of their Faith. Should a poor and obscure person, destitute of the attire of the men of learning, address them saying: "Follow ye, O people, the Messengers of God," they would, greatly surprised at such a statement, reply: "What! Meanest thou that all these divines, all these exponents of learning, with all their authority, their pomp, and pageantry, have erred, and failed to distinguish truth from falsehood? Dost thou, and people like thyself, pretend to have comprehended that which they have not understood?" If numbers and excellence of apparel be regarded as the criterions of learning and truth, the peoples of a bygone age, whom those of today have never surpassed in numbers, magnificence and power, should certainly be accounted a superior and worthier people. . . . Not one Prophet of God was made manifest Who did not fall a victim to the relentless hate, to the denunciation, denial and execration of the clerics of His day! Woe unto them for the iniquities their hands have formerly wrought! Woe unto them for that which they are now doing! What veils of glory more grievous than these embodiments of error! By the righteousness of God! To pierce such veils is the mightiest of all acts, and to rend them asunder the most meritorious of all deeds! . . . On their tongue the mention of God hath become an empty name; in their midst His holy Word a dead letter. Such is the sway of their desires, that the lamp of conscience and reason hath been quenched in their hearts. . . . No two are found to agree on one and the same law, for they seek no God but their own desire, and tread no path but the path of error. In leadership they have recognized the ultimate object of their endeavor, and account pride and haughtiness as the highest attainments of their hearts' desire. They have placed their sordid machinations above the Divine decree, have renounced resignation unto the will of God, busied themselves with selfish calculation, and walked in the way of the hypocrite. With all their power and strength they strive to secure themselves in their petty pursuits, fearful lest the least discredit undermine their authority or blemish the display of their magnificence.

Tablet to the People

O banished and faithful friend! Quench the thirst of heedlessness with the sanctified waters of My grace, and chase the gloom of remoteness through the morning-light of My Divine presence. Suffer not the habitation wherein dwelleth My undying love for thee to be destroyed through the tyranny of covetous desires, and overcloud not the beauty of the heavenly Youth with the dust of self and passion. Clothe thyself with the essence of righteousness, and let thine heart be afraid of none except God. Obstruct not the luminous spring of thy soul with the thorns and brambles of vain and inordinate affections, and impede not the flow of the living waters that stream from the fountain of thine heart. Set all thy hope in God, and cleave tenaciously to His unfailing mercy. Who else but Him can enrich the destitute, and deliver the fallen from his abasement?

O My servants! Were ye to discover the hidden, the shoreless oceans of My incorruptible wealth, ye would, of a certainty, esteem as nothing the world, nay, the entire creation. Let the flame of search burn with such fierceness within your hearts as to enable you to attain your supreme and most exalted goal—the station at which ye can draw nigh unto, and be united with, your Best-Beloved. . . .

O My servants! Let not your vain hopes and idle fancies sap the foundations of your belief in the All-Glorious God, inasmuch as such imaginings have been wholly unprofitable unto men, and failed to direct their steps unto the straight Path. Think ye, O My servants, that the Hand of My all-encompassing, My overshadowing, and transcendent sovereignty is chained up, that the flow of Mine ancient, My ceaseless, and all-pervasive mercy is checked, or that the clouds of My sublime and unsurpassed favors have ceased to rain their gifts upon men? Can ye imagine that the wondrous works that have proclaimed My divine and resistless power are withdrawn, or that the potency of My will and purpose hath been deterred from directing the destinies of mankind? If it be not so, wherefore, then, have ye striven to prevent the deathless Beauty of My sacred and gracious Countenance from being unveiled to men's eyes? Why have ye struggled to hinder the Manifestation of the Almighty and All-Glorious Being from shedding the radiance of His Revelation upon the earth? Were ye to be fair in your judgment, ye would readily recognize how the realities of all created things are inebriated with the joy of this new and wondrous Revelation, how all the atoms of the earth have been illuminated through the brightness of its glory. Vain and wretched is that which ye have imagined and still imagine!

Retrace your steps, O My servants, and incline your hearts to Him Who is the Source of your creation. Deliver yourselves from your evil and corrupt affections, and hasten to embrace the light of the undying Fire that gloweth on the Sinai of this mysterious and transcendent Revelation. Corrupt not the holy, the all-embracing, and primal Word of God, and seek not to profane its sanctity or to debase its exalted character. O heedless ones! Though the wonders of My mercy have encompassed all created things, both visible and invisible, and though the revelations of My grace and bounty have permeated every atom of the universe, yet the rod with which I can chastise the wicked is grievous, and the fierceness of Mine anger against them terrible. With ears that are sanctified from vain-glory and worldly desires hearken unto the counsels which I, in My merciful kindness, have revealed unto you, and with your inner and outer eyes contemplate the evidences of My marvelous Revelation. . . .

O My servants! Deprive not yourselves of the unfading and resplendent Light that shineth within the Lamp of Divine glory. Let the flame of the love of God burn brightly within your radiant hearts. Feed it with the oil of Divine guidance, and protect it within the shelter of your constancy. Guard it within the globe of trust and detachment from all else but God, so that the evil whisperings of the ungodly may not extinguish its light. O My servants! My holy, My divinely ordained Revelation may be likened unto an ocean in whose depths are concealed innumerable pearls of great price, of surpassing luster. It is the duty of every seeker to bestir himself and strive to attain the shores of this ocean, so that he may, in proportion to the eagerness of his search and the efforts he hath exerted, partake of such benefits as have been pre-ordained in God's irrevocable and hidden Tablets. If no one be willing to direct his steps towards its shores, if every one should fail to arise and find Him, can such a failure be said to have robbed this ocean of its power or to have lessened, to any degree, its treasures? How vain, how contemptible, are the imaginations which your hearts have devised, and are still devising! O My servants! The one true God is My witness! This most great, this fathomless and surging Ocean is near, astonishingly near, unto you. Behold it is closer to you than your life-vein! Swift as the twinkling of an eye ye can, if ye but wish it, reach and partake of this imperishable favor, this God-given grace, this incorruptible gift, this most potent and unspeakably glorious bounty.

O My servants! Could ye apprehend with what wonders of My munificence and bounty I have willed to entrust your souls, ye would, of a truth, rid yourselves of attachment to all created things, and would gain a true knowledge of your own selves—a knowledge which is the same as the comprehension of Mine own Being. Ye would find yourselves independent of all else but Me, and would perceive, with your inner and outer eye, and as manifest as the revelation of My effulgent Name, the seas of My loving-kindness and bounty moving within you. Suffer not your idle fancies, your evil passions, your insincerity and blindness of heart to dim the luster, or stain the sanctity, of so lofty a station. Ye are even as the bird which soareth, with the full force of its mighty wings and with complete and joyous confidence, through the immensity of the heavens, until, impelled to satisfy its hunger, it turneth longingly to the water and clay of the earth below it, and, having been entrapped in the mesh of its desire, findeth itself impotent to resume its flight to the realms whence it came. Powerless to shake off the burden weighing on its sullied wings, that bird, hitherto an inmate of the heavens is now forced to seek a dwelling-place upon the dust. Wherefore, O My servants, defile not your wings with the clay of waywardness and vain desires, and suffer them not to be stained with the dust of envy and hate, that ye may not be hindered from soaring in the heavens of My divine knowledge.

O My servants! Through the might of God and His power, and out of the treasury of His knowledge and wisdom, I have brought forth and revealed unto you the pearls that lay concealed in the depths of His everlasting ocean. I have summoned the Maids of Heaven to emerge from behind the veil of concealment, and have clothed them with these words of Mine—words of consummate power and wisdom. I have, moreover, with the hand of divine power, unsealed the choice wine of My Revelation, and have wafted its holy, its hidden, and musk-laden fragrance upon all created things. Who else but yourselves is to be blamed if ye choose to remain unendowed with so great an outpouring of God's transcendent and all-encompassing grace, with so bright a revelation of His resplendent mercy? . . .

O My servants! There shineth nothing else in Mine heart except the unfading light of the Morn of Divine guidance, and out of My mouth proceedeth naught but the essence of truth, which the Lord your God hath revealed. Follow not, therefore, your earthly desires, and violate not the Covenant of God, nor break your pledge to Him. With firm determination, with the whole affection of your heart, and with the full force of your words, turn ye unto Him, and walk not in the ways of the foolish. The world is but a show, vain and empty, a mere nothing, bearing the semblance of reality. Set not your affections upon it. Break not the bond that uniteth you with your Creator, and be not of those that have erred and strayed from His ways. Verily I say, the world is like the vapor in a desert, which the thirsty dreameth to be water and striveth after it with all his might, until when he cometh unto it, he findeth it to be mere illusion. It may, moreover, be likened unto the lifeless image of the beloved whom the lover hath sought and found, in the end, after long search and to his utmost regret, to be such as cannot "fatten nor appease his hunger."

O My servants! Sorrow not if, in these days and on this earthly plane, things contrary to your wishes have been ordained and manifested by God, for days of blissful joy, of heavenly delight, are assuredly in store for you. Worlds, holy and spiritually glorious, will be unveiled to your eyes. You are destined by Him, in this world and hereafter, to partake of their benefits, to share in their joys, and to obtain a portion of their sustaining grace. To each and every one of them you will, no doubt, attain.

CHAPTER TWO

THE PROMISED ONE

The Successive Revelations

Praised be Thou, O Lord my God! Every time I am reminded of Thee and muse on Thy virtues, I am seized with such ecstasies and am so enravished by Thee that I find myself unable to make mention of Thy name and to extol Thee. I am carried back to such heights that I recognize my self to be the same as the remembrance of Thee in Thy realm, and the essence of Thy praise among Thy servants. As long as that self endureth, so long will Thy praise continue to be shed abroad among Thy creatures and Thy remembrance glorified by Thy people.

Every man endued with insight among Thy servants is persuaded that my self liveth eternally and can never perish, inasmuch as remembrance of Thee is eternal and will endure so long as Thine own Self endureth, and Thy praise is everlasting and will last as long as Thine own sovereignty will last. By its means Thou art glorified by such of Thy chosen ones as call upon Thee and by the sincere among Thy servants. Nay, the praise wherewith any one, in the entire creation, praiseth Thee proceedeth from this exalted self and returneth unto it, even as the sun which, while it shineth, sheddeth its splendor upon whatsoever may be exposed to its rays. From this sun is generated, and unto it must return, the light which is shed over all things.

Exalted, immeasurably exalted art Thou above any attempt to measure the greatness of Thy Cause, above any comparison that one may seek to make, above the efforts of the human tongue to utter its import! From everlasting Thou hast existed, alone with no one else beside Thee, and wilt, to everlasting, continue to remain the same, in the sublimity of Thine essence and the inaccessible heights of Thy glory.

And when Thou didst purpose to make Thyself known unto men, Thou didst successively reveal the Manifestations of Thy Cause, and ordained each to be a sign of Thy Revelation among Thy people and the Day Spring of Thine invisible Self amidst Thy creatures, until the time when, as decreed by Thee, all Thy previous Revelations culminated in Him Whom Thou hast appointed as the Lord of all who are in the heaven of revelation and the kingdom of creation, Him Whom Thou hast established as the Sovereign Lord of all who are in the heavens and all who are on the earth. He it was Whom Thou hast determined to be the Herald of Thy Most Great Revelation and the Announcer of Thy Most Ancient Splendor. In this Thou hadst no other purpose except to try them who have manifested Thy most excellent titles unto all who are in heaven and on earth. He it was Whom Thou hast commanded to establish His covenant with all created things.

And when Thy promise came to pass and the set time was fulfilled, He Who is the Possessor of all Names and Attributes was made manifest unto men. Thereupon all that were in the heavens and all that were on the earth were terror-stricken save those whom Thou didst keep under Thy protection and preserve within the shelter of Thy power and gracious providence. There befell Him, at the hands of such of Thy creatures as have transgressed against Thee, that which the tongue of no one of Thy servants can recount.

Look down, then, upon Him, O my God, with the eye of Thy tender mercy, and send down upon Him and upon those that love Him all the good Thou didst ordain in the heaven of Thy will and the Tablet of Thy decree. Aid them, then, with Thy succor, for Thou art, verily, the Almighty, the Most Exalted, the All-Glorious, the All-Compelling.

Wishing to Reveal Thyself

Lauded be Thy name, O Lord my God! I testify that Thou wast a hidden Treasure wrapped within Thine immemorial Being and an impenetrable Mystery enshrined in Thine own Essence. Wishing to reveal Thyself, Thou didst call into being the Greater and the Lesser Worlds, and didst choose Man above all Thy creatures, and didst make Him a sign of both of these worlds, O Thou Who art our Lord, the Most Compassionate!

Thou didst raise Him up to occupy Thy throne before all the people of Thy creation. Thou didst enable Him to unravel Thy mysteries, and to shine with the lights of Thine inspiration and Thy Revelation, and to manifest Thy names and Thine attributes. Through Him Thou didst adorn the preamble of the book of Thy creation, O Thou Who art the Ruler of the universe Thou hast fashioned!

I bear witness that in His person solidity and fluidity have been joined and combined. Through His immovable constancy in Thy Cause, and His unwavering adherence to whatsoever Thou, in the plenitude of the light of Thy glory, didst unveil to His eyes, throughout the domains of Thy Revelation and creation, the souls of Thy servants were stirred up in their longing for Thy Kingdom, and the dwellers of Thy realms rushed forth to enter into Thy heavenly dominion. Through the restlessness He evinced in Thy path, the feet of all them that are devoted to Thee were steeled and confirmed to manifest Thy Cause amidst Thy creatures, and to demonstrate Thy sovereignty throughout Thy realm.

How great, O my God, is this Thy most excellent handiwork, and how consummate Thy creation, which hath caused every understanding heart and mind to marvel! And when the set time was fulfilled, and what had been preordained came to pass, Thou didst unloose His tongue to praise Thee, and to lay bare Thy mysteries before all Thy creation, O Thou Who art the Possessor of all names, and the Fashioner of earth and heaven! Through Him all created things were made to glorify Thee, and to celebrate Thy praise, and every soul was directed towards the kingdom of Thy revelation and Thy sovereignty.

At one time, Thou didst raise Him up, O my God, and didst attire Him with the ornament of the name of Him Who conversed with Thee (Moses), and didst through Him uncover all that Thy will had decreed and Thine irrevocable purpose ordained. At another time, Thou didst adorn Him with the name of Him Who was Thy Spirit (Jesus), and didst send Him down out of the heaven of Thy will, for the edification of Thy people, infusing thereby the spirit of life into the hearts of the sincere among Thy servants and the faithful among Thy creatures. Again, Thou didst reveal Him, decked forth by the name of Him Who was Thy Friend (Muḥammad), and caused Him to shine brightly above the horizon of Ḥijáz, as a token of Thy power and an evidence of Thy might. Through Him Thou didst send unto Thy servants what enabled them to scale the heights of Thy unity, and to yearn over the wonders of Thy manifold knowledge and wisdom.

I testify, O Thou Who art the Lord of the whole creation, and the Desire of whosoever hath sought Thee, that, amidst Thy creatures, they resemble the sun which no matter how often it riseth and setteth is still the one and the same sun. Whoso maketh any distinction between any of them hath truly failed to attain the ultimate purpose, and to reach the highest goal, and hath been deprived of the mysteries of unity and of the lights of sanctity and oneness. I testify, moreover, that Thou hast decreed that none on the face of the earth should equal them, and none of Thy creatures be able to be compared with any of them, in order that Thine own singleness and peerlessness might be recognized and established.

Glorified, immeasurably glorified be Thy name, O my God! How can I ever befittingly mention Thee or sufficiently praise Thee, that Thou hast manifested Him by the power of Thy might, and caused Him to shine above the horizon of Thy will, and made Him the Day Spring of Thy signs, and the Dawning-Place of the revelation of Thy names and Thine attributes? How bewilderingly mysterious, moreover, O my God, is His nature and all that Thou hast infused into Him, through Thy strength and by the power of Thy might! At one time He appeareth as the water which is Life indeed, sent down out of the heaven of Thy grace, and poured forth from the clouds of Thy mercy, that Thy creatures may be endued with new life, and live as long as Thine own Kingdom endureth. Every drop of that water would suffice to quicken the dead, and to set their faces in the direction of Thy favors and Thy gifts, and to rid them of all attachment to aught else except Thee. At another time He revealeth Himself as the Fire which Thou didst kindle in the tree of Thy unity, whose heat melted the hearts of Thine ardent lovers when He Who is the Day Star of the world shone forth above the horizon of 'Iráq. I testify, O my God, that through Him the veils of human fancy were burnt up, and the hearts of men were set towards the scene of Thy most resplendent glory.

I implore Thee, O Thou Who art the Supreme Ordainer, not to suffer me to be deprived of the breezes which are wafted in Thy days, the days whereon the sweet smell of the raiment of Thy mercy hath been shed abroad. Neither do Thou keep me back from Thy most great Ocean, every drop of which crieth out and saith: "Great is the blessedness that awaiteth him who hath been awakened from his sleep by the breath of God which, from the source of His mercy, hath blown over all such of His creatures as have set themselves towards Him!"

Thou seest, O my Lord, how Thy servants are held captive by their own selves and desires. Redeem them from their bondage, O my God, by the power of Thy sovereignty and might, that they may turn towards Thee when He Who is the Revealer of Thy names and attributes is manifested unto men.

Cast upon this poor and desolate creature, O my Lord, the glance of Thy wealth, and flood his heart with the beams of Thy knowledge, that he may apprehend the verities of the unseen world, and discover the mysteries of Thy heavenly realm, and perceive the signs and tokens of Thy kingdom, and behold the manifold revelations of this earthly life all set forth before the face of Him Who is the Revealer of Thine own Self. Direct, then, his eyes, O my God, towards the horizon of Thy loving-kindness, and make steadfast his heart in its attachment to Thee, and unloose his tongue to praise Thee, and make him able to hold fast the cord of Thy love, and to cling to the hem of Thy bounteousness, and to proclaim Thy name amidst Thy creatures, and to recount Thy virtues throughout Thy realm, in such wise that no obstacle will deter him from turning to Thy name, the All-Bountiful, and no veil shut him out from Thee, in Whose hand is the dominion of utterance and the kingdom of all names and attributes!

Hold Thou the hand of this seeker who hath set his face towards Thee, O my Lord, and draw him out of the depths of his vain imaginations, that the light of certainty may shine brightly above the horizon of his heart in the days whereon the sun of the knowledge of Thy creatures hath been darkened through the shining of the Day Star of Thy glory; the days whereon the moon of the world's wisdom hath been eclipsed through the appearance of Thy hidden knowledge, and the manifestation of Thy well-guarded secret, and the revelation of Thine enshrined mystery; the days whereon the stars of men's doings have fallen through the rising of the orb of Thy unity and the shedding of the radiance of Thy transcendent oneness.

I beg of Thee, O my God, by Thy most exalted Word which Thou hast ordained as the Divine Elixir unto all who are in Thy realm, the Elixir through whose potency the crude metal of human life hath been transmuted into purest gold, O Thou in Whose hands are both the visible and invisible kingdoms, to ordain that my choice be conformed to Thy choice and my wish to Thy wish, that I may be entirely content with that which Thou didst desire, and be wholly satisfied with what Thou didst destine for me by Thy bounteousness and favor. Potent art Thou to do as Thou willest. Thou, in very truth, art the All-Glorious, the All-Wise.

Happy is the man who hath recognized Thee, and discovered the sweetness of Thy fragrance, and set himself towards Thy kingdom, and tasted of the things that have been perfected therein by Thy grace and favor. Great is the blessedness of him who hath acknowledged Thy most excellent majesty, and whom the veils that have shut out the nations from Thee have not hindered from directing his eyes towards Thee, O Thou Who art the King of eternity and the Quickener of every moldering bone! Blessed, also, is he that hath inhaled Thy sweet savors, and been carried away by Thine utterances in Thy days. Blessed, moreover, be the man that hath turned unto Thee, and woe betide him that hath turned his back upon Thee.

Praised be Thou, the Lord of the worlds!

The Covenant Thou Hast Established

Glorified art Thou, O my God! Thou knowest that my sole aim in revealing Thy Cause hath been to reveal Thee and not my self, and to manifest Thy glory rather than my glory. In Thy path, and to attain Thy pleasure, I have scorned rest, joy, delight. At all times and under all conditions my gaze hath been fixed on Thy precepts, and mine eyes bent upon the things Thou hast bidden me observe in Thy Tablets. I have wakened every morning to the light of Thy praise and Thy remembrance, and reached every evening inhaling the fragrances of Thy mercy.

And when the entire creation was stirred up, and the whole earth was convulsed, and the sweet savors of Thy name, the All-Praised, had almost ceased to breathe over Thy realms, and the winds of Thy mercy had well-nigh been stilled throughout Thy dominions, Thou didst, through the power of Thy might, raise me up among Thy servants, and bid me to show forth Thy sovereignty amidst Thy people. Thereupon I arose before all Thy creatures, strengthened by Thy help and Thy power, and summoned all the multitudes unto Thee, and announced unto all Thy servants Thy favors and Thy gifts, and invited them to turn towards this Ocean, every drop of the waters of which crieth out, proclaiming unto all that are in heaven and on earth that He is, in truth, the Fountain of all life, and the Quickener of the entire creation, and the Object of the adoration of all worlds, and the Best-Beloved of every understanding heart, and the Desire of all them that are nigh unto Thee.

Though the fierce winds of the hatred of the wicked doers blew and beat on this Lamp, He was, at no time, in His love for Thy beauty, hindered from shedding the fragrance of His light. As the transgressions committed against Thee waxed greater and greater, my eagerness to reveal Thy Cause correspondingly increased, and as the tribulations deepened—and to this Thy glory beareth me witness—a fuller measure of Thy sovereignty and of Thy power was vouchsafed by me unto Thy creatures.

And finally, I was cast by the transgressors into the prison-city of 'Akká, and my kindred were made captives in Baghdád. The power of Thy might beareth me witness, O my God! Every trouble that hath touched me in Thy path hath added to my joy and increased my gladness. I swear by Thee, O Thou Who art the King of Kings! None of the kings of the earth hath power to hinder me from remembering Thee or from extolling Thy virtues. Were they to be leagued—as they have been leagued—against me, and to brandish their sharpest swords and most afflictive spears against me, I would not hesitate to magnify Thy name before all them that are in Thy heaven and on Thy earth. Nay rather, I would cry out and say: "This, O my Beloved, is my face which I have offered up for Thy face, and this is my spirit which I have sacrificed for Thy spirit, and this is my blood that seetheth in my veins, in its longing to be shed for love of Thee and in Thy path."

Though—as Thou beholdest me, O my God—I be dwelling in a place within whose walls no voice can be heard except the sound of the echo, though all the gates of ease and comfort be shut against us, and thick darkness appear to have compassed us on every side, yet my soul hath been so inflamed by its love for Thee, that nothing whatsoever can either quench the fire of its love or abate the consuming flame of its desire. Lifting up its voice, it crieth aloud amidst Thy servants, and calleth them, at all times and under all conditions, unto Thee.

I beseech Thee, by Thy Most Great Name, to open the eyes of Thy servants, that they may behold Thee shining above the horizon of Thy majesty and glory, and that they may not be hindered by the croaking of the raven from hearkening to the voice of the Dove of Thy sublime oneness, nor be prevented by the corrupt waters from partaking of the pure wine of Thy bounty and the everlasting streams of Thy gifts.

Gather them, then, together around this Divine Law, the covenant of which Thou hast established with all Thy Prophets and Thy Messengers, and Whose ordinances Thou hast written down in Thy Tablets and Thy Scriptures. Raise them up, moreover, to such heights as will enable them to perceive Thy Call.

Potent art Thou to do what pleaseth Thee. Thou art, verily, the Inaccessible, the All-Glorious.

Whom Thou Hast Chosen

Praised be Thou, O my God, that Thou hast been true to what the Pen of Thy Revelation hath inscribed upon the Tablets sent down by Thee unto them Whom Thou hast chosen above all Thy creatures, and through Whom Thou hast unlocked the doors of Thy mercy, and shed abroad the radiance of the light of Thy guidance. Glory to Thee that Thou hast laid bare what had from eternity been wrapped up within the Tabernacle of Thy majesty, Thine omnipotence and glory, and through which Thou hadst decked forth the heaven of Thy Revelation and adorned the pages of the book of Thy testimony.

And when the Pledge was fulfilled and the Promised One appeared, He was rejected by such of Thy servants as profess to have believed in Him in Whom Thy Godhead was manifested, Whom Thou didst ordain to be the Herald of this Revelation, and through Whose advent the eyes of the inmates of the sanctuary of Thy unity were cheered.

I know, O my Lord, neither their reasoning with which they have acknowledged Thee and believed in Thy signs, nor their argument whereby they have repudiated Thy sovereignty. Every time I call them to Thee and say: "O people! Consider the utterances of the Lord your God which are in your possession and those that have been sent down from the heaven of His will and power," they cavil at Thee, and turn their backs to Thee, though—as Thou art aware—each of the words that have gone out of the mouth of Thy will sheddeth the fragrance of the breaths of Thy mercy.

Some have chosen to cleave to him who is counted unworthy to converse with any of Thy servants that watch at Thy door (Mírzá Yaḥyá), how much more to enter into the court in which the Tongue of Thy majesty speaketh. Cleanse Thou their hearts and their eyes, O my Lord, that they may see with their eyes and understand with their hearts, that haply they may be attracted by Thine utterances to the Day-Spring of Thine inspiration, and draw nigh unto the soft-flowing stream of Thy knowledge.

Thou art He, O my Lord, Who hath, in every line of Thy Book, entered into covenant with them for me, and made it so sure that none of Thy creatures can any longer evade it. Thou didst say—and Thy word is the truth: "One single letter from Him excelleth all that hath been sent down in the Bayán."

Thou dost consider, therefore, O my God, how they have transgressed against Thy Cause, and beholdest what their hands have wrought in Thy days. They have so grievously wronged me that the Lote-Tree of Thy Revelation moaneth, and the inmates of the Tabernacle of Thy majesty and the dwellers of the cities of Thy names lament. I know not, O my God, for what reason they have risen up to oppress me, and by what proof they have turned aside from Him Who is the Day Spring of Thy signs. I beseech Thee, O Thou Who art the Lord of all names and the Creator of the heavens, to aid them to act equitably in Thy Cause, that haply they may discover the sweet smell of the robe of Thy mercy, and set their faces towards the horizon that shineth with the brightness of the light of Thy face. Weak are they, O my Lord, and Thou art the Lord of strength and power. They are but paupers, and Thou art the All-Possessing, the Most Generous.

Thou art well aware, O my God, that throughout my life I have sought no advantage for myself. I have offered up my spirit and my whole being for the exaltation of Thy word amidst Thy creatures and the glorification of Thy name among Thy servants. Thou didst send me with such a Testimony that they Who are the Exponents of Thy Revelation and the Day Springs of Thine inspiration were stirred up with vehement longing. Through it, Thy proof was established, and Thy bounty fulfilled, and Thy Cause perfected, and Thine utterances released, and Thy clear tokens uncovered.

Thou knowest, O my God, that I have wished only what Thou hast wished, and desire what Thou dost desire. Were I to speak forth before Thy servants the things wherewith Thou didst, through Thy bounty, inspire me and which Thou didst command me to utter amidst Thy creatures, the oppressors among Thy people would cavil at me. And were I to hold my peace and cease to celebrate the wonders of Thy praise, all the limbs of my body would be stirred up to extol Thee. I know not what the water is with which Thou didst create me, or what the fire Thou didst kindle within me. I swear by Thy glory! I shall not cease to mention Thee, though all that are in Thy heaven and on Thy earth rise up against me. Thee will I magnify, in all circumstances, with a heart wholly rid of all attachment to the world and all that is therein.

Praised be Thou, the Well-Beloved of the hearts of all such as have recognized Thee.

Thy Straight Path

I beseech Thee, O God of bounty and King of all created things, to guard Thy servants from the imaginations which their hearts may devise. Raise them up, then, to such heights that their footsteps may slip not in the face of the evidences of Thy handiwork, which the manifold exigencies of Thy wisdom have ordained, and whose secrets Thou hast hid from the face of Thy people and Thy creatures. Withhold them not, O my Lord, from the ocean of Thy knowledge, neither do Thou deprive them of what Thou didst destine for such of Thy chosen ones as have near access to Thee, and those of Thy trusted ones as are wholly devoted to Thy Self. Supply them, then, from Thy sea of certainty with what will calm the agitation of their hearts. Turn, O Lord my God, the darkness of their fancies into the brightness of certitude, and cause them to arise, and to walk steadfastly in Thy straight Path, that haply Thy Book may not hinder them from recognizing Him Who is its Revealer, and Thy names from acknowledging the One Who is their Creator, and their Provider, and their Origin, and their King, and their Begetter, and their Destroyer, and their Glorifier, and their Abaser, and their Governor, and the Sovereign Protector of their Bearers.

Thou Hast Sent Down Thy Book

Thou art the One, O my God and my Ruler, Who hast sent down Thy Book that Thou mayest manifest my Cause, and glorify my Word. Through it Thou didst enter into a Covenant, concerning me, with all that hath been created in Thy realm. Thou seest, O Beloved of the world, how the rebellious among Thy creatures have made of that Covenant a bulwark for themselves, and through it have withdrawn from Thy Beauty, and repudiated Thy signs.

Thou art He, O my God, Who hath commanded them in Thy great Book, and said: "Fear ye the Most Merciful, O people of the Bayán, and deny not Him for Whom I have ordained the Bayán to be one of the leaves of His Paradise. I, verily, esteem it as a gift from me unto Him. Were it His pleasure to accept it, He, truly, is the Most Bountiful; and if He cast it away and refuse to consider it, His verdict is just, and He, in very truth, is Praiseworthy in His acts, and meet to be obeyed in His behests. To none is given the right to cavil at Him."

The Tablet of Visitation

The praise which hath dawned from Thy most august Self, and the glory which hath shone forth from Thy most effulgent Beauty, rest upon Thee, O Thou Who art the Manifestation of Grandeur, and the King of Eternity, and the Lord of all who are in heaven and on earth! I testify that through Thee the sovereignty of God and His dominion, and the majesty of God and His grandeur, were revealed, and the Day Stars of ancient splendor have shed their radiance in the heaven of Thine irrevocable decree, and the Beauty of the Unseen hath shone forth above the horizon of creation. I testify, moreover, that with but a movement of Thy Pen Thine injunction "Be Thou" hath been enforced, and God's hidden Secret hath been divulged, and all created things have been called into being, and all the Revelations have been sent down.

I bear witness, moreover, that through Thy beauty the beauty of the Adored One hath been unveiled, and through Thy face the face of the Desired One hath shone forth, and that through a word from Thee Thou hast decided between all created things, causing them who are devoted to Thee to ascend unto the summit of glory, and the infidels to fall into the lowest abyss.

I bear witness that he who hath known Thee hath known God, and he who hath attained unto Thy presence hath attained unto the presence of God. Great, therefore, is the blessedness of him who hath believed in Thee, and in Thy signs, and hath humbled himself before Thy sovereignty, and hath been honored with meeting Thee, and hath attained the good pleasure of Thy will, and circled around Thee, and stood before Thy throne. Woe betide him that hath transgressed against Thee, and hath denied Thee, and repudiated Thy signs, and gainsaid Thy sovereignty, and risen up against Thee, and waxed proud before Thy face, and hath disputed Thy testimonies, and fled from Thy rule and Thy dominion, and been numbered with the infidels whose names have been inscribed by the fingers of Thy behest upon Thy holy Tablets.

Waft, then, unto me, O my God and my Beloved, from the right hand of Thy mercy and Thy loving-kindness, the holy breaths of Thy favors, that they may draw me away from myself and from the world unto the courts of Thy nearness and Thy presence. Potent art Thou to do what pleaseth Thee. Thou, truly, hast been supreme over all things.

The remembrance of God and His praise, and the glory of God and His splendor, rest upon Thee, O Thou who art His Beauty! I bear witness that the eye of creation hath never gazed upon one wronged like Thee. Thou wast immersed all the days of Thy life beneath an ocean of tribulations. At one time Thou wast in chains and fetters; at another Thou wast threatened by the sword of Thine enemies. Yet, despite all this, Thou didst enjoin upon all men to observe what had been prescribed unto Thee by Him Who is the All-Knowing, the All-Wise.

May my spirit be a sacrifice to the wrongs Thou didst suffer, and my soul be a ransom for the adversities Thou didst sustain. I beseech God, by Thee and by them whose faces have been illuminated with the splendors of the light of Thy countenance, and who, for love of Thee, have observed all whereunto they were bidden, to remove the veils that have come in between Thee and Thy creatures, and to supply me with the good of this world and the world to come. Thou art, in truth, the Almighty, the Most Exalted, the All-Glorious, the Ever-Forgiving, the Most Compassionate.

Bless Thou, O Lord my God, the Divine Lote-Tree and its leaves, and its boughs, and its branches, and its stems, and its offshoots, as long as Thy most excellent titles will endure and Thy most august attributes will last. Protect it, then, from the mischief of the aggressor and the hosts of tyranny. Thou art, in truth, the Almighty, the Most Powerful. Bless Thou, also, O Lord my God, Thy servants and Thy handmaidens who have attained unto Thee. Thou, truly, art the All-Bountiful, Whose grace is infinite. No God is there save Thee, the Ever-Forgiving, the Most Generous.

He Calleth the Nations

Praised be Thou, O my God! I beseech Thee by them who have circled round the throne of Thy will, and soared in the atmosphere of Thy good-pleasure, and turned with all their affections towards the Horizon of Thy Revelation and the Day Spring of Thine inspiration, and the Dawning-Place of Thy names, to aid Thy servants to observe what Thou hast commanded them in Thy days —commandments through which the sacredness of Thy Cause will be demonstrated unto Thy servants and the affairs of Thy creatures and of Thy realm will be set aright.

I testify, O my God, that this is the Day whereon Thy testimony hath been fulfilled, and Thy clear tokens have been manifested, and Thine utterances have been revealed, and Thy signs have been demonstrated, and the radiance of Thy countenance hath been diffused, and Thy proof hath been perfected, and Thine ascendancy hath been established, and Thy mercy hath overflowed, and the Day Star of Thy grace hath shone forth with such brilliance that Thou didst manifest Him Who is the Revealer of Thyself and the Treasury of Thy wisdom and the Dawning-Place of Thy majesty and power. Thou didst establish His covenant with every one who hath been created in the kingdoms of earth and heaven and in the realms of revelation and of creation. Thou didst raise Him up to such heights that the wrongs inflicted by the oppressors have been powerless to deter Him from revealing Thy sovereignty, and the ascendancy of the wayward hath failed to prevent Him from demonstrating Thy power and from exalting Thy Cause.

So highly didst Thou exalt Him that He openly delivered unto the kings Thy messages and commandments, and hath never for one moment sought His own protection, but striven to protect Thy servants from whatever might withhold them from approaching the kingdom of Thy nearness, and from setting their faces towards the horizon of Thy good-pleasure.

Thou seest, O my God, how, notwithstanding the swords that are drawn against Him, He calleth the nations unto Thee, and though Himself a prisoner summoneth them to turn in the direction of Thy gifts and bounties. With every fresh tribulation He manifested a fuller measure of Thy Cause, and exalted more highly Thy word.

I testify that through Him the Pen of the Most High was set in motion, and with His remembrance the Scriptures in the kingdom of names were embellished. Through Him Thy fragrances were wafted, and the sweet smell of Thy raiment was shed abroad amongst all the dwellers of the earth and the inmates of heaven. Thou seest and knowest full well, O my God, how He hath been made to dwell within the most desolate of cities, so that He may build up the hearts of Thy servants, and hath been willing to suffer the most grievous abasement, that Thy creatures may be exalted.

I pray Thee, O Thou Who causest the dawn to appear, by Thy Name through Which Thou hast subjected the winds, and sent down Thy Tablets, that Thou wilt grant that we may draw near unto what Thou didst destine for us by Thy favor and bounty, and to be far removed from whatsoever may be repugnant unto Thee. Give us, then, to drink from the hands of Thy grace every day and every moment of our lives of the waters that are life indeed, O Thou Who art the Most Merciful! Make us, then, to be of them who helped Thee when fallen into the hands of those Thine enemies who are numbered with the rebellious among Thy creatures and the wicked amidst Thy people. Write down, then, for us the recompense ordained for him that hath attained Thy presence, and gazed on Thy beauty, and supply us with every good thing ordained in Thy Book for such of Thy creatures as enjoy near access to Thee.

Brighten our hearts, O my Lord, with the splendor of Thy knowledge, and illumine our sight with the light of such eyes as are fixed upon the horizon of Thy grace and the Day Spring of Thy glory. Preserve us, then, by Thy Most Great Name, Which Thou didst cause to overshadow such nations as lay claim to what Thou hast forbidden in Thy Book. This, verily, is what Thou didst announce unto us in Thy Scriptures and Thy Tablets.

Cause us, then, to be so steadfast in our love towards Thee that we will turn to none except Thee, and will be reckoned amongst them that are brought nigh to Thee, and acknowledge Thee as One Who is exalted above every comparison and is holy beyond all likeness, and will lift up our voices amongst Thy servants and cry aloud that He is the one God, the Incomparable, the Ever-Abiding, the Most Powerful, the All-Glorious, the All-Wise.

Strengthen Thou, O my Lord, the hearts of them that love Thee, that they may not be affrighted by the hosts of the infidels that are turned back from Thee, but may follow Thee in whatsoever hath been revealed by Thee. Aid them, moreover, to remember and to praise Thee, and to teach Thy Cause with eloquence and wisdom. Thou art He Who hath called Himself the Most Merciful. Ordain, then, O my God, for me and for whosoever hath sought Thee what beseemeth the excellence of Thy glory and the greatness of Thy majesty. No God is there but Thee, the Ever-Forgiving, the Most Compassionate.

Darkness Hath Fallen

Lauded be Thy name, O Lord my God! Darkness hath fallen upon every land, and the forces of mischief have encompassed all the nations. Through them, however, I perceive the splendors of Thy wisdom, and discern the brightness of the light of Thy providence.

They that are shut out as by a veil from Thee have imagined that they have the power to put out Thy light, and to quench Thy fire, and to still the winds of Thy grace. Nay, and to this Thy might beareth me witness! Had not every tribulation been made the bearer of Thy wisdom, and every ordeal the vehicle of Thy providence, no one would have dared oppose us, though the powers of earth and heaven were to be leagued against us. Were I to unravel the wondrous mysteries of Thy wisdom which are laid bare before me, the reins of Thine enemies would be cleft asunder.

Glorified be Thou, then, O my God! I beseech Thee by Thy Most Great Name to assemble them that love Thee around the Law that streameth from the good-pleasure of Thy will, and to send down upon them what will assure their hearts.

Potent art Thou to do what pleaseth Thee. Thou art, verily, the Help in Peril, the Self-Subsisting.

The Eternity of Thy Majesty

How marvelous, then, are the manifold tokens of Thy might, and how great are the diverse evidences of Thy power! The learned have, without exception, admitted their ignorance when confronted with the radiance of the Luminary of Thy knowledge; and the mighty have all confessed their impotence in the face of the billowing Ocean of Thy power; and the rich have one and all acknowledged their poverty before the effusions of the Treasuries of Thy wealth; and the worldly wise have each recognized their nothingness beside the splendors of the Light of Thy beauty; and the exalted have all witnessed unto their abasement when face to face with the effulgence of the Day Star of Thy glory; and they who are in authority have borne witness to their own evanescence and to the evanescence of others, and discovered the eternity of Thy majesty, and of Thy sovereignty, and of Thy sublimity, and of Thy power.

This Divine Law

Praised be Thou, O Lord my God! I implore Thee by Them Who are the Tabernacles of Thy Divine holiness, Who are the Manifestations of Thy transcendent unity and the Day Springs of Thine inspiration and revelation, to grant that Thy servants may not be kept back from this Divine Law which, at Thy will and according to Thy pleasure, hath branched out from Thy most great Ocean. Do Thou, then, ordain for them that which Thou didst ordain for Thy chosen ones and for the righteous among Thy creatures, whose constancy in Thy Cause the tempests of trials have failed to shake, and whom the tumults of tests have been powerless to hinder from magnifying Thy most exalted Word—the Word through Which the heavens of men's idle fancies and vain imaginations have been split asunder. Thou art, verily, the Almighty, the All-Glorious, the All-Knowing.

Enable, then, Thy servants, O my God, to recognize the Day Star that hath shone forth above the horizon of Thine irrevocable decree and purpose, and suffer them not to be deprived of the Paradise which Thou, by Thy name, the All-Glorious, hast called into being in the heavens of Thine exalted omnipotence. Cause them, moreover, O my God, to hearken to Thy most sweet voice, that they may all hasten to recognize Thy unity and acknowledge Thy oneness, O Thou Who art the Beloved of the hearts of all that yearn after Thee, and the Object of the adoration of such as have known Thee!

I beseech Thee, by them that have cut down all the idols in this Revelation through which the Most Grievous Convulsion and the Great Terror have appeared, to assist, at all times, Thy servants with the signs of Thine almighty power and the evidences of Thy transcendent and all-compelling might. Grant, then, that their hearts may be made as strong as brass, that they may remain unmoved by the overpowering might of such as have transgressed against Him Who is the Manifestation of Thine Essence and the Day Spring of Thine invisible Self, and that they may all arise to glorify and help Thee, so that through them the ensigns of Thy triumph may be lifted up in Thy realm, and the standards of Thy Cause may be unfurled throughout Thy dominions. Thou art He who from everlasting hath, through the potency of His will, been all-powerful, and will continue to remain the same for ever and ever. Thou art, verily, the All-Glorious, the Most High. No God is there but Thee, the Most Powerful, the Most Exalted, the Help in Peril, the Most Great, the One Being, the Incomparable, the All-Glorious, the Unrestrained.

No Sooner Had He Revealed Himself

I beg of Thee, O my God, by Thy power, and Thy might, and Thy sovereignty, which have embraced all who are in Thy heaven and on Thy earth, to make known unto Thy servants this luminous Way and this straight Path, that they may acknowledge Thy unity and Thy oneness, with a certainty which the vain imaginations of the doubters will not impair, nor the idle fancies of the wayward obscure. Illumine, O my Lord, the eyes of Thy servants, and brighten their hearts with the splendors of the light of Thy knowledge, that they may apprehend the greatness of this most sublime station, and recognize this most luminous Horizon, that haply the clamor of men may fail to deter them from turning their gaze towards the effulgent light of Thy unity, and to hinder them from setting their faces toward the Horizon of detachment.

This is the Day, O my Lord, which Thou didst announce unto all mankind as the Day whereon Thou wouldst reveal Thy Self, and shed Thy radiance, and shine brightly over all Thy creatures. Thou hast, moreover, entered into a covenant with them, in Thy Books, and Thy Scriptures, and Thy Scrolls, and Thy Tablets, concerning Him Who is the Day Spring of Thy Revelation, and hast appointed the Bayán to be the Herald of this Most Great and all-glorious Manifestation, and this most resplendent and most sublime Appearance.

And when the world's horizon was illumined, and He Who is the Most Great Name was manifested, all disbelieved in Him and in His signs, except such as have been carried away by the sweetness of Thy glorification and praise. There befell Him what must remain inscrutable to everyone except Thee, Whose knowledge transcendeth all who are in Thy heaven and all who are on Thy earth.

Thou well knowest, O my God, that the Revealer of the Bayán (the Báb) hath commanded all mankind concerning Thy Cause, and Thy Revelation, and Thy Sovereignty. He hath said, and sweet is His speech: "Beware lest the Bayán and its Letters keep you back from Him Who is the Most Merciful and from His sovereignty." He, moreover, hath written: "Were He to produce no more than one verse, ye must not deny Him. Haste ye towards Him, that haply He may cause to descend upon you what He pleaseth, as a token of His grace unto you. He truly is the Possessor of His servants, and the King of creation."

Thou seest, then, O Thou Who art the Beloved of the world and the Revealer of the Most Great Name, how He hath come down with the kingdom of His signs, and in a manner that hath caused the atoms of the earth to testify that the whole world hath been filled with these signs. And yet, notwithstanding this most manifest and all-glorious Revelation, and these signs which none can appraise except Thee, O Thou the King of names, Thou beholdest how they have broken off from Him Who is the Day Spring of Thine Essence, and have caviled at the One Who is the Fountain-Head of Thy wisdom and of Thine utterance. They were so seized with thirst for fame, that they rejected Thy tokens, and Thy testimonies, and Thy signs, which every man of insight perceiveth in whatsoever declareth Thy greatness, and Thy sovereignty, and acknowledgeth Thy Revelation and Thy might. They have so traduced Him as to cause the inmates of the all-glorious Tabernacle and the Concourse on high to lament, and have uttered such calumnies against Him that the souls of Thy chosen Ones and the hearts of them that are dear to Thee have melted. They have erred so grievously that they cast away Thy most resplendent signs, and clung to their idle fancies, O Thou Who art the Possessor of Names and the Lord of the Throne on high and of earth below!

Thou art, O my God and the Exultation of my heart, the One Who hath adorned Thy Tablet, of which none is aware except Thee, with the mention of this Day which Thou didst call after Thy name, that haply none may on that day be seen save Thy most august Self, and naught else be brought to mind except Thy most sweet remembrance.

No sooner had He revealed Himself than the foundations of the kindreds of the earth shook and trembled, and the learned swooned away, and the wise were bewildered, except such as have, through the power of Thy might, drawn nigh unto Thee, and received the choice wine of Thy Revelation from the hand of Thy grace, and have quaffed it in Thy name, and exclaimed: "Praise be unto Thee, O Thou the Desire of the worlds! and glory be to Thee, O Thou Who art the Exultation of the hearts that pant after Thee!"

My God, my Master, my Highest Hope, and the Goal of my desire! Thou seest and hearest the sighing of this wronged One, from this darksome well which the vain imaginations of Thine adversaries have built, and from this blind pit which the idle fancies of the wicked among Thy creatures have digged. By Thy Beauty, O Thou Whose glory is uncovered to the face of men! I am not impatient in the troubles that touch me in my love for Thee, neither in the adversities which I suffer in Thy path. Nay, I have, by Thy power, chosen them for mine own self, and I glory in them amongst such of Thy creatures as enjoy near access to Thee, and those of Thy servants that are wholly devoted to Thy Self.

The Fire of Thy Love

Thou art He, O my God, Who hath raised me up at Thy behest, and bidden me to occupy Thy seat, and to summon all men to the court of Thy mercy. It is Thou Who hast commanded me to tell out the things Thou didst destine for them in the Tablet of Thy decree and didst inscribe with the pen of Thy Revelation, and Who hast enjoined on me the duty of kindling the fire of Thy love in the hearts of Thy servants, and of drawing all the peoples of the earth nearer to the habitation of Thy throne.

And when, as bidden by Thee, I arose and called out, by Thy leave, all Thy creatures, the wayward among Thy servants opposed me. Some turned away from me, others disowned my claim, a few hesitated, while others were sore perplexed, notwithstanding that Thy testimony was set forth before the followers of all religions, and Thy proof demonstrated unto all the peoples of the earth, and the signs of Thy might so powerfully manifested as to encompass the entire creation.

I was, moreover, opposed by mine own kindred, although, as Thou knowest, they were dear to me and I had desired for them that which I had desired for mine own self. These are the ones who, when learning that I had been cast into prison, perpetrated against me what no man else on earth had perpetrated.

I entreat Thee, therefore, O my God, by Thy name by which Thou hast separated between truth and denial, to purify their hearts of all evil suggestions, and to enable them to draw nigh unto Him Who is the Day Spring of Thy names and Thine attributes.

Thou knowest, O my God, that I have severed every tie that bindeth me to any of Thy creatures except that most exalted tie that uniteth me with whosoever cleaveth unto Thee, in this the day of the revelation of Thy most august Self, that hath appeared in Thy name, the All-Glorious. Thou knowest that I have dissolved every bond that knitteth me to any one of my kindred except such as have enjoyed near access to Thy most effulgent face.

I have no will but Thy will, O my Lord, and cherish no desire except Thy desire. From my pen floweth only the summons which Thine own exalted pen hath voiced, and my tongue uttereth naught save what the Most Great Spirit hath itself proclaimed in the kingdom of Thine eternity. I am stirred by nothing else except the winds of Thy will, and breathe no word except the words which, by Thy leave and Thine inspiration, I am led to pronounce.

Praise be to Thee, O Thou Who art the Well-Beloved of all that have known Thee, and the Desire of the hearts of such as are devoted to Thee, inasmuch as Thou hast made me a target for the ills that I suffer in my love for Thee, and the object of the assaults launched against me in Thy path. Thy glory beareth me witness! I can, on no account, feel impatient of the adversities that I have borne in my love for Thee. From the very day Thou didst reveal Thyself unto me, I have accepted for myself every manner of tribulation. Every moment of my life my head crieth out to Thee and saith: "Would, O my Lord, that I could be raised on the spear-point in Thy path!" while my blood entreateth Thee saying: "Dye the earth with me, O my God, for the sake of Thy love and Thy pleasure!" Thou knowest that I have, at no time, sought to guard my body against any affliction, nay rather I have continually anticipated the things Thou didst ordain for me in the Tablet of Thy decree.

Behold, then, O my God, my loneliness among Thy servants and my remoteness from Thy friends and Thy chosen ones. I beseech Thee, by the showers of the clouds of Thy mercy, whereby Thou hast caused the blossom of Thy praise and utterance and the flowers of Thy wisdom and testimony to spring forth in the hearts of all them that have recognized Thy oneness, to supply Thy servants and my kindred with the fruits of the tree of Thy unity, in these days when Thou hast been established upon the throne of Thy mercy. Hinder them not, O my Lord, from attaining unto the things Thou dost possess, and write down for them that which will aid them to scale the heights of Thy grace and favor. Give them, moreover, to drink of the living waters of Thy knowledge, and ordain for them the good of this world and of the world to come.

Thou art, verily, the Lord of Bahá, and the Beloved of his heart, and the Object of his desire, and the Inspirer of his tongue, and the Source of his soul. No God is there but Thee, the Inaccessible, the Most High. Thou art, verily, the Almighty, the Most Exalted, the Ever-Forgiving, the Most Merciful.

No Refuge Can Be Found

My God, my Well-Beloved! No place is there for any one to flee to when once Thy laws have been sent down, and no refuge can be found by any soul after the revelation of Thy commandments. Thou hast inspired the Pen with the mysteries of Thine eternity, and bidden it teach man that which he knoweth not, and caused him to partake of the living waters of truth from the cup of Thy Revelation and Thine inspiration.

No sooner, however, had the Pen traced upon the tablet one single letter of Thy hidden wisdom, than the voice of the lamentation of Thine ardent lovers was lifted up from all directions. Thereupon, there befell the just what hath caused the inmates of the tabernacle of Thy glory to weep and the dwellers of the cities of Thy revelation to groan.

Thou dost consider, O my God, how He Who is the Manifestation of Thy names is in these days threatened by the swords of Thine adversaries. In such a state He crieth out and summoneth all the inhabitants of Thine earth and the denizens of Thy heaven unto Thee.

Purify, O my God, the hearts of Thy creatures with the power of Thy sovereignty and might, that Thy words may sink deep into them. I know not what is in their hearts, O my God, nor can tell the thoughts they think of Thee. Methinks that they imagine that Thy purpose in calling them to Thine all-highest horizon is to heighten the glory of Thy majesty and power. For had they been satisfied that Thou summonest them to that which will recreate their hearts and immortalize their souls, they would never have fled from thy governance, nor deserted the shadow of the tree of Thy oneness. Clear away, then, the sight of Thy creatures, O my God, that they may recognize Him Who showeth forth the Godhead as One Who is sanctified from all that pertaineth unto them, and Who, wholly for Thy sake, is summoning them to the horizon of Thy unity, at a time when every moment of His life is beset with peril. Had His aim been the preservation of His own Self, He would never have left it at the mercy of Thy foes.

I swear by Thy glory! I have accepted to be tried by manifold adversities for no purpose except to regenerate all that are in Thy heaven and on Thy earth. Whoso hath loved Thee, can never feel attached to his own self, except for the purpose of furthering Thy Cause; and whoso hath recognized Thee can recognize naught else except Thee, and can turn to no one save Thee.

Enable Thy servants, O my God, to discover the things Thou didst desire for them in Thy Kingdom. Acquaint them, moreover, with what He Who is the Origin of Thy most excellent titles hath, in His love for Thee, been willing to bear for the sake of the regeneration of their souls, that they may haste to attain the River that is Life indeed, and turn their faces in the direction of Thy Name, the Most Merciful. Abandon them not to themselves, O my God! Draw them, by Thy bountiful favor, to the heaven of Thine inspiration. They are but paupers, and Thou art the All-Possessing, the Ever-Forgiving, the Most Compassionate.

Entities of a New Creation

How great is Thy power! How exalted Thy sovereignty! How lofty Thy might! How excellent Thy majesty! How supreme is Thy grandeur—a grandeur which He Who is Thy Manifestation hath made known and wherewith Thou hast invested Him as a sign of Thy generosity and bountiful favor. I bear witness, O my God, that through Him Thy most resplendent signs have been uncovered, and Thy mercy hath encompassed the entire creation. But for Him, how could the Celestial Dove have uttered its songs or the Heavenly Nightingale, according to the decree of God, have warbled its melody?

I testify that no sooner had the First Word proceeded, through the potency of Thy will and purpose, out of His mouth, and the First Call gone forth from His lips than the whole creation was revolutionized, and all that are in the heavens and all that are on earth were stirred to the depths. Through that Word the realities of all created things were shaken, were divided, separated, scattered, combined and reunited, disclosing, in both the contingent world and the heavenly kingdom, entities of a new creation, and revealing, in the unseen realms, the signs and tokens of Thy unity and oneness. Through that Call Thou didst announce unto all Thy servants the advent of Thy most great Revelation and the appearance of Thy most perfect Cause.

No sooner had that Revelation been unveiled to men's eyes than the signs of universal discord appeared among the peoples of the world, and commotion seized the dwellers of earth and heaven, and the foundations of all things were shaken. The forces of dissension were released, the meaning of the Word was unfolded, and every several atom in all created things acquired its own distinct and separate character. Hell was made to blaze, and the delights of Paradise were uncovered to men's eyes. Blessed is the man that turneth towards Thee, and woe betide him who standeth aloof from Thee, who denieth Thee and repudiateth Thy signs in this Revelation wherein the faces of the exponents of denial have turned black and the faces of the exponents of truthfulness have turned white, O Thou Who art the Possessor of all names and attributes, Who holdest in Thy grasp the empire of whatever hath been created in heaven and on earth!

He Hath Entrusted Every Created Thing

How wondrous is the unity of the Living, the Ever-Abiding God—a unity which is exalted above all limitations, that transcendeth the comprehension of all created things! He hath, from everlasting, dwelt in His inaccessible habitation of holiness and glory, and will unto everlasting continue to be enthroned upon the heights of His independent sovereignty and grandeur. How lofty hath been His incorruptible Essence, how completely independent of the knowledge of all created things, and how immensely exalted will it remain above the praise of all the inhabitants of heavens and the earth!

From the exalted source, and out of the essence of His favor and bounty He hath entrusted every created thing with a sign of His knowledge, so that none of His creatures may be deprived of its share in expressing, each according to its capacity and rank, this knowledge. This sign is the mirror of His beauty in the world of creation. The greater the effort exerted for the refinement of this sublime and noble mirror, the more faithfully will it be made to reflect the glory of the names and attributes of God, and reveal the wonders of His signs and knowledge. Every created thing will be enabled (so great is this reflecting power) to reveal the potentialities of its pre-ordained station, will recognize its capacity and limitations, and will testify to the truth that "He, verily is God; there is none other God besides Him." . . .

There can be no doubt whatever that, in consequence of the efforts which every man may consciously exert and as a result of the exertion of his own spiritual faculties, this mirror can be so cleansed from the dross of earthly defilements and purged from satanic fancies as to be able to draw nigh unto the meads of eternal holiness and attain the courts of everlasting fellowship. In pursuance, however, of the principle that for every thing a time hath been fixed, and for every fruit a season hath been ordained, the latent energies of such a bounty can best be released and the vernal glory of such a gift can only be manifested, in the Days of God. Invested though each day may be with its pre-ordained share of God's wondrous grace, the Days immediately associated with the Manifestatiton of God possess a unique distinction and occupy a station which no mind can ever comprehend. Such is the virtue infused into them that, if the hearts of all that dwell in the heavens and the earth were, in those days of everlasting delight, to be brought face to face with that Day Star of unfading glory and attuned to His Will, each would find itself exalted above all earthly things, radiant with His light, and sanctified through His grace. All hail to this grace which no blessing, however great, can excel, and all honor to such a loving-kindness the like of which the eye of creation hath not seen! Exalted is He above that which they attribute unto Him or recount about Him!

It is for this reason that, in those days, no man shall ever stand in need of his neighbor. It hath already been abundantly demonstrated that in that divinely-appointed Day the majority of them that have sought and attained His holy court have revealed such knowledge and wisdom, a drop of which none else besides these holy and sanctified souls, however long he may have taught or studied, hath grasped or will ever comprehend. It is by virtue of this power that the beloved of God have, in the days of the Manifestation of the Day Star of Truth, been exalted above, and made independent of, all human learning. Nay, from their hearts and the springs of their innate powers hath gushed out unceasingly the inmost essence of human learning and wisdom.

The Best-Beloved Is Come

O My servants! It behoveth you to refresh and revive your souls through the gracious favors which, in this Divine, this soul-stirring Springtime, are being showered upon you. The Day Star of His great glory hath shed its radiance upon you, and the clouds of His limitless grace have overshadowed you. How high the reward of him that hath not deprived himself of so great a bounty, nor failed to recognize the beauty of his Best-Beloved in this, His new attire.

Say: O people! The Lamp of God is burning; take heed, lest the fierce winds of your disobedience extinguish its light. Now is the time to arise and magnify the Lord, your God. Strive not after bodily comforts, and keep your heart pure and stainless. The Evil One is lying in wait, ready to entrap you. Gird yourselves against his wicked devices, and, led by the light of the name of the one true God, deliver yourselves from the darkness that surroundeth you. Center your thoughts in the Well-Beloved, rather than in your own selves.

Say: O ye that have strayed and lost your way! The Divine Messenger, Who speaketh naught but the truth, hath announced unto you the coming of the Best-Beloved. Behold, He is now come. Wherefore are ye downcast and dejected? Why remain despondent when the Pure and Hidden One hath appeared unveiled amongst you? He Who is both the Beginning and the End, He Who is both Stillness and Motion, is now manifest before your eyes. Behold how, in this Day, the Beginning is reflected in the End, how out of Stillness Motion hath been engendered. This motion hath been generated by the potent energies which the words of the Almighty have released throughout the entire creation. Whoso hath been quickened by its vitalizing power, will find himself impelled to attain the court of the Beloved; and whoso hath deprived himself therefrom, will sink into irretrievable despondency. He is truly wise whom the world and all that is therein have not deterred from recognizing the light of this Day, who will not allow men's idle talk to cause him to swerve from the way of righteousness. He is indeed as one dead who, at the wondrous dawn of this Revelation, hath failed to be quickened by its soul-stirring breeze. He is indeed a captive who hath not recognized the Supreme Redeemer, but hath suffered his soul to be bound, distressed and helpless, in the fetters of his desires.

O My servants! Whoso hath tasted of this Fountain hath attained unto everlasting Life, and whoso hath refused to drink therefrom is even as the dead. Say: O ye workers of iniquity! Covetousness hath hindered you from giving a hearing ear unto the sweet voice of Him Who is the All-Sufficing. Wash it away from your hearts, that His Divine secret may be made known unto you. Behold Him manifest and resplendent as the sun in all its glory.

Say: O ye that are bereft of understanding! A severe trial pursueth you, and will suddenly overtake you. Bestir yourselves, that haply it may pass and inflict no harm upon you. Acknowledge the exalted character of the name of the Lord, your God, Who hath come unto you in the greatness of His glory. He, verily, is the All-Knowing, the All-Possessing, the Supreme Protector.

The Signs of Revelation

Know thou that every created thing is a sign of the revelation of God. Each, according to its capacity, is, and will ever remain, a token of the Almighty. Inasmuch as He, the sovereign Lord of all, hath willed to reveal His sovereignty in the kingdom of names and attributes, each and every created thing hath, through the act of the Divine Will, been made a sign of His glory. So pervasive and general is this revelation that nothing whatsoever in the whole universe can be discovered that doth not reflect His splendor. Under such conditions every consideration of proximity and remoteness is obliterated. . . . Were the Hand of Divine power to divest of this high endowment all created things, the entire universe would become desolate and void.

Behold, how immeasurably exalted is the Lord your God above all created things! Witness the majesty of His sovereignty, His ascendancy, and supreme power. If the things which have been created by Him—magnified be His glory—and ordained to be the manifestations of His names and attributes, stand, by virtue of the grace with which they have been endowed, exalted beyond all proximity and remoteness, how much loftier must be that Divine Essence that hath called them into being? . . .

Meditate on what the poet hath written: "Wonder not, if my Best-Beloved be closer to me than mine own self; wonder at this, that I, despite such nearness, should still be so far from Him." . . . Considering what God hath revealed, that "We are closer to man than his life-vein," the poet hath, in allusion to this verse, stated that, though the revelation of my Best-Beloved hath so permeated my being that He is closer to me than my life-vein, yet, notwithstanding my certitude of its reality and my recognition of my station, I am still so far removed from Him. By this he meaneth that his heart, which is the seat of the All-Merciful and the throne wherein abideth the splendor of His revelation, is forgetful of its Creator, hath strayed from His path, hath shut out itself from His glory, and is stained with the defilement of earthly desires.

It should be remembered in this connection that the one true God is in Himself exalted beyond and above proximity and remoteness. His reality transcendeth such limitations. His relationship to His creatures knoweth no degrees. That some are near and others are far is to be ascribed to the Manifestations themselves.

That the heart is the throne, in which the Revelation of God the All-Merciful is centered, is attested by the holy utterances which We have formerly revealed. Among them is this saying: "Earth and heaven cannot contain Me; what can alone contain Me is the heart of him that believeth in Me, and is faithful to My Cause." How often hath the human heart, which is the recipient of the light of God and the seat of the revelation of the All-Merciful, erred from Him Who is the Source of that light and the Well Spring of that revelation. It is the waywardness of the heart that removeth it far from God, and condemneth it to remoteness from Him. Those hearts, however, that are aware of His Presence, are close to Him, and are to be regarded as having drawn nigh unto His throne.

Consider, moreover, how frequently doth man become forgetful of his own self, whilst God remaineth, through His all-encompassing knowledge, aware of His creature, and continueth to shed upon him the manifest radiance of His glory. It is evident, therefore, that, in such circumstances, He is closer to him than his own self. He will, indeed, so remain for ever, for, whereas the one true God knoweth all things, perceiveth all things, and comprehendeth all things, mortal man is prone to err, and is ignorant of the mysteries that lie enfolded within him. . . .

Let no one imagine that by Our assertion that all created things are the signs of the revelation of God is meant that—God forbid—all men, be they good or evil, pious or infidel, are equal in the sight of God. Nor doth it imply that the Divine Being—magnified be His name and exalted be His glory—is, under any circumstances, comparable unto men, or can, in any way, be associated with His creatures. Such an error hath been committed by certain foolish ones who, after having ascended into the heavens of their idle fancies, have interpreted Divine Unity to mean that all created things are the signs of God, and that, consequently, there is no distinction whatsoever between them. Some have even outstripped them by maintaining that these signs are peers and partners of God Himself. Gracious God! He, verily, is one and indivisible; one in His essence, one in His attributes. Everything besides Him is as nothing when brought face to face with the resplendent revelation of but one of His names, with no more than the faintest intimation of His glory—how much less when confronted with His own Self!

By the righteousness of My name, the All-Merciful! The Pen of the Most High trembleth with a great trembling and is sore shaken at the revelation of these words. How puny and insignificant is the evanescent drop when compared with the waves and billows of God's limitless and everlasting Ocean and how utterly contemptible must every contingent and perishable thing appear when brought face to face with the uncreated, the unspeakable glory of the Eternal! We implore pardon of God, the All-Powerful, for them that entertain such beliefs, and give utterance to such words. Say: O people! How can a fleeting fancy compare with the Self-Subsisting, and how can the Creator be likened unto His creatures, who are but as the script of His Pen? Nay, His script excelleth all things, and is sanctified from, and immeasurably exalted above, all creatures.

Furthermore, consider the signs of the revelation of God in their relation one to another. Can the sun, which is but one of these signs, be regarded as equal in rank to darkness? The one true God beareth Me witness! No man can believe it, unless he be of those whose hearts are straitened, and whose eyes have become deluded. Say: Consider your own selves. Your nails and eyes are both parts of your bodies. Do ye regard them of equal rank and value? If ye say, yea; say, then: ye have indeed charged with imposture, the Lord, my God, the All-Glorious, inasmuch as ye spare the one, and cherish the other as dearly as your own life.

To transgress the limits of one's own rank and station is, in no wise, permissible. The integrity of every rank and station must needs be preserved. By this is meant that every created thing should be viewed in the light of the station it hath been ordained to occupy.

It should be borne in mind, however, that when the light of My Name, the All-Pervading, hath shed its radiance upon the universe, each and every created thing hath, according to a fixed decree, been endowed with the capacity to exercise a particular influence, and been made to possess a distinct virtue. Consider the effect of poison. Deadly though it is, it possesseth the power of exerting, under certain conditions, a beneficial influence. The potency infused into all created things is the direct consequence of the revelation of this most blessed Name. Glorified be He, Who is the Creator of all names and attributes! Cast into the fire the tree that hath rot and dried up, and abide under the shadow of the green and goodly Tree, and partake of the fruit thereof.

The people living in the days of the Manifestations of God have, for the most part, uttered such unseemly sayings. These have been set down circumstantially in the revealed Books and Holy Scriptures.

He is really a believer in the Unity of God who recognizeth in each and every created thing the sign of the revelation of Him Who is the Eternal Truth, and not he who maintaineth that the creature is indistinguishable from the Creator.

Consider, for instance, the revelation of the light of the Name of God, the Educator. Behold, how in all things the evidences of such a revelation are manifest, how the betterment of all beings dependeth upon it. This education is of two kinds. The one is universal. Its influence pervadeth all things and sustaineth them. It is for this reason that God hath assumed the title, "Lord of all worlds." The other is confined to them that have come under the shadow of this Name, and sought the shelter of this most mighty Revelation. They, however, that have failed to seek this shelter, have deprived themselves of this privilege, and are powerless to benefit from the spiritual sustenance that hath been sent down through the heavenly grace of this Most Great Name. How great the gulf fixed between the one and the other! If the veil were lifted, and the full glory of the station of those that have turned wholly towards God, and have, in their love for Him, renounced the world, were made manifest, the entire creation would be dumbfounded. The true believer in the Unity of God will, as it hath already been explained, recognize, in the believer and the unbeliever, the evidences of the revelation of both of these Names. Were this revelation to be withdrawn, all would perish.

Consider, in like manner, the revelation of the light of the Name of God, the Incomparable. Behold, how this light hath enveloped the entire creation, how each and every thing manifesteth the sign of His Unity, testifieth to the reality of Him Who is the Eternal Truth, proclaimeth His sovereignty, His oneness, and His power. This revelation is a token of His mercy that hath encompassed all created things. They that have joined partners with Him, however, are unaware of such a revelation, and are deprived of the Faith through which they can draw near unto, and be united with, Him. Witness how the divers peoples and kindreds of the earth bear witness to His unity, and recognize His oneness. But for the sign of the Unity of God within them, they would have never acknowledged the truth of the words, "There is none other God but God." And yet, consider how grievously they have erred, and strayed from His path. Inasmuch as they have failed to recognize the Sovereign Revealer, they have ceased to be reckoned among those who may be regarded as true believers in the Unity of God.

This sign of the revelation of the Divine Being in them that have joined partners with Him may, in a sense, be regarded as a reflection of the glory with which the faithful are illumined. None, however, can comprehend this truth save men endued with understanding. They that have truly recognized the Unity of God should be regarded as the primary manifestations of this Name. It is they who have quaffed the wine of Divine Unity from the cup which the hand of God hath proffered unto them, and who have turned their faces towards Him. How vast the distance that separateth these sanctified beings from those men that are so far away from God! . . .

God grant that, with a penetrating vision, thou mayest perceive, in all things, the sign of the revelation of Him Who is the Ancient King, and recognize how exalted and sanctified from the whole creation is that most holy and sacred Being. This, in truth, is the very root and essence of belief in the unity and singleness of God. "God was alone; there was none else besides Him." He, now, is what He hath ever been. There is none other God, but Him, the One, the Incomparable, the Almighty, the Most Exalted, the Most Great.

The Generating Impulse of Creation

All-praise to the unity of God, and all-honor to Him, the sovereign Lord, the incomparable and all-glorious Ruler of the universe, Who, out of utter nothingness, hath created the reality of all things, Who, from naught, hath brought into being the most refined and subtle elements of His creation, and Who, rescuing His creatures from the abasement of remoteness and the perils of ultimate extinction, hath received them into His kingdom of incorruptible glory. Nothing short of His all-encompassing grace, His all-pervading mercy, could have possibly achieved it. How could it, otherwise, have been possible for sheer nothingness to have acquired by itself the worthiness and capacity to emerge from its state of non-existence into the realm of being?

Having created the world and all that liveth and moveth therein, He, through the direct operation of His unconstrained and sovereign Will, chose to confer upon man the unique distinction and capacity to know Him and to love Him—a capacity that must needs be regarded as the generating impulse and the primary purpose underlying the whole of creation. . . . Upon the inmost reality of each and every created thing He hath shed the light of one of His names, and made it a recipient of the glory of one of His attributes. Upon the reality of man, however, He hath focused the radiance of all of His names and attributes, and made it a mirror of His own Self. Alone of all created things man hath been singled out for so great a favor, so enduring a bounty.

These energies with which the Day Star of Divine bounty and Source of heavenly guidance hath endowed the reality of man lie, however, latent within him, even as the flame is hidden within the candle and the rays of light are potentially present in the lamp. The radiance of these energies may be obscured by worldly desires even as the light of the sun can be concealed beneath the dust and dross which cover the mirror. Neither the candle nor the lamp can be lighted through their own unaided efforts, nor can it ever be possible for the mirror to free itself from its dross. It is clear and evident that until a fire is kindled the lamp will never be ignited, and unless the dross is blotted out from the face of the mirror it can never represent the image of the sun nor reflect its light and glory.

And since there can be no tie of direct intercourse to bind the one true God with His creation, and no resemblance whatever can exist between the transient and the Eternal, the contingent and the Absolute, He hath ordained that in every age and dispensation a pure and stainless Soul be made manifest in the kingdoms of earth and heaven. Unto this subtle, this mysterious and ethereal Being He hath assigned a twofold nature; the physical, pertaining to the world of matter, and the spiritual, which is born of the substance of God Himself. He hath, moreover, conferred upon Him a double station. The first station, which is related to His innermost reality, representeth Him as One Whose voice is the voice of God Himself. To this testifieth the tradition: "Manifold and mysterious is My relationship with God. I am He, Himself, and He is I, Myself, except that I am that I am, and He is that He is." And in like manner, the words: "Arise, O Muḥammad, for lo, the Lover and the Beloved are joined together and made one in Thee." He similarly saith: "There is no distinction whatsoever between Thee and Them, except that They are Thy Servants." The second station is the human station, exemplified by the following verses: "I am but a man like you." "Say, praise be to my Lord! Am I more than a man, an apostle?" These Essences of Detachment, these resplendent Realities are the channels of God's all-pervasive grace. Led by the light of unfailing guidance, and invested with supreme sovereignty, they are commissioned to use the inspiration of their words, the effusions of their infallible grace and the sanctifying breeze of their Revelation for the cleansing of every longing heart and receptive spirit from the dross and dust of earthly cares and limitations. Then, and only then, will the Trust of God, latent in the reality of man, emerge, as resplendent as the rising Orb of Divine Revelation, from behind the veil of concealment, and implant the ensign of its revealed glory upon the summits of men's hearts.

From the foregoing passages and allusions it hath been made indubitably clear that in the kingdoms of earth and heaven there must needs be manifested a Being, an Essence Who shall act as a Manifestation and Vehicle for the transmission of the grace of the Divinity Itself, the Sovereign Lord of all. Through the Teachings of this Day Star of Truth every man will advance and develop until he attaineth the station at which he can manifest all the potential forces with which his inmost true self hath been endowed. It is for this very purpose that in every age and dispensation the Prophets of God and His chosen Ones have appeared amongst men, and have evinced such power as is born of God and such might as only the Eternal can reveal.

Can one of sane mind ever seriously imagine that, in view of certain words the meaning of which he cannot comprehend, the portal of God's infinite guidance can ever be closed in the face of men? Can he ever conceive for these Divine Luminaries, these resplendent Lights either a beginning or an end? What outpouring flood can compare with the stream of His all-embracing grace, and what blessing can excel the evidences of so great and pervasive a mercy? There can be no doubt whatever that if for one moment the tide of His mercy and grace were to be withheld from the world, it would completely perish. For this reason, from the beginning that hath no beginning the portals of Divine mercy have been flung open to the face of all created things, and the clouds of Truth will continue to the end that hath no end to rain on the soil of human capacity, reality and personality their favors and bounties. Such hath been God's method continued from everlasting to everlasting.

The Morn of Divine Guidance

O my brother! When a true seeker determineth to take the step of search in the path leading unto the knowledge of the Ancient of Days, he must, before all else, cleanse his heart, which is the seat of the revelation of the inner mysteries of God, from the obscuring dust of all acquired knowledge, and the illusions of the embodiments of satanic fancy. He must purge his breast, which is the sanctuary of the abiding love of the Beloved, of every defilement, and sanctify his soul from all that pertaineth to water and clay, from all shadowy and ephemeral attachments. He must so cleanse his heart that no remnant of either love or hate may linger therein, lest that love blindly incline him to error, or that hate repel him away from the truth. Even as thou dost witness in this Day how most of the people, because of such love and hate. are bereft of the immortal Face, have strayed far from the Embodiments of the Divine mysteries, and, shepherdless, are roaming through the wilderness of oblivion and error.

That seeker must, at all times, put his trust in God, must renounce the peoples of the earth, must detach himself from the world of dust, and cleave unto Him Who is the Lord of Lords. He must never seek to exalt himself above any one, must wash away from the tablet of his heart every trace of pride and vainglory, must cling unto patience and resignation, observe silence and refrain from idle talk. For the tongue is a smoldering fire, and excess of speech a deadly poison. Material fire consumeth the body, whereas the fire of the tongue devoureth both heart and soul. The force of the former lasteth but for a time, whilst the effects of the latter endureth a century.

That seeker should, also, regard backbiting as grievous error, and keep himself aloof from its dominion, inasmuch as backbiting quencheth the light of the heart, and extinguisheth the life of the soul. He should be content with little, and be freed from all inordinate desire. He should treasure the companionship of them that have renounced the world, and regard avoidance of boastful and worldly people a precious benefit. At the dawn of every day he should commune with God, and, with all his soul, persevere in the quest of his Beloved. He should consume every wayward thought with the flame of His loving mention, and, with the swiftness of lightning, pass by all else save Him. He should succor the dispossessed, and never withhold his favor from the destitute. He should show kindness to animals, how much more unto his fellow-man, to him who is endowed with the power of utterance. He should not hesitate to offer up his life for his Beloved, nor allow the censure of the people to turn him away from the Truth. He should not wish for others that which he doth not wish for himself, nor promise that which he doth not fulfil. With all his heart he should avoid fellowship with evil-doers, and pray for the remission of their sins. He should forgive the sinful, and never despise his low estate, for none knoweth what his own end shall be. How often hath a sinner attained, at the hour of death, to the essence of faith, and, quaffing the immortal draught, hath taken his flight unto the Concourse on high! And how often hath a devout believer, at the hour of his soul's ascension, been so changed as to fall into the nethermost fire!

Our purpose in revealing these convincing and weighty utterances is to impress upon the seeker that he should regard all else beside God as transient, and count all things save Him, Who is the Object of all adoration, as utter nothingness.

These are among the attributes of the exalted, and constitute the hall-mark of the spiritually-minded. They have already been mentioned in connection with the requirements of the wayfarers that tread the path of Positive Knowledge. When the detached wayfarer and sincere seeker hath fulfilled these essential conditions, then and only then can he be called a true seeker. Whensoever he hath fulfilled the conditions implied in the verse: "Whoso maketh efforts for Us," he shall enjoy the blessings conferred by the words: "In Our Ways shall We assuredly guide him."

Only when the lamp of search, of earnest striving, of longing desire, of passionate devotion, of fervid love, of rapture, and ecstasy, is kindled within the seeker's heart, and the breeze of His loving-kindness is wafted upon his soul, will the darkness of error be dispelled, the mists of doubts and misgivings be dissipated, and the lights of knowledge and certitude envelop his being. At that hour will the Mystic Herald, bearing the joyful tidings of the Spirit, shine forth from the City of God resplendent as the morn, and, through the trumpet-blast of knowledge, will awaken the heart, the soul, and the spirit from the slumber of heedlessness. Then will the manifold favors and outpouring grace of the holy and everlasting Spirit confer such new life upon the seeker that he will find himself endowed with a new eye, a new ear, a new heart, and a new mind. He will contemplate the manifest signs of the universe, and will penetrate the hidden mysteries of the soul. Gazing with the eye of God, he will perceive within every atom a door that leadeth him to the stations of absolute certitude. He will discover in all things the mysteries of Divine Revelation, and the evidences of an everlasting Manifestation.

I swear by God! Were he that treadeth the path of guidance and seeketh to scale the heights of righteousness to attain unto this glorious and exalted station, he would inhale, at a distance of a thousand leagues, the fragrance of God, and would perceive the resplendent morn of a Divine guidance rising above the Day Spring of all things. Each and every thing, however small, would be to him a revelation, leading him to his Beloved, the Object of his quest. So great shall be the discernment of this seeker that he will discriminate between truth and falsehood, even as he doth distinguish the sun from shadow. If in the uttermost corners of the East the sweet savors of God be wafted, he will assuredly recognize and inhale their fragrance, even though he be dwelling in the uttermost ends of the West. He will, likewise, clearly distinguish all the signs of God—His wondrous utterances, His great works, and mighty deeds—from the doings, the words and ways of men, even as the jeweler who knoweth the gem from the stone, or the man who distinguisheth the spring from autumn, and heat from cold. When the channel of the human soul is cleansed of all worldly and impeding attachments, it will unfailingly perceive the breath of the Beloved across immeasurable distances, and will, led by its perfume, attain and enter the City of Certitude.

Therein he will discern the wonders of His ancient Wisdom, and will perceive all the hidden teachings from the rustling leaves of the Tree that flourisheth in that City. With both his inner and outer ear, he will hear from its dust the hymns of glory and praise ascending unto the Lord of Lords, and with his inner eye will he discover the mysteries of "return" and "revival."

How unspeakably glorious are the signs, the tokens, the revelations, and splendors which He, Who is the King of Names and Attributes, hath destined for that City! The attainment unto this City quencheth thirst without water, and kindleth the love of God without fire. Within every blade of grass are enshrined the mysteries of an inscrutable Wisdom, and upon every rose-bush a myriad nightingales pour out, in blissful rapture, their melody. Its wondrous tulips unfold the mystery of the undying Fire in the Burning Bush, and its sweet savors of holiness breathe the perfume of the Messianic Spirit. It bestoweth wealth without gold, and conferreth immortality without death. In each one of its leaves ineffable delights are treasured, and within every chamber unnumbered mysteries lie hidden.

They that valiantly labor in quest of God, will, when once they have renounced all else but Him, be so attached and wedded unto that City, that a moment's separation from it would to them be unthinkable. They will hearken unto infallible proofs from the Hyacinth of that assembly, and will receive the surest testimonies from the beauty of its Rose, and the melody of its Nightingale. Once in about a thousand years shall this City be renewed and re-adorned. . . .

That City is none other than the Word of God revealed in every age and dispensation. In the days of Moses it was the Pentateuch; in the days of Jesus, the Gospel; in the days of Muḥammad, the Messenger of God, the Qur'án; in this day, the Bayán; and in the

Dispensation of Him Whom God will make manifest, His own Book—the Book unto which all the Books of former Dispensations must needs be referred, the Book that standeth amongst them all transcendent and supreme.

The Hosts of Divine Inspiration

O wayfarer in the path of God! Take thou thy portion of the ocean of His grace, and deprive not thyself of the things that lie hidden in its depths. Be thou of them that have partaken of its treasures. A dewdrop out of this ocean would, if shed upon all that are in the heavens and on the earth, suffice to enrich them with the bounty of God, the Almighty, the All-Knowing, the All-Wise. With the hands of renunciation draw forth from its life-giving waters, and sprinkle therewith all created things, that they may be cleansed from all man-made limitations and may approach the mighty seat of God, this hallowed and resplendent Spot.

Be not grieved if thou performest it thyself alone. Let God be all-sufficient for thee. Commune intimately with His Spirit, and be thou of the thankful. Proclaim the Cause of thy Lord unto all who are in the heavens and on the earth. Should any man respond to thy call, lay bare before him the pearls of the wisdom of the Lord, thy God, which His Spirit hath sent down unto thee, and be thou of them that truly believe. And should any one reject thy offer, turn thou away from him, and put thy trust and confidence in the Lord, thy God, the Lord of all worlds.

By the righteousness of God! Whoso openeth his lips in this Day and maketh mention of the name of his Lord, the hosts of Divine inspiration shall descend upon him from the heaven of My name, the All-Knowing, the All-Wise. On him shall also descend the Concourse on high, each bearing aloft a chalice of pure light. Thus hath it been fore-ordained in the realm of God's Revelation, by the behest of Him Who is the All-Glorious, the Most Powerful.

There lay concealed within the Holy Veil, and prepared for the service of God, a company of His chosen ones who shall be manifested unto men, who shall aid His Cause, who shall be afraid of no one, though the entire human race rise up and war against them. These are the ones who, before the gaze of the dwellers on earth and the denizens of heaven, shall arise and, shouting aloud, acclaim the name of the Almighty, and summon the children of men to the path of God, the All-Glorious, the All-Praised. Walk thou in their way, and let no one dismay thee. Be of them whom the tumult of the world, however much it may agitate them in the path of their Creator, can never sadden, whose purpose the blame of the blamer will never defeat.

Go forth with the Tablet of God and His signs, and rejoin them that have believed in Me, and announce unto them tidings of Our most holy Paradise. Warn, then, those that have joined partners with Him. Say: I am come to you, O people, from the Throne of glory, and bear you an announcement from God, the Most Powerful, the Most Exalted, the Most Great. In mine hand I carry the testimony of God, your Lord and the Lord of your sires of old. Weigh it with the just Balance that ye possess, the Balance of the testimony of the Prophets and Messengers of God. If ye find it to be established in truth, if ye believe it to be of God, beware, then, lest ye cavil at it, and render your works vain, and be numbered with the infidels. It is indeed the sign of God that hath been sent down through the power of truth, through which the validity of His Cause hath been demonstrated unto His creatures, and the ensigns of purity lifted up betwixt earth and heaven.

Say: This is the sealed and mystic Scroll, the repository of God's irrevocable Decree, bearing the words which the Finger of Holiness hath traced, that lay wrapt within the veil of impenetrable mystery, and hath now been sent down as a token of the grace of Him Who is the Almighty, the Ancient of Days. In it have We decreed the destinies of all the dwellers of the earth and the denizens of heaven, and written down the knowledge of all things from first to last. Nothing whatsoever can escape or frustrate Him, whether created in the past or to be created in the future, could ye but perceive it.

Say: The Revelation sent down by God hath most surely been repeated, and the outstretched Hand of Our power hath overshadowed all that are in the heavens and all that are on the earth. We have, through the power of truth, the very truth, manifested an infinitesimal glimmer of Our impenetrable Mystery, and lo, they that have recognized the radiance of the Sinaic splendor expired, as they caught a lightening glimpse of this Crimson Light enveloping the Sinai of Our Revelation. Thus hath He Who is the Beauty of the All-Merciful come down in the clouds of His testimony, and the decree accomplished by virtue of the Will of God, the All-Glorious, the All-Wise.

Say: Step out of Thy holy chamber, O Maid of Heaven, inmate of the Exalted Paradise! Drape thyself in whatever manner pleaseth Thee in the silken Vesture of Immortality, and put on, in the name of the All-Glorious, the broidered Robe of Light. Hear, then, the sweet, the wondrous accent of the Voice that cometh from the Throne of Thy Lord, the Inaccessible, the Most High. Unveil Thy face, and manifest the beauty of the black-eyed Damsel, and suffer not the servants of God to be deprived of the light of Thy shining countenance. Grieve not if Thou hearest the sighs of the dwellers of the earth, or the voice of the lamentation of the denizens of heaven. Leave them to perish on the dust of extinction. Let them be reduced to nothingness, inasmuch as the flame of hatred hath been kindled within their breasts. Intone, then, before the face of the peoples of earth and heaven, and in a most melodious voice, the anthem of praise, for a remembrance of Him Who is the King of the names and attributes of God. Thus have We decreed Thy destiny. Well able are We to achieve Our purpose.

Beware that Thou divest not Thyself, Thou Who art the Essence of Purity, of Thy robe of effulgent glory. Nay, enrich Thyself increasingly, in the kingdom of creation, with the incorruptible vestures of Thy God, that the beauteous image of the Almighty may be reflected through Thee in all created things and the grace of Thy Lord be infused in the plenitude of its power into the entire creation.

If Thou smellest from any one the smell of the love of Thy Lord, offer up Thyself for him, for We have created Thee to this end, and have covenanted with Thee, from time immemorial, and in the presence of the congregation of Our well-favored ones, for this very purpose. Be not impatient if the blind in heart hurl down the shafts of their idle fancies upon Thee. Leave them to themselves, for they follow the promptings of the evil ones.

Cry out before the gaze of the dwellers of heaven and of earth: I am the Maid of Heaven, the Offspring begotten by the Spirit of Bahá. My habitation is the Mansion of His Name, the All-Glorious. Before the Concourse on high I was adorned with the ornament of His names. I was wrapt within the veil of an inviolable security, and lay hidden from the eyes of men. Methinks that I heard a Voice of divine and incomparable sweetness, proceeding from the right hand of the God of Mercy, and lo, the whole Paradise stirred and trembled before Me, in its longing to hear its accents, and gaze on the beauty of Him that uttered them. Thus have We revealed in this luminous Tablet, and in the sweetest of languages, the verses which the Tongue of Eternity was moved to utter in the Qayyúm-i-Asmá.

Say: He ordaineth as He pleaseth, by virtue of His sovereignty, and doeth whatsoever He willeth at His own behest. He shall not be asked of the things it pleaseth Him to ordain. He, in truth, is the Unrestrained, the All-Powerful, the All-Wise.

They that have disbelieved in God and rebelled against His sovereignty are the helpless victims of their corrupt inclinations and desires. These shall return to their abode in the fire of hell: wretched is the abode of the deniers!

CHAPTER THREE

THE LIFE OF THE SOUL

The Power of Regeneration

The vitality of men's belief in God is dying out in every land; nothing short of His wholesome medicine can ever restore it. The corrosion of ungodliness is eating into the vitals of human society; what else but the Elixir of His potent Revelation can cleanse and revive it? Is it within human power, O Ḥakím, to effect in the constituent elements of any of the minute and indivisible particles of matter so complete a transformation as to transmute it into purest gold? Perplexing and difficult as this may appear, the still greater task of converting satanic strength into heavenly power is one that We have been empowered to accomplish. The Force capable of such a transformation transcendeth the potency of the Elixir itself. The Word of God, alone, can claim the distinction of being endowed with the capacity required for so great and far-reaching a change.

A Fixed Time to Turn to God

We have a fixed time for you, O peoples. If ye fail, at the appointed hour, to turn towards God, He, verily, will lay violent hold on you, and will cause grievous afflictions to assail you from every direction. How severe, indeed, is the chastisement with which your Lord will then chastise you!

An Ever-Advancing Civilization

O Kamál! The heights which, through the most gracious favor of God, mortal man can attain, in this Day, are as yet unrevealed to his sight. The world of being hath never had, nor doth it yet possess the capacity for such a revelation. The day, however, is approaching when the potentialities of so great a favor will, by virtue of His behest, be manifested unto men. Though the forces of the nations be arrayed against Him, though the kings of the earth be leagued to undermine His Cause, the power of His might shall stand unshaken. He, verily, speaketh the truth, and summoneth all mankind to the way of Him Who is the Incomparable, the All-Knowing.

All men have been created to carry forward an ever-advancing civilization. The Almighty beareth Me witness: To act like the beasts of the field is unworthy of man. Those virtues that befit his dignity are forbearance, mercy, compassion and loving-kindness towards all the peoples and kindreds of the earth. Say: O friends! Drink your fill from this crystal stream that floweth through the heavenly grace of Him Who is the Lord of Names. Let others partake of its waters in My name, that the leaders of men in every land may fully recognize the purpose for which the Eternal Truth hath been revealed, and the reason for which they themselves have been created.

As One Soul and One Body

He Who is your Lord, the All-Merciful, cherisheth in His heart the desire of beholding the entire human race as one soul and one body. Haste ye to win your share of God's good grace and mercy in this Day that eclipseth all other created Days. How great the felicity that awaiteth the man that forsaketh all he hath in a desire to obtain the things of God! Such a man, We testify, is among God's blessed ones.

The Paradise of His Presence

Release yourselves, O nightingales of God, from the thorns and brambles of wretchedness and misery, and wing your flight to the rose-garden of unfading splendor. O My friends that dwell upon the dust! Haste forth unto your celestial habitation. Announce unto yourselves the joyful tidings: "He Who is the Best-Beloved is come! He hath crowned Himself with the glory of God's Revelation, and hath unlocked to the face of men the doors of His ancient Paradise." Let all eyes rejoice, and let every ear be gladdened, for now is the time to gaze on His beauty, now is the fit time to hearken to His voice. Proclaim unto every longing lover: "Behold, your Well-Beloved hath come among men!" and to the messengers of the Monarch of love impart the tidings: "Lo, the Adored One hath appeared arrayed in the fullness of His glory!" O lovers of His beauty! Turn the anguish of your separation from Him into the joy of an everlasting reunion, and let the sweetness of His presence dissolve the bitterness of your remoteness from His court.

Behold how the manifold grace of God, which is being showered from the clouds of Divine glory, hath, in this day, encompassed the world. For whereas in days past every lover besought and searched after his Beloved, it is the Beloved Himself Who now is calling His lovers and is inviting them to attain His presence. Take heed lest ye forfeit so precious a favor; beware lest ye belittle so remarkable a token of His grace. Abandon not the incorruptible benefits, and be not content with that which perisheth. Lift up the veil that obscureth your vision, and dispel the darkness with which it is enveloped, that ye may gaze on the naked beauty of the Beloved's face, may behold that which no eye hath beheld, and hear that which no ear hath heard.

Hear Me, ye mortal birds! In the Rose-Garden of changeless splendor a Flower hath begun to bloom, compared to which every other flower is but a thorn, and before the brightness of Whose glory the very essence of beauty must pale and wither. Arise, therefore, and, with the whole enthusiasm of your hearts, with all the eagerness of your souls, the full fervor of your will, and the concentrated efforts of your entire being, strive to attain the paradise of His presence, and endeavor to inhale the fragrance of the incorruptible Flower, to breathe the sweet savors of holiness, and to obtain a portion of this perfume of celestial glory. Whoso followeth this counsel will break his chains asunder, will taste the abandonment of enraptured love, will attain unto his heart's desire, and will surrender his soul into the hands of his Beloved. Bursting through his cage, he will, even as the bird of the spirit, wing his flight to his holy and everlasting nest.

Night hath succeeded day, and day hath succeeded night, and the hours and moments of your lives have come and gone, and yet none of you hath, for one instant, consented to detach himself from that which perisheth. Bestir yourselves, that the brief moments that are still yours may not be dissipated and lost. Even as the swiftness of lightning your days shall pass, and your bodies shall be laid to rest beneath a canopy of dust. What can ye then achieve? How can ye atone for your past failure?

The everlasting Candle shineth in its naked glory. Behold how it hath consumed every mortal veil. O ye moth-like lovers of His light! Brave every danger, and consecrate your souls to its consuming flame. O ye that thirst after Him! Strip yourselves of every earthly affection, and hasten to embrace your Beloved. With a zest that none can equal make haste to attain unto Him. The Flower, thus far hidden from the sight of men, is unveiled to your eyes. In the open radiance of His glory He standeth before you. His voice summoneth all the holy and sanctified beings to come and be united with Him. Happy is he that turneth thereunto; well is it with him that hath attained, and gazed on the light of so wondrous a countenance.

Man's Perfection and Nobility

Whatever is in the heavens and whatever is on the earth is a direct evidence of the revelation within it of the attributes and names of God, inasmuch as within every atom are enshrined the signs that bear eloquent testimony to the revelation of that Most Great Light. Methinks, but for the potency of that revelation, no being could ever exist. How resplendent the luminaries of knowledge that shine in an atom, and how vast the oceans of wisdom that surge within a drop! To a supreme degree is this true of man, who, among all created things, hath been invested with the robe of such gifts, and hath been singled out for the glory of such distinction. For in him are potentially revealed all the attributes and names of God to a degree that no other created being hath excelled or surpassed. All these names and attributes are applicable to him. Even as He hath said: "Man is My mystery, and I am his mystery." Manifold are the verses that have been repeatedly revealed in all the Heavenly Books and the Holy Scriptures, expressive of this most subtle and lofty theme. Even as He hath revealed: "We will surely show them Our signs in the world and within themselves." Again He saith: "And also in your own selves: will ye not, then, behold the signs of God?" And yet again He revealeth: "And be ye not like those who forget God, and whom He hath therefore caused to forget their own selves." In this connection, He Who is the eternal King—may the souls of all that dwell within the mystic Tabernacle be a sacrifice unto Him—hath spoken: "He hath known God who hath known himself."

. . . From that which hath been said it becometh evident that all things, in their inmost reality, testify to the revelation of the names and attributes of God within them. Each according to its capacity, indicateth, and is expressive of, the knowledge of God. So potent and universal is this revelation, that it hath encompassed all things visible and invisible. Thus hath He revealed: "Hath aught else save Thee a power of revelation which is not possessed by Thee, that it could have manifested Thee? Blind is the eye which doth not perceive Thee." Likewise hath the eternal King spoken: "No thing have I perceived, except that I perceived God within it, God before it, or God after it." Also in the tradition of Kumayl it is written: "Behold, a light hath shone forth out of the morn of eternity, and lo, its waves have penetrated the inmost reality of all men." Man, the noblest and most perfect of all created things, excelleth them all in the intensity of this revelation, and is a fuller expression of its glory. And of all men, the most accomplished, the most distinguished, and the most excellent are the Manifestations of the Sun of Truth. Nay, all else besides these Manifestations, live by the operation of their Will, and move and have their being through the outpourings of their grace.

Re-Created By His Spirit

The Most Great Name beareth Me witness! How sad if any man were, in this Day, to rest his heart on the transitory things of this world! Arise, and cling firmly to the Cause of God. Be most loving one to another. Burn away, wholly for the sake of the Well-Beloved, the veil of self with the flame of the undying Fire, and with faces, joyous and beaming with light, associate with your neighbor. Ye have well observed, in all its aspects, the behavior of Him Who is the Word of Truth amidst you. Ye know full well how hard it is for this Youth to allow, though it be for one night, the heart of any one of the beloved of God to be saddened by Him.

The Word of God hath set the heart of the world afire; how regrettable if ye fail to be enkindled with its flame! Please God, ye will regard this blessed night as the night of unity, will knit your souls together, and resolve to adorn yourselves with the ornament of a goodly and praiseworthy character. Let your principal concern be to rescue the fallen from the slough of impending extinction, and to help him embrace the ancient Faith of God. Your behavior towards your neighbor should be such as to manifest clearly the signs of the one true God, for ye are the first among men to be re-created by His Spirit, the first to adore and bow the knee before Him, the first to circle round His throne of glory. I swear by Him Who hath caused Me to reveal whatever hath pleased Him! Ye are better known to the inmates of the Kingdom on high than ye are known to your own selves. Think ye these words to be vain and empty? Would that ye had the power to perceive the things your Lord, the All-Merciful, doth see—things that attest the excellence of your rank, that bear witness to the greatness of your worth, that proclaim the sublimity of your station! God grant that your desires and unmortified passions may not hinder you from that which hath been ordained for you.

Every Man Endowed with Capacity

Tear asunder, in My Name, the veils that have grievously blinded your vision, and, through the power born of your belief in the unity of God, scatter the idols of vain imitation. Enter, then, the holy paradise of the good-pleasure of the All-Merciful. Sanctify your souls from whatsoever is not of God, and taste ye the sweetness of rest within the pale of His vast and mighty Revelation, and beneath the shadow of His supreme and infallible authority. Suffer not yourselves to be wrapt in the dense veils of your selfish desires, inasmuch as I have perfected in every one of you My creation, so that the excellence of My handiwork may be fully revealed unto men. It follows, therefore, that every man hath been, and will continue to be, able of himself to appreciate the Beauty of God, the Glorified. Had he not been endowed with such a capacity, how could he be called to account for his failure? If, in the Day when all the peoples of the earth will be gathered together, any man should, whilst standing in the presence of God, be asked: "Wherefore hast thou disbelieved in My Beauty and turned away from My Self," and if such a man should reply and say: "Inasmuch as all men have erred, and none hath been found willing to turn his face to the Truth, I, too, following their example, have grievously failed to recognize the Beauty of the Eternal," such a plea will, assuredly, be rejected. For the faith of no man can be conditioned by any one except himself.

The Result of Volition

And now, concerning thy question regarding the creation of man. Know thou that all men have been created in the nature made by God, the Guardian, the Self-Subsisting. Unto each one hath been prescribed a pre-ordained measure, as decreed in God's mighty and guarded Tablets. All that which ye potentially possess can, however, be manifested only as a result of your own volition. Your own acts testify to this truth. Consider, for instance, that which hath been forbidden, in the Bayán, unto men. God hath in that Book, and by His behest, decreed as lawful whatsoever He hath pleased to decree, and hath, through the power of His sovereign might, forbidden whatsoever He elected to forbid. To this testifieth the text of that Book. Will ye not bear witness? Men, however, have wittingly broken His law. Is such a behavior to be attributed to God, or to their proper selves? Be fair in your judgment. Every good thing is of God, and every evil thing is from yourselves.

The Soul's Power

Thou hast asked Me whether man, as apart from the Prophets of God and His chosen ones, will retain, after his physical death, the self-same individuality, personality, consciousness, and understanding that characterize his life in this world. If this should be the case, how is it, thou hast observed, that whereas such slight injuries to his mental faculties as fainting and severe illness deprive him of his understanding and consciousness, his death, which must involve the decomposition of his body and the dissolution of its elements, is powerless to destroy that understanding and extinguish that consciousness? How can any one imagine that man's consciousness and personality will be maintained, when the very instruments necessary to their existence and function will have completely disintegrated?

Know thou that the soul of man is exalted above, and is independent of all infirmities of body or mind. That a sick person showeth signs of weakness is due to the hindrances that interpose themselves between his soul and his body, for the soul itself remaineth unaffected by any bodily ailments. Consider the light of the lamp. Though an external object may interfere with its radiance, the light itself continueth to shine with undiminished power. In like manner, every malady afflicting the body of man is an impediment that preventeth the soul from manifesting its inherent might and power. When it leaveth the body, however, it will evince such ascendency, and reveal such influence as no force on earth can equal. Every pure, every refined and sanctified soul will be endowed with tremendous power, and shall rejoice with exceeding gladness.

Consider the lamp which is hidden under a bushel. Though its light be shining, yet its radiance is concealed from men. Likewise, consider the sun which hath been obscured by the clouds. Observe how its splendor appeareth to have diminished, when in reality the source of that light hath remained unchanged. The soul of man should be likened unto this sun, and all things on earth should be regarded as his body. So long as no external impediment interveneth between them, the body will, in its entirety, continue to reflect the light of the soul, and to be sustained by its power. As soon as, however, a veil interposeth itself between them, the brightness of that light seemeth to lessen.

Consider again the sun when it is completely hidden behind the clouds. Though the earth is still illumined with its light, yet the measure of light which it receiveth is considerably reduced. Not until the clouds have dispersed, can the sun shine again in the plenitude of its glory. Neither the presence of the cloud nor its absence can, in any way, affect the inherent splendor of the sun. The soul of man is the sun by which his body is illumined, and from which it draweth its sustenance, and should be so regarded.

Consider, moreover, how the fruit, ere it is formed, lieth potentially within the tree. Were the tree to be cut into pieces, no sign nor any part of the fruit, however small, could be detected. When it appeareth, however, it manifesteth itself, as thou hast observed, in its wondrous beauty and glorious perfection. Certain fruits, indeed, attain their fullest development only after being severed from the tree.

A Sign of God

Thou hast asked Me concerning the nature of the soul. Know, verily, that the soul is a sign of God, a heavenly gem whose reality the most learned of men hath failed to grasp, and whose mystery no mind, however acute, can ever hope to unravel. It is the first among all created things to declare the excellence of its Creator, the first to recognize His glory, to cleave to His truth, and to bow down in adoration before Him. If it be faithful to God, it will reflect His light, and will, eventually, return unto Him. If it fail, however, in its allegiance to its Creator, it will become a victim to self and passion, and will, in the end, sink in their depths.

The Gift of Understanding

Know thou that, according to what thy Lord, the Lord of all men, hath decreed in His Book, the favors vouchsafed by Him unto mankind have been, and will ever remain, limitless in their range. First and foremost among these favors, which the Almighty hath conferred upon man, is the gift of understanding. His purpose in conferring such a gift is none other except to enable His creature to know and recognize the one true God—exalted be His glory. This gift giveth man the power to discern the truth in all things, leadeth him to that which is right, and helpeth him to discover the secrets of creation. Next in rank, is the power of vision, the chief instrument whereby his understanding can function. The senses of hearing, of the heart, and the like, are similarly to be reckoned among the gifts with which the human body is endowed. Immeasurably exalted is the Almighty Who hath created these powers, and revealed them in the body of man.

Every one of these gifts is an undoubted evidence of the majesty, the power, the ascendancy, the all-embracing knowledge of the one true God—exalted be His glory. Consider the sense of touch. Witness how its power hath spread itself over the entire human body. Whereas the faculties of sight and of hearing are each localized in a particular center, the sense of touch embraceth the whole human frame. Glorified be His power, magnified be His sovereignty!

These gifts are inherent in man himself. That which is preeminent above all other gifts, is incorruptible in nature, and pertaineth to God Himself, is the gift of Divine Revelation. Every bounty conferred by the Creator upon man, be it material or spiritual, is subservient unto this. It is, in its essence, and will ever so remain, the Bread which cometh down from Heaven. It is God's supreme testimony, the clearest evidence of His truth, the sign of His consummate bounty, the token of His all-encompassing mercy, the proof of His most loving providence, the symbol of His most perfect grace. He hath, indeed, partaken of this highest gift of God who hath recognized His Manifestation in this Day.

Render thanks unto thy Lord for having vouchsafed unto thee so great a bounty. Lift up thy voice and say: All praise be to Thee, O Thou, the Desire of every understanding heart!

Chosen From the Whole World

Say: Deliver your souls, O people, from the bondage of self, and purify them from all attachment to anything besides Me.

Remembrance of Me cleanseth all things from defilement, could ye but perceive it. Say: Were all created things to be entirely divested of the veil of worldly vanity and desire, the Hand of God would in this Day clothe them, one and all, with the robe "He doeth whatsoever He willeth in the kingdom of creation," that thereby the sign of His sovereignty might be manifested in all things. Exalted then be He, the Sovereign Lord of all, the Almighty, the Supreme Protector, the All-Glorious, the Most Powerful.

Intone, O My servant, the verses of God that have been received by thee, as intoned by them who have drawn nigh unto Him, that the sweetness of thy melody may kindle thine own soul, and attract the hearts of all men. Whoso reciteth, in the privacy of his chamber, the verses revealed by God, the scattering angels of the Almighty shall scatter abroad the fragrance of the words uttered by his mouth, and shall cause the heart of every righteous man to throb. Though he may, at first, remain unaware of its effect, yet the virtue of the grace vouchsafed unto him must needs sooner or later exercise its influence upon his soul. Thus have the mysteries of the Revelation of God been decreed by virtue of the Will of Him Who is the Source of power and wisdom.

O Khalil! God beareth Me witness. Though My Pen be still moving on My Tablet, yet, in its very heart, it weepeth and is sore distressed. The lamp burning before the Throne, likewise, weepeth and groaneth by reason of the things which the Ancient Beauty hath suffered at the hands of them who are but a creation of His Will. God, Himself, knoweth and testifieth to the truth of My words. No man that hath purged his ear from the loud clamor of the infidels, and inclined it to all created things, can fail to hear the voice of their lamentation and weeping over the trouble that hath befallen Us at the hands of those of Our servants that have disbelieved in, and rebelled against, Us. Thus have We disclosed to thee a glimmer of the woes that have come upon us, that thou mayest be made aware of Our sufferings, and patiently endure thy sorrows.

Arise to aid thy Lord at all times and in all circumstances, and be thou one of His helpers. Admonish, then, the people to lend a hearing ear to the words which the Spirit of God hath uttered in this irradiant and resplendent Tablet. Say: Sow not, O people, the seeds of dissension amongst men, and contend not with your neighbor. Be patient under all conditions, and place your whole trust and confidence in God. Aid ye your Lord with the sword of wisdom and of utterance. This indeed well becometh the station of man. To depart from it would be unworthy of God, the Sovereign Lord of all, the Glorified. The people, however, have been led astray, and are truly of the heedless.

Unlock, O people, the gates of the hearts of men with the keys of the remembrance of Him Who is the Remembrance of God and the Source of wisdom amongst you. He hath chosen out of the whole world the hearts of His servants, and made them each a seat for the revelation of His glory. Wherefore, sanctify them from every defilement, that the things for which they were created may be engraven upon them. This indeed is a token of God's bountiful favor.

Beautify your tongues, O people, with truthfulness, and adorn your souls with the ornament of honesty. Beware, O people, that ye deal not treacherously with any one. Be ye the trustees of God amongst His creatures, and the emblems of His generosity amidst His people. They that follow their lusts and corrupt inclinations, have erred and dissipated their efforts. They, indeed, are of the lost. Strive, O people, that your eyes may be directed towards the mercy of God, that your hearts may be attuned to His wondrous remembrance, that your souls may rest confidently upon His grace and bounty, that your feet may tread the path of His good-pleasure. Such are the counsels which I bequeath unto you. Would that ye might follow My counsels!

The Flood of Grace

This is the Day whereon the Ocean of God's mercy hath been manifested unto men, the Day in which the Day Star of His loving-kindness hath shed its radiance upon them, the Day in which the clouds of His bountiful favor have overshadowed the whole of mankind. Now is the time to cheer and refresh the down-cast through the invigorating breeze of love and fellowship, and the living waters of friendliness and charity.

They who are the beloved of God, in whatever place they gather and whomsoever they may meet, must evince, in their attitude towards God, and in the manner of their celebration of His praise and glory, such humility and submissiveness that every atom of the dust beneath their feet may attest the depth of their devotion. The conversation carried on by these holy souls should be informed with such power that these same atoms of dust will be thrilled by its influence. They should conduct themselves in such manner that the earth upon which they tread may never be allowed to address them such words as these: "I am to be preferred above you. For witness, how patient I am in bearing the burden which the husbandman layeth upon me. I am the instrument that continually imparteth unto all beings the blessings with which He Who is the Source of all grace hath entrusted me. Notwithstanding the honor conferred upon me, and the unnumbered evidences of my wealth—a wealth that supplieth the needs of all creation—behold the measure of my humility, witness with what absolute submissiveness I allow myself to be trodden beneath the feet of men . . ."

Show forbearence and benevolence and love to one another. Should any one amongst you be incapable of grasping a certain truth, or be striving to comprehend it, show forth, when conversing with him, a spirit of extreme kindliness and good-will. Help him to see and recognize the truth, without esteeming yourself to be, in the least, superior to him, or to be possessed of greater endowments.

The whole duty of man in this Day is to attain that share of the flood of grace which God poureth forth for him. Let none, therefore, consider the largeness or smallness of the receptacle. The portion of some might lie in the palm of a man's hand, the portion of others might fill a cup, and of others even a gallon-measure.

Every eye, in this Day, should seek what will best promote the Cause of God. He, Who is the Eternal Truth, beareth Me witness! Nothing whatever can, in this Day, inflict a greater harm upon this Cause than dissension and strife, contention, estrangement and apathy, among the loved ones of God. Flee them, through the power of God and His sovereign aid, and strive to knit together the hearts of men, in His Name, the Unifier, the All-Knowing, the All-Wise.

Beseech ye the one true God to grant that ye may taste the

savor of such deeds as are performed in His path, and partake of the sweetness of such humility and submissiveness as are shown for His sake. Forget your own selves, and turn your eyes towards your neighbor. Bend your energies to whatever may foster the education of men. Nothing is, or can ever be, hidden from God. If ye follow in His way, His incalculable and imperishable blessings will be showered upon you. This is the luminous Tablet, whose verses have streamed from the moving Pen of Him Who is the Lord of all worlds. Ponder it in your hearts, and be of them that observe its precepts.

Two Duties Laid Upon Man

The first duty prescribed by God for His servants is the recognition of Him Who is the Day Spring of His Revelation and the Fountain of His laws, Who representeth the Godhead in both the Kingdom of His Cause and the world of creation. Whoso achieveth this duty hath attained unto all good; and whoso is deprived thereof, hath gone astray, though he be the author of every righteous deed. It behoveth every one who reacheth this most sublime station, this summit of transcendent glory, to observe every ordinance of Him Who is the Desire of the world. These twin duties are inseparable. Neither is acceptable without the other. Thus hath it been decreed by Him Who is the Source of Divine inspiration.

They whom God hath endued with insight will readily recognize that the precepts laid down by God constitute the highest means for the maintenance of order in the world and the security of its peoples. He that turneth away from them, is accounted among the abject and foolish. We, verily, have commanded you to refuse the dictates of your evil passions and corrupt desires, and not to transgress the bounds which the Pen of the Most High hath fixed, for these are the breath of life unto all created things. The seas of Divine wisdom and divine utterance have risen under the breath of the breeze of the All-Merciful. Hasten to drink your fill, O men of understanding! They that have violated the Covenant of God by breaking His commandments, and have turned back on their heels, these have erred grievously in the sight of God, the All-Possessing, the Most High.

O ye peoples of the world! Know assuredly that My commandments are the lamps of My loving providence among My servants, and the keys of My mercy for My creatures. Thus hath it been sent down from the heaven of the Will of your Lord, the Lord of Revelation. Were any man to taste the sweetness of the words which the lips of the All-Merciful have willed to utter, he would, though the treasures of the earth be in his possession, renounce them one and all, that he might vindicate the truth of even one of His commandments, shining above the day spring of His bountiful care and loving-kindness.

Say: From My laws the sweet smelling savor of My garment can be smelled, and by their aid the standards of victory will be planted upon the highest peaks. The Tongue of My power hath, from the heaven of My omnipotent glory, addressed to My creation these words: "Observe My commandments, for the love of My beauty." Happy is the lover that hath inhaled the divine fragrance of his Best-Beloved from these words, laden with the perfume of a grace which no tongue can describe. By My life! He who hath drunk the choice wine of fairness from the hands of My bountiful favor, will circle around My commandments that shine above the Day Spring of My creation.

Think not that We have revealed unto you a mere code of laws. Nay, rather, We have unsealed the choice Wine with the fingers of might and power. To this beareth witness that which the Pen of Revelation hath revealed. Meditate upon this, O men of insight!

Whenever My laws appear like the sun in the heaven of Mine utterance, they must be faithfully obeyed by all, though My decree be such as to cause the heaven of every religion to be cleft asunder. He doeth what He pleaseth. He chooseth; and none may question His choice. Whatsoever He, the Well-Beloved, ordaineth, the same is, verily, beloved. To this He Who is the Lord of all creation beareth Me witness. Whoso hath inhaled the sweet fragrance of the All-Merciful, and recognized the Source of this utterance, will welcome with his own eyes the shafts of the enemy, that he may establish the truth of the laws of God amongst men. Well is it with him that hath turned thereunto, and apprehended the meaning of His decisive decree.

The Spirit That Animateth the Heart

The first and foremost duty prescribed unto men, next to the recognition of Him Who is the Eternal Truth, is the duty of steadfastness in His Cause. Cleave thou unto it, and be of them whose minds are firmly fixed and grounded in God. No act, however meritorious, did or can ever compare unto it. It is the king of all acts, and to this thy Lord, the All-Highest, the Most Powerful, will testify. . . .

The virtues and attributes pertaining unto God are all evident and manifest, and have been mentioned and described in all the heavenly Books. Among them are trustworthiness, truthfulness, purity of heart while communing with God, forbearance, resignation to whatever the Almighty hath decreed, contentment with the things His Will hath provided, patience, nay thankfulness in the midst of tribulation, and complete reliance, in all circumstances, upon Him. These rank, according to the estimate of God, among the highest and most laudable of all acts. All other acts are, and will ever remain, secondary and subordinate unto them. . . .

The spirit that animateth the human heart is the knowledge of God, and its truest adorning is the recognition of the truth that "He doeth whatsoever He willeth, and ordaineth that which He pleaseth." Its raiment is the fear of God, and its perfection steadfastness in His Faith. Thus God instructeth whosoever seeketh Him. He, verily, loveth the one that turneth towards Him. There is none other God but Him, the Forgiving, the Most Bountiful. All praise be to God, the Lord of all worlds.

Potentialities Inherent in Man

The All-Merciful hath conferred upon man the faculty of vision, and endowed him with the power of hearing. Some have described him as the "lesser world," when, in reality, he should be regarded as the "greater world." The potentialities inherent in the station of man, the full measure of his destiny on earth, the innate excellence of his reality, must all be manifested in this promised Day of God.

Endowed With Constancy

Blessed is the man that hath acknowledged his belief in God and in His signs, and recognized that "He shall not be asked of His doings." Such a recognition hath been made by God the ornament of every belief, and its very foundation. Upon it must depend the acceptance of every goodly deed. Fasten your eyes upon it, that haply the whisperings of the rebellious may not cause you to slip.

Were He to decree as lawful the thing which from time immemorial had been forbidden, and forbid that which had, at all times, been regarded as lawful, to none is given the right to question His authority. Whoso will hesitate, though it be for less than a moment, should be regarded as a transgressor.

Whoso hath not recognized this sublime and fundamental verity, and hath failed to attain this most exalted station, the winds of doubt will agitate him, and the sayings of the infidels will distract his soul. He that hath acknowledged this principle will be endowed with the most perfect constancy. All-honor to this all-glorious station, the remembrance of which adorneth every exalted Tablet. Such is the teaching which God bestoweth on you, a teaching that will deliver you from all manner of doubt and perplexity, and enable you to attain unto salvation in both this world and in the next. He, verily, is the Ever-Forgiving, the Most Bountiful.

Establish Unity

The voice of the Divine Herald, proceeding out of the throne of God, declareth: O ye My loved ones! Suffer not the hem of My sacred vesture to be smirched and mired with the things of this world, and follow not the promptings of your evil and corrupt desires. The Day Star of Divine Revelation, that shineth in the plenitude of its glory in the heaven of this Prison, beareth Me witness. They whose hearts are turned towards Him Who is the Object of the adoration of the entire creation must needs, in this Day, pass beyond and be sanctified from all created things, visible and invisible. If they arise to teach My Cause, they must let the breath of Him Who is the Unconstrained, stir them and must spread it abroad on the earth with high resolve, with minds that are wholly centered in Him, and with hearts that are completely detached from and independent of all things, and with souls that are sanctified from the world and its vanities. It behoveth them to choose as the best provision for their journey reliance upon God, and to clothe themselves with the love of their Lord, the Most Exalted, the All-Glorious. If they do so, their words shall influence their hearers.

How great, how very great, the gulf that separateth Us from them who, in this Day, are occupied with their evil passions, and have set their hopes on the things of the earth and its fleeting glory! Many a time hath the court of the All-Merciful been to outward seeming so denuded of the riches of this world that they who lived in close association with Him suffered from dire want. Despite their sufferings, the Pen of the Most High hath, at no time, been willing to refer, nor even to make the slightest allusion, to the things that pertain to this world and its treasures. And if, at any time, any gift were presented to Him, that gift was accepted as a token of His grace unto him that offered it. Should it ever please Us to appropriate to Our own use all the treasures of the earth, to none is given the right to question Our authority, or to challenge Our right. It would be impossible to conceive any act more contemptible than soliciting, in the name of the one true God, the riches which men possess.

It is incumbent upon thee, and upon the followers of Him Who is the Eternal Truth, to summon all men to whatsoever shall sanctify them from all attachment to the things of the earth and purge them from its defilements, that the sweet smell of the raiment of the All-Glorious may be smelled from all them that love Him.

They who are possessed of riches, however, must have the utmost regard for the poor, for great is the honor destined by God for those poor who are steadfast in patience. By My life! There is no honor, except what God may please to bestow, that can compare to this honor. Great is the blessedness awaiting the poor that endure patiently and conceal their sufferings, and well is it with the rich who bestow their riches on the needy and prefer them before themselves.

Please God, the poor may exert themselves and strive to earn the means of livelihood. This is a duty which, in this most great Revelation, hath been prescribed unto every one, and is accounted in the sight of God as a goodly deed. Whoso observeth this duty, the help of the invisible One shall most certainly aid him. He can enrich, through His grace, whomsoever He pleaseth. He, verily, hath power over all things. . . .

Tell, O 'Alí, the loved ones of God that equity is the most fundamental among human virtues. The evaluation of all things must needs depend upon it. Ponder a while on the woes and afflictions which this Prisoner hath sustained. I have, all the days of My life, been at the mercy of Mine enemies, and have suffered each day, in the path of the love of God, a fresh tribulation. I have patiently endured until the fame of the Cause of God was spread abroad on the earth. If any one should now arise and, prompted by the vain imaginations his heart hath devised, endeavor, openly or in secret, to sow the seeds of dissension amongst men—can such a man be said to have acted with equity? No, by Him Whose might extendeth over all things! By My life! Mine heart groaneth and mine eyes weep sore for the Cause of God and for them that understand not what they say and imagine what they cannot comprehend.

It beseemeth all men, in this Day, to take firm hold on the Most Great Name, and to establish the unity of all mankind. There is no place to flee to, no refuge that any one can seek, except Him. Should any man be led to utter such words as will turn away the people from the shores of God's limitless ocean, and cause them to fix their hearts on anything except this glorious and manifest Being, that hath assumed a form subject to human limitations—such a man, however lofty the station he may occupy, shall be denounced by the entire creation as one that hath deprived himself of the sweet savors of the All-Merciful.

Say: Observe equity in your judgment, ye men of understanding heart! He that is unjust in his judgment is destitute of the characteristics that distinguish man's station. He Who is the Eternal Truth knoweth well what the breasts of men conceal. His long forbearance hath emboldened His creatures, for not until the appointed time is come will He rend any veil asunder. His surpassing mercy hath restrained the fury of His wrath, and caused most people to imagine that the one true God is unaware of the things they have privily committed. By Him Who is the All-Knowing, the All-Informed! The mirror of His knowledge reflecteth, with complete distinctness, precision and fidelity, the doings of all men. Say: Praise be to Thee, O Concealer of the sins of the weak and helpless! Magnified be Thy name, O Thou that forgivest the heedless ones that trespass against Thee!

We have forbidden men to walk after the imaginations of their hearts, that they may be enabled to recognize Him Who is the sovereign Source and Object of all knowledge, and may acknowledge whatsoever He may be pleased to reveal. Witness how they have entangled themselves with their idle fancies and vain imaginations. By My life! They are themselves the victims of what their own hearts have devised, and yet they perceive it not. Vain and profitless is the talk of their lips, and yet they understand not.

We beseech God that He may graciously vouchsafe His grace unto all men, and enable them to attain the knowledge of Him and of themselves. By My life! Whoso hath known Him shall soar in the immensity of His love, and shall be detached from the world and all that is therein. Nothing on earth shall deflect him from his course, how much less they who, prompted by their vain imaginations, speak those things which God hath forbidden.

Say: This is the Day when every ear must needs be attentive to His voice. Hearken ye to the Call of this wronged One, and magnify ye the name of the one true God, and adorn yourselves with the ornament of His remembrance, and illumine your hearts with the light of His love. This is the key that unlocketh the hearts of men, the burnish that shall cleanse the souls of all beings. He that is careless of what hath poured out from the finger of the Will of

God liveth in manifest error. Amity and rectitude of conduct, rather than dissension and mischief, are the marks of true faith.

Proclaim unto men what He, Who speaketh the truth and is the Bearer of the Trust of God, hath bidden thee observe. My glory be with thee, O thou that callest upon My name, whose eyes are directed towards My court, and whose tongue uttereth the praise of thy Lord, the Beneficent.

The Root of Knowledge

O, would that the world could believe Me! Were all the things that lie enshrined within the heart of Bahá, and which the Lord, His God, the Lord of all names, hath taught Him, to be unveiled to mankind, every man on earth would be dumbfounded.

How great the multitude of truths which the garment of words can never contain! How vast the number of such verities as no expression can adequately describe, whose significance can never be unfolded, and to which not even the remotest allusions can be made! How manifold are the truths which must remain unuttered until the appointed time is come! Even as it hath been said: "Not everything that a man knoweth can be disclosed, nor can everything that he can disclose be regarded as timely, nor can every timely utterance be considered as suited to the capacity of those who hear it."

Of these truths some can be disclosed only to the extent of the capacity of the repositories of the light of Our knowledge, and the recipients of Our hidden grace. We beseech God to strengthen thee with His power, and enable thee to recognize Him Who is the Source of all knowledge, that thou mayest detach thyself from all human learning, for, "what would it profit any man to strive after learning when he hath already found and recognized Him Who is the Object of all knowledge?" Cleave to the Root of Knowledge, and to Him Who is the Fountain thereof, that thou mayest find thyself independent of all who claim to be well versed in human learning, and whose claim no clear proof, nor the testimony of any enlightening book, can support.

Union With God

O thou who hast surrendered thy will to God! By self-surrender and perpetual union with God is meant that men should merge their will wholly in the Will of God, and regard their desires as utter nothingness beside His Purpose. Whatsoever the Creator commandeth His creatures to observe, the same must they diligently, and with the utmost joy and eagerness, arise and fulfil. They should in no wise allow their fancy to obscure their judgment, neither should they regard their own imaginings as the voice of the Eternal. In the Prayer of Fasting We have revealed: "Should Thy Will decree that out of Thy mouth these words proceed and be addressed unto them, 'Observe, for My Beauty's sake, the fast, O people, and set no limit to its duration,' I swear by the majesty of Thy glory, that every one of them will faithfully observe it, will abstain from whatsoever will violate Thy law, and will continue to do so until they yield up their souls unto Thee." In this consisteth the complete surrender of one's will to the Will of God. Meditate on this, that thou mayest drink in the waters of everlasting life which flow through the words of the Lord of all mankind, and mayest testify that the one true God hath ever been immeasurably exalted above His creatures. He, verily, is the Incomparable, the Ever-Abiding, the Omniscient, the All-Wise.

A Safe Approach to God

Know ye that by "the world" is meant your unawareness of Him Who is your Maker, and your absorption in aught else but Him. The "life to come," on the other hand, signifieth the things that give you a safe approach to God, the All-Glorious, the Incomparable. Whatsoever deterreth you, in this Day, from loving God is nothing but the world. Flee it, that ye may be numbered with the blest. Should a man wish to adorn himself with the ornaments of the earth, to wear its apparels, or partake of the benefits it can bestow, no harm can befall him, if he alloweth nothing whatever to intervene between him and God, for God hath ordained every good thing, whether created in the heavens or in the earth, for such of His servants as truly believe in Him. Eat ye, O people, of the good things which God hath allowed you, and deprive not yourselves from His wondrous bounties. Render thanks and praise unto him, and be of them that are truly thankful.

By Which the Truth Is Distinguished

The ordinances of God have been sent down from the heaven of His most august Revelation. All must diligently observe them. Man's supreme distinction, his real advancement, his final victory, have always depended, and will continue to depend, upon them. Whoso keepeth the commandments of God shall attain everlasting felicity.

A twofold obligation resteth upon him who hath recognized the Day Spring of the Unity of God, and acknowledged the truth of Him Who is the Manifestation of His oneness. The first is steadfastness in His love, such steadfastness that neither the clamor of the enemy nor the claims of the idle pretender can deter him from cleaving unto Him Who is the Eternal Truth, a steadfastness that taketh no account of them whatever. The second is strict observance of the laws He hath prescribed—laws which He hath always ordained, and will continue to ordain, unto men, and through which the truth may be distinguished and separated from falsehood.

Unless One Love God

Say: O people of the Bayán! Did We not admonish you, in all Our Tablets and in all Our hidden Scriptures, not to follow your evil passions and corrupt inclinations, but to keep your eyes directed towards the Scene of transcendent glory, on the Day when the Most Mighty Balance shall be set, the Day when the sweet melodies of the Spirit of God shall be poured out from the right hand of the throne of your Lord, the omnipotent Protector, the All-Powerful, the Holy of Holies? Did We not forbid you to cleave to the things that would shut you out from the Manifestation of our Beauty, in its subsequent Revelation, be they the embodiments of the names of God and all their glory, or the revealers of His attributes and their dominion? Behold, how, as soon as I revealed Myself, ye have rejected My truth and turned away from Me, and been of them that have regarded the signs of God as a play and pastime!

By My Beauty! Nothing whatsoever shall, in this Day, be accepted from you, though ye continue to worship and prostrate yourselves before God throughout the eternity of His dominion. For all things are dependent upon His Will, and the worth of all acts is conditioned upon His acceptance and pleasure. The whole universe is but a handful of clay in His grasp. Unless one recognize God and love Him, his cry shall not be heard by God in this Day. This is of the essence of His Faith, did ye but know it.

Actions of the Righteous

Be generous in prosperity, and thankful in adversity. Be worthy of the trust of thy neighbor, and look upon him with a bright and friendly face. Be a treasure to the poor, an admonisher to the rich, an answerer of the cry of the needy, a preserver of the sanctity of thy pledge. Be fair in thy judgment, and guarded in thy speech. Be unjust to no man, and show all meekness to all men. Be as a lamp unto them that walk in darkness, a joy to the sorrowful, a sea for the thirsty, a haven for the distressed, an upholder and defender of the victim of oppression. Let integrity and uprightness distinguish all thine acts. Be a home for the stranger, a balm to the suffering, a tower of strength for the fugitive. Be eyes to the blind, and a guiding light unto the feet of the erring. Be an ornament to the countenance of truth, a crown to the brow of fidelity, a pillar of the temple of righteousness, a breath of life to the body of mankind, an ensign of the hosts of justice, a luminary above the horizon of virtue, a dew to the soil of the human heart, an ark on the ocean of knowledge, a sun in the heaven of bounty, a gem on the diadem of wisdom, a shining light in the firmament of thy generation, a fruit upon the tree of humility.

True Liberty

Consider the pettiness of men's minds. They ask for that which injureth them, and cast away the thing that profiteth them. They are, indeed, of those that are far astray. We find some men desiring liberty, and priding themselves therein. Such men are in the depths of ignorance.

Liberty must, in the end, lead to sedition, whose flames none can quench. Thus warneth you He Who is the Reckoner, the All-Knowing. Know ye that the embodiment of liberty and its symbol is the animal. That which beseemeth man is submission unto such restraints as will protect him from his own ignorance, and guard him against the harm of the mischief-maker. Liberty causeth man to overstep the bounds of propriety, and to infringe on the dignity of his station. It debaseth him to the level of extreme depravity and wickedness.

Regard men as a flock of sheep that need a shepherd for their protection. This, verily, is the truth, the certain truth. We approve of liberty in certain circumstances, and refuse to sanction it in others. We, verily, are the All-Knowing.

Say: True liberty consisteth in man's submission unto My commandments, little as ye know it. Were men to observe that which We have sent down unto them from the Heaven of Revelation, they would, of a certainty, attain unto perfect liberty. Happy is the man that hath apprehended the Purpose of God in whatever He hath revealed from the Heaven of His Will, that pervadeth all created things. Say: The liberty that profiteth you is to be found nowhere except in complete servitude unto God, the Eternal Truth. Whoso hath tasted of its sweetness will refuse to barter it for all the dominion of earth and heaven.

In Amity and Concord

It is Our wish and desire that every one of you may become a source of all goodness unto men, and an example of uprightness to mankind. Beware lest ye prefer yourselves above your neighbors. Fix your gaze upon Him Who is the Temple of God amongst men. He, in truth, hath offered up His life as a ransom for the redemption of the world. He, verily, is the All-Bountiful, the Gracious, the Most High. If any differences arise amongst you, behold Me standing before your face, and overlook the faults of one another for My name's sake and as a token of your love for My manifest and resplendent Cause. We love to see you at all times consorting in amity and concord within the paradise of My good-pleasure, and to inhale from your acts the fragrance of friendliness and unity, of loving-kindness and fellowship. Thus counselleth you the All-Knowing, the Faithful. We shall always be with you; if We inhale the perfume of your fellowship, Our heart will assuredly rejoice, for naught else can satisfy Us. To this beareth witness every man of true understanding.

The Reason They Were Created

Shake off, O heedless ones, the slumber of negligence, that ye may behold the radiance which His glory hath spread through the world. How foolish are those who murmur against the premature birth of His light. O ye who are inly blind! Whether too soon or too late, the evidences of His effulgent glory are now actually manifest. It behoveth you to ascertain whether or not such a light hath appeared. It is neither within your power nor mine to set the time at which it should be made manifest. God's inscrutable Wisdom hath fixed its hour beforehand. Be content, O people, with that which God hath desired for you and predestined unto you.

The Principle of Moderation

Whoso cleaveth to justice, can, under no circumstances, transgress the limits of moderation. He discerneth the truth in all things, through the guidance of Him Who is the All-Seeing. The civilization, so often vaunted by the learned exponents of arts and sciences, will, if allowed to overleap the bounds of moderation, bring great evil upon men. Thus warneth you He Who is the All-Knowing. If carried to excess, civilization will prove as prolific a source of evil as it had been of goodness when kept within the restraints of moderation. Meditate on this, O people, and be not of them that wander distraught in the wilderness of error. The day is approaching when its flame will devour the cities, when the Tongue of Grandeur will proclaim: "The Kingdom is God's, the Almighty, the All-Praised!"

All other things are subject to this same principle of moderation. Render thanks unto thy Lord Who hath remembered thee in this wondrous Tablet. All-Praise be to God, the Lord of the glorious throne.

Were any man to ponder in his heart that which the Pen of the Most High hath revealed and to taste of its sweetness, he would, of a certainty, find himself emptied and delivered from his own desires, and utterly subservient to the Will of the Almighty. Happy is the man that hath attained so high a station, and hath not deprived himself of so bountiful a grace.

In this Day, We can neither approve the conduct of the fearful that seeketh to dissemble his faith, nor sanction the behavior of the avowed believer that clamorously asserteth his allegiance to this Cause. Both should observe the dictates of wisdom, and strive diligently to serve the best interests of the Faith.

The Advancement of the World

Every man of insight will, in this day, readily admit that the counsels which the Pen of this wronged One hath revealed constitute the supreme animating power for the advancement of the world and the exaltation of its peoples. Arise, O people, and by the power of God's might, resolve to gain the victory over your own selves, that haply the whole earth may be freed and sanctified from its servitude to the gods of its idle fancies—gods that have inflicted such loss upon, and are responsible for the misery of, their wretched worshipers. These idols form the obstacle that impeded man in his efforts to advance in the path of perfection. We cherish the hope that the Hand of Divine power may lend its assistance to mankind, and deliver it from its state of grievous abasement.

In one of the Tablets these words have been revealed: O people of God! Do not busy yourselves in your own concerns; let your thoughts be fixed upon that which will rehabilitate the fortunes of mankind and sanctify the hearts and souls of men. This can best be achieved through a virtuous life and a goodly behavior. Valiant acts will insure the triumph of this Cause, and a saintly character will reinforce its power. Cleave unto righteousness, O people of Bahá! This, verily, is the commandment which this wronged One hath given unto you, and the first choice of His unrestrained Will for every one of you.

The Essence of Justice

Know verily that the essence of justice and the source thereof are both embodied in the ordinances prescribed by Him who is the Manifestation of the Self of God amongst men, if ye be of them that recognize this truth. He doth verily incarnate the highest, the infallible standard of justice unto all creation. Were His law to be such as to strike terror into the hearts of all that are in heaven and on earth, that law is naught but manifest justice. The fears and agitation which the revelation of this law provoke in men's hearts should indeed be likened to the cries of the suckling babe weaned from his mother's milk, if ye be of them that perceive. Were men to discover the motivating purpose of God's Revelation, they would assuredly cast away their fears, and, with hearts filled with gratitude, rejoice with exceeding gladness.

Words of Wisdom

The source of all good is trust in God, submission unto His command, and contentment in His holy will and pleasure.

The essence of wisdom is the fear of God, the dread of His scourge and the apprehension of His justice and decree.

The essence of religion is to testify unto that which the Lord hath revealed, and follow that which He hath ordained in His mighty Book.

The source of all glory is acceptance of whatsoever the Lord hath bestowed, and contentment with that which God hath ordained.

The essence of love is for man to turn his heart to the Beloved

One, and sever himself from all else but God, and desire naught save that which is the desire of his Lord.

True remembrance is to make mention of the Lord, the All-Praised, and forget all else beside Him.

True reliance is for the servant to pursue his profession and calling in this world, to hold fast unto the Lord, to seek naught but His grace, inasmuch as in His hands is the destiny of all His servants.

The essence of detachment is for man to turn his face toward the courts of the Lord, to enter His presence, behold His countenance, and stand as witness before Him.

The essence of understanding is to testify to one's poverty, and submit to the will of the Lord, the Sovereign, the Gracious, the All-Powerful.

The source of courage and power is the promotion of the Word of God, and steadfastness in His Love.

The essence of charity is for the servant to recount the blessings of his Lord, and to render thanks unto Him at all times, and under all conditions.

The essence of wealth is love for Me. Whoso loveth Me is the possessor of all things, and he that loveth Me not is, indeed, of the poor and needy. This is that which the Finger of Glory and Splendor hath revealed . . .

The essence of faith is fewness of words and abundance of deeds; he whose words exceed his deeds, know verily his death is better than his life . . .

The source of all evil is for man to turn away from his Lord and set his heart on things ungodly.

The most burning fire is to question the signs of God, to dispute idly that which He hath revealed, to deny Him and carry one's self proudly before Him.

The source of all learning is the knowledge of God, exalted be His Glory, and this cannot be attained save through the knowledge of His Divine Manifestation. The essence of abasement is to pass from under the shadow of the Merciful, and seek the shelter of the Evil One.

The source of error is to disbelieve in the one true God, rely upon aught else but Him, and flee from His Decree.

True loss is for him whose days have been spent in utter ignorance of his true self.

The essence of all that We have revealed for thee is Justice, is for man to free himself from idle fancies and imitation, discern with the eye of oneness His glorious handiwork, and look into all things with a searching eye.

Thus have We instructed thee, manifested unto thee words of wisdom, that thou mayest be thankful unto the Lord, thy God, and glory therein amidst all peoples.

Prayers

Glorified art Thou, O Lord my God! I beseech Thee by Him Who is Thy Most Great Name, Who hath been sorely afflicted by such of Thy creatures as have repudiated Thy truth, and Who hath been hemmed in by sorrows which no tongue can describe, to grant that I may remember Thee and celebrate Thy praise, in these days when all have turned away from Thy beauty, have disputed with Thee, and turned away disdainfully from Him Who is the Revealer of Thy Cause. None is there, O my Lord, to help Thee except Thine own Self, and no power to succor Thee save Thine own power.

I entreat Thee to enable me to cleave steadfastly to Thy Love and Thy remembrance. This is, verily, within my power, and Thou art the One that knoweth all that is in me. Thou, in truth, art knowing, apprised of all. Deprive me not, O my Lord, of the splendors of the light of Thy face, whose brightness hath illuminated the whole world. No God is there beside Thee, the Most Powerful, the All-Glorious, the Ever-Forgiving.

Magnified be Thy name, O Lord my God! Thou art He Whom all things worship and Who worshipeth no one, Who is the Lord of all things and is the vassal of none, Who knoweth all things and is known of none. Thou didst wish to make Thyself known unto men; therefore, Thou didst, through a word of Thy mouth, bring creation into being and fashion the universe. There is none other

God except Thee, the Fashioner, the Creator, the Almighty, the Most Powerful.

I implore Thee, by this very word that hath shone forth above the horizon of Thy will, to enable me to drink deep of the living waters through which Thou hast vivified the hearts of Thy chosen ones and quickened the souls of them that love Thee, that I may, at all times and under all conditions, turn my face wholly towards Thee.

Thou art the God of power, of glory and bounty. No God is there beside Thee, the Supreme Ruler, the All-Glorious, the Omniscient.

Praise be to Thee, O Lord my God! I swear by Thy might! Successive afflictions have withheld the pen of the Most High from laying bare that which is hidden from the eyes of Thy creatures, and incessant trials have hindered the tongue of the Divine Ordainer from proclaiming the wonders of Thy glorification and praise. With a stammering tongue, therefore, I call upon Thee, O my God, and with this my afflicted pen I occupy myself in remembrance of Thy name.

Is there any man of insight, O my God, that can behold Thee with Thine own eye, and where is the thirsty one who can direct his face towards the living waters of Thy love? I am the one, O my God, who hath blotted out from his heart the remembrance of all except Thee, and hath graven upon it the mysteries of Thy love. Thine own might beareth me witness! But for tribulations, how could the assured be distinguished from the doubters among Thy servants? They who have been inebriated with the wine of Thy knowledge, these, verily, hasten to meet every manner of adversity in their longing to pass into Thy presence. I implore Thee, O Beloved of my heart and the Object of my soul's adoration, to shield them that love me from the faintest trace of evil and corrupt desires. Supply them, then, with the good of this world and of the next.

Thou art, verily, He Whose grace hath guided them aright, He Who hath declared Himself to be the All-Merciful. No God is there but Thee, the All-Glorious, the Supreme Helper.

O my Lord! Make Thy beauty to be my food, and Thy presence my drink, and Thy pleasure my hope, and praise of Thee my action, and remembrance of Thee my companion, and the power of Thy sovereignty my succorer, and Thy habitation my home, and my dwelling-place the seat Thou hast sanctified from the limitations imposed upon them who are shut out as by a veil from Thee.

Thou art, verily, the Almighty, the All-Glorious, the Most Powerful.

O Thou Whose face is the object of the adoration of all that yearn after Thee, Whose presence is the hope of such as are wholly devoted to Thy will, Whose nearness is the desire of all that have drawn nigh unto Thy court, Whose countenance is the companion of those who have recognized Thy truth, Whose name is the mover of the souls that long to behold Thy face, Whose voice is the true life of Thy lovers, the words of Whose mouth are as the waters of life unto all who are in heaven and on earth!

I beseech Thee, by the wrong Thou hast suffered and the ills inflicted upon Thee by the hosts of wrongful doers, to send down upon me from the clouds of Thy mercy that which will purify me of all that is not of Thee, that I may be worthy to praise Thee and fit to love Thee.

Withhold not from me, O my Lord, the things Thou didst ordain for such of Thy handmaidens as circle around Thee, and on whom are poured continually the splendors of the sun of Thy beauty and the beams of the brightness of Thy face. Thou art He Who from everlasting hath succored whosoever hath sought Thee, and bountifully favored him who hath asked Thee.

No God is there beside Thee, the Mighty, the Ever-Abiding, the All-Bounteous, the Most Generous.

Praised be Thou, O Lord my God! This is Thy servant who hath quaffed from the hands of Thy grace the wine of Thy tender mercy, and tasted of the savor of Thy love in Thy days. I beseech Thee, by the embodiments of Thy names whom no grief can hinder from rejoicing in Thy love or from gazing on Thy face, and whom all the hosts of the heedless are powerless to cause to turn aside from the path of Thy pleasure, to supply him with the good things Thou dost possess, and to raise him up to such heights that he will regard the world even as a shadow that vanisheth swifter than the twinkling of an eye.

Keep him safe also, O my God, by the power of Thine immeasurable majesty, from all that Thou abhorrest. Thou art, verily, his Lord and the Lord of all worlds.

Praised be Thou, O Lord my God! I implore Thee, by Thy Most Great Name through Which Thou didst stir up thy servants and build up Thy cities, and by Thy most excellent titles, and Thy most august attributes, to assist Thy people to turn in the direction of Thy manifold bounties, and set their faces towards the Tabernacle of Thy wisdom. Heal Thou the sicknesses that have assailed the souls on every side, and have deterred them from directing their gaze towards the Paradise that lieth in the shelter of Thy shadowing Name, which Thou didst ordain to be the King of all names unto all who are in heaven and all who are on earth. Potent art Thou to do as pleaseth Thee. In Thy hands is the empire of all names. There is none other God but Thee, the Mighty, the Wise.

I am but a poor creature, O my Lord; I have clung to the hem of Thy riches. I am sore sick; I have held fast the cord of Thy healing. Deliver me from the ills that have encircled me, and wash me thoroughly with the waters of Thy graciousness and mercy, and attire me with the raiment of wholesomeness, through Thy forgiveness and bounty. Fix, then, mine eyes upon Thee, and rid me of all attachment to aught else except Thyself. Aid me to do what Thou desirest, and to fulfill what Thou pleasest.

Thou art truly the Lord of this life and of the next. Thou art, in truth, the Ever-Forgiving, the Most Merciful.

Thy name is my healing, O my God, and remembrance of Thee is my remedy. Nearness to Thee is my hope, and love for Thee is my companion. Thy mercy to me is my healing and my succor in both this world and the world to come. Thou, verily, art the All-Bountiful, the All-Knowing, the All-Wise.

Thou beholdest, O my God, the Day Star of Thy Word shining above the horizon of Thy prison-city, inasmuch as within its walls He who is the Manifestation of Thy Self and the Day-Spring of the light of Thy unity hath raised His voice and uttered Thy praise. The fragances of Thy love have thereby been wafted over Thy cities and have encompassed all the dwellers of Thy realm.

Since Thou hast revealed Thy grace, O my God, deter not Thy servants from directing their eyes towards it. Consider not, O my God, their estate, and their concerns and their works. Consider the greatness of Thy glory, and the plenteousness of Thy gifts, and the power of Thy might, and the excellence of Thy favors. I swear by Thy glory! Wert Thou to look upon them with the eye of justice, all would deserve Thy wrath and the rod of Thine anger. Hold Thou Thy creatures, O my God, with the hands of Thy grace, and make Thou known unto them what is best for them of all the things that have been created in the kingdom of Thy invention.

We testify, O my God, that Thou art God, and that there is no God besides Thee. From eternity Thou hast existed with none to equal or rival Thee, and wilt abide for ever the same. I beseech Thee, by the eyes which see Thee established upon the throne of unity and the seat of oneness, to aid all them that love Thee by Thy Most Great Name, and to lift them up unto such heights that they will testify with their own beings and with their tongues that Thou art God alone, the Incomparable, the One, the Ever-Abiding. Thou hast had at no time any peer or partner. Thou, in truth, art the All-Glorious, the Almighty, Whose help is implored by all men.

Many a chilled heart, O my God, hath been set ablaze with the fire of Thy Cause, and many a slumberer hath been wakened by the sweetness of Thy voice. How many are the strangers who have sought shelter beneath the shadow of the tree of Thy oneness, and how numerous the thirsty ones who have panted after the fountain of Thy living waters in Thy days!

Blessed is he that hath set himself towards Thee, and hasted to attain the Day-Spring of the lights of Thy face. Blessed is he who with all his affections hath turned to the Dawning-Place of Thy Revelation and the Fountain-Head of Thine inspiration. Blessed is he that hath expended in Thy path what Thou didst bestow upon him through Thy bounty and favor. Blessed is he who, in his sore longing after Thee, hath cast away all else except Thyself. Blessed is he who hath enjoyed intimate communion with Thee, and rid himself of all attachment to any one save Thee.

I beseech Thee, O my Lord, by Him Who is Thy Name, Who, through the power of Thy sovereignty and might, hath risen above the horizon of His prison, to ordain for every one what becometh Thee and beseemeth Thine exaltation.

Thy might, in truth, is equal to all things.

Praise be unto Thee, O my God! Thou art He Who by a word of His mouth hath revolutionized the entire creation, and by a stroke of His pen hath divided Thy servants one from another. I bear witness, O my God, that through a word spoken by Thee in this Revelation all created things were made to expire, and through yet another word all such as Thou didst wish were, by Thy grace and bounty, endued with new life.

I render Thee thanks, therefore, and extol Thee, in the name of all them that are dear to Thee, for that Thou hast caused them to be born again, by reason of the living waters which have flowed down out of the mouth of Thy will. Since Thou didst quicken them by Thy bounteousness, O my God, make them steadfastly inclined, through Thy graciousness, towards Thy will; and since Thou didst suffer them to enter into the Tabernacle of Thy Cause, grant by Thy grace that they may not be kept back from Thee.

Unlock, then, to their hearts, O my God, the portals of Thy knowledge, that they may recognize Thee as One Who is far above the reach and ken of the understanding of Thy creatures, and immeasurably exalted above the strivings of Thy people to hint at Thy nature, and may not follow every clamorous impostor that presumeth to speak in Thy name. Enable them, moreover, O my Lord, to cleave so tenaciously to Thy Cause that they may remain unmoved by the perplexing suggestions of them who, prompted by their desires, utter what hath been forbidden unto them in Thy Tablets and Thy Scriptures.

Thou art well aware, O my Lord, that I hear the howling of the wolves which appear in Thy servants' clothing. Keep safe, therefore, Thy loved ones from their mischief, and enable them to cling steadfastly to whatsoever hath been manifested by Thee in this Revelation, which no other Revelation within Thy knowledge hath excelled.

Do Thou destine for them, O my Lord, that which will profit them. Illumine, then, their eyes with the light of Thy knowledge, that they may see Thee visibly supreme over all things, and resplendent amidst Thy creatures, and victorious over all that are in Thy heaven and all that are on Thy earth. Powerful art Thou to do Thy pleasure. No God is there but Thee, the All-Glorious, Whose help is implored by all men.

Praised be Thou, Who art the Lord of all creation.

Lauded be Thy name, O my God and the God of all things, my Glory and the Glory of all things, my Desire and the Desire of all things, my Strength and the Strength of all things, my King and the King of all things, my Possessor and the Possessor of all things, my Aim and the Aim of all things, my Mover and the Mover of all things! Suffer me not, I implore Thee, to be kept back from the ocean of Thy tender mercies, nor to be far removed from the shores of nearness to Thee.

Aught else except Thee, O my Lord, profiteth me not, and near access to any one save Thyself availeth me nothing. I entreat Thee by the plenteousness of Thy riches, whereby Thou didst dispense with all else except Thyself, to number me with such as have set their faces towards Thee, and arisen to serve Thee.

Forgive, then, O my Lord, Thy servants and Thy handmaidens. Thou, truly, art the Ever-Forgiving, the Most Compassionate.

God testifieth to the unity of His Godhood and to the singleness of His own Being. On the throne of eternity, from the inaccessible heights of His station, His tongue proclaimeth that there is none other God but Him. He Himself, independently of all else, hath ever been a witness unto His own oneness, the revealer of His own nature, the glorifier of His own essence. He, verily, is the All-Powerful, the Almighty, the Beauteous.

He is supreme over His servants, and standeth over His creatures. In His hand is the source of authority and truth. He maketh men alive by His signs, and causeth them to die through His wrath. He shall not be asked of His doings and His might is equal unto all things. He is the Potent, the All-Subduing. He holdeth within his grasp the empire of all things, and on His right hand is fixed the Kingdom of His Revelation. His power, verily, embraceth the whole of creation. Victory and overlordship are His; all might and dominion are His; all glory and greatness are His. He, of a truth, is the All-Glorious, the Most Powerful, the Unconditioned.

All praise, O my God, be to Thee Who art the Source of all glory and majesty, of greatness and honor, of sovereignty and dominion, of loftiness and grace, of awe and power. Whomsoever Thou willest Thou causest to draw nigh unto the Most Great Ocean, and on whomsoever Thou desirest Thou conferrest the honor of recognizing Thy Most Ancient Name. Of all who are in heaven and on earth, none can withstand the operation of Thy sovereign Will. From all eternity Thou didst rule the entire creation, and Thou wilt continue for evermore to exercise Thy dominion over all created things. There is none other God but Thee, the Almighty, the Most Exalted, the All-Powerful, the All-Wise.

Illumine, O Lord, the faces of Thy servants, that they may behold Thee; and cleanse their hearts that they may turn unto the court of Thy heavenly favors, and recognize Him Who is the Manifestation of Thy Self and the Day Spring of Thine Essence. Verily, Thou art the Lord of all worlds. There is no God but Thee, the Unconstrained, the All-Subduing.

Glorified art Thou, O Lord my God! I beseech Thee by Thy Name, the Restrainer, to withhold from us the maleficence of Thine adversaries who have disbelieved in Thy testimony, and caviled at Thy beauty. Overpower by Thy Name, the All-Subduing, such as have wronged Thy Previous Manifestation Who hath now appeared invested with Thy title, the All-Glorious. Lay hold, by Thy name, the Chastiser, on them that have treated Thy Cause with scorn, have jested at Thy most mighty utterances, and were hindered from attaining this most exalted station. Enable Thy loved ones, by Thy Name, the Victorious, to prevail against Thine enemies and the infidels among Thy creatures. Rend asunder, by Thy Name, the Cleaver, the veil that hideth the doings of them that have besmirched Thine honor and undermined Thy Faith among Thy people. Bind, by Thy Name, the Restorer, the broken hearts of them that love Thee, and graciously bless them in their affairs. Teach them, by Thy Name, the All-Knowing, the wonders of Thy wisdom, that they may cleave steadfastly to Thy Faith and walk in the ways of Thy pleasure. Keep them safe, by Thy Name, the Withholder, from the tyranny of the oppressor and the wickedness of the evil-doers and the malice of the stirrers of mischief. Shield them, by Thy Name, the Preserver, within the stronghold of Thy might and power, that haply they may be protected from the darts of doubt that are hurled by such as have rebelled against Thee. Sanctify for Thy servants, by Thy Name which Thou hast blessed above all other names, which Thou hast singled out for Thy favor, and by which Thou didst reveal Thy beauty, these days of which the Pen of Thy decree hath distinctly written, and which, according to Thy will and wisdom, have been preordained in Thine irrevocable Tablet. Subject to Thy rule, by Thy Name, the Conqueror, the people of Thy realm, that all may turn towards Thy face and forsake their all for love of Thee and for the sake of Thy pleasure.

Glorified art Thou, O Lord my God! Rain down, I beseech Thee, from the clouds of Thine overflowing grace, that which shall cleanse the hearts of Thy servants from whatever may prevent their beholding Thy face, or may prevent them from turning unto Thee, that they may all recognize Him Who is their Fashioner and Creator. Help them, then, O God, to reach forth, through the power of Thy sovereign might, towards such a station that can readily distinguish every foul smell from the fragrance of the raiment of Him Who is the Bearer of Thy most lofty and exalted name, that they may turn with all their affections toward Thee, and may enjoy such intimate communion with Thee that if all that is in heaven and on earth were given them they would regard it as unworthy of their notice, and would refuse to cease from remembering Thee and from extolling Thy virtues.

Shield, I pray Thee, O my Beloved, my heart's Desire, Thy servant who hath sought Thy face, from the darts of them that have denied Thee and from the shafts of such as have repudiated Thy Truth. Cause him, then, to be wholly devoted to Thee, to declare Thy name, and to fix his gaze upon the sanctuary of Thy Revelation. Thou art, in truth, He Who, at no time, hath turned away those who have set their hopes in Thee from the door of Thy mercy, nor prevented such as have sought Thee from attaining the court of Thy grace. No God is there but Thee, the Most Powerful, the All-Highest, the Help in Peril, the All-Glorious, the All-Compelling, the Unconditioned.

Glory to Thee, O Thou Who art the Lord of all worlds, and the Beloved of all such as have recognized Thee! Thou seest me sitting under a sword hanging on a thread, and art well aware that in such a state I have not fallen short of my duty towards Thy Cause, nor failed to shed abroad Thy praise, and declare Thy virtues, and deliver all Thou hadst prescribed unto me in Thy Tablets. Though the sword be ready to fall on my head, I call Thy loved ones with such a calling that the hearts are carried away towards the horizon of Thy majesty and grandeur.

Purge out thoroughly their ears, O my Lord, that they may hearken unto the sweet melodies that have ascended from the right hand of the throne of Thy glory. I swear by Thy might! Were any one to attune his ears to their harmony he would soar up to the kingdom of Thy revelation, wherein every created thing proclaimeth that Thou art God, and that there is none other God save Thee, the Omnipotent, the Help in Peril, the Self-Subsisting. Cleanse Thou, O my God, the eyes of Thy servants, and so transport them by the sweetness of Thine utterances that calamities will be powerless to hinder them from turning unto Thee, and from directing their eyes towards the horizon of Thy Revelation.

Darkness hath encompassed every land, O my God, and caused most of Thy servants to tremble. I beseech Thee, by Thy Most Great Name, to raise in every city a new creation that shall turn towards Thee, and shall remember Thee amidst Thy servants, and shall unfurl by virtue of their utterances and wisdom the ensigns of Thy victory, and shall detach themselves from all created things.

Potent art Thou to do Thy pleasure. No God is there but Thee, the Most Powerful, He Whose help is implored by all men.

Praise be to Thee, O Lord my God! I am the one who hath sought the good pleasure of Thy will, and directed his steps towards the seat of Thy gracious favors. I am he who hath forsaken his all, who hath fled to Thee for shelter, who hath set his face towards the tabernacle of Thy revelation and the adored sanctuary of Thy glory. I beseech Thee, O my Lord, by Thy call whereby they who recognized Thy unity have sought the shadow of Thy most gracious providence, and the sincere have fled far from themselves unto Thy name, the Most Exalted, the All-Glorious, through which Thy verses were sent down, and Thy word fulfilled, and Thy proof manifested, and the sun of Thy beauty risen, and Thy testimony established, and Thy signs uncovered,—I beseech Thee to grant that I may be numbered with them that have quaffed the wine that is life indeed from the hands of Thy gracious providence, and have rid themselves, in Thy path, of all attachment to Thy creatures, and been so inebriated with Thy manifold wisdom that they hastened to the field of sacrifice with Thy praise on their lips and Thy remembrance in their hearts. Send down, also, upon me, O my God, that which will wash me from anything that is not of Thee, and deliver me from Thine enemies who have disbelieved in Thy signs.

Potent art Thou to do what Thou willest. No God is there beside Thee, the Help in Peril, the Self-Subsisting.

O Thou Whose tests are a healing medicine to such as are nigh unto Thee, Whose sword is the ardent desire of all them that love

Thee, Whose dart is the dearest wish of those hearts that yearn after Thee, Whose decree is the sole hope of them that have recognized Thy truth! I implore Thee, by Thy divine sweetness and by the splendors of the glory of Thy face, to send down upon us from Thy retreats on high that which will enable us to draw nigh unto Thee. Set, then, our feet firm, O my God, in Thy Cause, and enlighten our hearts with the effulgence of Thy knowledge, and illumine our breasts with the brightness of Thy names.

Lauded be Thy Name, O Lord my God! I am Thy servant who hath laid hold on the cord of Thy tender mercies, and clung to the hem of Thy bounteousness. I entreat Thee by Thy name whereby Thou hast subjected all created things, both visible and invisible, and through which the breath that is life indeed was wafted over the entire creation, to strengthen me by Thy power which hath encompassed the heavens and the earth, and to guard me from all sickness and tribulation. I bear witness that Thou art the Lord of all names, and the Ordainer of all that may please Thee. There is none other God but Thee, the Almighty, the All-Knowing, the All-Wise.

Do Thou ordain for me, O my Lord, what will profit me in every world of Thy worlds. Supply me, then, with what Thou hast written down for the chosen ones among Thy creatures, whom neither the blame of the blamer, nor the clamor of the infidel nor the estrangement of such as have withdrawn from Thee, hath deterred from turning towards Thee.

Thou, truly, art the Help in Peril through the power of Thy sovereignty. No God is there save Thee, the Almighty, the Most Powerful.

Create in me a pure heart, O my God, and renew a tranquil conscience within me, O my Hope! Through the spirit of power confirm Thou me in Thy Cause, O my Best-Beloved, and by the light of Thy glory reveal unto me Thy path, O Thou the Goal of my desire! Through the power of Thy transcendent might lift me up unto the heaven of Thy holiness, O Source of my being, and by the breezes of Thine eternity gladden me, O Thou

Who art my God! Let Thine everlasting melodies breathe tranquillity on me, O my Companion, and let the riches of Thine ancient countenance deliver me from all except Thee, O my Master, and let the tidings of the revelation of Thine incorruptible Essence bring me joy, O Thou Who art the most manifest of the manifest and the most hidden of the hidden!

O God, my God! Be Thou not far from me, for tribulation upon tribulation hath gathered about me. O God, my God! Leave me not to myself, for the extreme of adversity hath come upon me. Out of the pure milk, drawn from the breasts of Thy loving-kindness, give me to drink, for my thirst hath utterly consumed me. Beneath the shadow of the wings of Thy mercy shelter me, for all mine adversaries with one consent have fallen upon me. Keep me near to the throne of Thy majesty, face to face with the revelation of the signs of Thy glory, for wretchedness hath grievously touched me. With the fruits of the Tree of Thine Eternity nourish me, for uttermost weakness hath overtaken me. From the cups of joy, proffered by the hands of Thy tender mercies, feed me, for manifold sorrows have laid mighty hold upon me. With the broidered robe of Thine omnipotent sovereignty attire me, for poverty hath altogether despoiled me. Lulled by the cooing of the Dove of Thine Eternity, suffer me to sleep, for woes at their blackest have befallen me. Before the throne of Thy oneness, amid the blaze of the beauty of Thy countenance, cause me to abide, for fear and trembling have violently crushed me. Beneath the ocean of Thy forgiveness, faced with the restlessness of the leviathan of glory, immerse me, for my sins have utterly doomed me.

O Thou Whose face is the object of my adoration, Whose beauty is my sanctuary, Whose habitation is my goal, Whose praise is my hope, Whose providence is my companion, Whose love is the cause of my being, Whose mention is my solace, Whose nearness is my desire, Whose presence is my dearest wish and highest aspiration, I entreat Thee not to withhold from me the things

Thou didst ordain for the chosen ones among Thy servants. Supply me, then, with the good of this world and of the next.

Thou, truly, art the King of all men. There is no God but Thee, the Ever-Forgiving, the Most Generous.

O God, my God! I beg of Thee by the ocean of Thy healing, and by the splendors of the Day Star of Thy grace, and by Thy Name through which Thou didst subdue Thy servants, and by the pervasive power of Thy most exalted Word and the potency of Thy most august Pen, and by Thy mercy that hath preceded the creation of all who are in heaven and on earth, to purge me with the waters of Thy bounty from every affliction and disorder, and from all weakness and feebleness.

Thou seest, O my Lord, Thy suppliant waiting at the door of Thy bounty, and him who hath set his hopes on Thee clinging to the cord of Thy generosity. Deny him not, I beseech Thee, the things he seeketh from the ocean of Thy grace and the Day Star of Thy loving-kindness.

Powerful art Thou to do what pleaseth Thee. There is none other God save Thee, the Ever-Forgiving, the Most Generous.

THE HIDDEN WORDS

HE IS THE GLORY OF GLORIES

This is that which hath descended from the realm of glory, uttered by the tongue of power and might, and revealed unto the Prophets of old. We have taken the inner essence thereof and clothed it in the garment of brevity, as a token of grace unto the righteous, that they may stand faithful unto the Covenant of God, may fulfill in their lives His trust and in the realm of spirit obtain the gem of Divine virtue.

O SON OF SPIRIT!

My first counsel is this: Possess a pure, kindly and radiant heart, that thine may be a sovereignty ancient, imperishable and everlasting.

O SON OF SPIRIT!

The best beloved of all things in My sight is Justice; turn not away therefrom if thou desirest Me, and neglect it not that I may confide in thee. By its aid thou shalt see with thine own eyes and not through the eyes of others, and shalt know of thine own knowledge and not through the knowledge of thy neighbor. Ponder this in thy heart; how it behoveth thee to be. Verily justice is My gift to thee and the sign of My loving-kindness. Set it then before thine eyes.

O SON OF MAN!

Veiled in My immemorial being and in the ancient eternity of My essence, I knew My love for thee; therefore I created thee, have engraved on thee Mine image and revealed to thee My beauty.

O SON OF MAN!

I loved thy creation, hence I created thee. Wherefore, do thou love Me, that I may name thy name and fill thy soul with the spirit of life.

O SON OF BEING!

Love Me, that I may love thee. If thou lovest Me not, My love can in no wise reach thee. Know this, O servant.

O SON OF BEING!

Thy Paradise is My love; thy heavenly home, reunion with Me. Enter therein and tarry not. This is that which hath been destined for thee in Our kingdom above and Our exalted dominion.

O SON OF MAN!

If thou lovest Me, turn away from thyself; and if thou seekest My pleasure, regard not thine own; that thou mayest die in Me and I may eternally live in thee.

O SON OF SPIRIT!

There is no peace for thee save by renouncing thyself and turning unto Me; for it behoveth thee to glory in My name, not in thine own; to put thy trust in Me and not in thyself, since I desire to be loved alone and above all that is.

O SON OF BEING!

My love is My stronghold; he that entereth therein is safe and secure, and he that turneth away shall surely stray and perish.

O SON OF UTTERANCE!

Thou art My stronghold; enter therein that thou mayest abide in safety. My love is in thee, know it, that thou mayest find Me near unto thee.

O SON OF BEING!

Thou art My lamp and My light is in thee. Get thou from it thy radiance and seek none other than Me. For I have created thee rich and have bountifully shed My favor upon thee.

O SON OF BEING!

With the hands of power I made thee and with the fingers of strength I created thee; and within thee have I placed the essence of My light. Be thou content with it and seek naught else, for My work is perfect and My command is binding. Question it not, nor have a doubt thereof.

O SON OF SPIRIT!

I created thee rich, why dost thou bring thyself down to poverty? Noble I made thee, wherewith dost thou abase thyself? Out of the essence of knowledge I gave thee being, why seekest thou enlightenment from anyone beside Me? Out of the clay of love I molded thee, how dost thou busy thyself with another? Turn thy sight unto thyself, that thou mayest find Me standing within thee, mighty, powerful and self-subsisting.

O SON OF MAN!

Thou art My dominion and My dominion perisheth not, wherefore fearest thou thy perishing? Thou art My light and My light shall never be extinguished, why dost thou dread extinction? Thou art My glory and My glory fadeth not; thou art My robe and My robe shall never be outworn. Abide then in thy love for Me, that thou mayest find Me in the realm of glory.

O SON OF UTTERANCE!

Turn thy face unto Mine and renounce all save Me; for My sovereignty endureth and My dominion perisheth not. If thou seekest another than Me, yea, if thou searchest the universe for evermore, thy quest will be in vain.

O SON OF LIGHT!

Forget all save Me and commune with My spirit. This is of the essence of My command, therefore turn unto it.

O SON OF MAN!

Be thou content with Me and seek no other helper. For none but Me can ever suffice thee.

O SON OF SPIRIT!

Ask not of Me that which We desire not for thee, then be content with what We have ordained for thy sake, for this is that which profiteth thee, if therewith thou dost content thyself.

O SON OF THE WONDROUS VISION!

I have breathed within thee a breath of My own Spirit, that thou mayest be My lover. Why hast thou forsaken Me and sought a beloved other than Me?

O SON OF SPIRIT!

My claim on thee is great, it cannot be forgotten. My grace to thee is plenteous, it cannot be veiled. My love has made in thee its home, it cannot be concealed. My light is manifest to thee, it cannot be obscured.

O SON OF MAN!

Upon the tree of effulgent glory I have hung for thee the choicest fruits, wherefore hast thou turned away and contented thyself with that which is less good? Return then unto that which is better for thee in the realm on high.

O SON OF SPIRIT!

Noble have I created thee, yet thou hast abased thyself. Rise then unto that for which thou wast created.

O SON OF THE SUPREME!

To the eternal I call thee, yet thou dost seek that which perisheth. What hath made thee turn away from Our desire and seek thine own?

O SON OF MAN!

Transgress not thy limits, nor claim that which beseemeth thee not. Prostrate thyself before the countenance of thy God, the Lord of might and power.

O SON OF SPIRIT!

Vaunt not thyself over the poor, for I lead him on his way and behold thee in thy evil plight and confound thee for evermore.

O SON OF BEING!

How couldst thou forget thine own faults and busy thyself with the faults of others? Whoso doeth this is accursed of Me.

O SON OF MAN!

Breathe not the sins of others so long as thou art thyself a sinner. Shouldst thou transgress this command, accursed wouldst thou be, and to this I bear witness.

O SON OF SPIRIT!

Know thou of a truth: He that biddeth men be just and himself committeth iniquity is not of Me, even though he bear My name.

O SON OF BEING!

Ascribe not to any soul that which thou wouldst not have ascribed to thee, and say not that which thou doest not. This is My command unto thee, do thou observe it.

O Son of Man!

Deny not My servant should he ask anything from thee, for his face is My face; be then abashed before Me.

O Son of Being!

Bring thyself to account each day ere thou art summoned to a reckoning; for death, unheralded, shall come upon thee and thou shalt be called to give account for thy deeds.

O Son of the Supreme!

I have made death a messenger of joy to thee. Wherefore dost thou grieve? I made the light to shed on thee its splendor. Why dost thou veil thyself therefrom?

O Son of Spirit!

With the joyful tidings of light I hail thee: rejoice! To the court of holiness I summon thee; abide therein that thou mayest live in peace for evermore.

O Son of Spirit!

The spirit of holiness beareth unto thee the joyful tidings of reunion; wherefore dost thou grieve? The spirit of power confirmeth thee in His cause; why dost thou veil thyself? The light of His countenance doth lead thee; how canst thou go astray?

O Son of Man!

Sorrow not save that thou art far from Us. Rejoice not save that thou art drawing near and returning unto Us.

O Son of Man!

Rejoice in the gladness of thine heart, that thou mayest be worthy to meet Me and to mirror forth My beauty.

O Son of Man!

Divest not thyself of My beauteous robe, and forfeit not thy portion from My wondrous fountain, lest thou shouldst thirst for evermore.

O Son of Being!

Walk in My statutes for love of Me and deny thyself that which thou desirest if thou seekest My pleasure.

O Son of Man!

Neglect not my commandments if thou lovest My beauty, and forget not My counsels if thou wouldst attain My good pleasure.

O Son of Man!

Wert thou to speed through the immensity of space and traverse the expanse of heaven, yet thou wouldst find no rest save in submission to Our command and humbleness before Our Face.

O Son of Man!

Magnify My cause that I may reveal unto thee the mysteries of My greatness and shine upon thee with the light of eternity.

O Son of Man!

Humble thyself before Me, that I may graciously visit thee. Arise for the triumph of My cause, that while yet on earth thou mayest obtain the victory.

O Son of Being!

Make mention of Me on My earth, that in My heaven I may remember thee, thus shall Mine eyes and thine be solaced.

O Son of the Throne!

Thy hearing is My hearing, hear thou therewith. Thy sight is My sight, do thou see therewith, that in thine inmost soul thou mayest testify unto My exalted sanctity, and I within Myself may bear witness unto an exalted station for thee.

O Son of Being!

Seek a martyr's death in My path, content with My pleasure and thankful for that which I ordain, that thou mayest repose with Me beneath the canopy of majesty behind the tabernacle of glory.

O Son of Man!

Ponder and reflect. Is it thy wish to die upon thy bed, or to shed thy life-blood on the dust, a martyr in My path, and so become the manifestation of My command and the revealer of My light in the highest paradise? Judge thou aright, O servant!

O Son of Man!

By My beauty! To tinge thy hair with thy blood is greater in My sight than the creation of the universe and the light of both worlds. Strive then to attain this, O servant!

O Son of Man!

For everything there is a sign. The sign of love is fortitude under My decree and patience under My trials.

O Son of Man!

The true lover yearneth for tribulation even as doth the rebel for forgiveness and the sinful for mercy.

O Son of Man!

If adversity befall thee not in My path, how canst thou walk in the ways of them that are content with My pleasure? If trials afflict thee not in thy longing to meet Me how wilt thou attain the light in thy love for My beauty?

O Son of Man!

My calamity is My providence, outwardly it is fire and vengeance, but inwardly it is light and mercy. Hasten thereunto that thou mayest become an eternal light and an immortal spirit. This is My command unto thee, do thou observe it.

O Son of Man!

Should prosperity befall thee, rejoice not, and should abasement come upon thee, grieve not, for both shall pass away and be no more.

O Son of Being!

If poverty overtake thee, be not sad; for in time the Lord of wealth shall visit thee. Fear not abasement, for glory shall one day rest on thee.

O Son of Being!

If thine heart be set upon this eternal, imperishable dominion, and this ancient, everlasting life, forsake this mortal and fleeing sovereignty.

O Son of Being!

Busy not thyself with this world, for with fire We test the gold, and with gold We test Our servants.

O Son of Man!

Thou dost wish for gold and I desire thy freedom from it. Thou thinkest thyself rich in its possession, and I recognize thy wealth in thy sanctity therefrom. By My life! This is My knowledge, and that is thy fancy; how can My way accord with thine?

O Son of Man!

Bestow My wealth upon My poor, that in heaven thou mayest draw from stores of unfading splendor and treasures of imperishable glory. But by My life! To offer up thy soul is a more glorious thing couldst thou but see with Mine eye.

O Son of Man!

The temple of being is My throne; cleanse it of all things, that there I may be established and there I may abide.

O Son of Being!

Thy heart is My home; sanctify it for My descent. Thy spirit is My place of revelation; cleanse it for My manifestation.

O Son of Man!

Put thy hand into My bosom, that I may rise above thee, radiant and resplendent.

O Son of Man!

Ascend unto My heaven, that thou mayest obtain the joy of reunion, and from the chalice of imperishable glory quaff the peerless wine.

O Son of Man!

Many a day hath passed over thee whilst thou hast busied thyself with thy fancies and idle imaginings. How long art thou to slumber on thy bed? Lift up thy head from slumber, for the Sun hath risen to the zenith, haply it may shine upon thee with the light of beauty.

O Son of Man!

The light hath shone on thee from the horizon of the sacred Mount and the spirit of enlightenment hath breathed in the Sinai of thy heart. Wherefore, free thyself from the veils of idle fancies and enter into My court, that thou mayest be fit for everlasting life and worthy to meet Me. Thus may death not come upon thee, neither weariness nor trouble.

O Son of Man!

My eternity is My creation, I have created it for thee. Make it the garment of thy temple. My unity is My handiwork; I have wrought it for thee; clothe thyself therewith, that thou mayest be to all eternity the revelation of My everlasting being.

O Son of Man!

My majesty is My gift to thee, and My grandeur the token of My mercy unto thee. That which beseemeth Me none shall understand, nor can any one recount. Verily, I have preserved it in My hidden storehouses and in the treasuries of My command, as a sign of My loving-kindness unto My servants and My mercy unto My people.

O Children of the Divine and Invisible Essence!

Ye shall be hindered from loving Me and souls shall be perturbed as they make mention of Me. For minds cannot grasp Me nor hearts contain Me.

O Son of Beauty!

By My spirit and by My favor! By My mercy and by My beauty! All that I have revealed unto thee with the tongue of power, and have written for thee with the pen of might, hath been in accordance with thy capacity and understanding, not with My state and the melody of My voice.

O Children of Men!

Know ye not why We created you all from the same dust? That no one should exalt himself over the other. Ponder at all times in your hearts how ye were created. Since We have created you all from one same substance it is incumbent on you to be even as one soul, to walk with the same feet, eat with the same mouth and dwell in the same land, that from your inmost being, by your deeds and actions, the signs of oneness and the essence of detachment may be made manifest. Such is My counsel to you, O concourse of light! Heed ye this counsel that ye may obtain the fruit of holiness from the tree of wondrous glory.

O Ye Sons of Spirit!

Ye are My treasury, for in you I have treasured the pearls of My mysteries and the gems of My knowledge. Guard them from the strangers amidst My servants and from the ungodly amongst My people.

O Son of Him That Stood by His Own Entity in the Kingdom of His Self!

Know thou, that I have wafted unto thee all the fragrances of holiness, have fully revealed to thee My word, have perfected through thee My bounty and have desired for thee that which I have desired for My Self. Be then content with My pleasure and thankful unto Me.

O Son of Man!

Write all that We have revealed unto thee with the ink of light upon the tablet of thy spirit. Should this not be in thy power, then make thine ink of the essence of thy heart. If this thou canst not do, then write with that crimson ink that hath been shed in My path. Sweeter indeed is this to Me than all else, that its light may endure for ever.

CHAPTER FOUR

LAWS OF THE NEW AGE

TABLET OF TARÁZÁT

In My Name, the Protector over all Names!

Praise and glory belong unto the King of Names and the Creator of heavens, the waves of the sea of Whose appearance are manifest and evident before the faces of all in the world. The sun of His command is submitted to no covering, and His word of affirmation is beyond the reach of negation. Neither the restriction of tyrants nor the oppression wrought by Pharaohs could withhold Him from His Will. Glorified is His Power and great is His Grandeur!

Praise be unto God! Although Signs have encompassed the world, and proofs and arguments are shining forth and manifest from all directions like unto the light, yet ignorant servants are found heedless, nay, even contradictory. O that they were content with mere contradicting! Nay, but they are all the time plotting to cut down the Blessed Tree. From the beginning of this Dispensation the manifestors of selfishness have exerted themselves with all tyranny and injustice to extinguish the light of God; but, verily, God prevented them therefrom, and through His power caused the light to appear and protected it through His might, until the heaven and earth were illuminated with its radiance and brightness! Praise be unto Him under all circumstances!

Glory be unto Thee, O Thou God of the world and desire of nations, O Thou Who hast become manifest in the Greatest Name, whereby the pearls of wisdom and utterance have appeared from the shells of the great sea of Thy knowledge, and the heavens of religions are adorned with the light of the appearance of the sun of Thy countenance!

I beg of Thee—by that Word, by reason of which Thy proof

was made perfect among Thy creatures and Thine argument among Thy servants—to strengthen Thy people in that, whereby the face of the Cause will radiate in Thy dominion and the standards of Thy power and the banners of Thy guidance will be planted in Thy lands and among Thy servants!

O my God! Thou beholdest them clinging to the rope of Thy grace and holding fast unto the hem of the mantle of Thy beneficence. Ordain for them that which may draw them nearer unto Thee, and withhold them from all else save Thee.

I beg of Thee, O Thou king of existence and protector of the seen and unseen, to make whosoever arises to serve Thy Cause as a sea moving by Thy desire; ablaze with the fire of Thy Sadrat, shining from the horizon of the heaven of Thy will. Verily, Thou art the mighty One, whom neither the power of all the world, nor the strength of nations can weaken. There is no God but Thee, the one, the single, the protector, the self-subsistent!

O thou who hast drunk the choice wine of My utterance from the cup of My knowledge!

In this day, the following words were heard from the rustling of the Sadratu'l-Muntahá, which is planted by the hand of power of the King of Names, in the exalted paradise:

The First Taráz

and the First Tajallí, which has risen from the horizon of the Mother-Book, is that man should know his own self, and know those things which lead to loftiness or to baseness, to shame or to honor, to affluence or to poverty. After man has realized his own being and become mature, then for him wealth is needed. If this wealth is acquired through a craft and profession, it is approvable and worthy of praise to men of wisdom, especially to those servants who arise to train the world and beautify the souls of nations. These are the cup-bearers of the kawthér of knowledge and the guides to the ideal path. They direct the people of the whole world unto the right path, and instruct them in that which is conducive to the elevation and progress of being.

The right path is a path which leads man to the day spring of perception and dawning-place of knowledge and directs him to that which is the cause of honor and glory and greatness. We hope that, by the providence of the wise Physician, the dust will be removed from his eyes and the clearness of his sight will increase; so that he may discover that for which he has been created. In this day that which will decrease blindness and increase sight is worthy of attention. To the possessors of wisdom this spiritual sight is the minister and guide of knowledge. The apprehension of knowledge is due to the power of insight. The people of Bahá must, in all cases, act and advise people in that which is worthy.

The Second Taráz

is to consort with the people of religions with joy and fragrance; to show forth that which is declared by the Speaker of the Mount; and to render justice in affairs. The followers of sincerity and faithfulness must consort with all the people of the world with joy and fragrance; for association is always conducive to union and harmony, and union and harmony are the cause of the order of the world and the life of nations. Blessed are they who hold fast to the rope of compassion and kindness and are detached from animosity and hatred!

This oppressed One exhorts the people of the world to forbearance and benevolence. These are as two lights for the darkness of the world and as two teachers to lead nations to knowledge. Blessed are those who attain thereto, and woe unto those who are heedless!

The Third Taráz

is concerning good character. Good character is, verily, the best mantle for men on the part of God; by this, God adorns the temples of His friends. By My life, the light of good character surpasses the light of the sun and its effulgence. He who attains thereto is accounted as the essence of men. Upon this the honor and glory of the world are based and are dependent. Good character is the means of guiding men to the right path and the great message. Blessed is he who is adorned with the attributes and virtues of the Supreme Concourse!

Gaze toward justice and equity under all circumstances. This exalted Utterance has been revealed, from the Pen of ABHÁ, in the "Hidden Words":

"O Son of Spirit!

"The best of all to Me is Justice. Desire thou not to cast it away if thou desirest Me, and neglect it not, that thou may'st be faithful to Me, for by it thou wilt attain to see the things with thine own eyes and not by the eyes of the creatures, and know them by thine own knowledge and not by the knowledge of any in the world. Meditate on this—how thou oughtest to be. Justice is one of My gifts to thee and one of My cares over thee, therefore put it before thine eyes continually."

The possessors of justice and equity occupy the highest station and loftiest rank: the lights of righteousness and piety radiate and shine from such souls. It is hoped that nations and countries may not be deprived of the lights of these two orbs.

THE FOURTH TARÁZ

is on trustworthiness. Verily, this is the door of tranquillity to all in the world, and the sign of glory from the presence of the merciful One. Whosoever attains thereto has attained to treasuries of wealth and affluence. Trustworthiness is the greatest door to the security and tranquillity of mankind. The stability of every affair always depends on it, and the worlds of honor, glory and affluence are illuminated by its light.

Sometime since, this sweet Utterance was revealed from the Supreme Pen:

"Verily, We mention unto thee Trustworthiness and the place it occupies before God, thy Lord and the Lord of the Great Throne. One day We repaired unto our Green Island. When We entered therein, We found its streams flowing, its trees in full foliage, and the sun playing through the interstices.

"Turning our Face to the right, We beheld that which the pen fails to describe, nor can it set forth that which was witnessed by the eye of the Lord of mankind in that place, which is the most pure, the most honored, the most blessed, the most lofty.

"We then advanced toward the left. There We beheld one of the countenances of the exalted Paradise, standing on a pillar of light, and calling out in the loudest voice, saying: 'O ye concourse of heaven and earth, gaze upon my beauty, my light, my appearance and my effulgence. By God, the true One, I am Trustworthiness, its manifestation and its beauty, and I am the reward to him who clings thereto, who knoweth its rank and position and holdeth fast unto its hem. I am the most great ornament to the people of Bahá, and the mantle of honor to all in the kingdom of emanation. I am the greatest cause for the affluence of the world, and the horizon of tranquillity to the people of existence.' Thus have We revealed unto thee that which will draw mankind near unto the Lord of creation!

"O people of Bahá! Trustworthiness is the best garment for your temples and the most splendid crown for your heads. Adhere thereto by the command of the omnipotent commander!"

The Fifth Taráz

regards the preservation and protection of the stations of the servants of God. They must not make light of any matter, but speak in truthfulness and sincerity. The people of Bahá must not refuse to discharge the due reward of any one, and must respect possessors of talent; and they must not stain their tongues with slander like unto the former community. In this day the sun of arts and crafts is manifest from the horizon of the heaven of the Occident, and the river of skill is flowing from the sea of that part. One must speak with justice and recognize the worth of benefits. By the life of God, the word Justice is shining and luminous like unto the sun: We beg of God to illuminate all with its lights. Verily, He is powerful in all things and is worthy to grant!

In these days, truthfulness and sincerity are captive in the claws of falsehood, and justice is oppressed by the scourges of injustice. The smoke of corruption has so enveloped the world that naught is seen from any direction save armies and naught is heard from any region except the clashing of swords. We beg of God to assist the appearances of His power in that which is conducive to the reformation of the world and the welfare of nations.

The Sixth Taráz

Knowledge is one of the greatest benefits of God. To acquire knowledge is incumbent on all. These visible arts and present implements are from the results of His knowledge and wisdom, which have been revealed from the Supreme Pen. The Supreme Pen is that pen from the treasury of which the gems of wisdom and utterance, and the arts of all the world have appeared and become manifest. In this day the mysteries of this earth are unfolded and visible before the eyes, and the pages of swiftly appearing newspapers are indeed the mirror of the world; they display the doings and actions of the different nations; they both illustrate them and cause them to be heard. Newspapers are as a mirror which is endowed with hearing, sight and speech; they are a wonderful phenomenon and a great matter. But it behoveth the writers thereof to be sanctified from the prejudice of egotism and desire and to be adorned with the ornament of equity and justice; they must inquire into matters as much as possible, in order that they may be informed of the real facts, and commit the same to writing.

Concerning this oppressed One, whatever the newspapers have mentioned is mostly devoid of truth. Good speech and truthfulness are, in loftiness of position and rank, like unto the sun which hath risen from the horizon of the heaven of knowledge. The waves of this sea are visible before the faces of all in the world, and the traces of the Pen of wisdom and utterance are manifest.

They have written in newspapers that this servant hath fled from Írán and gone to 'Iráq Arabie! Praise be to God, this servant hath not concealed Himself even for an instant and hath been always standing and present before all faces. Verily, We have not fled, nor do We flee; nay, rather, the ignorant servants have fled from Us! We left our native land, and horsemen, commissioned by the Íránian and Russian governments, escorted us until We arrived at 'Iráq with glory and power. Praise be to God, the matter of this Oppressed One is exalted like unto heaven and is shining and luminous as the sun. Concealment hath no access to this Station, and dread and silence have no place therein!

The Mysteries of the Resurrection Day and the Signs of the "Hour" have all become manifest, but the people are heedless and veiled. . . .

TABLET OF THE WORLD

In My Name, The Speaker in the Kingdom of Bayán!

Praise and glorification behoveth the manifest King who hath adorned the Strong Prison with the presence of his holiness 'Alí-Kabli-Akbar and his holiness Ameen, and ornamented it with the lights of assurance, steadfastness and tranquillity. The Glory of God and the glory of all in the heaven and earth be upon both of them!

Light and glory, greeting and praise be upon the hands of His Cause, through whom the light of long-suffering hath shone forth, and the declaration of authority is proven of God, the powerful, the mighty, the independent; and through whom the sea of bestowal hath moved, and the breeze of the favor of God, the Lord of mankind, hath wafted. We beg of Him—Exalted is He—to protect them through His hosts, to guard them by His dominion, and to assist them by His power which hath conquered all things. The dominion belongs to God, the Maker of Heaven, and the King of the Kingdom of Names!

THE GREAT MESSAGE commands:

O ye people of Írán! Ye have been the day springs of mercy and the dawning-places of compassion and love; and the regions of existence have been illuminated and adorned with the light of your knowledge and wisdom. How is it that you have arisen to destroy yourselves and your friends with your own hands?

O my Afnán! Upon thee be my Bahá and favor! The tent of

the Divine Cause is great; it shall envelop all the nations of the world. The day is your day, and a thousand Tablets are your evidence. Arise to assist the Cause, and be engaged in subduing the minds and souls of the people of the world through the host of utterance. You must show forth that which will be conducive to the welfare and tranquillity of the helpless ones of the world. Gird up the loins of effort; perchance the slaves may be emancipated from bondage and find freedom. In this day, the cry of justice is raised and the lamentation of equity is heard. The dark smoke of oppression hath enveloped the world and nations. Through the motion of the Supreme Pen a new life of significances is breathed into the body of words by the command of the ideal commander, and the effects thereof are visible and manifest in all the things of the world. This is the most great glad-tidings which hath flowed from the Pen of this oppressed One.

Say: O friends! Why fear, and whom shall ye dread? These clay-pieces of the world shall be disintegrated by a slight moisture. Your union itself will be conducive to scattering superstitious souls. Strife and conflict are characteristic of the ferocious beasts of the earth. By the assistance of God, the sharp swords of the Bábí community have been returned to the scabbards through good words and pleasing deeds. The righteous have always, through good words, taken possession of the gardens of existence.

Say: O friends! Do not forsake wisdom. Hearken to the exhortations of the Supreme Pen with the ear of intelligence. No one of all the people of the world should suffer harm from your hands or tongues.

Concerning the Land of Ta we have revealed in the Book of Aqdas that which is conducive to warning all in the world. The unjust ones of the world have usurped the rights of nations, and are with all power and strength occupied with their own lustful desires. The tyrant of the land of Ya wrought that wherefore the eyes of the Supreme Concourse shed tears of blood.

O thou who art drinking the choice wine of My utterance and gazing toward the horizon of My Manifestation! How is it that the people of Írán, notwithstanding their precedence in sciences and arts, are now found to be the lowest among all the peoples of the world? O people! In this blessed, brilliant day, deprive not yourselves of the bounties of the bounteous One. In this day, the rains of wisdom and utterance are descending from the clouds of mercy of the merciful One. Blessed is he who renders justice in the matter, and woe unto those who are unjust!

In this day every knowing one testifies that the utterances, which are revealed from the Pen of this oppressed One, are the greatest cause for the elevation of the world and the development of nations. Say: O people! Arise to assist yourselves through the heavenly power, that perchance the earth may be purified and purged from the idols of superstitions and imaginations which are, forsooth, the cause of the failure and humiliation of the helpless people. These idols intervene and withhold the people from progress and loftiness. It is hoped that the hand of power will assist, and will deliver the creatures from the great baseness.

It is revealed in one of the Tablets: "O people of God! Be not occupied with yourselves. Be intent on the betterment of the world and the training of nations." The betterment of the world can be accomplished through pure and excellent deeds and well-approved and agreeable conduct. The helper of the Cause is deeds and its assistant is good character. O people of Bahá! Hold fast unto piety! This is that which is commanded by this oppressed One and chosen by the potent One.

O friends! in this soul-refreshing springtime, it behoveth you to be refreshed and verdant through the Divine vernal shower. A great sun has diffused its rays and the cloud of mercy is overspread. Successful is he who did not make himself portionless, and recognized the Friend in this garment.

Say: The Ahrimans are lurking in ambush: be ye aware and deliver yourselves from every darkness through the light of the name of the discerning One. Have ye regard for the world, and not for yourselves. Ahrimans are such souls as intervene and interpose between men and exaltation and loftiness in their positions. In this day, it is incumbent and obligatory upon all to adhere to that which is conducive to the progress and elevation of the just government and people. In every one of the Verses, the Supreme Pen hath opened doors of love and union. We have said—and

Our saying is truth—"Consort with all the people of religions with joy and fragrance." Through this utterance, whatever was the cause of foreignness, discord and disunion has been removed.

Concerning the progress of existence and the development of men We have revealed that which is the greatest door to the training of the people of the world. All that hath been formerly revealed from the tongue or pen of the people of the past, the king thereof is indeed revealed in this Most Great Manifestation from the heaven of will of the Lord of pre-existence. In former ages it has been said: "To love one's native land is faith." But the Tongue of grandeur hath said in the day of this Manifestation: "Glory is not his who loves his native land; but glory is his who loves his kind." By these exalted words He taught the birds of souls a new flight and effaced restriction and blind imitation from the Book. This oppressed One hath forbidden the people of God to engage in strife and conflict, and summoned them to good deeds, and to spiritual and pleasing morals. In this day the hosts which assist the Cause are good deeds and good morals. Blessed are they who adhere thereto, and woe unto those who reject them!

O people of God! I exhort you to courtesy. Courtesy is, in the primary station, the lord of all virtues. Blessed is he who is illumined with the light of courtesy, and is adorned with the mantle of uprightness! He who is endowed with courtesy is endowed with a great station. It is hoped that this oppressed One, and all, will attain to it, adhere to it, hold unto it, and observe it. This is the irrefutable command which hath flowed and is revealed from the Pen of the Greatest Name.

This day is a day wherein the gems of steadfastness must appear from the mine of man. O people of justice! Ye must be luminous like unto light, and be ablaze as the fire of the Sinaitic tree. This fire of love will assemble all the different peoples in one court; but the fire of animosity is the cause of disunion and conflict. We beg of God to protect His servants from the evil of His enemies. Verily, He is powerful in all things!

Praise be to God! The true One—exalted is His glory!—hath opened the doors of the minds and souls through the key of the Supreme Pen. Every one of the revealed Verses is a manifest door to the appearance of spiritual virtues and holy deeds. This voice and this utterance is not particularized to one country or one city. The people of the world in general must adhere to that which is revealed and hath appeared, so that they may attain to the real freedom. The world is illuminated with the lights of the orb of Manifestation; for in the "year sixty" (1844) the Precursor—may the lives of all else save Him be a sacrifice to Him!—announced the glad-tidings of the new life, and in the "year eighty" (1863) the world attained to the new light and the wonderful life. Now most of the people of the lands are prepared to hearken unto the exalted Word, upon which depends and is based the resuscitation and resurrection of all.

In the Prison, 'Akká, We have revealed in the Red Epistle that which is conducive to the elevation of men and to the cultivation of countries. Among others, these utterances have been revealed therein, from the Pen of the King of existence.

The greatest foundations upon which depends the administration of people are the following:

First: The ministers of the House of Justice must promote the Most Great Peace, in order that the world may be freed from onerous expenditures. This matter is obligatory and indispensable; for warfare and conflict are the foundation of trouble and distress.

Second: Languages must be reduced to one, and that one language must be taught in all the schools of the world.

Third: All must adhere to the means which is conducive to love and unity.

Fourth: Men and women must place a part of what they earn by trade, agriculture or other business, in charge of a trustworthy person, to be spent in the education and instruction of the children. That deposit must be invested in the education of the children, under the advice of the trustees of the House of Justice.

Fifth: Complete regard should be had to the matter of agriculture. Although this matter is mentioned in the fifth, yet in reality it is endowed with the first station. Agriculture is greatly developed in foreign countries, but in Írán it has still remained unheeded. It is hoped that the Sháh—May God assist him!—will concern himself with this great and important matter.

To resume: Were they to adhere to that which has been revealed by the Supreme Pen in the Red Epistle, they shall find themselves independent of all the laws of the world. Certain utterances have repeatedly poured forth from the Supreme Pen, that perchance the day springs of power and dawning-places of the Divine might may, sometime, be enabled to enforce them. Were seekers to be found, all that hath appeared from the absolute penetrative Will would be declared sincerely to please God; but where is the seeker, where is the inquirer, where is the just one? Now, every day, a fire of oppression is ablaze, and a sword of bloodshed is unsheathed. Praise be to God! The grandees of Írán and the high nobility glory in savage qualities. "Such stories add astonishment to astonishment!"

This oppressed One is night and day engaged in thanking and praising the Lord of mankind, for it is witnessed that Our exhortations and advice have produced effect, and the conduct and manners of this community have attained to the rank of God's acceptance; because an event has occurred which is the means of illumining the eyes of all in the world: it is this, that the friends have interceded for the enemies before the princes and rulers. Good deeds bear witness to the truth of words. It is hoped that the righteous will illuminate the world through the light of deeds. I beg of God—exalted and blessed is He!—to enable all, in His days, to be steadfast in His love and in His Cause. Verily, He is the friend of the sincere and of those who practice!

O people of God! The Supreme Pen hath caused worlds to appear, and hath bestowed ideal light on the eyes. But most of the people in Írán have ever been bereft of profitable utterances and holy sciences and arts.

In the preceding day, this exalted word was especially revealed for one of the friends from the Supreme Pen, that perchance the people of denial may attain unto faith, and penetrate the intricacies of fundamental divine matters, and be thereby admonished.

The deniers and contradictors hold to four words:

First: Destroying men's lives.

Second: Burning the Books.

Third: Shunning other nations.

Fourth: Exterminating other communities.

Now, by the grace and authority of the Word of God, these four great barriers have been demolished. These four manifest decrees have been effaced from the Book, and God hath changed brutal manners into spiritual qualities. Glorified is His will! Exalted is His power! Great is His dominion!

Now, beg ye of God—exalted is His Glory!—and We beg of Him also to guide the Shiite community and to deliver them from unworthy attributes. In every day the tongue of every individual of that community uttereth many a curse; and the word "Mal'oon," pronounced with guttural "o," is one of their daily foods.

O my God! O my God! Thou hearest the cry of Thy Bahá and His lamentation in days and nights; and Thou knowest that, verily, He hath not desired aught for Himself, but hath desired to sanctify the souls of Thy servants and deliver them from the fire of hatred and animosity, which surrounds them at all times. O my Lord! The hands of the chosen ones are, verily, stretched toward the heaven of Thy bounty, and those of the sincere ones toward the firmament of Thy Bestowal. I beg of Thee not to disappoint them in that which they have desired from the sea of Thy gift, from the heaven of Thy grace, and from the sun of Thy generosity. O my Lord! Strengthen them in such virtues, whereby their stations may be exalted among nations. Verily, Thou art the powerful, the mighty, the bestower!

O people of God! Hearken unto that, the hearing of which is conducive to the deliverance, tranquillity, security, exaltation and loftiness of all men in general!

Certain laws and principles are necessary and indispensable for Írán; but it is suitable that these should be accomplished in accord with the wish of His Majesty the Sháh—May God assist him!—the eminent doctors and the great state authorities. Under their advice a place must be appointed, and they must assemble together in that place, and hold fast to the rope of consultation, and decide upon and execute that which is conducive to the people's security, affluence, welfare and tranquillity. For, if this matter be managed otherwise, it would lead to discord and tumult. In the principal laws and commandments which have, ere this, been revealed in the Book of Aqdas and other Tablets affairs have been placed in charge of just kings and chiefs, and of the trustees of the House of Justice. Upon reflection, men of equity and discernment will witness, with outward and inward eyes, the effulgence of the orb of justice in all that We have revealed. At present that form of government followed by the British nation seems good; for that nation is illuminated both with the light of kingdom and consultation.

In Our laws and principles a chapter has been devoted to the law of retaliation which is the cause of the protection and preservation of people; but the people's dread of that law withholds them only outwardly from committing base and unseemly deeds. But that which prevents and guards men both outwardly and inwardly from base deeds is the fear of God.

The fear of God is the real guardian and the ideal protector. Men must adhere and hold fast unto that which is conducive to the appearance of this great gift. Blessed is he who hearkens unto what My Supreme Pen hath uttered, and acts in accord with that which is commanded on the part of the ancient commander.

O people of God! Hearken unto the exhortations of the unique Friend with the ear of the soul. The Word of God is like unto a tree: its planting-ground must be the hearts of the people: cultivate it through the kawthar of wisdom and utterance, so that its roots may become firm, and its branches surpass the firmament.

O ye people of the world! The virtue of this Most Great Manifestation is that We have effaced from the Book whatever was the cause of difference, corruption and discord, and recorded therein that which leads to unity, harmony and accord. Joy unto those who practice!

We have repeatedly exhorted the friends to avoid, nay, to flee from that which is redolent of sedition. The world is in confusion, and the opinions of men are discordant. I beg of God to adorn them with the light of His justice, and to make known unto them that which will profit them under all circumstances. Verily, He is the self-sufficient, the most high! . . .

WORDS OF PARADISE

. . . The Word of God, as described and recorded by the Pen of Abhá on the First Leaf of the Exalted Paradise:

Truly, I say, the fear of God hath ever been the perspicuous protection and solid fortress for the whole community of the world. It is the greatest means for the protection of mankind, and the chief cause of the preservation of humanity. Yea, there exists a sign in the being of man which guards and protects him from that which is unworthy and unbecoming. That sign is called modesty. But this virtue is assigned to a few; for all are not endowed with this station.

The Word of God in the Second Leaf of the Exalted Paradise:

At this moment the Supreme Pen exhorts the day springs of power and dawning-places of authority, *to-wit*: kings, rulers, chiefs, princes, learned men and mystics, and commands them to hold fast to religion. Religion is the greatest instrument for the order of the world and the tranquillity of all existent beings. The weakness of the pillars of religion has encouraged the ignorant and rendered them audacious and arrogant. Truly, I say, whatever lowers the lofty station of religion will increase heedlessness in the wicked, and finally result in anarchy. Hear, O ye possessors of perception! Then be admonished, O ye endowed with sight!

The Word of God in the Third Leaf of the Exalted Paradise:

O Son of Man! If thou lookest toward mercy, regard not that which benefits thee, and hold to that which will benefit the servants. If thou lookest toward justice, choose thou for others what thou choosest for thyself. Verily, through meekness, man is elevated to the heaven of power; and again, pride degrades him to the lowest station of humiliation and abasement. O people of God! The day is great, and the call is mighty! In one of the Tablets this exalted Word is revealed from the heaven of Will: "Were the power of the soul entirely transformed into the sense of hearing, then it could be said that it were able to hear this Call which is raised from the Supreme Horizon, otherwise these polluted ears are not worthy to hear it." Blessed are those who hear, and woe unto them who are heedless!

The Word of God in the Fourth Leaf of the Exalted Paradise:

O people of God!—Exalted is His Glory!—Ask God to guard the sources of power and authority against the evil of egotism and lust, and to illumine them with the lights of justice and guidance. Two abominable deeds proceeded from His Highness Muḥammad S͟háh, notwithstanding the loftiness of his position. One was the exile of the King of the dominions of bounty and grace, His Holiness the First Point; the second was the murder of the lord of the city of counsel and of belles lettres. In brief, his error and bounty were great.

A king whom the pride of authority and independence does not withhold from being just, and whom benefits, opulence, glory, hosts and legions do not deprive of the splendors of the orb of equity—such a king shall possess a lofty station and an exalted rank in the Supreme Concourse: it is incumbent on all to assist and love such a blessed being. Blessed is the ruler who controls the reins of the ego, and overcomes his wrath; who prefers justice to oppression and equity to tyranny!

The Word of God in the Fifth Leaf of the Exalted Paradise:

The greatest gift and the highest blessing, in the primary station, is wisdom. It is the protector of existence, and its support and helper. Wisdom is the messenger of the merciful One, and the Manifestor of the Name, the "All-Wise." Through wisdom the station of man is evident and manifest. It is the knower and the first teacher in the school of existence, and it is the guide, the possessor of a lofty rank. Under the auspices of its training the element earth was endowed with pure soul and surpassed the firmament. Wisdom is the first orator in the city of justice; and in the "year nine" (1853) it illuminated the world with the glad-tidings of the Manifestation. Wisdom is the peerless wise one who, in the beginning of the world, ascended the ladder of significances; and when, by the Divine will, it occupied the pulpit of utterance, it spoke in two words. From the first word appeared the glad-tidings of promise, and from the second the fear of threat. From promise and threat, fear and hope became manifest, and by these two the foundation of the order of the world was established and consolidated. Exalted is the Wise One, the possessor of great bounty!

The Word of God in the Sixth Leaf of the Exalted Paradise:

The light of men is justice; quench it not with the contrary winds of oppression and tyranny. The purpose of justice is the appearance of unity among people. In this exalted Word, the sea of God's wisdom is moving: all the books of the world are not sufficient to contain its interpretation.

If the world is adorned with this mantle, the sun of the saying —"On that day God will satisfy them all with His abundance"— will appear and shine from the horizon of the heaven of the world. Know ye the station of this utterance, for it is from the loftiest fruits of the tree of the Supreme Pen. Happy is he who heareth and attaineth!

Truly, I say, all that has descended from the heaven of the Divine Will is conducive to the order of the world, and to the furtherance of unity and harmony among its people. Thus hath the tongue of this wronged One spoken in His Great Prison!

The Word of God in the Seventh Leaf of the Exalted Paradise:

O ye wise men among nations! Turn your eyes away from foreignness and gaze unto oneness, and hold fast unto the means which conduce to the tranquillity and security of the people of the whole world. This span-wide world is but one native land and one locality. Abandon that glory which is the cause of discord, and turn unto that which promotes harmony. To the people of Bahá glory is in knowledge, good deeds, good morals and wisdom —not in native land, or station. O people of the earth; appreciate the worth of this heavenly Word, for it is like unto a ship for the sea of knowledge, and is as the sun to the universe of perception.

The Word of God in the Eighth Leaf of the Exalted Paradise:

Schools must first train the children in the principles of religion, so that the Promise and the Threat, recorded in the Books of God, may prevent them from the things forbidden and adorn them with the mantle of the commandments: But this in such a measure that it may not injure the children by resulting in ignorant fanaticism and bigotry.

It is incumbent upon the Trustees of the House of Justice to take counsel together regarding such laws as have not been expressly revealed in the Book. Of these whatever they deem advisable and proper that must they enforce. Verily, God will inspire them with that which He willeth, and He is the ruler, the knower! We have formerly declared that speech was decreed to be in two languages, and that there should be an effort to reduce it into one. So, likewise, should it be with the writings of the world, in order that people may not waste and lavish their lives in the study of various languages, and that the whole earth may be considered as one city and one land.

The Word of God in the Ninth Leaf of the Exalted Paradise:

Truly I say: Moderation is desirable in every affair, and when it is exceeded it leads to detriment. Consider the civilization of the people of the Occident—how it has occasioned commotion and agitation to the people of the world. There has appeared an infernal instrument, and such atrocity is displayed in the destruction of life, the like of which was not seen by the eye of the world, nor heard by the ears of nations. It is impossible to reform these violent, overwhelming evils, except the peoples of the world become united in affairs, or in one religion. Hearken ye unto the voice of this oppressed One, and adhere to the Most Great Peace!

A strange and wonderful instrument exists in the earth; but it is concealed from minds and souls. It is an instrument which has the power to change the atmosphere of the whole earth, and its infection causes destruction.

Praise be to God! A wonderful thing is perceived: the lightning and similar forces are subdued by a conductor, and act by his command. Exalted is the mighty One who hath made manifest that which He desired, through His absolute, invincible command!

O people of Bahá! Each one of the revealed commands is a strong fortress for the protection of the world. Verily, this oppressed One only wishes your security and elevation.

We exhort the men of the House of Justice, and command them to guard and protect the servants, maid-servants and children. They must, under all circumstances have regard for the interests of the servants. Blessed is the prince who succors a captive, the rich one who favors the needy, the just man who secures the right of a wronged one from the oppressor, and the trustee who performs what he is commanded on the part of the Pre-existent Commander!

O Ḥaydar-Kabli-'Alí! Upon thee be my Bahá and praise! My commands and exhortations have encompassed the world; nevertheless they have caused sorrows, not joy and happiness: because some of those who pretend to love Me have arisen in oppression, and inflicted that which was not wrought by even the former nations, nor by the Íránian doctors of religion. We have formerly said: "My imprisonment is not My affliction, nor is it what I have suffered from Mine enemies, but rather the deeds done by My friends who have related themselves to My Person, and commit that whereby My heart and My pen lament."

We have repeatedly revealed similar utterances, but they have not profited the heedless ones, for they are found to be captives to egotism and lust. Ask thou God to enable all of them to repent and return. As long as the ego is subject to carnal desires, sin and error continue. It is hoped that the hand of the Divine mercy, and the blessings of the compassionate One may assist them all, and adorn them with the garment of forgiveness and favor; and that He may also guard them from that which impairs His Cause among His servants. Verily, He is the powerful, the mighty, and He is the forgiving, the merciful!

The Word of God in the Tenth Leaf of the Exalted Paradise:

O people of the earth! A solitary life and severe discipline do not meet God's approval. The possessors of perception and knowledge should look unto the means which are conducive to joy and fragrance. Such practices come forth and proceed from the loins of superstition and the womb of fancy, and are not worthy the people of knowledge. Some of the people of the past and of later times dwelt in mountain caves, and others frequented the tombs during the night. Say: Hearken to the advice of this oppressed One. Abandon that which ye hold, and adhere unto what the trustworthy counsellor commands. Deprive not yourselves of that which is created for you.

Charity is beloved and acceptable before God, and is accounted the chief among all good deeds. Consider, and then remember that which the merciful One has revealed in the Qur'án: "But they prefer the poor before themselves, although there be indigence among them. He who is preserved from the covetousness of his own soul, such shall surely prosper." Indeed, this blessed Word is, in this connection, a sun among words: Blessed is he who prefers his brother before himself: Such an one is of the people of Bahá, in the Red Ark, on the part of God, the Knower, the Wise!

The Word of God in the Eleventh Leaf of the Exalted Paradise:

We command the appearance of names and attributes to adhere henceforth unto that which has been revealed in this Most Great Manifestation, and not to become a cause of discord, and to look unto the horizon of this luminous Word, as revealed in this Epistle, unto the end beyond which there is no end. Discord is the cause of bloodshed and entails revolution among the servants. Hearken to the Voice of this wronged One, and depart not therefrom.

If one ponders over that which is revealed in this Manifestation from the Supreme Pen, he will know for a certainty that, in all that this wronged One hath spoken, He has had no intention to establish any position or rank for Himself. But it has been Our aim to uplift men through exalted Words unto the Supreme Horizon, and prepare them to hearken unto that which conduces to the sanctifying and purifying of the people of the world from the strife and discord which result from differences in religions. Whereunto My heart and My pen, My manifest and My hidden being bear witness. God willing, they all will turn unto the treasuries which are deposited within themselves.

O people of Bahá! The reflective faculty is the depository of crafts, arts and sciences. Exert yourselves, so that the gems of knowledge and wisdom may proceed from this ideal mine, and conduce to the tranquillity and union of the different nations of the world.

Under all circumstances—whether in adversity or comfort, in glory or affliction—this wronged One has commanded all to show forth love and affection, compassion and union. Whenever any exaltation and loftiness appeared, those hidden behind coverings would come forth and speak calumniating words which were sharper than a sword. They cling to false and rejected words, and are deprived and withheld from the sea of the Divine verses. If such coverings had not intervened Írán would have been subdued by the Divine utterance in hardly more than two years, the position of both the State and the people would have become exalted, and the intended aim would have appeared in its fullest manifestation without concealment or covering.

In brief, We have said all that was necessary to be said, formerly by allusion, and recently in explicit words. And after Persia had been reformed, then the fragrances of the Word would have been diffused in other countries. For all that has flowed from the Supreme Pen has been and is conducive to the elevation, exaltation and training of all the people of the world, and is the greatest antidote for all diseases—were they to understand and perceive. . . .

TABLET OF TAJALLÍYÁT

He is the Hearer from His Supreme Horizon!

I testify that verily there is no God save He! and He who hath come is verily the hidden mystery, the concealed secret, the most great Book for the nations, and the heaven of beneficence to the world: He is the mighty sign among mankind, and the dawning-place of highest attributes in the world of emanation. Through Him hath appeared that which was concealed from all eternity and was hidden from men of discernment. Verily, He is the One whose Manifestation was announced by the Books of God in former and in latter times.

Whoever acknowledges Him, His signs, and His evidences hath verily acknowledged that which the Tongue of Grandeur hath uttered before the creation of heaven and earth, and before the appearance of the kingdom of Names. Through Him the sea of knowledge hath moved among mankind, and the running water of wisdom hath flowed from the presence of God, the King of Days. Blessed is the discerning one who witnessed and perceived, the hearing one who heard His sweet voice, and the hand that took hold of the Book through the power of its Lord, the king of this world and of the world to come! Blessed is the hastener who hastened toward His Supreme horizon, and the strong one whom neither the influence of princes nor the clamor of religious doctors did weaken! But woe unto him who disbelieved the grace of God and His bounty, His mercy and His power! Verily, such an one is of those who reject the proof of God and His argument throughout all eternity.

Joy unto him who, in this Day, casts away that which is possessed by the people, and holds fast to that which is commanded on the part of God, the King of Names and the Creator of things, *viz.*: The One who hath come from the heaven of pre-existence with the Greatest Name, and with a power that the hosts of the earth fail to withstand—whereunto testifies the "Mother-Book" in the Highest Station.

O 'Alí-Kabli-Akbar! We have heard thy voice repeatedly, and We have responded to thee in that which the sayings of the world cannot equal, and from which the sincere ones find the perfume of the utterance of the clement One, the lovers the fragrances of union, and the thirsty ones the murmur of the kawther of life. Blessed is he who attains thereto, and discovers that sweet fragrance which is now being diffused from the Pen of God, the protector, the mighty, the bestower!

We testify that verily thou hast advanced, hast journeyed until thou arrived and presented thyself here, and hast hearkened unto the voice of the oppressed One who is imprisoned because of that which was wrought by the hands of those who denied the Verses of God and His commands and rejected this grace by which the regions of the world are illuminated.

Blessed is thy face, for it turned unto Our direction; thine ears, for they heard; and thy tongue, for it uttered the praise of God, the Lord of Lords! We beg of God to make thee a banner for assistance of His Cause, and to draw thee nearer unto Him under all circumstances. We make mention of the friends of God and His beloved ones in that place, and we gladden them through that which is revealed unto them from the kingdom of the utterance of their Lord, the king of the day of judgment.

Remember them on My part, and illumine them with the lights of the orb of My utterance. Verily thy Lord is the mighty, the gracious!

O thou who art speaking My praise! Hearken to that which the oppressors say in My days. Some say, "Verily he hath claimed divinity!" others say, "He hath calumniated God," and still others say, "He hath appeared for corruption." Woe unto them! Grief unto them! Are they not the worshippers of imaginations?

Verily, We now desire to leave the "Eloquent Language." Verily thy Lord is the powerful, the independent! It is our desire to speak in the Íránian language, so that perchance the people of Persia may all hear the Utterance of the Clement One, and may come forth and find the truth.

The First Tajallí

which hath shone forth from the Sun of Truth is the knowledge of God—exalted is His Glory!—and the knowledge of the King of Pre-existence cannot be attained except by knowing the Greatest Name. He is the speaker of the Mount who is established and seated upon the throne of Manifestation, and He is the hidden, invisible One, the concealed Mystery.

All the former and later Books of God are adorned with His commemoration and speak His praise. Through Him the standard of knowledge is planted in the world, and the banner of unity is hoisted among nations. The meeting of God cannot be obtained except through meeting Him. Through Him appeared all that was hidden and invisible from all eternity.

Verily, He hath appeared in Truth, and hath uttered a Word whereby "all in the heavens and earth—except those whom God wished—are stunned." Faith in God, and the knowledge of Him cannot be fully realized except through believing in all that hath proceeded from Him, and by practicing all that He hath commanded and all that is revealed in the Book from the Supreme Pen. Those submerged in the sea of Divine utterance must at all times observe the commands and prohibitions of God. His commandments are the greatest fortress for the protection of the world and for the preservation of mankind. Light is upon those who confess and acknowledge them, and fire is on those who reject and oppose them.

The Second Tajallí

is steadfastness in the Cause of God and in His love—exalted is His glory! This cannot be attained except through knowledge of Him, and a perfect knowledge of Him cannot be obtained except by confessing the blessed Word: "God doeth that which He willeth." He who adheres to this exalted Word, and drinks from the kawther of divine utterance which is deposited therein, will find himself so steadfast that all the books of the world shall not withhold him from the "Mother-Book." Oh! Great is this lofty station, exalted position, and furthermost end!

O 'Alí-Kabli-Akbar! Think how low is the station of the deniers. All of them speak the blessed Words: "Verily, He is to be praised in His deeds, and to be obeyed in His Command;" nevertheless, if something may appear, in the least degree against their lust and desire, they will reject it. Say: No one is informed of the expediencies of the consummate wisdom of God. Verily, were He to declare the earth to be heaven, no one hath the right to contradict Him. This is that whereunto the Point of El-Bayán (the Báb) hath testified in all that was revealed unto Him on the part of God, the cleaver of dawns.

The Third Tajallí

is concerning sciences, crafts and arts. Knowledge is like unto wings for the being, and is as a ladder for ascending. To acquire knowledge is incumbent on all, but of those sciences which may profit the people of the earth, and not such sciences as begin in mere words, and end in mere words. The possessors of sciences and arts have a great right among the people of the world. Whereunto testifies the mother of divine utterance in the day of return. Joy unto those who hear!

Indeed, the real treasury of man is his knowledge. Knowledge is the means of honor, prosperity, joy, gladness, happiness and exultation. Thus hath the Tongue of Grandeur spoken in this Great Prison!

The Fourth Tajallí

concerns the declaration of divinity, lordship, and similar statements. Were one endowed with perception to gaze upon this evident, blessed Tree, and upon its fruits, he would verily become independent of all else save It, and would acknowledge that which the speaker of the mount hath uttered on the throne of Manifestation.

O 'Alí-Kabli-Akbar! Speak unto people concerning the signs of thy Lord, and make known unto them His right path and His great Message. Say: O servants! If ye are the people of justice and equity, ye will confess all that has flowed from the Supreme Pen. If ye are of the people of Bayán, the Persian Bayán will guide you and suffice you, and, if ye are of the people of El-Forkan, reflect upon the "Splendor" and the "Voice" revealed in the Sinaitic Tree for the Son of Imran.

Praise be to God! It was supposed that at the manifestation of God knowledge had waxed perfect and mature, and had reached the furthermost end. Now it has become evident that knowledge has decreased among the deniers, and has remained immature.

O 'Alí! They refuse to accept from the Tree of being that which they accepted from the Tree of Sinai! Say: O people of Bayán! Speak not after the self and desire! Most of the peoples of the world confess the blessed Word which has proceeded from the Tree. By the life of God, were it not for the mention of "Divinity" made by the Precursor (the Báb), this oppressed One would not have spoken in that which is the cause of distraction and destruction of the ignorant.

In the beginning of the Bayán, He says in description of "He-whom-God-shall-manifest": *"Verily, He is the One who shall utter in all grades—'Verily, I am God. There is no God but Me, the Lord of all things, and all besides Me is created by Me! O ye, My creatures! Ye are to worship Me.'"* Likewise, in another place, in speaking of "He-whom-God-shall-manifest," He says: *"Verily, I am the first one of those who worship Him."*

Now, man must reflect upon the "Worshipper," and the "Worshipped One": perchance the people of the earth may attain to a drop of the sea of knowledge, and comprehend the station of this manifestation. Verily, He hath appeared, and hath spoken in truth. Blessed is he who confesses and acknowledges, and woe unto every remote denier!

O ye concourse of the earth! Hearken to the voice of the Sadrat, the shade of which hath encompassed the loftiest positions of the world; and be not of the tyrants of the earth who denied the manifestation of God and His power, and renounced His bounty. Are they not of the contemptible, in the Book of God, the Lord of the creatures?

Glory, shining from the heaven of My Providence, be upon thee, and upon him who is with thee and hearkens to thy saying in the Cause of God, the mighty, the praiseworthy!

THE GLAD-TIDINGS

This is the voice of El-Abhá, which is being raised from the supreme horizon, in the prison 'Akká!

He is the declarer, the knower, the omniscient!

God testifies and the appearance of His names and attributes bears witness that, by the raising of the voice and by the exalted Word, it has been our aim that the ears of the people of the world should be purified through the kawt͟her of divine utterance from false narrations and be prepared to hearken unto the blessed, pure, exalted Word which hath appeared from the treasury of the knowledge of the maker of heaven and creator of names. Blessed are those who are just!

O, people of the earth!

The First Glad-Tidings

which is conferred in this most great Manifestation on all the people of the world, from the "Mother-Book," is the abolishing of the decree of religious warfare from the Book. Exalted is the beneficent One, the possessor of great bounty—the One through whom the door of grace is opened before all in the Heaven and earth!

THE SECOND GLAD-TIDINGS:

It is sanctioned that all the nations of the world consort with each other with joy and fragrance. Consort ye, O people, with all religions with joy and fragrance! Thus hath the orb of permission and desire shone forth from the horizon of the heaven of the command of God, the Lord of the creatures!

THE THIRD GLAD-TIDINGS

is the study of various languages. This command hath formerly flowed from the Supreme Pen. Their majesties, the kings—may God assist them—or the counsellors of the earth must consult together, and appoint one of the existing languages, or a new language, and instruct the children therein, in all the schools of the world; and the same must be done in respect to writing also. In such case the earth will be considered as one. Blessed is he who heareth the Voice and fulfilleth that which is commanded on the part of God, the Lord of the great throne!

THE FOURTH GLAD-TIDINGS:

Let every one of the kings—May God strengthen them—arise to protect and assist this oppressed community. Each must precede the other in serving and showing love unto them. This matter is obligatory upon all. Blessed are those who practice!

THE FIFTH GLAD-TIDINGS:

In every country or government where any of this community reside, they must behave toward that government with faithfulness, trustfulness and truthfulness. This is that which is revealed from the presence of the Ancient Commander! It is obligatory and incumbent on the people of the world in general to assist this most great cause—which has descended from the heaven of the will of the king of pre-existence—that perchance the fire of animosity which is ablaze in the hearts of some of the nations, may be quenched through the water of divine wisdom and lordly commands and exhortations, and that the light of union and accord may irradiate and illuminate the regions. It is hoped that through the favor of the appearances of the power of God the armaments of the world will be changed into peace and corruption and conflict will vanish from among men.

The Sixth Glad-Tidings

is the Most Great Peace, the account of which has been formerly revealed from the Supreme Pen. Joy unto whosoever adhereth thereto and practices that whereunto he is commanded on the part of God, the knower, the wise!

The Seventh Glad-Tidings:

Men are permitted to have their choice in the manner of habiliment, and in the cut of the beard and its dressing. But, beware, O people, not to make yourselves as playthings to the ignorant!

The Eighth Glad-Tidings:

The pious practices of the monks and priests among the people of His Holiness the Spirit—upon Him is the peace of God and His glory!—are remembered before God; but, in this day, they must abandon solitude for open places, and engage in that which may profit both themselves and other men. We have conferred permission on them all to engage in matrimony, so that there may appear from them those who may celebrate the praise of God, the Lord of the seen and unseen and the Lord of the lofty throne!

The Ninth Glad-Tidings:

The sinner, when in a state wherein he finds himself free and severed from all else save God, must beg for forgiveness and pardon. It is not allowable to declare one's sins and transgressions before any man, inasmuch as this has not been, nor is, conducive to securing God's forgiveness and pardon. At the same time such confession before the creatures leads to one's humiliation and abasement, and God—exalted in His glory!—does not wish for the humiliation of His servants. Verily He is compassionate and beneficent!

A sinner must, between himself and God, beg for mercy from the Sea of Mercy and ask forgiveness from the Heaven of Beneficence, and then say:

Oh my God! Oh my God! I beg of Thee—by the blood of Thy lovers, who were so attracted by Thy sweet utterance that they betook themselves unto the lofty summit, the place of great martyrdom, and by the mysteries concealed in Thy knowledge, and by the pearls deposited in the Sea of Thy bestowal—to forgive me, and my father and my mother. Verily Thou art the most merciful of the merciful! There is no God but Thee, the forgiving, the beneficent!

Oh, my Lord! Thou beholdest the essence of error advancing toward the sea of Thy gift, and the weak one toward the kingdom of Thy power, and the poor one toward the sun of Thy wealth. Oh, my Lord! Disappoint him not of Thy generosity and bounty; deprive him not of the graces of Thy days, and turn him not away from Thy door which Thou hast opened before all in Thy heaven and earth.

Alas! Alas! My transgressions have prevented me from drawing nigh unto the court of Thy sanctity, and my trespasses have kept me afar from turning unto the tents of Thy glory. I have indeed wrought that which Thou hast forbidden me; I have neglected that which Thou hast commanded me! I beg of Thee by the King of Names to decree for me from the Pen of grace and bestowal that which will draw me near unto Thee and will purify me from my sins which have intervened between me and Thy forgiveness and pardon. Verily, Thou are the powerful, the bounteous! There is no God but Thee, the mighty, the gracious!

THE TENTH GLAD-TIDINGS:

We have removed from the Epistles and Tablets the decree of

effacing the books as a favor from the presence of God, the sender of this great message!

THE ELEVENTH GLAD-TIDINGS:

To study sciences and arts of all descriptions is allowable; but such sciences as are profitable, which lead and conduce to the elevation of mankind. Thus has the matter been decreed on the part of God, the commander, the wise!

THE TWELFTH GLAD-TIDINGS:

It is made incumbent on every one of you to engage in some one occupation, such as arts, trades, and the like. We have made this—your occupation—identical with the worship of God, the True One. Reflect, O people, upon the mercy of God and upon His favors, then thank Him in mornings and evenings.

Waste not your time in idleness and indolence, and occupy yourselves with that which will profit yourselves and others beside yourself. Thus hath the matter been decreed in this Tablet from the horizon of which the sun of wisdom and divine utterance is gleaming! The most despised of men before God is he who sits and begs. Cling unto the rope of means, relying upon God, the causer of causes. Every soul who occupies himself in an art or trade—this will be accounted an act of worship before God. Verily this is from no other than His great and abundant favor!

THE THIRTEENTH GLAD-TIDINGS:

The affairs of the people are placed in charge of the men of the House of Justice of God. They are the trustees of God among His servants and the day springs of command in His countries.

O people of God! The trainer of the world is justice, for it consists of two pillars: Reward and retribution. These two pillars are two fountains for the life of the people of the world. Inasmuch as for each time and day a particular decree and order is expedient, affairs are therefore entrusted to the ministers of the House of Justice, so that they may execute that which they deem advisable at the time. Those souls who arise to serve the Cause sincerely to please God will be inspired by the divine, invisible inspirations. It is incumbent upon all to obey.

Administrative affairs are all in charge of the House of Justice; but acts of worship must be observed according as they are revealed in the Book.

O, people of Bahá! Ye are day springs of the love, and dawning-places of the providence of God. Defile not the tongue with cursing or execrating any one and guard your eyes against that which is not worthy. Show forth that which ye possess. If it is accepted, the aim is attained, and, if not, interference with those who reject it is not allowable, but leave them to themselves and advance toward God, the protector, the self-subsistent.

Be not the cause of sorrow, how much less of sedition and strife. It is hoped that ye may be trained under the shadow of the Tree of divine providence, and act in that which is desired by God. Ye are all leaves of one tree and drops of one sea.

The Fourteenth Glad-Tidings:

To undertake journeys for the sake of visiting the tombs of the dead is not necessary. If those who have means and wealth should give to the House of Justice the amount which would otherwise be expended on such journeys, this would be acceptable and agreeable before God. Happy are those who practice!

The Fifteenth Glad-Tidings:

Although a republican form of government profits all the people of the world, yet the majesty of kingship is one of the signs of God. We do not wish that the countries of the world should be deprived thereof. If statesmen combine the two into one form, their reward will be great before God.

Agreeable to the requirements of former times, the former religions confirmed and commanded religious warfare, prohibited association and intercourse with other peoples, and forbade the reading of certain books, but in this most great Manifestation and mighty message, favors and gifts of God have pervaded all and the irrefutable command is revealed in that which already has been mentioned from the horizon of the will of the Lord of pre-existence. We praise God—Exalted and Glorified is He!—for that which He hath revealed in this day, the blessed, the mighty, the wonderful! Were all the people of the world each to possess a hundred thousand tongues and speak in God's praise and glorification until the day which hath no end, verily all their thanks will not equal what is due even a single one of the favors mentioned in this Epistle!—whereunto testifies every man of knowledge and discernment and every man of wisdom and understanding. I beg of God—exalted in His glory!—and entreat Him to enable the kings and sovereigns, who are dawning-places of power and day-springs of might, to execute His precepts and commands.

Verily, He is the powerful, the mighty and worthy to grant!

TABLET OF ISHRÁQÁT

. . . O Jaleel! The oppressed One of the world says: The orb of justice is concealed; the sun of equity is behind the clouds; thieves occupy the position of guardians and protectors, and traitors are seated in the place of trustworthy ones. In the preceding year, a tyrant occupied the seat of the governorship of this city. At every instance We suffered a harm from him. By the life of God, he wrought that which caused the greatest dread. But the tyranny of the whole world can never withhold the Supreme Pen. Out of especial grace and mercy to the princes and counsellors of the earth We wrote that which is conducive to protection, security, tranquillity and composure—perchance the servants may be protected from the wickedness of tyrants. Verily He is the guardian, the helper, the confirmer!

The men of the House of Justice of God must, night and day, gaze toward that which hath been revealed from the horizon of the heaven of the Supreme Pen for the training of the servants, for the upbuilding of countries, for the protection of men and for the preservation of human honor.

THE FIRST ISHRÁQ:

When the sun of wisdom dawned from the horizon of administration, it spoke in these exalted words:

The people of wealth and men of honor and power must have the best possible regard for the respect of religion. Religion is a manifest light and a strong fortress for the protection and tranquillity of the people of the world. For the fear of God commands people to do that which is just and forbids them that which is evil. If the lamp of Religion remain concealed agitation and anarchy would prevail, and the orb of justice and equity and the sun of peace and tranquillity would be withheld from giving light. Every man of discernment testifies to that which is mentioned.

THE SECOND ISHRÁQ:

We have commanded the Most Great Peace, which is the greatest means for the protection of mankind. The rulers of the world must, in one accord, adhere to this command which is the main cause for the security and tranquillity of the world. They are daysprings of the power and dawning-places of the authority of God. We beg of God to assist them in that which is conducive to the peace of the servants.

The account of this subject has been previously revealed from the Supreme Pen. Blessed are those who act accordingly!

THE THIRD ISHRÁQ

commands the executing of the penal laws, for this is the primary means for the maintenance of the world. The heaven of divine wisdom is illumined and shining with two orbs, consultation and kindness. And the tent of the order of the world is hoisted and established on two pillars: reward and retribution.

THE FOURTH ISHRÁQ:

In this manifestation, victorious hosts are worthy deeds and morals, and the leader and commander of these hosts is godlike piety. This comprehends all and rules over all!

The Fifth Ishráq

is that governments must be acquainted with the conditions of the officials and must confer upon them dignity and positions in accord with due measure and merit. To have regard for this matter is obligatory and incumbent on every chief and ruler. Thus, perchance, traitors shall not usurp the place of trustworthy men, or spoilers occupy the seat of guardians.

In this Most Great Prison, among the officials formerly and recently appointed, some have been—Praise be to God!—adorned with the ornament of Justice; but some others of them——. We take refuge in God! We beg of God that He may guide them all, perchance they may not be deprived of the fruits of the tree of trustworthiness and integrity, nor withheld from the lights of the sun of equity and justice.

The Sixth Ishráq

is concerning union and harmony among mankind. Through union the regions of the world have ever been illuminated with the light of the Cause. The greatest means is that the peoples should be familiar with each other's writing and language.

We have formerly commanded, in the Tablets, that the trustees of the House of Justice must select one tongue out of the present languages, or a new language, and likewise select one among the various writings and teach them to children in the schools of the world, so that the whole world may thereby be considered as one native land and one part.

The most splendid fruit of the tree of Knowledge is this exalted Word: Ye are all fruits of one tree and leaves of one branch. Glory is not his who loves his own country, but glory is his who loves his kind.

In this connection We have formerly revealed that which is the means for the prosperity of the world and the unification of nations. Blessed are those who attain! Blessed are those who practice!

THE SEVENTH ISHRÁQ:

The Supreme Pen enjoins upon all to instruct and educate the children. Upon Our arrival in the Prison, the following verses have in this connection been revealed in the Book of Aqdas, from the heaven of the divine will: It is decreed that every father must educate his sons and daughters in learning and in writing and also in that which hath been ordained in the Tablet. He who neglects that which hath been commanded, if he is rich, it is incumbent on the trustees to recover from him the amount required for the education of the children; otherwise the matter shall devolve on the House of Justice. Verily We have made it an asylum for the poor and needy.

He who educates his son, or any other's children, it is as though he hath educated one of My children. Upon such an one be My Bahá, My providence and My mercy, which hath embraced all in the world!

THE EIGHTH ISHRÁQ:

This passage is written, at this time, by the Supreme Pen and is accounted of the Book of Aqdas. The affairs of the people are in charge of the men of the House of Justice of God. They are the trustees of God among His servants and the sources of command in His countries.

O people of God! The trainer of the world is justice for it consists of two pillars, reward and retribution. These two pillars are two fountains for the life of the people of the world.

Inasmuch as for each day and time a particular decree or order is expedient, affairs are therefore entrusted to the House of Justice, so that it may execute that which it deems advisable at the time. Those souls who arise to serve the Cause sincerely, to please God, shall be inspired by the invisible inspiration of God. It is incumbent upon all to obey them.

Administrative affairs are all in charge of the House of Justice, and devotional acts must be observed according as they are revealed in the Book.

O people of Bahá! Ye are dawning-places of the love and day-springs of the favor of God. Defile not the tongues with cursing and execrating anyone and guard your eyes from that which is not worthy. Show forth that which ye possess. If it is accepted, the aim is attained; if not, interference with those who reject it is not allowable. Leave him to himself, and advance toward God, the protector, the self-subsistent. Be not the cause of sorrow, how much less of sedition and strife! It is hoped ye may be trained under the shadow of the tree of divine favor and act in that which God desireth. Ye are all leaves of one tree and drops of one sea.

The Ninth Ishráq:

The religion of God and the creed of God hath been revealed and made manifest from the heaven of the will of the king of pre-existence for the sake of union and harmony among the people of the world; make it not a means for disagreement and discord!

The religion of God and His law is the greatest cause and mightiest means for the appearance and effulgence of the orb of unity. The development of the world, the training of nations, the tranquillity of the servants and the security of the people of all lands have been due to the divine precepts and ordinances. Religion is the greatest cause for the appearance of this great gift. It bestows the cup of vitality, confers immortal life and imparts eternal benefit to the people. The rulers of the earth, especially the trustees of the House of Justice, must make abundant effort to preserve this station and guard and promote it. Likewise it is necessary that they should inquire into the conditions of the subjects and be acquainted with the deeds and affairs of every one in the communities.

We ask the manifestors of the divine power, that is, kings and leaders, to endeavor, perchance discord may vanish and the world be illumined with the light of accord. All must adhere to and practice that which hath been revealed from the Supreme Pen. The true One testifies and the atoms of the universe bear witness that We have spoken and revealed in Tablets and Epistles from the Supreme Pen that which is conducive to the exaltation, elevation, training, protection and progress of the people of the earth. We beg of God to strengthen the servants. What this oppressed One requires of all is justice and equity. Let them not satisfy themselves with mere hearing, but reflect upon that which hath proceeded from this oppressed One. I swear by the sun of divine utterance which hath arisen from the horizon of the kingdom of the clement One, that were there an exponent or speaker to be found We would not have made ourself an object of censure, derision and calumnies on the part of the people.

Upon Our arrival at 'Iráq, the Cause of God was in a state of inactivity and the fragrances of Revelation had ceased. Most of the believers were found to be withered, nay dead! Therefore, the Trumpet was sounded "for a second time" and this blessed Word flowed from the Tongue of Grandeur: "We have blown in the trumpet for a second time." Thus We quickened the world with the fragrances of revelation and inspiration!

Now, from behind every covering, souls have emerged, intent upon persecuting this wronged One. They have obstructed the flowing of this mighty benefit and have rejected it!

O people of justice! If this matter were to be denied, what matter in this earth can be worthy of demonstration, or deserves to be acknowledged? The contradictors are collecting the verses of this Manifestation, and with whomsoever they have found them, have seized them by the means of showing love. With every sect, they account themselves of the same sect! Say, die ye in your wrath; verily, He hath come with a matter which no possessor of sight, bearing, perspicacity, justice and equity can deny. Whereunto testifieth the Pen of pre-existence at this manifest time!

O Jalál! Upon thee be My glory! We commend the friends of the true One to good deeds; perchance they may succeed and act in accord with that which hath been revealed from the heaven of command. The benefit of the utterance of the merciful One goes to those who practice. We beg of God to strengthen them in that which He loveth and approveth, to enable them to act with justice and equity in this irrefutable command, to make known unto them His signs and to direct them unto His right path.

His Holiness, the Precursor (the Báb)—May the lives of all

else save Him be a sacrifice to Him!—hath revealed Ordinances, but the world of Command hath been made dependent upon Our acceptance. This wronged One has, therefore, enforced some of them and revealed them in a different text, in the Book of Aqdas, while We have not adopted some others. The matter is in His hand. He doeth whatsoever He willeth and ordereth whatsoever He desireth, and He is the mighty, the praised One!

Some other commandments have been also revealed in the style of prayer. Blessed are those who attain! Blessed are those who practice! . . .

CHAPTER FIVE

THE MYSTERY OF GOD

TABLET OF THE BRANCH

He is Eternal in His Abhá Horizon!

Verily, the Cause of God hath come upon the clouds of utterances and the polytheists are in this day in great torment! Verily, the hosts of revelation have descended with banners of inspiration from the heaven of the Tablet in the name of God, the powerful, the mighty! At this time the monotheists all rejoice in the victory of God and His dominion, and the deniers will then be in manifest perplexity.

O ye people! Do ye flee from the mercy of God after it has encompassed the existent things created between the heavens and earths? Beware lest ye prefer your own selves before the mercy of God, and deprive not yourselves thereof! Verily, whosoever turneth away therefrom will be in great loss. Verily, mercy is like unto verses which have descended from the one heaven, and from them the monotheists drink the choice wine of life, whilst the polytheists drink from the fiery water; and when the verses of God are read unto them, the fire of hatred is enkindled within their breasts. Thus have they preferred their own selves before the mercy of God, and are of those who are heedless.

Enter, O people, beneath the shelter of the Word! Then drink therefrom the choice wine of inner significances and utterances; for therein is hidden the kawt͟her of the glorious One—and it hath appeared from the horizon of the Will of your Lord, the merciful, with wonderful lights.

Say: Verily, the ocean of pre-existence hath branched forth from this most great Ocean. Blessed, therefore, is he who abides upon Its shores, and is of those who are established thereon. Verily, this most sacred temple of Abhá—the Branch of Holiness—hath branched forth from the Sadratu'l-Muntahá. Blessed is whosoever sought shelter beneath it and is of those who rest therein.

Say: Verily, the branch of command hath sprung forth from this root which God hath firmly planted in the ground of the will, the limb of which has been elevated to a station which encompasses all existence. Therefore, exalted be He for this creation, the lofty, the blessed, the inaccessible, the mighty!

O ye people! Draw nigh unto It, and taste the fruits of its knowledge and wisdom on the part of the mighty, the knowing One. Whosoever will not taste thereof shall be deprived of the bounty, even though he hath partaken of all that is in the earth—were ye of those who know.

Say: Verily a word hath gone forth in favor from the most great Tablet and God has adorned It with the mantle of Himself, and made it sovereign over all in the earth and a sign of His grandeur and omnipotence among the creatures; in order that, through it, the people shall praise their Lord, the mighty, the powerful, the wise; and that, through it, they shall glorify their creator and sanctify the self of God which standeth within all things. Verily, this is naught but a Revelation upon the part of the wise, the ancient One!

Say: O people, praise ye God, for its Manifestation, for verily it is the most great favor upon you and the most perfect blessing upon you; and through Him every moldering bone is quickened. Whosoever turns to Him hath surely turned unto God, and whosoever turneth away from Him hath turned away from My beauty, denied My proof and is of those who transgress. Verily, He is the remembrance of God amongst you and His trust within you, and His manifestation unto you and His appearance among the servants who are nigh. Thus have I been commanded to convey to you the message of God, your Creator; and I have delivered to you that of which I was commanded. Whereupon, thereunto testifieth God, then His angels, then His messengers, and then His holy servants.

Inhale the fragrances of the Riḍván from His roses and be not of those who are deprived. Appreciate the bounty of God upon you and be not veiled therefrom—and, verily, We have sent Him forth in the temple of man. Thus praise ye the Lord, the Originator of whatsoever He willeth through His wise and inviolable Command!

Verily, those who withhold themselves from the shelter of the Branch are indeed lost in the wilderness of perplexity; and are consumed by the heat of self-desire, and are of those who perish.

Hasten, O people, unto the shelter of God, in order that He may protect you from the heat of the Day whereon none shall find for himself any refuge or shelter except beneath the shelter of His Name, the clement, the forgiving! Clothe yourselves, O people, with the garment of assurance, in order that He may protect you from the dart of doubts and superstitions, and that ye may be of those who are assured in those days wherein none shall ever be assured and none shall be firmly established in the Cause, except by severing himself from all that is possessed by the people and turning unto the holy and radiant Outlook.

O ye people! Do ye take unto yourselves the Jebt as a helper other than God, and do ye seek the Taghoot as a Lord besides your Lord the almighty, the omnipotent? Forsake, O people, their mention, then hold the chalice of life in the Name of your Lord, the merciful. Verily, by God, the existent world is quickened through a drop thereof, were ye of those who know.

Say: In that Day there is no refuge for any one save the command of God, and no salvation for any soul but God. Verily, this is the truth and there is naught after truth but manifest error.

Verily, God hath made it incumbent upon every soul to deliver His Cause according to his ability. Thus hath the command been recorded by the finger of might and power upon the Tablet of majesty and greatness.

Whosoever quickens one soul in this Cause is like unto one quickening all the servants and the Lord shall bring him forth in the day of resurrection into the Riḍván of oneness, adorned with the Mantle of Himself, the protector, the mighty, the generous! Thus will ye assist your Lord, and naught else save this shall ever be mentioned in this day before God, your Lord and the Lord of your forefathers.

As to thee, O servant, hearken unto the admonition given unto thee in the Tablet; then seek the grace of thy Lord at all times. Then spread the Tablet among those who believe in God and in His verses; so that they may follow that which is contained therein, and be of those who are praiseworthy.

Say: O people, cause no corruption in the earth and dispute not with men; for, verily, this is not worthy of those who have chosen in the shelter of their Lord a station which shall indeed remain secure.

If ye find one athirst, give him to drink from the chalice of Kawtha and Tasneen; and if ye find one endowed with an attentive ear, read unto him the verses of God, the mighty, the merciful, the compassionate! Unloose the tongue with excellent utterance, then admonish the people if ye find them advancing unto the sanctuary of God; otherwise abandon them unto themselves and forsake them in the abyss of hell. Beware lest ye scatter the pearls of inner significance before every barren, dumb one. Verily, the blind are deprived of witnessing the lights and are unable to distinguish between the stone and the holy, precious pearl.

Verily, wert thou to read the most mighty, wonderful verses to the stone for a thousand years, will it understand, or will they take any effect therein? No! by thy Lord, the merciful, the clement! If thou readest all the verses of God unto the deaf, will he hear a single letter? No! Verily, by the beauty, the mighty, the ancient!

Thus have We delivered unto thee some of the jewels of wisdom and utterance, in order that thou mayest gaze unto the direction of thy Lord and be severed from all the creatures. May the spirit and glory rest upon thee, and upon those who dwell upon the plain of holiness and who remain in the Cause of their Lord in manifest steadfastness!

KITÁB-I-'AHD

Although the Most High Horizon is devoid of trivial possessions of the earth, we have nevertheless bequeathed unto our heirs a noble and peerless heritage within the treasure-house of trust and resignation.

We have left no treasure nor have we added to man's pains.

By the Life of God! In earthly riches fear is hidden and peril is concealed. Consider, then take warning by what the God of Mercy hath revealed in the Qur'án:—

"Woe unto those who malign and speak evil of their fellows; who hoard earthly goods and count their riches."

Earthly possessions are unstable; wherefore whatsoever passeth or suffereth vicissitudes is unworthy of regard except to a limited measure.

In bearing hardships and tribulations and in revealing verses and expounding proofs, it has been the purpose of this oppressed One to extinguish the fire of hate and animosity, that, haply, the horizons of the hearts of mankind be illumined with the light of concord and attain real tranquillity.

The light of the following utterance shineth from the horizon of the Divine Tablet, which should be observed by all: Oh people of the world! I counsel you to act in a manner which shall tend to elevate your stations. Cling to divine virtue and obey the divine law. Truly I say, the tongue is for mentioning that which is good; do not defile it by evil speech. "God hath forgiven your past ways." You must henceforth speak that which is worthy. Shun reviling, maligning, and whatsoever will offend your fellowmen.

Man's station is great. Ere this, the following exalted words have flowed forth from the Pen of Abhá:

This is a Day great and blessed. Whatsoever was hidden in man is today being revealed. The station of man is great, were he to cling to truth and righteousness and be firm and steadfast in the Cause. Before the God of Mercy, a true man appears like unto heaven. The sun and the moon of that heaven are his sight and hearing and its stars are his shining attributes. His station is the highest and his signs are the educator of the world.

In this Day, every believer who discovered the fragrance of the garment and turned with a pure heart unto the most high horizon is indeed recorded in the Crimson Tablet as of the people of Bahá.

Hold the chalice of My grace in My name. Then drain it in My mention, the mighty, the wonderful!

Oh people of the world! The religion of God is to create love and unity; do not make it the cause of enmity and discord. All that is regarded by men of insight and the people of the most lofty outlook as the means for safeguarding and effecting the peace and tranquillity of man, has flowed from the Supreme Pen. But the ignorant ones who are the victim of self and desire, are heedless of the consummate wisdom of the truly wise One, and their words and deeds are prompted by fancy and superstition.

Oh ye chosen of God and His trusted ones! Kings are the manifestors of God's power and the source of His majesty and affluence. Pray ye in their behalf. The government of the earth has been vouchsafed unto them. But the hearts of men He decreed unto Himself. He forbade conflict and strife—a rigid prohibition in the Book. This is the Decree of God in this most great Manifestation; and God hath preserved it from annulment and clothed it with the broidered garment of confirmation. Verily, He is the all-knowing, the all-wise!

It is incumbent upon all to support those rulers and chiefs of state who are adorned with the raiment of justice and equity. Blessed are the rulers and the learned in el-Bahá! They verily are My trustees amongst My servants, and the sources of My Decrees amongst My people. Upon them rest My Bahá, My mercy, and My grace which hath encircled the world!

Anent this matter, we have revealed in the Book of Aqdas the following words which radiate the light of divine mercy:

Oh my Branches! A mighty power and supreme potency is hidden and concealed in the world of being. Focus your gaze upon it and upon the direction of its unity, not upon the differences which are apparent therein.

God's Will and Testament enjoins upon the branches, the twigs, and the kinsfolk, one and all, to gaze unto the most great Branch. Consider what we have revealed in my Book of Aqdas, to wit:

"When the sea of My Presence is exhausted and the Book of Origin hath reached its end, turn you unto him ('Abdu'l-Bahá) who is desired by God—he who is issued from this ancient Root."

The purpose of this sacred verse is the most great Branch. Thus have we declared the matter as a favor on our part, and we are the gracious, the beneficent!

God hath, verily, decreed the station of the great Branch next to that of the most great Branch. Verily He is the wise ordainer. We have chosen el-Akbar after the el'A'sam, as a command on the part of God, the all-knowing, the omniscient.

All must regard the other Branches with affection, but God hath not decreed unto them any right to the people's property.

Oh my branches, my twigs, and my kinsfolk! I counsel you to manifest divine virtue, and to act in accord with the Law, and with whatsoever is befitting and will elevate your stations.

Truly I say, virtue is the greatest commander which leads the Cause of God to victory, and the legions which deserve this commander are pure, sanctified and praiseworthy deeds and attributes.

Say: Oh servants! Do not make the cause of order a cause for disorder, nor the means of unity a means for disunity. It is hoped that the people of Bahá will observe the sacred verse: "Say, all are created by God." This lofty utterance is like unto water for quenching the fire of hate and hostility which is hidden and stored in men's hearts and minds. This single utterance will cause the various sects and creeds to attain the light of true unity. Verily He speaketh truth and guideth to the right path; and He is the mighty, the glorious, the omnipotent.

For the honor of the Cause and the promotion of the Word—it is necessary that all shall respect and have regard for the Branches. This command has been recorded once and again in the divine Book. Blessed is he who obeys whatsoever hath been ordained on the part of God, the ancient ruler. All shall also have respect for the women-members of Our household and for the afnán and kinsfolk. We likewise counsel you to serve mankind and bring peace to the world.

All that leads to the quickening of the peoples and the salvation of the world hath been revealed from the kingdom of utterance by the Lord of mankind. Hearken to the exhortations of the Supreme Pen with ideal ears. These are preferable unto you above all that is on the earth. Whereunto beareth witness my Book, the blessed, the glorious!

Whoso Layeth Claim to a Revelation

Whoso layeth claim to a Revelation direct from God, ere the expiration of a full thousand years, such a man is assuredly a lying impostor. We pray God that He may graciously assist him to retract and repudiate such claim. Should he repent, God will, no doubt, forgive him. If, however, he persisteth in his error, God will, assuredly, send down one who will deal mercilessly with him. Terrible, indeed, is God in punishing! Whosoever interpreteth this verse otherwise than its obvious meaning is deprived of the Spirit of God and of His mercy which encompasseth all created things. Fear God, and follow not your idle fancies. Nay, rather follow the bidding of your Lord, the Almighty, the All-Wise.

II

WORDS OF ‘ABDUL-BAHÁ

CHAPTER SIX

THE FAITH OF BAHÁ'U'LLÁH

Mankind Is in Danger

O people of the world!

The dawn of the Sun of Reality is assuredly for the illumination of the world and for the manifestation of mercy. In the assemblage of the family of Adam results and fruits are praiseworthy, and the holy bestowals of every bounty are abundant. It is an absolute mercy and a complete bounty, the illumination of the world, fellowship and harmony, love and union; nay, rather, mercifulness and oneness, the elimination of discord and the unity of whosoever are on the earth in the utmost of freedom and dignity. The Blessed Beauty said: "All are the fruits of one tree and the leaves of one branch." He likened the world of existence to one tree and all the souls to leaves, blossoms and fruits. Therefore all the branches, leaves, blossoms and fruits must be in the utmost of freshness, and the bringing about of this delicacy and sweetness depends upon union and fellowship. Therefore they must assist each other with all their power and seek everlasting life. Thus the friends of God must manifest the mercy of the Compassionate Lord in the world of existence and must show forth the bounty of the visible and invisible King. They must purify their sight, and look upon mankind as the leaves, blossoms and fruits of the tree of creation, and must always be thinking of doing good to someone, of love, consideration, affection and assistance to somebody. They must see no enemy and count no one as an ill wisher. They must consider every one on the earth as a friend; regard the stranger as an intimate, and the alien as a companion. They must not be bound by any tie, nay, rather, they should be free from every bond. In this day the one who is favored in the threshold of grandeur is the one who offers the cup of faithfulness and bestows the pearl of gift to the enemies, even to the fallen oppressor, lends a helping hand, and considers every bitter foe as an affectionate friend.

These are the commands of the Blessed Beauty, these are the counsels of the Greatest Name. O ye dear friends! The world is engaged in war and struggle, and mankind is in the utmost conflict and danger. The darkness of unfaithfulness has enshrouded the earth and the illumination of faithfulness has become concealed. All nations and tribes of the world have sharpened their claws and are warring and fighting with each other. The edifice of man is shattered. Thousands of families are wandering disconsolate. Thousands of souls are besmeared with dust and blood in the arena of battle and struggle every year, and the tent of happiness and life is overthrown. The prominent men become commanders and boast of bloodshed, and glory in destruction. One says: "I have severed with my sword the necks of a nation," and one: "I have levelled a kingdom to the dust"; and another: "I have overthrown the foundation of a government." This is the pivot around which the pride and glory of mankind are revolving. In all regions friendship and uprightness are denounced and reconciliation and regard for truth are despised. The herald of peace, reformation, love and reconciliation is the Religion of the Blessed Beauty which has pitched its tent on the apex of the world and proclaimed its summons to the people.

Then, O ye friends of God! Appreciate the value of this precious Revelation, move and act in accordance with it and walk in the straight path and the right way. Show it to the people. Raise the melody of the Kingdom and spread abroad the teachings and ordinances of the loving Lord so that the world may become another world, the darkened earth may become illumined and the dead body of the people may obtain new life. Every soul may seek everlasting life through the breath of the Merciful. Life in this mortal world will quickly come to an end, and this earthly glory, wealth, comfort and happiness will soon vanish and be no more. Summon ye the people to God and call the souls to the manners and conduct of the Supreme Concourse. To the orphans be ye kind fathers, and to the unfortunate a refuge and shelter. To the poor be a treasure of wealth, and to the sick a remedy and healing. Be a helper of every oppressed one, the protector of every destitute one, be ye ever mindful to serve any soul of mankind. Attach no importance to self-seeking, rejection, arrogance, oppression and enmity. Heed them not. Deal in the contrary way. Be kind in truth, not only in appearance and outwardly. Every soul of the friends of God must concentrate his mind on this, that he may manifest the mercy of God and the bounty of the Forgiving One. He must do good to every soul whom he encounters, and render benefit to him, becoming the cause of improving the morals and correcting the thoughts so that the light of guidance may shine forth and the bounty of His Holiness the Merciful One may encompass. Love is light in whatsoever house it may shine and enmity is darkness in whatsoever abode it dwell.

O friends of God! Strive ye so that this darkness may be utterly dispelled and the Hidden Mystery may be revealed and the realities of things made evident and manifest.

I Have Come With This Mission

I have come from distant lands to visit the meetings and assemblies of this country. In every meeting I find people gathered loving each other; therefore I am greatly pleased. The bond of union is evidenced in this assembly today where the power of God has brought together in faith, agreement and concord those who are engaged in furthering the development of the human world. It is my hope that all mankind may become similarly united in the bond and agreement of love. Unity is the expression of the loving power of God and reflects the reality of divinity. It is resplendent in this day through the bestowals of light upon humanity.

Throughout the universe the divine power is effulgent in endless images and pictures. The world of creation, the world of humanity may be likened to the earth itself and the divine power to the sun. This Sun has shone upon all mankind. In the endless variety of its reflections the divine will is manifested. Consider how all are recipients of the bounty of the same Sun. At most the difference between them is that of degree, for the effulgence is one effulgence, the one light emanating from the Sun. This will express the oneness of the world of humanity. The body-politic or the social unity of the human world may be likened to an ocean and each member, each individual a wave upon that same ocean.

The light of the sun becomes apparent in each object according to the capacity of that object. The difference is simply one of degree and receptivity. The stone would be a recipient only to a limited extent; another created thing might be as a mirror wherein the sun is fully reflected; but the same light shines upon both.

The most important thing is to polish the mirrors of hearts in order that they may become illumined and receptive of the divine light. One heart may possess the capacity of the polished mirror; another be covered and obscured by the dust and dross of this world. Although the same Sun is shining upon both, in the mirror which is polished, pure and sanctified you may behold the Sun in all its fullness, glory and power revealing its majesty and effulgence, but in the mirror which is rusted and obscured there is no capacity for reflection although so far as the Sun itself is concerned it is shining thereon and is neither lessened nor deprived. Therefore our duty lies in seeking to polish the mirrors of our hearts in order that we shall become reflectors of that light and recipients of the divine bounties which may be fully revealed through them.

This means the oneness of the world of humanity. That is to say, when this human body-politic reaches a state of absolute unity, the effulgence of the eternal Sun will make its fullest light and heat manifest. Therefore we must not make distinctions between individual members of the human family. We must not consider any soul as barren or deprived. Our duty lies in educating souls so that the Sun of the bestowals of God shall become resplendent in them, and this is possible through the power of the oneness of humanity. The more love is expressed among mankind and the stronger the power of unity, the greater will be this reflection and revelation, for the greatest bestowal of God is love. Love is the source of all the bestowals of God. Until love takes possession of the heart no other divine bounty can be revealed in it.

All the prophets have striven to make love manifest in the hearts of men. His Holiness Jesus Christ sought to create this love in the hearts. He suffered all difficulties and ordeals that perchance the human heart might become the fountain-source of love. Therefore we must strive with all our heart and soul that this love may take possession of us so that all humanity whether it be in the east or in the west may be connected through the bond of this divine affection; for we are all the waves of one sea; we have come into being through the same bestowal and are recipients from the same center. The lights of earth are all acceptable, but the center of effulgence is the sun and we must direct our gaze to the sun. God is the supreme center. The more we turn toward this center of light, the greater will be our capacity.

In the Orient there were great differences among races and peoples. They hated each other and there was no association among them. Various and divergent sects were hostile, irreconcilable. The different races were in constant war and conflict. About sixty years ago Bahá’u’lláh appeared upon the eastern horizon. He caused love and unity to become manifest among these antagonistic peoples. He united them with the bond of love; their former hatred and animosity passed away; love and unity reigned instead. It was a dark world; it became radiant. A new springtime appeared through him, for the Sun of Truth had risen again. In the fields and meadows of human hearts variegated flowers of inner significance were blooming and the good fruits of the kingdom of God became manifest.

I have come here with this mission; that through your endeavors, through your heavenly morals, through your devoted efforts a perfect bond of unity and love may be established between the east and the west, so that the bestowals of God may descend upon all and that all may be seen to be the parts of the same tree,—the great tree of the human family. For mankind may be likened to the branches, leaves, blossoms and fruit of that tree.

The favors of God are unending, limitless. Infinite bounties have encompassed the world. We must emulate the bounties of God, and just as each one of them—the bounty of life for instance—surrounds and encompasses all, so likewise must we be connected and blended together until each part shall become the expression of the whole.

Consider; we plant a seed. A complete and perfect tree appears from it, and from each seed of this tree another tree can be produced. Therefore the part is expressive of the whole, for this seed was a part of the tree, but therein potentially was the whole tree. So each one of us may become expressive or representative of all the bounties of life to mankind. This is the unity of the world of humanity. This is the bestowal of God. This is the felicity of the human world and this is the manifestation of the divine favor.

The Blessed Perfection, Bahá'u'lláh

The Blessed Perfection Bahá'u'lláh belonged to the royal family of Írán. From earliest childhood He was distinguished among His relatives and friends. They said: "This child has extraordinary power." In wisdom, intelligence and as a source of new knowledge He was advanced beyond His age and superior to His surroundings. All who knew Him were astonished at his precocity. It was usual for them to say: "Such a child will not live," for it is commonly believed that precocious children do not reach maturity. During the period of youth the Blessed Perfection did not enter school. He was not willing to be taught. This fact is well established among the Íránians of Ṭihrán. Nevertheless He was capable of solving the difficult problems of all who came to Him. In whatever meeting, scientific assembly or theological discussion He was found, He became the authority of explanation upon intricate and abstruse questions presented.

Until His father passed away Bahá'u'lláh did not seek position or political station notwithstanding His connection with the government. This occasioned surprise and comment. It was frequently said: "How is it that a young man of such keen intelligence and subtle perception does not seek lucrative appointments? As a matter of fact every position is open to him." This is a historical statement fully attested by the people of Írán.

He was most generous, giving abundantly to the poor. None who came to Him were turned away. The doors of His house were open to all. He always had many guests. This unbounded generosity was conducive to greater astonishment from the fact that He sought neither position nor prominence. In commenting upon this His friends said He would become impoverished, for His expenses were many and His wealth becoming more and more limited. "Why is he not thinking of his own affairs?", they inquired of each other; but some who were wise declared: "This personage is connected with another world; he has something sublime within him that is not evident now; the day is coming when it will be manifested." In truth the Blessed Perfection was a refuge for every weak one, a shelter for every fearing one, kind to every indigent one, lenient and loving to all creatures.

He became well known in regard to these qualities before His Holiness the Báb appeared. Then Bahá'u'lláh declared the Báb's mission to be true and promulgated His teachings. The Báb announced that the greater manifestation would take place after Him and called the promised one: "Him whom God would manifest," saying that nine years later the reality of His own mission would become apparent. In His writings He stated that in the ninth year this expected one would be known; in the ninth year they would attain to all glory and felicity; in the ninth year they would advance rapidly. Between Bahá'u'lláh and the Báb there was communication privately. The Báb wrote a letter containing three hundred and sixty derivatives of the root "Bahá." The Báb was martyred in Tabríz, and Bahá'u'lláh exiled into 'Iráq-Arabie in 1852, announced Himself in Baghdád. For the Íránian Government had decided that as long as He remained in Írán the peace of the country would be disturbed; therefore He was exiled in the expectation that Írán would become quiet. His banishment, however, produced the opposite effect. New tumult arose and the mention of His greatness and influence spread everywhere throughout the country. The proclamation of His manifestation and mission was made in Baghdád. He called his friends together there and spoke to them of God. Afterward He left the city and went alone into the mountains of Kurdistán where He made his abode in caves and grottoes. A part of this time He lived in the city of Sulimaniyye. Two years passed during which neither His friends nor family knew just where He was.

Although solitary, secluded and unknown in His retirement, the report spread throughout Kurdistán that this was a most remarkable and learned personage gifted with a wonderful power of attraction. In a short time Kurdistán was magnetized with His love. During this period Bahá'u'lláh lived in poverty. His garments were those of the poor and needy. His food was that of the indigent and lowly. An atmosphere of majesty haloed Him as the sun at midday. Everywhere He was greatly revered and beloved.

After two years He returned to Baghdád. Friends He had known in Sulimaniyye came to visit Him. They found Him in his accustomed environment of ease and affluence and were astonished at the appointments of one who had lived in seclusion under such frugal conditions in Kurdistán.

The Íránian government believed the banishment of the Blessed Perfection from Írán would be the extermination of His Cause in that country. These rulers now realized that it spread more rapidly. His prestige increased, His teachings became more widely circulated. The chiefs of Írán then used their influence to have Bahá'u'lláh exiled from Baghdád. He was summoned to Constantinople by the Turkish authorities. While in Constantinople He ignored every restriction, especially the hostility of ministers of state and clergy. The official representatives of Írán again brought their influence to bear upon the Turkish authorities and succeeded in having Bahá'u'lláh banished from Constantinople to Adrianople, the object being to keep Him as far away as possible from Írán and render His communication with that country more difficult. Nevertheless the Cause still spread and strengthened.

Finally they consulted together and said: "We have banished Bahá'u'lláh from place to place but each time he is exiled his cause is more widely extended, his proclamation increases in power and day by day his lamp is becoming brighter. This is due to the fact that we have exiled him to large cities and populous centers. Therefore we will send him to a penal colony as a prisoner so that all may know he is the associate of murderers, robbers and criminals; in a short time he and his followers will perish." The sultan of Turkey then banished Him to the prison of 'Akká in Syria.

When Bahá'u'lláh arrived at 'Akká, through the power of God He was able to hoist His banner. His light at first had been a star;

now it became a mighty sun and the illumination of His Cause expanded from the east to the west. Inside prison walls He wrote epistles to all the kings and rulers of nations summoning them to arbitration and Universal Peace. Some of the kings received His words with disdain and contempt. One of these was the sultan of the Ottoman kingdom. Napoleon III of France did not reply. A second epistle was addressed to him. It stated: "I have written you an epistle before this, summoning you to the cause of God but you are of the heedless. You have proclaimed that you were the defender of the oppressed; now it hath become evident that you are not. Nor are you kind to your own suffering and oppressed people. Your actions are contrary to your own interests and your kingly pride must fall. Because of your arrogance God shortly will destroy your sovereignty. France will flee away from you and you will be overwhelmed by a great conquest. There will be lamentation and mourning, women bemoaning the loss of their sons." This arraignment of Napoleon III was published and spread.

Read it and consider: One prisoner, single and solitary, without assistant or defender, a foreigner and stranger imprisoned in the fortress of 'Akká writing such letters to the emperor of France and sultan of Turkey. Reflect upon this how Bahá'u'lláh upraised the standard of His Cause in prison. Refer to history. It is without parallel. No such thing has happened before that time nor since; a prisoner and an exile advancing His Cause and spreading His teachings broadcast so that eventually He became powerful enough to conquer the very king who banished Him.

His Cause spread more and more. The Blessed Perfection was a prisoner twenty-five years. During all this time He was subjected to the indignities and revilement of the people. He was persecuted, mocked and put in chains. In Írán His properties were pillaged and His possessions confiscated. First, banishment from Írán to Baghdád; then to Constantinople; then Adrianople; finally from Roumelia to the prison fortress of 'Akká.

During His lifetime He was intensely active. His energy was unlimited. Scarcely one night was passed in restful sleep. He bore these ordeals, suffered these calamities and difficulties in order that a manifestation of selflessness and service might become apparent in the world of humanity; that the Most Great Peace should become a reality; that human souls might appear as the angels of heaven; that heavenly miracles would be wrought among men; that human faith should be strengthened and perfected; that the precious, priceless bestowal of God, the human mind, might be developed to its fullest capacity in the temple of the body; and man become the reflection and likeness of God, even as it hath been revealed in the Bible: "We shall create man in Our own image."

Briefly; the Blessed Perfection bore all these ordeals and calamities in order that our hearts might become enkindled and radiant, our spirits be glorified, our faults become virtues, our ignorance transformed into knowledge; in order that we might attain the real fruits of humanity and acquire heavenly graces; although pilgrims upon earth we should travel the road of the heavenly kingdom; although needy and poor we might receive the treasures of life eternal. For this has He borne these difficulties and sorrows.

Trust all to God. The lights of God are resplendent. The blessed epistles are spreading. The blessed teachings are promulgated throughout the east and west. Soon you will see that the heavenly words have established the oneness of the world of humanity. The banner of the Most Great Peace has been unfurled and the "great community" is appearing.

Religion Is Progressive

Religion is the outer expression of the divine reality. Therefore it must be living, vitalized, moving and progressive. If it be without motion and non-progressive it is without the divine life; it is dead. The divine institutes are continuously active and evolutionary; therefore the revelation of them must be progressive and continuous. All things are subject to re-formation. This is a century of life and renewal. Sciences and arts, industry and invention have been reformed. Law and ethics have been reconstituted, reorganized. The world of thought has been regenerated. Sciences of former ages and philosophies of the past are useless today. Present exigencies demand new methods of solution; world problems are without precedent. Old ideas and modes of thought are fast becoming obsolete. Ancient laws and archaic ethical systems will not meet the requirements of modern conditions, for this is clearly the century of a new life, the century of the revelation of the reality and therefore the greatest of all centuries. Consider how the scientific developments of fifty years have surpassed and eclipsed the knowledge and achievements of all the former ages combined. Would the announcements and theories of ancient astronomers explain our present knowledge of the sun-worlds and planetary systems? Would the mask of obscurity which beclouded mediaeval centuries meet the demand for clear-eyed vision and understanding which characterizes the world today? Will the despotism of former governments answer the call for freedom which has risen from the heart of humanity in this cycle of illumination? It is evident that no vital results are now forthcoming from the customs, institutions and standpoints of the past. In view of this, shall blind imitations of ancestral forms and theological interpretations continue to guide and control the religious life and spiritual development of humanity today? Shall man gifted with the power of reason unthinkingly follow and adhere to dogma, creeds and hereditary beliefs which will not bear the analysis of reason in this century of effulgent reality? Unquestionably this will not satisfy men of science, for when they find premise or conclusion contrary to present standards of proof and without real foundation, they reject that which has been formerly accepted as standard and correct and move forward from new foundations.

The divine prophets have revealed and founded religion. They have laid down certain laws and heavenly principles for the guidance of mankind. They have taught and promulgated the knowledge of God, established praiseworthy ethical ideals and inculcated the highest standards of virtues in the human world. Gradually these heavenly teachings and foundations of reality have been beclouded by human interpretations and dogmatic imitations of ancestral beliefs. The essential realities which the prophets labored so hard to establish in human hearts and minds while undergoing ordeals and suffering tortures of persecution, have now well nigh vanished. Some of these heavenly messengers have been killed, some imprisoned; all of them despised and rejected while proclaiming the reality of divinity. Soon after their departure from this world, the essential truth of their teachings was lost sight of and dogmatic imitations adhered to.

Inasmuch as human interpretations and blind imitations differ widely, religious strife and disagreement have arisen among mankind, the light of true religion has been extinguished and the unity of the world of humanity destroyed. The prophets of God voiced the spirit of unity and agreement. They have been the founders of divine reality. Therefore if the nations of the world forsake imitations and investigate the reality underlying the revealed Word of God they will agree and become reconciled. For reality is one and not multiple.

The nations and religions are steeped in blind and bigoted imitations. A man is a Jew because his father was a Jew. The Muḥammadan follows implicitly the footsteps of his ancestors in belief and observance. The Buddhist is true to his heredity as a Buddhist. That is to say they profess religious belief blindly and without investigation, making unity and agreement impossible. It is evident therefore that this condition will not be remedied without a reformation in the world of religion. In other words the fundamental reality of the divine religions must be renewed, reformed, revoiced to mankind.

From the seed of reality, religion has grown into a tree which has put forth leaves and branches, blossoms and fruit. After a time this tree has fallen into a condition of decay. The leaves and blossoms have withered and perished; the tree has become stricken and fruitless. It is not reasonable that man should hold to the old tree, claiming that its life forces are undiminished, its fruit unequalled, its existence eternal. The seed of reality must be sown again in human hearts in order that a new tree may grow therefrom and new divine fruits refresh the world. By this means the nations and peoples now divergent in religion will be brought into unity, imitations will be forsaken and a universal brotherhood in the reality itself will be established. Warfare and strife will cease among mankind; all will be reconciled as servants of God. For all are sheltered beneath the tree of His providence and mercy. God is kind to all; He is the giver of bounty to all alike, even as His

Holiness Jesus Christ has declared that God "sendeth rain on the just and on the unjust"; that is to say, the mercy of God is universal. All humanity is under the protection of His love and favor, and unto all He has pointed the way of guidance and progress.

Progress is of two kinds, material and spiritual. The former is attained through observation of the surrounding existence and constitutes the foundation of civilization. Spiritual progress is through the breaths of the Holy Spirit and is the awakening of the conscious soul of man to perceive the reality of divinity. Material progress insures the happiness of the human world. Spiritual progress insures the happiness and eternal continuance of the soul. The prophets of God have founded the laws of divine civilization. They have been the root and fundamental source of all knowledge. They have established the principles of human brotherhood or fraternity which is of various kinds, such as the fraternity of family, of race, of nation and of ethical motives. These forms of fraternity, these bonds of brotherhood are merely temporal and transient in association. They do not insure harmony and are usually productive of disagreement. They do not prevent warfare and strife; on the contrary they are selfish, restricted and fruitful causes of enmity and hatred among mankind. The spiritual brotherhood which is enkindled and established through the breaths of the Holy Spirit unites nations and removes the cause of warfare and strife. It transforms mankind into one great family and establishes the foundations of the oneness of humanity. It promulgates the spirit of international agreement and insures Universal Peace. Therefore we must investigate the foundation reality of this heavenly fraternity. We must forsake all imitations and promote the reality of the divine teachings. In accordance with these principles and actions and by the assistance of the Holy Spirit, both material and spiritual happiness shall become realized. Until all nations and peoples become united by the bonds of the Holy Spirit in this real fraternity, until national and international prejudices are effaced in the reality of this spiritual brotherhood, true progress, prosperity and lasting happiness will not be attained by man. This is the century of new and universal nationhood. Sciences have advanced, industries have progressed, politics have been reformed, liberty has been proclaimed, justice is awakening. This is the century of motion, divine stimulus and accomplishment; the century of human solidarity and altruistic service; the century of Universal Peace and the reality of the divine kingdom.

This Radiant Century

In the estimation of historians this radiant century is equivalent to one hundred centuries of the past. If comparison be made with the sum total of all former human achievements it will be found that the discoveries, scientific advancement and material civilization of this present century have equaled, yea far exceeded the progress and outcome of one hundred former centuries. The production of books and compilations of literature alone bear witness that the output of the human mind in this century has been greater and more enlightening than all the past centuries together. It is evident therefore that this century is of paramount importance. Reflect upon the miracles of accomplishment which have already characterized it, the discoveries in every realm of human research, inventions, scientific knowledge, ethical reforms and regulations established for the welfare of humanity, mysteries of nature explored, invisible forces brought into visibility and subjection, a veritable wonder-world of new phenomena and conditions heretofore unknown to man now open to his uses and further investigation. The east and west can communicate instantly. A human being can soar in the skies or speed in submarine depths. The power of steam has linked the continents. Trains cross the deserts and pierce the barriers of mountains; ships find unerring pathways upon the trackless oceans. Day by day discoveries are increasing. What a wonderful century this is! It is an age of universal reformation. Laws and statutes of governments civil and federal are in process of change and transformation. Sciences and arts are being moulded anew. Thoughts are metamorphosed. The foundations of human society are changing and strengthening. Today sciences of the past are useless. The Ptolemaic system of astronomy, numberless other systems and theories of scientific and philosophical explanation are discarded, known to be false and worthless. Ethical precedents and principles cannot be applied to the needs of the modern world. Thoughts and theories of past ages are fruitless now. Thrones and governments are crumbling and falling. All conditions and requisites of the past unfitted and inadequate for the present time, are undergoing radical reform. It is evident therefore that counterfeit and spurious religious teaching, antiquated forms of belief and ancestral imitations which are at variance with the foundation of divine reality must also pass away and be reformed. They must be abandoned and new conditions be recognized. The morals of humanity must undergo change. New remedy and solution for human problems must be adopted. Human intellects themselves must change and be subject to the universal reformation. Just as the thoughts and hypotheses of past ages are fruitless today, likewise dogmas and codes of human invention are obsolete and barren of product in religion. Nay, it is true that they are the cause of enmity and conducive to strife in the world of humanity; war and bloodshed proceed from them and the oneness of mankind finds no recognition in their observance. Therefore it is our duty in this radiant century to investigate the essentials of divine religion, seek the realities underlying the oneness of the world of humanity and discover the source of fellowship and agreement which will unite mankind in the heavenly bond of love. This unity is the radiance of eternity, the divine spirituality, the effulgence of God and the bounty of the Kingdom. We must investigate the divine source of these heavenly bestowals and adhere unto them steadfastly. For if we remain fettered and restricted by human inventions and dogmas, day by day the world of mankind will be degraded, day by day warfare and strife will increase and satanic forces converge toward the destruction of the human race.

If love and agreement are manifest in a single family, that family will advance, become illumined and spiritual; but if enmity and hatred exist within it destruction and dispersion are inevitable. This is likewise true of a city. If those who dwell within it manifest a spirit of accord and fellowship it will progress steadily and human conditions become brighter whereas through enmity and strife it will be degraded and its inhabitants scattered. In the same way the people of a nation develop and advance toward civilization and enlightenment through love and accord, and are disintegrated by war and strife. Finally, this is true of humanity itself in the aggregate. When love is realized and the ideal spiritual bonds unite the hearts of men, the whole human race will be uplifted, the world will continually grow more spiritual and radiant and the happiness and tranquillity of mankind be immeasurably increased. Warfare and strife will be uprooted, disagreement and dissension pass away and Universal Peace unite the nations and peoples of the world. All mankind will dwell together as one family, blend as the waves of one sea, shine as stars of one firmament and appear as fruits of the same tree. This is the happiness and felicity of humankind. This is the illumination of man, the glory eternal and life everlasting; this is the divine bestowal. I desire this station for you and I pray God that the people of America may achieve this great end in order that the virtue of this democracy may be insured and their names be glorified eternally. May the confirmations of God uphold them in all things and their memories become revered throughout the east and the west. May they become the servants of the Most High God, near and dear to Him in the oneness of the heavenly Kingdom.

His Holiness Bahá'u'lláh endured ordeals and hardships sixty years. There was no persecution, vicissitude or suffering He did not experience at the hand of His enemies and oppressors. All the days of His life were passed in difficulty and tribulation; at one time in prison, another in exile, sometimes in chains. He willingly endured these difficulties for the unity of mankind, praying that the world of humanity might realize the radiance of God, the oneness of humankind become a reality, strife and warfare cease and peace and tranquillity be realized by all. In prison He hoisted the banner of human solidarity, proclaiming Universal Peace, writing to the kings and rulers of nations summoning them to international unity and counselling arbitration. His life was a vortex of persecution and difficulty, yet catastrophes, extreme ordeals and vicissitudes did not hinder the accomplishment of His work and mission. Nay, on the contrary His power became greater and greater, His efficiency and influence spread and increased until His glorious light shone throughout the Orient, love and unity were established and the differing religions found a center of contact and reconciliation.

Therefore we also must strive in this pathway of love and service, sacrificing life and possessions, passing our days in devotion, consecrating our efforts wholly to the cause of God, so that, God willing, the ensign of universal religion may be uplifted in the world of mankind and the oneness of the world of humanity be established.

In your hearts I have beheld the reflection of a great and wonderful love. The Americans have shown me uniform kindness and I entertain a deep spiritual love for them. I am pleased with the susceptibilities of your hearts. I will pray for you asking divine assistance and then say farewell.

O my God! O my God! verily these servants are turning to Thee, supplicating Thy kingdom of mercy. Verily they are attracted by Thy holiness and set aglow with the fire of Thy love, seeking confirmation from Thy wondrous kingdom and hoping for attainment in Thy heavenly realm. Verily they long for the descent of Thy bestowal, desiring illumination from the Sun of Reality. O Lord! make them radiant lamps, merciful signs, fruitful trees and shining stars. May they come forth in Thy service and be connected with Thee by the bonds and ties of thy love, longing for the lights of Thy favor. O Lord! make them signs of guidance, standards of Thy immortal kingdom, waves of the sea of Thy mercy, mirrors of the light of Thy majesty. Verily Thou art the generous! Verily Thou art the merciful! Verily Thou art the precious, the beloved!

The Most Great Peace

Today there is no greater glory for man than that of service in the cause of the "Most Great Peace." Peace is light whereas war is darkness. Peace is life; war is death. Peace is guidance; war is error. Peace is the foundation of God; war is satanic institution. Peace is the illumination of the world of humanity; war is the destroyer of human foundations. When we consider outcomes in the world of existence we find that peace and fellowship are factors of upbuilding and betterment whereas war and strife are the causes of destruction and disintegration. All created things are expressions of the affinity and cohesion of elementary substances, and non-existence is the absence of their attraction and agreement. Various elements unite harmoniously in composition but when these elements become discordant, repelling each other, decomposition and non-existence result. Everything partakes of this nature and is subject to this principle, for the creative foundation in all its degrees and kingdoms is an expression or outcome of love. Consider the restlessness and agitation of the human world today because of war. Peace is health and construction; war is disease and dissolution. When the banner of truth is raised, peace becomes the cause of the welfare and advancement of the human world. In all cycles and ages war has been a factor of derangement and discomfort whereas peace and brotherhood have brought security and consideration of human interests. This distinction is especially pronounced in the present world conditions, for warfare in former centuries had not attained the degree of savagery and destructiveness which now characterizes it. If two nations were at war in olden times, ten or twenty thousand would be sacrificed but in this century the destruction of one hundred thousand lives in a day is quite possible. So perfected has the science of killing become and so efficient the means and instruments of its accomplishment that a whole nation can be obliterated in a short time. Therefore comparison with the methods and results of ancient warfare is out of the question.

According to an intrinsic law, all phenomena of being attain to a summit and degree of consummation, after which a new order and condition is established. As the instruments and science of war have reached the degree of thoroughness and proficiency, it is hoped that the transformation of the human world is at hand and that in the coming centuries all the energies and inventions of man will be utilized in promoting the interests of peace and brotherhood. Therefore may this esteemed and worthy society for the establishment of international peace be confirmed in its sincere intentions and empowered by God. Then will it hasten the time when the banner of universal agreement will be raised and international welfare will be proclaimed and consummated so that the darkness which now encompasses the world shall pass away.

Sixty years ago His Holiness Bahá'u'lláh was in Írán. Seventy years ago His Holiness the Báb appeared there. These two blessed souls devoted their lives to the foundation of international peace and love among mankind. They strove with heart and soul to establish the teachings by which divergent people might be brought together and no strife, rancor or hatred prevail. His Holiness Bahá'u'lláh addressing all humanity, said that Adam the parent of mankind may be likened to the tree of nativity upon which you are the leaves and blossoms. Inasmuch as your origin was one, you must now be united and agreed; you must consort with each other in joy and fragrance. He pronounced prejudice, whether religious, racial, patriotic, political, the destroyer of the body-politic. He said that man must recognize the oneness of humanity, for all in origin belong to the same household and all are servants of the same God. Therefore mankind must continue in the state of fellowship and love, emulating the institutions of God and turning away from satanic promptings, for the divine bestowals bring forth unity and agreement whereas satanic leadings induce hatred and war.

This remarkable personage was able by these principles to establish a bond of unity among the differing sects and divergent people of Írán. Those who followed His teachings no matter from what denomination or faction they came were conjoined by the ties of love, until now they cooperate and live together in peace and agreement. They are real brothers and sisters. No distinctions of class are observed among them and complete harmony prevails. Daily this bond of affinity is strengthening and their spiritual fellowship continually develops. In order to insure the progress of mankind and to establish these principles His Holiness Bahá'u'lláh suffered every ordeal and difficulty. His Holiness the Báb became a martyr, and over twenty thousand men and women sacrificed their lives for their faith. His Holiness Bahá'u'lláh was imprisoned and subjected to severe persecutions. Finally he was exiled from Írán to Mesopotamia; from Baghdád He was sent to Constantinople and

Adrianople and from thence to the prison of 'Akká in Syria. Through all these ordeals He strove day and night to proclaim the oneness of humanity and promulgate the message of Universal Peace. From the prison of 'Akká He addressed the kings and rulers of the earth in lengthy letters summoning them to international agreement and explicitly stating that the standard of the "Most Great Peace" would surely be upraised in the world.

This has come to pass. The powers of earth cannot withstand the privileges and bestowals which God has ordained for this great and glorious century. It is a need and exigency of the time. Man can withstand anything except that which is divinely intended and indicated for the age and its requirements. Now, praise be to God! in all countries of the world, lovers of peace are to be found and these principles are being spread among mankind, especially in this country. Praise be to God! this thought is prevailing and souls are continually arising as defenders of the oneness of humanity, endeavoring to assist and establish international peace. There is no doubt that this wonderful democracy will be able to realize it and the banner of international agreement will be unfurled here to spread onward and outward among all the nations of the world. I give thanks to God that I find you imbued with such susceptibilities and lofty aspirations and I hope that you will be the means of spreading this light to all men. Thus may the Sun of Reality shine upon the east and west. The enveloping clouds shall pass away and the heat of the divine rays will dispel the mist. The reality of man shall develop and come forth as the image of God his creator. The thoughts of man shall take such upward flight that former accomplishments shall appear as the play of children;—for the ideas and beliefs of the past and the prejudices regarding race and religion have ever been lowering and destructive to human evolution. I am most hopeful that in this century these lofty thoughts shall be conducive to human welfare. Let this century be the sun of previous centuries the effulgences of which shall last forever, so that in times to come they shall glorify the twentieth century, saying the twentieth century was the century of lights, the twentieth century was the century of life, the twentieth century was the century of international peace, the twentieth century was the century of divine bestowals and the twentieth century has left traces which shall last forever.

Man and Nature

From the time of the creation of Adam to this day there have been two pathways in the world of humanity; one the natural or materialistic, the other the religious or spiritual. The pathway of nature is the pathway of the animal realm. The animal acts in accordance with the requirements of nature, follows its own instincts and desires. Whatever its impulses and proclivities may be it has the liberty to gratify them; yet it is a captive of nature. It cannot deviate in the least degree from the road nature has established. It is utterly minus spiritual susceptibilities, ignorant of divine religion and without knowledge of the kingdom of God. The animal possesses no power of ideation or conscious intelligence; it is a captive of the senses and deprived of that which lies beyond them. It is subject to what the eye sees, the ear hears, the nostrils sense, the taste detects and touch reveals. These sensations are acceptable and sufficient for the animal. But that which is beyond the range of the senses, that realm of phenomena through which the conscious pathway to the kingdom of God leads, the world of spiritual susceptibilities and divine religion,—of these the animal is completely unaware, for in its highest station it is a captive of nature.

One of the strangest things witnessed is that the materialists of today are proud of their natural instincts and bondage. They state that nothing is entitled to belief and acceptance except that which is sensible or tangible. By their own statements they are captives of nature, unconscious of the spiritual world, uninformed of the divine Kingdom and unaware of heavenly bestowals. If this be a virtue the animal has attained it to a superlative degree, for the animal is absolutely ignorant of the realm of spirit and out of touch with the inner world of conscious realization. The animal would agree with the materialist in denying the existence of that which transcends the senses. If we admit that being limited to the plane of the senses is a virtue the animal is indeed more virtuous than man, for it is entirely bereft of that which lies beyond, absolutely oblivious of the kingdom of God and its traces whereas God has deposited within the human creature an illimitable power by which he can rule the world of nature.

Consider how all other phenomenal existence and beings are captives of nature. The sun, that colossal center of our solar system, the giant stars and planets, the towering mountains, the earth itself and its kingdoms of life lower than the human,—all are captives of nature except man. No other created thing can deviate in the slightest degree from obedience to natural law. The sun in its glory and greatness millions of miles away is held prisoner in its orbit of universal revolution, captive of universal natural control. Man is the ruler of nature. According to natural law and limitation he should remain upon the earth, but behold how he violates this command and soars above the mountains in aeroplanes. He sails in ships upon the surface of the ocean and dives into its depths in submarines. Man makes nature his servant; harnesses the mighty energy of electricity for instance and imprisons it in a small lamp for his uses and convenience. He speaks from the east to the west through a wire. He is able to store and preserve his voice in a phonograph. Though he is a dweller upon earth he penetrates the mysteries of starry worlds inconceivably distant. He discovers latent realities within the bosom of the earth, uncovers treasures, penetrates secrets and mysteries of the phenomenal world and brings to light that which according to nature's jealous laws should remain hidden, unknown and unfathomable. Through an ideal inner power man brings these realities forth from the invisible plane to the visible. This is contrary to nature's law.

It is evident therefore that man is ruler over nature's sphere and province. Nature is inert, man is progressive. Nature has no consciousness, man is endowed with it. Nature is without volition and acts perforce whereas man possesses a mighty will. Nature is incapable of discovering mysteries or realities whereas man is especially fitted to do so. Nature is not in touch with the realm of God, man is attuned to its evidences. Nature is uninformed of God, man is conscious of Him. Man acquires divine virtues, nature is denied them. Man can voluntarily discontinue vices, nature has no power to modify the influence of its instincts. Altogether it is evident that man is more noble and superior; that in him there is an ideal power surpassing nature. He has consciousness, volition, memory, intelligent power, divine attributes and virtues of which nature is completely deprived, bereft and minus; therefore man is higher and nobler by reason of the ideal and heavenly force latent and manifest in him.

How strange then it seems that man, notwithstanding his endowment with this ideal power, will descend to a level beneath him and declare himself no greater than that which is manifestly inferior to his real station. God has created such a conscious spirit within him that he is the most wonderful of all contingent beings. In ignoring these virtues he descends to the material plane, considers matter the ruler of existence and denies that which lies beyond. Is this virtue? In its fullest sense this is animalistic, for the animal realizes nothing more. In fact from this standpoint the animal is the greater philosopher because it is completely ignorant of the kingdom of God, possesses no spiritual susceptibilities and is uninformed of the heavenly world. In brief, this is a view of the pathway of nature.

The second pathway is that of religion, the road of the divine Kingdom. It involves the acquisition of praiseworthy attributes, heavenly illumination and righteous actions in the world of humanity. This pathway is conducive to the progress and uplift of the world. It is the source of human enlightenment, training and ethical improvement; the magnet which attracts the love of God because of the knowledge of God it bestows. This is the road of the holy Manifestations of God for they are in reality the foundation of the divine religion of oneness. There is no change or transformation in this pathway. It is the cause of human betterment, the acquisition of heavenly virtues and the illumination of mankind.

Alas! that humanity is completely submerged in imitations and unrealities notwithstanding the truth of divine religion has ever remained the same. Superstitions have obscured the fundamental reality, the world is darkened and the light of religion is not apparent. This darkness is conducive to differences and dissensions;

rites and dogmas are many and various; therefore discord has arisen among the religious systems whereas religion is for the unification of mankind. True religion is the source of love and agreement amongst men, the cause of the development of praiseworthy qualities; but the people are holding to the counterfeit and imitation, negligent of the reality which unifies; so they are bereft and deprived of the radiance of religion. They follow superstitions inherited from their fathers and ancestors. To such an extent has this prevailed that they have taken away the heavenly light of divine truth and sit in the darkness of imitations and imaginations. That which was meant to be conducive to life has become the cause of death; that which should have been an evidence of knowledge is now a proof of ignorance; that which was a factor in the sublimity of human nature has proved to be its degradation. Therefore the realm of the religionist has gradually narrowed and darkened and the sphere of the materialist has widened and advanced; for the religionist has held to imitation and counterfeit, neglecting and discarding holiness and the sacred reality of religion. When the sun sets it is the time for bats to fly. They come forth because they are creatures of the night. When the lights of religion become darkened the materialists appear. They are the bats of night. The decline of religion is their time of activity; they seek the shadows when the world is darkened and clouds have spread over it.

His Holiness Bahá'u'lláh has risen from the eastern horizon. Like the glory of the sun He has come into the world. He has reflected the reality of divine religion, dispelled the darkness of imitations, laid the foundation of new teachings and resuscitated the world.

The first teaching of Bahá'u'lláh is the investigation of reality. Man must seek the reality himself, forsaking imitations and adherence to mere hereditary forms. As the nations of the world are following imitations in lieu of truth and as imitations are many and various, differences of belief have been productive of strife and warfare. So long as these imitations remain the oneness of the world of humanity is impossible. Therefore we must investigate the reality in order that by its light the clouds and darkness may be dispelled. Reality is one reality; it does not admit multiplicity or division. If the nations of the world investigate reality they will agree and become united. Many people and sects in Írán have sought reality through the guidance and teaching of Bahá'u'lláh. They have become united and now live in a state of agreement and love; among them there is no longer the least trace of enmity and strife.

The Jews were expecting the appearance of the Messiah, looking forward to it with devotion of heart and soul but because they were submerged in imitations they did not believe in His Holiness Jesus Christ when he appeared. Finally they rose against Him even to the extreme of persecution and shedding His blood. Had they investigated reality they would have accepted their promised Messiah. These blind imitations and hereditary prejudices have invariably become the cause of bitterness and hatred and have filled the world with darkness and violence of war. Therefore we must seek the fundamental truth in order to extricate ourselves from such conditions and then with illumined faces find the pathway to the kingdom of God.

The second teaching of Bahá'u'lláh concerns the unity of mankind. All are the servants of God and members of one human family. God has created all and all are His children. He rears, nourishes, provides for and is kind to all. Why should we be unjust and unkind? This is the policy of God, the lights of which have shone throughout the world. His sun bestows its effulgence unsparingly upon all, His clouds send down rain without distinction or favor, His breezes refresh the whole earth. It is evident that humankind without exception is sheltered beneath His mercy and protection. Some are imperfect; they must be perfected. The ignorant must be taught, the sick healed, the sleepers awakened. The child must not be oppressed or censured because it is undeveloped; it must be patiently trained. The sick must not be neglected because they are ailing; nay, rather, we must have compassion upon them and bring them healing. Briefly; the old conditions of animosity, bigotry and hatred between the religious systems must be dispelled and the new conditions of love, agreement and spiritual brotherhood be established among them.

The third teaching of Bahá'u'lláh is that religion must be the source of fellowship, the cause of unity and the nearness of God to man. If it rouses hatred and strife it is evident that absence of religion is preferable and an irreligious man better than one who professes it. According to the divine will and intention religion should be the cause of love and agreement, a bond to unify all mankind for it is a message of peace and good-will to man from God.

The fourth teaching of Bahá'u'lláh is the agreement of religion and science. God has endowed man with intelligence and reason whereby he is required to determine the verity of questions and propositions. If religious beliefs and opinions are found contrary to the standards of science they are mere superstitions and imaginations; for the antithesis of knowledge is ignorance, and the child of ignorance is superstition. Unquestionably there must be agreement between true religion and science. If a question be found contrary to reason, faith and belief in it are impossible and there is no outcome but wavering and vacillation.

Bahá'u'lláh has also taught that prejudices, whether religious, racial, patriotic or political are destructive to the foundations of human development. Prejudices of any kind are the destroyers of human happiness and welfare. Until they are dispelled the advancement of the world of humanity is not possible, yet racial, religious and national bias are observed everywhere. For thousands of years the world of humanity has been agitated and disturbed by prejudices. As long as it prevails, warfare, animosity and hatred will continue. Therefore if we seek to establish peace we must cast aside this obstacle, for otherwise agreement and composure are not to be attained.

Fifth: Bahá'u'lláh set forth principles of guidance and teaching for economic readjustment. Regulations were revealed by Him which insure the welfare of the commonwealth. As the rich man enjoys his life surrounded by ease and luxuries, so the poor man must likewise have a home and be provided with sustenance and comforts commensurate with his needs. This readjustment of the social economic is of the greatest importance inasmuch as it insures the stability of the world of humanity; and until it is effected, happiness and prosperity are impossible.

Sixth: Bahá'u'lláh teaches that an equal standard of human rights must be recognized and adopted. In the estimation of God all men are equal; there is no distinction or preferment for any soul in the dominion of His justice and equity.

Seventh: Education is essential and all standards of training and teaching throughout the world of mankind should be brought into conformity and agreement; a universal curriculum should be established and the basis of ethics be the same.

Eighth: A universal language shall be adopted and be taught by all the schools and institutions of the world. A committee appointed by national bodies of learning shall select a suitable language to be used as a medium of international communication. All must acquire it. This is one of the great factors in the unification of man.

Ninth: Bahá'u'lláh emphasized and established the equality of man and woman. Sex is not particularized to humanity; it exists throughout the animate kingdoms but without distinction or preference. In the vegetable kingdom there is complete equality between male and female of species. Likewise in the animal plane equality exists; all are under the protection of God. Is it becoming to man that he, the noblest of creatures, should observe and insist upon such distinction? Woman's lack of progress and proficiency has been due to her need of equal education and opportunity. Had she been allowed this equality there is no doubt she would be the counterpart of man in ability and capacity. The happiness of mankind will be realized when women and men coordinate and advance equally, for each is the complement and helpmeet of the other.

The world of humanity cannot advance through mere physical powers and intellectual attainments; nay, rather, the Holy Spirit is essential. The divine Father must assist the human world to attain maturity. The body of man is in need of physical and mental energy but his spirit requires the life and fortification of the Holy Spirit. Without its protection and quickening the human world would be extinguished. His Holiness Jesus Christ declared, "Let the dead bury their dead." He also said, "That which is born of the flesh is flesh, and that which is born of the spirit is spirit." It is evident therefore according to His Holiness that the human spirit which is not fortified by the presence of the Holy Spirit is dead and in need of resurrection by that divine power; otherwise though materially advanced to high degrees man cannot attain full and complete progress.

Science and Spiritual Development

If we look with a perceiving eye upon the world of creation, we find that all existing things may be classified as follows: First—Mineral—that is to say matter or substance appearing in various forms of composition. Second—Vegetable—possessing the virtues of the mineral plus the power of augmentation or growth, indicating a degree higher and more specialized than the mineral. Third—Animal—possessing the attributes of the mineral and vegetable plus the power of sense perception. Fourth—Human—the highest specialized organism of visible creation, embodying the qualities of the mineral, vegetable and animal plus an ideal endowment absolutely minus and absent in the lower kingdoms—the power of intellectual investigation into the mysteries of outer phenomena. The outcome of this intellectual endowment is science which is especially characteristic of man. This scientific power investigates and apprehends created objects and the laws surrounding them. It is the discoverer of the hidden and mysterious secrets of the material universe and is peculiar to man alone. The most noble and praiseworthy accomplishment of man therefore is scientific knowledge and attainment.

Science may be likened to a mirror wherein the images of the mysteries of outer phenomena are reflected. It brings forth and exhibits to us in the arena of knowledge all the product of the past. It links together past and present. The philosophical conclusions of bygone centuries, the teachings of the prophets and wisdom of former sages are crystallized and reproduced in the scientific advancement of today. Science is the discoverer of the past. From its premises of past and present we deduce conclusions as to the future. Science is the governor of nature and its mysteries, the one agency by which man explores the institutions of material creation. All created things are captives of nature and subject to its laws. They cannot transgress the control of these laws in one detail or particular. The infinite starry worlds and heavenly bodies are nature's obedient subjects. The earth and its myriad organisms, all minerals, plants and animals are thralls of its dominion. But man through the exercise of his scientific, intellectual power can rise out of this condition, can modify, change and control nature according to his own wishes and uses. Science, so to speak, is the "breaker" of the laws of nature.

Consider, for example, that man according to natural law should dwell upon the surface of the earth. By overcoming this law and restriction however he sails in ships over the ocean, mounts to the zenith in aeroplanes and sinks to the depths of the sea in submarines. This is against the fiat of nature and a violation of her sovereignty and dominion. Nature's laws and methods, the hidden secrets and mysteries of the universe, human inventions and discoveries, all our scientific acquisitions should naturally remain concealed and unknown, but man through his intellectual acumen searches them out of the plane of the invisible, draws them into the plane of the visible, exposes and explains them. For instance, one of the mysteries of nature is electricity. According to nature this force, this energy should remain latent and hidden, but man scientifically breaks through the very laws of nature, arrests it and even imprisons it for his use.

In brief, man through the possession of this ideal endowment of scientific investigation is the most noble product of creation, the governor of nature. He takes the sword from nature's hand and uses it upon nature's head. According to natural law, night is a period of darkness and obscurity, but man by utilizing the power of electricity, by wielding this electric sword overcomes the darkness and dispels the gloom. Man is superior to nature and makes nature do his bidding. Man is a sensitive being; nature is minus sensation. Man has memory and reason; nature lacks them. Man is nobler than nature. There are powers within him of which nature is devoid. It may be claimed that these powers are from nature itself and that man is a part of nature. In answer to this statement we will say that if nature is the whole and man is a part of that whole, how could it be possible for a part to possess qualities and virtues which are absent in the whole? Undoubtedly the part must be endowed with the same qualities and properties as the whole.

For example, the hair is a part of the human anatomy. It cannot contain elements which are not found in other parts of the body, for in all cases the component elements of the body are the same. Therefore it is manifest and evident that man, although in body a part of nature, nevertheless in spirit possesses a power transcending nature; for if he were simply a part of nature and limited to material laws he could possess only the things which nature embodies. God has conferred upon and added to man a distinctive power, the faculty of intellectual investigation into the secrets of creation, the acquisition of higher knowledge, the greatest virtue of which is scientific enlightenment.

This endowment is the most praiseworthy power of man, for through its employment and exercise, the betterment of the human race is accomplished, the development of the virtues of mankind is made possible and the spirit and mysteries of God become manifest. Therefore I am greatly pleased with my visit to this university. Praise be to God! that this country abounds in such institutions of learning where the knowledge of sciences and arts may readily be acquired.

As material and physical sciences are taught here and are constantly unfolding in wider vistas of attainment, I am hopeful that spiritual development may also follow and keep pace with these outer advantages. As material knowledge is illuminating those within the walls of this great temple of learning, so also may the light of the spirit, the inner and divine light of the real philosophy glorify this institution. The most important principle of divine philosophy is the oneness of the world of humanity, the unity of mankind, the bond conjoining east and west, the tie of love which blends human hearts.

Therefore it is our duty to put forth our greatest efforts and summon all our energies in order that the bonds of unity and accord may be established among mankind. For thousands of years we have had bloodshed and strife. It is enough; it is sufficient. Now is the time to associate together in love and harmony. For thousands of years we have tried the sword and warfare; let mankind for a time at least live in peace. Review history and consider how much savagery, how much bloodshed and battle the world has witnessed. It has been either religious warfare, political warfare or some other clash of human interests. The world of humanity has never enjoyed the blessing of Universal Peace. Year by year the implements of warfare have been increased and perfected. Consider the wars of past centuries; only ten, fifteen or twenty thousand at the most were killed but now it is possible to kill one hundred thousand in a single day. In ancient times warfare was carried on with the sword; today it is the smokeless gun. Formerly battleships were sailing vessels; today they are dreadnoughts. Consider the increase and improvement in the weapons of war. God has created us all human and all countries of the world are parts of the same globe. We are all his servants. He is kind and just to all. Why should we be unkind and unjust to each other? He provides for all. Why should we deprive one another? He protects and preserves all. Why should we kill our fellow-creatures? If this warfare and strife be for the sake of religion, it is evident that it violates the spirit and basis of all religion. All the divine Manifestations have proclaimed the oneness of God and the unity of mankind. They have taught that men should love and mutually help each other in order that they might progress. Now if this conception of religion be true, its essential principle is the oneness of humanity. The fundamental truth of the Manifestations is peace. This underlies all religion, all justice. The divine purpose is that men should live in unity, concord and agreement and should love one another. Consider the virtues of the human world and realize that the oneness of humanity is the primary foundation of them all. Read the Gospel and the other holy books. You will find their fundamentals are one and the same. Therefore unity is the essential truth of religion and when so understood embraces all the virtues of the human world. Praise be to God! this knowledge has been spread, eyes have been opened and ears have become attentive. Therefore we must endeavor to promulgate and practice the religion of God which has been founded by all the prophets. And the religion of God is absolute love and unity.

Teachings of Bahá’u’lláh

I will speak to you concerning the special teachings of Bahá’u-’lláh. All the divine principles announced by the tongue of the prophets of the past are to be found in the words of Bahá'u'lláh; but in addition to these, He has revealed certain new teachings which are not found in any of the sacred books of former times. I shall mention some of them; the others which are many in number may be found in the books, tablets and epistles written by Bahá'u'lláh, such as the Hidden Words, the Glad-Tidings, the Words of Paradise, Tajallíyát, Tarázát and others. Likewise in the Book of Aqdas there are new teachings which cannot be found in any of the past books or epistles of the prophets.

A fundamental teaching of Bahá'u'lláh is the oneness of the world of humanity. Addressing mankind, He says: "Ye are all leaves of one tree and the fruits of one branch." By this it is meant that the world of humanity is like a tree, the nations or peoples are the different limbs or branches of that tree and the individual human creatures are as the fruits and blossoms thereof. In this way His Holiness Bahá'u'lláh expressed the oneness of humankind whereas in all religious teachings of the past, the human world has been represented as divided into two parts, one known as the people of the Book of God or the pure tree and the other the people of infidelity and error or the evil tree. The former were considered as belonging to the faithful and the others to the hosts of the irreligious and infidel; one part of humanity the recipients of divine mercy and the other the object of the wrath of their Creator. His Holiness Bahá'u'lláh removed this by proclaiming the oneness of the world of humanity and this principle is specialized in His teachings for He has submerged all mankind in the sea of divine generosity. Some are asleep; they need to be awakened. Some are ailing; they need to be healed. Some are immature as children; they need to be trained. But all are recipients of the bounty and bestowals of God.

Another new principle revealed by His Holiness Bahá'u'lláh is the injunction to investigate truth; that is to say, no man should blindly follow his ancestors and forefathers. Nay, each must see with his own eyes, hear with his own ears and investigate the truth himself in order that he may follow the truth instead of blind acquiescence and imitation of ancestral beliefs.

His Holiness Bahá'u'lláh has announced that the foundation of all the religions of God is one; that oneness is truth and truth is oneness which does not admit of plurality. This teaching is new and specialized to this Manifestation.

He sets forth a new principle for this day in the announcement that religion must be the cause of unity, harmony and agreement among mankind. If it be the cause of discord and hostility, if it leads to separation and creates conflict, the absence of religion would be preferable in the world.

Furthermore He proclaims that religion must be in harmony with science and reason. If it does not conform to science and reconcile with reason it is superstition. Down to the present day it has been customary for man to accept a religious teaching even though it were not in accord with human reason and judgment. The harmony of religious belief with reason is a new vista which Bahá'u'lláh has opened for the soul of man.

He establishes the equality of man and woman. This is peculiar to the teachings of Bahá'u'lláh, for all other religions have placed man above woman.

A new religious principle is that prejudice and fanaticism whether sectarian, denominational, patriotic or political are destructive to the foundation of human solidarity; therefore man should release himself from such bonds in order that the oneness of the world of humanity may become manifest.

Universal Peace is assured by Bahá'u'lláh as a fundamental accomplishment of the religion of God; that peace shall prevail among nations, governments and peoples, among religions, races and all conditions of mankind. This is one of the special characteristics of the Word of God revealed in this Manifestation.

Bahá'u'lláh declares that all mankind should attain knowledge and acquire an education. This is a necessary principle of religious belief and observance characteristically new in this dispensation.

He has set forth the solution and provided the remedy for the economic question. No religious books of the past Prophets speak of this important human problem.

He has ordained and established the House of Justice which is endowed with a political as well as a religious function, the consummate union and blending of church and state. This institution is under the protecting power of Bahá'u'lláh Himself. A universal or international House of Justice shall also be organized. Its rulings shall be in accordance with the commands and teachings of Bahá'u'lláh, and that which the universal House of Justice ordains shall be obeyed by all mankind. This international House of Justice shall be appointed and organized from the Houses of Justice of the whole world, and all the world shall come under its administration.

As to the most great characteristic of the revelation of Bahá'u'lláh—a specific teaching not given by any of the Prophets of the past—it is the ordination and appointment of the Center of the Covenant. By this appointment and provision He has safeguarded and protected the religion of God against differences and schisms, making it impossible for any one to create a new sect or faction of belief. To insure unity and agreement He has entered into a Covenant with all the people of the world including the Interpreter and Explainer of His teachings so that no one may interpret or explain the religion of God according to his own view or opinion and thus create a sect founded upon his individual understanding of the divine words. The Book of the Covenant or Testament of Bahá'u'lláh is the means of preventing such a possibility, for whosoever shall speak from the authority of himself alone shall be degraded. Be ye informed and cognizant of this.

The Educators of Mankind

According to the statement of philosophers the difference in degree of humankind from lowest to highest is due to education. The proofs they advance are these: The civilization of Europe and America is an evidence and outcome of education whereas the semi-civilized and barbarous peoples of Africa bear witness in their condition that they have been deprived of its advantages. Education makes the ignorant wise, the tyrant just, promotes happiness, strengthens the mind, develops the will and makes fruitless trees of humanity fruitful. Therefore in the human world some have attained lofty degrees while others grope in the abyss of despair. Nevertheless the highest attainment is possible for every member of the human race even to the station of the prophets. This is the statement and reasoning of the philosophers.

The prophets of God are the first educators. They bestow universal education upon man and cause him to rise from lowest levels of savagery to the highest pinnacles of spiritual development. The philosophers too are educators along lines of intellectual training. At most they have only been able to educate themselves and a limited number about them, to improve their own morals and, so to speak, civilize themselves; but they have been incapable of universal education. They have failed to cause an advancement for any given nation from savagery to civilization.

It is evident that although education improves the morals of mankind, confers the advantages of civilization and elevates man from lowest degrees to the station of sublimity, there is nevertheless a difference in the intrinsic or natal capacity of individuals. Ten children of the same age, with equal station of birth, taught in the same school, partaking of the same food, in all respects subject to the same environment, their interests equal and in common, will evidence separate and distinct degrees of capability and advancement; some exceedingly intelligent and progressive, some of mediocre ability, others limited and incapable. One may become a learned professor while another under the same course of education proves dull and stupid. From all standpoints the opportunities have been equal but the results and outcomes vary from the highest to lowest degree of advancement. It is evident therefore that mankind differs in natal capacity and intrinsic intellectual endowment. Nevertheless, although capacities are not the same, every member of the human race is capable of education.

His Holiness Jesus Christ was an educator of humanity. His teachings were altruistic; His bestowal universal. He taught mankind by the power of the Holy Spirit and not through human agency, for the human power is limited whereas the divine power is illimitable and infinite. The influence and accomplishment of Christ will attest this. Galen the Greek physician and philosopher who lived in the second century A. D., wrote a treatise upon the civilization of nations. He was not a Christian but he has borne testimony that religious beliefs exercise an extraordinary effect upon the problems of civilization. In substance he says: "There are certain people among us, followers of Jesus the Nazarene who was killed in Jerusalem. These people are truly imbued with moral principles which are the envy of philosophers. They believe in God and fear Him. They have hopes in His favors, therefore they shun all unworthy deeds and actions and incline to praiseworthy ethics and morals. Day and night they strive that their deeds may be commendable and that they may contribute to the welfare of humanity; therefore each one of them is virtually a philosopher, for these people have attained unto that which is the essence and purport of philosophy. These people have praiseworthy morals even though they may be illiterate."

The purpose of this is to show that the holy Manifestations of God, the divine prophets, are the first teachers of the human race. They are universal educators and the fundamental principles they have laid down are the causes and factors of the advancement of nations. Forms and imitations which creep in afterward are not conducive to that progress. On the contrary these are destroyers of human foundations established by the heavenly educators. These are clouds which obscure the Sun of Reality. If you reflect upon the essential teachings of Jesus you will realize that they are the light of the world. Nobody can question their truth. They are the very source of life and the cause of happiness to the human race. The forms and superstitions which appeared and obscured the light did not affect the reality of Christ. For example, His Holiness Jesus Christ said: "Put up the sword into the sheath." The meaning is that warfare is forbidden and abrogated; but consider the Christian wars which took place afterward. Christian hostility and inquisition spared not even the learned; he who proclaimed the revolution of the earth was imprisoned; he who announced the new astronomical system was persecuted as a heretic; scholars and scientists became objects of fanatical hatred and many were killed and tortured. How do these actions conform with the teachings of Jesus Christ and what relation do they bear to his own example? For Christ declared: "Love your enemies, and pray for them that persecute you that you may be sons of your Father which is in Heaven; for He maketh His sun to rise on the evil and the good, and sendeth rain on the just and the unjust." How can hatred, hostility and persecution be reconciled with Christ and His teachings?

Therefore there is need of turning back to the original foundation. The fundamental principles of the prophets are correct and true. The imitations and superstitions which have crept in are at wide variance with the original precepts and commands. His Holiness Bahá'u'lláh has revoiced and re-established the quintessence of the teachings of all the prophets, setting aside the accessories and purifying religion from human interpretation. He has written a book entitled Hidden Words. The preface announces that it contains the essences of the words of the prophets of the past clothed in the garment of brevity for the teaching and spiritual guidance of the people of the world. Read it that you may understand the true foundations of religion and reflect upon the inspiration of the messengers of God. It is light upon light.

We must not look for truth in the deeds and actions of nations; we must investigate truth at its divine source and summon all mankind to unity in the reality itself.

The Divine Standard of Knowledge

During my visit to London and Paris last year I had many talks with the materialistic philosophers of Europe. The basis of all their conclusions is that the acquisition of knowledge of phenomena is according to a fixed, invariable law,—a law mathematically exact in its operation through the senses. For instance, the eye sees a chair; therefore there is no doubt of the chair's existence. The eye looks up into the heavens and beholds the sun; I see flowers upon this table; I smell their fragrance; I hear sounds outside, etc, etc. This, they say, is a fixed mathematical law of perception and deduction, the operation of which admits of no doubt whatever; for inasmuch as the universe is subject to our sensing, the proof is self-evident that our knowledge of it must be gained through the avenues of the senses. That is to say, the materialists announce, that the criterion and standard of human knowledge is sense perception. Among the Greeks and Romans the criterion of knowledge was reason; that whatever is provable and acceptable by reason must necessarily be admitted as true. A third standard or criterion is the opinion held by theologians that traditions or prophetic statement and interpretations constitute the basis of human knowing. There is still another, a fourth criterion, upheld by religionists and metaphysicians who say that the source and channel of all human penetration into the unknown is through inspiration. Briefly then, these four criterions according to the declarations of men are: First—Sense Perception; Second—Reason; Third—Traditions; Fourth—Inspiration.

In Europe I told the philosophers and scientists of materialism that the criterion of the senses is not reliable. For instance, consider a mirror and the images reflected in it. These images have no actual corporeal existence. Yet if you had never seen a mirror you would firmly insist and believe that they were real. The eye sees a mirage upon the desert as a lake of water but there is no reality in it. As we stand upon the deck of a steamer the shore appears to be moving, yet we know the land is stationary and we are moving. The earth was believed to be fixed and the sun revolving about it but although this appears to be so, the reverse is now known to be true. A whirling torch makes a circle of fire appear before the eye, yet we realize there is but one point of light. We behold a shadow moving upon the ground but it has no material existence, no substance. In deserts the atmospheric effects are particularly productive of illusions which deceive the eye. Once I saw a mirage in which a whole caravan appeared traveling upward into the sky. In the far north other deceptive phenomena appear and baffle human vision. Sometimes three or four suns called by scientists "mock suns" will be shining at the same time whereas we know the great solar orb is one and that it remains fixed and single. In brief, the senses are continually deceived and we are unable to separate that which is reality from that which is not.

As to the second criterian, reason, this likewise is unreliable and not to be depended upon. This human world is an ocean of varying opinions. If reason is the perfect standard and criterion of knowledge, why are opinions at variance and why do philosophers disagree so completely with each other? This is a clear proof that human reason is not to be relied upon as an infallible criterion. For instance, great discoveries and announcements of former centuries are continually upset and discarded by the wise men of today. Mathematicians, astronomers, chemical scientists continually disprove and reject the conclusions of the ancients; nothing is fixed, nothing final; everything continually changing because human reason is progressing along new roads of investigation and arriving at new conclusions every day. In the future much that is announced and accepted as true now will be rejected and disproved. And so it will continue ad infinitum.

When we consider the third criterion, traditions, upheld by theologians as the avenue and standard of knowledge, we find this source equally unreliable and unworthy of dependence. For religious traditions are the report and record of understanding and interpretation of the Book. By what means has this understanding, this interpretation been reached? By the analysis of human reason. When we read the Book of God the faculty of comprehension by which we form conclusions is reason. Reason is mind. If we are not endowed with perfect reason, how can we comprehend the meanings of the Word of God? Therefore human reason, as already pointed out, is by its very nature finite and faulty in conclusions. It cannot surround the Reality Itself, the Infinite Word. Inasmuch as the source of traditions and interpretations is human reason, and human reason is faulty, how can we depend upon its findings for real knowledge?

The fourth criterion I have named is inspiration through which it is claimed the reality of knowledge is attainable. What is inspiration? It is the influx of the human heart. But what are satanic promptings which afflict mankind? They are the influx of the heart also. How shall we differentiate between them? The question arises, How shall we know whether we are following inspiration from God or satanic promptings of the human soul? Briefly, the point is that in the human material world of phenomena these four are the only existing criterions or avenues of knowledge, and all of them are faulty and unreliable. What then remains? How shall we attain the reality of knowledge? By the breaths and promptings of the Holy Spirit which is light and knowledge Itself. Through it the human mind is quickened and fortified into true conclusions and perfect knowledge. This is conclusive argument showing that all available human criterions are erroneous and defective, but the divine standard of knowledge is infallible. Therefore man is not justified in saying: "I know because I perceive through my senses"; or: "I know because it is proved through my faculty of reason"; or: "I know because it is according to tradition and interpretation of the holy book"; or: "I know because I am inspired." All human standard of judgment is faulty, finite.

The Sun of Reality

In our solar system, the center of illumination is the sun itself. Through the will of God this central luminary is the one source of the existence and development of all phenomenal things. When we observe the organisms of the material kingdoms we find that their growth and training are dependent upon the heat and light of the sun. Without this quickening impulse there would be no growth of tree or vegetation, neither would the existence of animal or human being be possible; in fact no forms of created life would be manifest upon the earth. But if we reflect deeply we will perceive that the great bestower and giver of life is God; the sun is the intermediary of His will and plan. Without the bounty of the sun therefore the world would be in darkness. All illumination of our planetary system proceeds or emanates from the solar center.

Likewise in the spiritual realm of intelligence and idealism there must be a center of illumination, and that center is the everlasting, ever-shining Sun, the Word of God. Its lights are the lights of reality which have shone upon humanity, illumining the realm of thought and morals, conferring the bounties of the divine world upon man. These lights are the cause of the education of souls and the source of the enlightenment of hearts, sending forth in effulgent radiance the message of the glad-tidings of the kingdom of God. In brief, the moral and ethical world and the world of spiritual regeneration are dependent for their progressive being upon that heavenly center of illumination. It gives forth the light of religion and bestows the life of the spirit, imbues humanity with archetypal virtues and confers eternal splendors. This Sun of Reality, this center of effulgences is the prophet or Manifestation of God. Just as the phenomenal sun shines upon the material world producing life and growth, likewise the spiritual or prophetic Sun confers illumination upon the human world of thought and intelligence, and unless it rose upon the horizon of human existence the kingdom of man would become dark and extinguished.

The Sun of Reality is one Sun but it has different dawning-places, just as the phenomenal sun is one although it appears at various points of the horizon. During the time of spring the luminary of the physical world rises far to the north of the equinoctial; in summer it dawns midway and in winter it appears in the most southerly point of its zodiacal journey. These day springs or dawning-points differ widely but the sun is ever the same sun whether it be the phenomenal or spiritual luminary. Souls who focus their vision upon the Sun of Reality will be the recipients of light no matter from what point it rises, but those who are fettered by adoration of the dawning-point are deprived when it appears in a different station upon the spiritual horizon.

Furthermore, just as the solar cycle has its four seasons the cycle of the Sun of Reality has its distinct and successive periods. Each brings its vernal season or springtime. When the Sun of Reality returns to quicken the world of mankind a divine bounty descends from the heaven of generosity. The realm of thoughts and ideals is set in motion and blessed with new life. Minds are developed, hopes brighten, aspirations become spiritual, the virtues of the human world appear with freshened power of growth and the image and likeness of God become visible in man. It is the springtime of the inner world. After the spring, summer comes with its fullness and fruitage spiritual; autumn follows with its withering winds which chill the soul; the Sun seems to be going away until at last the mantle of winter overspreads and only faint traces of the effulgence of that divine Sun remain. Just as the surface of the material world becomes dark and dreary, the soil dormant, the trees naked and bare and no beauty or freshness remain to cheer the darkness and desolation, so the winter of the spiritual cycle witnesses the death and disappearance of divine growth and extinction of the light and love of God. But again the cycle begins and a new springtime appears. In it the former springtime has returned, the world is resuscitated, illumined and attains spirituality; religion is renewed and reorganized, hearts are turned to God, the summons of God is heard and life is again bestowed upon man. For a long time the religious world had been weakened and materialism had advanced; the spiritual forces of life were waning, moralities were becoming degraded, composure and peace had vanished from souls and satanic qualities were dominating hearts; strife and hatred overshadowed humanity, bloodshed and violence prevailed. God was neglected; the Sun of Reality seemed to have gone completely; deprivation of the bounties of heaven was a fact; and so the season of winter fell upon mankind. But in the generosity of God a new springtime dawned, the lights of God shone forth, the effulgent Sun of Reality returned and became manifest, the realm of thoughts and kingdom of hearts became exhilarated, a new spirit of life breathed into the body of the world and continuous advancement became apparent.

I hope that the lights of the Sun of Reality will illumine the whole world so that no strife and warfare, no battles and bloodshed remain. May fanaticism and religious bigotry be unknown, all humanity enter the bond of brotherhood, souls consort in perfect agreement, the nations of earth at last hoist the banner of truth and the religions of the world enter the divine temple of oneness, for the foundations of the heavenly religions are one reality. Reality is not divisible; it does not admit multiplicity. All the holy Manifestations of God have proclaimed and promulgated the same reality. They have summoned mankind to reality itself and reality is one. The clouds and mists of imitations have obscured the Sun of Truth. We must forsake these imitations, dispel these clouds and mists and free the Sun from the darkness of superstition. Then will the Sun of Truth shine most gloriously; then all the inhabitants of the world will be united, the religions will be one, sects and denominations will reconcile, all nationalities will flow together in the recognition of one Fatherhood and all degrees of humankind gather in the shelter of the same tabernacle, under the same banner.

Until the heavenly civilization is founded, no result will be forthcoming from material civilization, even as you observe. See what catastrophes overwhelm mankind. Consider the wars which disturb the world. Consider the enmity and hatred. The existence of these wars and conditions indicates and proves that the heavenly civilization has not yet been established. If the civilization of the Kingdom be spread to all the nations, this dust of disagreement will be dispelled, these clouds will pass away and the Sun of Reality in its greatest effulgence and glory will shine upon mankind.

The Source of Unity

What is real unity? When we observe the human world we find various collective expressions of unity therein. For instance, man is distinguished from the animal by his degree or kingdom. This comprehensive distinction includes all the posterity of Adam and constitutes one great household or human family which may be considered the fundamental or physical unity of mankind. Furthermore, a distinction exists between various groups of humankind according to lineage, each group forming a racial unity separate from the others. There is also the unity of tongue among those who use the same language as a means of communication; national unity where various peoples live under one form of government such as French, German, British, etc.; and political unity which conserves the civil rights of parties or factions of the same government. All these unities are imaginary and without real foundation, for no real result proceeds from them. The purpose of true unity is real and divine outcomes. From these limited unities mentioned only limited outcomes proceed whereas unlimited unity produces unlimited result. For instance, from the limited unity of race or nationality the results at most are limited. It is like a family living alone and solitary; there are no unlimited or universal outcomes from it.

The unity which is productive of unlimited results is first a unity of mankind which recognizes that all are sheltered beneath the overshadowing glory of the All-Glorious; that all are servants of one God; for all breathe the same atmosphere, live upon the same earth, move beneath the same heavens, receive effulgence from the same sun and are under the protection of one God. This is the most great unity, and its results are lasting if humanity adheres to it; but mankind has hitherto violated it, adhering to sectarian or other limited unities such as racial, patriotic or unity of self-interests; therefore no great results have been forthcoming. Nevertheless it is certain that the radiance and favors of God are encompassing, minds have developed, perceptions have become acute, sciences and arts are widespread and capacity exists for the proclamation and promulgation of the real and ultimate unity of mankind which will bring forth marvelous results. It will reconcile all religions, make warring nations loving, cause hostile kings to become friendly and bring peace and happiness to the human world. It will cement together the Orient and Occident, remove forever the foundations of war and upraise the ensign of the Most Great Peace. These limited unities are therefore signs of that great unity which will make all the human family one by being productive of the attractions of conscience in mankind.

Another unity is the spiritual unity which emanates from the breaths of the Holy Spirit. This is greater than the unity of mankind. Human unity or solidarity may be likened to the body whereas unity from the breaths of the Holy Spirit is the spirit animating the body. This is a perfect unity. It creates such a condition in mankind that each one will make sacrifices for the other and the utmost desire will be to forfeit life and all that pertains to it in behalf of another's good. This is the unity which existed among the disciples of His Holiness Jesus Christ and bound together the prophets and holy souls of the past. It is the unity which through the influence of the divine spirit is permeating the Bahá'ís so that each offers his life for the other and strives with all sincerity to attain his good-pleasure. This is the unity which caused twenty thousand people in Írán to give their lives in love and devotion to it. It made the Báb the target of a thousand arrows and caused Bahá'u'lláh to suffer exile and imprisonment forty years. This unity is the very spirit of the body of the world. It is impossible for the body of the world to become quickened with life without its vivification. His Holiness Jesus Christ—may my life be a sacrifice to Him!—promulgated this unity among mankind. Every soul who believed in Jesus Christ became revivified and resuscitated through this spirit, attained to the zenith of eternal glory, realized the life everlasting, experienced the second birth and rose to the acme of good fortune.

In the Word of God there is still another unity, the oneness of the Manifestations of God, His Holiness Abraham, Moses, Jesus Christ, Muḥammad, the Báb and Bahá’u’lláh. This is a unity divine, heavenly, radiant, merciful; the one reality appearing in its successive manifestations. For instance, the sun is one and the same but its points of dawning are various. During the summer season it rises from the northern point of the ecliptic; in winter it appears from the southern point of rising. Each month between it appears from a certain zodiacal position. Although these dawning-points are different, the sun is the same sun which has appeared from them all. The significance is the reality of prophethood which is symbolized by the sun, and the holy Manifestations are the dawning-places or zodiacal points.

There is also the divine unity or entity which is sanctified above all concept of humanity. It cannot be comprehended nor conceived because it is infinite reality and cannot become finite. Human minds are incapable of surrounding that reality because all thoughts and conceptions of it are finite, intellectual creations and not the reality of divine being which alone knows itself. For example, if we form a conception of divinity as a living, almighty, self-subsisting, eternal being, this is only a concept apprehended by a human intellectual reality. It would not be the outward, visible reality which is beyond the power of human mind to conceive or encompass. We ourselves have an external, visible entity but even our concept of it is the product of our own brain and limited comprehension. The reality of divinity is sanctified above this degree of knowing and realization. It has ever been hidden and secluded in its own holiness and sanctity above our comprehending. Although it transcends our realization, its lights, bestowals, traces and virtues have become manifest in the realities of the prophets, even as the sun becomes resplendent in various mirrors. These holy realities are as reflectors, and the reality of divinity is as the sun which although it is reflected from the mirrors, and its virtues and perfections become resplendent therein, does not stoop from its own station of majesty and glory and seek abode in the mirrors; it remains in its heaven of sanctity. At most it is this, that its lights become manifest and evident in its mirrors or manifestations. Therefore its bounty proceeding from them is one bounty but the recipients of that bounty are many. This is the unity of God; this is oneness;—unity of divinity, holy above ascent or descent, embodiment, comprehension or idealization;—divine unity. The prophets are its mirrors; its lights are revealed through them; its virtues become resplendent in them, but the Sun of Reality never descends from its own highest point and station. This is unity, oneness, sanctity; this is glorification whereby we praise and adore God.

The Quickening Spirit

The greatest power in the realm and range of human existence is spirit,—the divine breath which animates and pervades all things. It is manifested throughout creation in different degrees or kingdoms. In the vegetable kingdom it is the spirit augmentative or power of growth, the animus of life and development in plants, trees and organisms of the floral world. In this degree of its manifestation, spirit is unconscious of the powers which qualify the kingdom of the animal. The distinctive virtue or plus of the animal is sense perception; it sees, hears, smells, tastes and feels but is incapable in turn, of conscious ideation or reflection which characterize and differentiate the human kingdom. The animal neither exercises nor apprehends this distinctive human power and gift. From the visible it cannot draw conclusions regarding the invisible whereas the human mind from visible and known premises attains knowledge of the unknown and invisible. For instance, Christopher Columbus from information based upon known and provable facts drew conclusions which led him unerringly across the vast ocean to the unknown continent of America. Such power of accomplishment is beyond the range of animal intelligence. Therefore this power is a distinctive attribute of the human spirit and kingdom. The animal spirit cannot penetrate and discover the mysteries of things. It is a captive of the senses. No amount of teaching, for instance, would enable it to grasp the fact that the sun is stationary and the earth moves around it. Likewise the human spirit has its limitations. It cannot comprehend the phenomena of the kingdom transcending the human station, for it is a captive of powers and life forces which have their operation upon its own plane of existence and it cannot go beyond that boundary.

There is however another spirit which may be termed the divine, to which Jesus Christ refers when He declares that man must be born of its quickening and baptized with its living fire. Souls deprived of that spirit are accounted as dead, though they are possessed of the human spirit. His Holiness Jesus Christ has pronounced them dead inasmuch as they have no portion of the divine spirit. He says: "Let the dead bury their dead." In another instance He declares: "That which is born of the flesh is flesh; and that which is born of the spirit is spirit." By this He means that souls though alive in the human kingdom are nevertheless dead if devoid of this particular spirit of divine quickening. They have not partaken of the divine life of the higher kingdom; for the soul which partakes of the power of the divine spirit is verily living.

This quickening spirit has spontaneous emanation from the Sun of Truth, from the reality of divinity and is not a revelation or a manifestation. It is like the rays of the sun. The rays are emanations from the sun. This does not mean that the sun has become divisible; that a part of the sun has come out into space. This plant beside me has risen from the seed; therefore it is a manifestation and unfoldment of the seed. The seed, as you can see, has unfolded in manifestation and the result is this plant. Every leaf of the plant is a part of the seed. But the reality of divinity is indivisible and each individual of human kind cannot be a part of it as is often claimed. Nay, rather, the individual realities of mankind when spiritually born are emanations from the reality of divinity, just as the flame, heat and light of the sun are the effulgence of the sun and not a part of the sun itself. Therefore a spirit has emanated from the reality of divinity, and its effulgences have become visible in human entities or realities. This ray and this heat are permanent. There is no cessation in the effulgence. As long as the sun exists the heat and light will exist, and inasmuch as eternality is a property of divinity, this emanation is everlasting. There is no cessation in its outpouring. The more the world of humanity develops, the more the effulgences or emanations of divinity will become revealed, just as the stone when it becomes polished and pure as a mirror will reflect in fuller degree the glory and splendor of the sun.

The mission of the prophets, the revelation of the holy books, the manifestation of the heavenly teachers and the purpose of divine philosophy all center in the training of the human realities so that they may become clear and pure as mirrors and reflect the light and love of the Sun of Reality. Therefore I hope that whether you be in the east or the west you will strive with heart and soul in order that day by day the world of humanity may become glorified, more spiritual, more sanctified; and that the splendor of the Sun of Reality may be revealed fully in human hearts as in a mirror. This is worthy of the world of mankind. This is the true evolution and progress of humanity. This is the supreme bestowal. Otherwise, by simple development along material lines man is not perfected. At most, the physical aspect of man, his natural or material conditions may become stabilized and improved but he will remain deprived of the spiritual or divine bestowal. He is then like a body without a spirit, a lamp without the light, an eye without the power of vision, an ear that hears no sound, a mind incapable of perceiving, an intellect minus the power of reason.

Man has two powers, and his development two aspects. One power is connected with the material world and by it he is capable of material advancement. The other power is spiritual and through its development his inner, potential nature is awakened. These powers are like two wings. Both must be developed, for flight is impossible with one wing. Praise be to God! material advancement has been evident in the world but there is need of spiritual advancement in like proportion. We must strive unceasingly and without rest to accomplish the development of the spiritual nature in man, and endeavor with tireless energy to advance humanity toward the nobility of its true and intended station. For the body of man is accidental; it is of no importance. The time of its disintegration will inevitably come. But the spirit of man is essential and therefore eternal. It is a divine bounty. It is the effulgence of the Sun of Reality and therefore of greater importance than the physical body.

Spiritual Existence Is Immortality

According to divine philosophy, there are two important and universal conditions in the world of material phenomena; one which concerns life, the other concerning death; one relative to existence, the other non-existence; one manifest in composition, the other in decomposition. Some define existence as the expression of reality or being, and non-existence as non-being, imagining that death is annihilation. This is a mistaken idea, for total annihilation is an impossibility. At most, composition is ever subject to decomposition or distintegration; that is to say, existence implies the grouping of material elements in a form or body, and non-existence is simply the de-composing of these groupings. This is the law of creation in its endless forms and infinite variety of expression. Certain elements have formed the composite creature man. This composite association of the elements in the form of a human body is therefore subject to disintegration which we call death, but after disintegration the elements themselves persist unchanged. Therefore total annihilation is an impossibility, and existence can never become non-existence. This would be equivalent to saying that light can become darkness, which is manifestly untrue and impossible. As existence can never become non-existence, there is no death for man; nay, rather, man is everlasting and everliving. The rational proof of this is that the atoms of the material elements are transferable from one form of existence to another, from one degree and kingdom to another, lower or higher. For example, an atom of the soil or dust of earth may traverse the kingdoms from mineral to man by successive incorporations into the bodies of the organisms of those kingdoms. At one time it enters into the formation of the mineral or rock; it is then absorbed by the vegetable kingdom and becomes a constituent of the body and fibre of a tree; again it is appropriated by the animal, and at a still later period is found in the body of man. Throughout these degrees of its traversing the kingdoms from one form of phenomenal being to another, it retains its atomic existence and is never annihilated nor relegated to non-existence.

Non-existence therefore is an expression applied to change of form, but this transformation can never be rightly considered annihilation, for the elements of composition are ever present and existent as we have seen in the journey of the atom through successive kingdoms, unimpaired; hence there is no death; life is everlasting. So to speak, when the atom entered into the composition of the tree, it died to the mineral kingdom, and when consumed by the animal, it died to the vegetable kingdom, and so on until its transference or transmutation into the kingdom of man; but throughout its traversing it was subject to transformation and not annihilation. Death therefore is applicable to a change or transference from one degree or condition to another. In the mineral realm there was a spirit of existence; in the world of plant life and organisms it reappeared as the vegetative spirit; thence it attained the animal spirit and finally aspired to the human spirit. These are degrees and changes but not obliteration; and this is a rational proof that man is everlasting, everliving. Therefore death is only a relative term implying change. For example, we will say that this light before me, having reappeared in another incandescent lamp, has died in the one and lives in the other. This is not death in reality. The perfections of the mineral are translated into the vegetable and from thence into the animal, the virtue always attaining a plus or superlative degree in the upward change. In each kingdom we find the same virtues manifesting themselves more fully, proving that the reality has been transferred from a lower to a higher form and kingdom of being. Therefore non-existence is only relative and absolute non-existence inconceivable. This rose in my hand will become disintegrated and its symmetry destroyed, but the elements of its composition remain changeless; nothing affects their elemental integrity. They cannot become non-existent; they are simply transferred from one state to another.

Through his ignorance, man fears death; but the death he shrinks from is imaginary and absolutely unreal; it is only human imagination.

The bestowal and grace of God have quickened the realm of existence with life and being. For existence there is neither change nor transformation; existence is ever existence; it can never be translated into non-existence. It is gradation; a degree below a higher degree is considered as non-existence. This dust beneath our feet, as compared with our being is non-existent. When the human body crumbles into dust we can say it has become non-existent; therefore its dust in relation to living forms of human being is as non-existent but in its own sphere it is existent, it has its mineral being. Therefore it is well proved that absolute non-existence is impossible; it is only relative.

The purpose is this;—that the everlasting bestowal of God vouchsafed to man is never subject to corruption. Inasmuch as He has endowed the phenomenal world with being, it is impossible for that world to become non-being, for it is the very genesis of God; it is the realm of origination; it is a creational and not a subjective world, and the bounty descending upon it is continuous and permanent. Therefore man the highest creature of the phenomenal world is endowed with that continuous bounty bestowed by divine generosity without cessation. For instance, the rays of the sun are continuous, the heat of the sun emanates from it without cessation; no discontinuance of it is conceivable. Even so the bestowal of God is descending upon the world of humanity, never ceasing, continuous, forever. If we say that the bestowal of existence ceases or falters it is equivalent to saying that the sun can exist with cessation of its effulgence. Is this possible? Therefore the effulgences of existence are ever-present and continuous.

The conception of annihilation is a factor in human degradation, a cause of human debasement and lowliness, a source of human fear and abjection. It has been conducive to the dispersion and weakening of human thought whereas the realization of existence and continuity has upraised man to sublimity of ideals, established the foundations of human progress and stimulated the development of heavenly virtues; therefore it behoves man to abandon thoughts of non-existence and death which are absolutely imaginary and see himself ever living, everlasting in the divine purpose of his creation. He must turn away from ideas which degrade the human soul, so that day by day and hour by hour he may advance upward and higher to spiritual perception of the continuity of the human reality. If he dwells upon the thought of non-existence he will become utterly incompetent; with weakened will-power his ambition for progress will be lessened and the acquisition of human virtues will cease.

Therefore you must thank God that He has bestowed upon you the blessing of life and existence in the human kingdom. Strive diligently to acquire virtues befitting your degree and station. Be as lights of the world which cannot be hid and which have no setting in horizons of darkness. Ascend to the zenith of an existence which is never beclouded by the fears and forebodings of non-existence. When man is not endowed with inner perception he is not informed of these important mysteries. The retina of outer vision though sensitive and delicate may nevertheless be a hindrance to the inner eye which alone can perceive. The bestowals of God which are manifest in all phenomenal life are sometimes hidden by intervening veils of mental and mortal vision which render man spiritually blind and incapable but when those scales are removed and the veils rent asunder, then the great signs of God will become visible and he will witness the eternal light filling the world. The bestowals of God are all and always manifest. The promises of heaven are ever present. The favors of God are all-surrounding but should the conscious eye of the soul of man remain veiled and darkened he will be led to deny these universal signs and remain deprived of these manifestations of divine bounty. Therefore we must endeavor with heart and soul in order that the veil covering the eye of inner vision may be removed, that we may behold the manifestations of the signs of God, discern His mysterious graces, and realize that material blessings as compared with spiritual bounties are as nothing. The spiritual blessings of God are greatest. When we were in the mineral kingdom, although endowed with certain gifts and powers, they were not to be compared with the blessings of the human kingdom. In the matrix of the mother we were the recipients of endowments and blessings of God, yet these were as nothing compared to the powers and graces bestowed upon us after birth into this human world. Likewise if we are born from the matrix of this physical and phenomenal environment into the freedom and loftiness of the life and vision spiritual, we shall consider this mortal existence and its blessings as worthless by comparison.

In the spiritual world, the divine bestowals are infinite, for in that realm there is neither separation nor disintegration which characterize the world of material existence. Spiritual existence is absolute immortality, completeness and unchangeable being. Therefore we must thank God that He has created for us both material blessings and spiritual bestowals. He has given us material gifts and spiritual graces, outer sight to view the lights of the sun and inner vision by which we may perceive the glory of God. He has designed the outer ear to enjoy the melodies of sound and the inner hearing wherewith we may hear the voice of our creator. We must strive with energies of heart, soul and mind to develop and manifest the perfections and virtues latent within the realities of the phenomenal world, for the human reality may be compared to a seed. If we sow the seed, a mighty tree appears from it. The virtues of the seed are revealed in the tree; it puts forth branches, leaves, blossoms, and produces fruits. All these virtues were hidden and potential in the seed. Through the blessing and bounty of cultivation these virtues became apparent. Similarly the merciful God our creator has deposited within human realties certain virtues latent and potential. Through education and culture, these virtues deposited by the loving God will become apparent in the human reality even as the unfoldment of the tree from within the germinating seed.

RACE UNITY, ASSURANCE OF WORLD PEACE

Today I am most happy, for I see here a gathering of the servants of God. I see the white and colored people together. In the estimation of God there is no distinction of color; all are one in the color and beauty of servitude to him. Color is not important; the heart is all-important. It matters not what the exterior may be if the heart be pure and white within. God does not behold differences of hue and complexion; He looks at the hearts. He whose morals and virtues are praiseworthy is preferred in the presence of God; he who is devoted to the Kingdom is most beloved. In the realm of genesis and creation the question of color is of least importance.

The mineral kingdom abounds with many-colored substances and compositions but we find no strife among them on that account. In the kingdom of the plant and vegetable, distinct and variegated hues exist but the fruit and flowers are not in conflict for that reason. Nay, rather, the very fact that there is difference and variety lends a charm to the garden. If all were of the same color the effect would be monotonous and depressing. When you enter a rose-garden the wealth of color and variety of floral forms spread before you a picture of wonder and beauty. The world of humanity is like a garden and the various races are the flowers which constitute its adornment and decoration. In the animal kingdom also we find variety of color. See how the doves differ in beauty yet they live together in perfect peace, and love each other. They do not make difference of color a cause of discord and strife. They view each other as the same species and kind. They know they are one in kind. Often a white dove soars aloft with a black one. Throughout the animal kingdom we do not find the creatures separated because of color. They recognize unity of species and oneness of kind. If we do not find color distinction drawn in a kingdom of lower intelligence and reason, how can it be justified among human beings, especially when we know that all have come from the same source and belong to the same household? In origin and intention of creation mankind is one. Distinctions of race and color have arisen afterward.

Therefore today I am exceedingly glad that both white and colored people have gathered here and I hope the time will come when they shall live together in the utmost peace, unity and friendship. I wish to say one thing of importance to both in order that the white race may be just and kind to the colored and that the colored race may in turn be grateful and appreciative toward the white. The great proclamation of liberty and emancipation from slavery was made upon this continent. A long bloody war was fought by white men for the sake of colored people. These white men forfeited their possessions and sacrificed their lives by thousands in order that colored men might be freed from bondage. The colored population of the United States of America are possibly not fully informed of the wide-reaching effect of this freedom and emancipation upon their colored brethren in Asia and Africa where even more terrible conditions of slavery existed. Influenced and impelled by the example of the United States, the European powers proclaimed universal liberty to the colored race and slavery ceased to exist. This effort and accomplishment by the white nations should never be lost sight of. Both races should rejoice in gratitude, for the institution of liberty and equality here became the cause of liberating your fellow-beings elsewhere. The colored people of this country are especially fortunate, for, praise be to God! conditions here are so much higher than in the East and comparatively few differences exist in the possibility of equal attainments with the white race. May both develop toward the highest degree of equality and altruism. May you be drawn together in friendship and may extraordinary development make brotherhood a reality and truth. I pray in your behalf that there shall be no name other than that of humanity among you. For instance we say "a flock of doves," without mention or distinction as to white or black; we apply the name "horse," "deer," "gazelle" to other creatures, referring to species and not to their variance in color. It is my hope that through love and fellowship we may advance to such a degree of mutual recognition and estimate, that the oneness of the human world may be realized in each and all present in this meeting.

Therefore strive earnestly and put forth your greatest endeavor toward the accomplishment of this fellowship and the cementing of this bond of brotherhood between you. Such an attainment is not possible without will and effort on the part of each; from one, expressions of gratitude and appreciation; from the other kindliness and recognition of equality. Each one should endeavor to develop and assist the other toward mutual advancement. This is possible only by conjoining of effort and inclination. Love and unity will be fostered between you, thereby bringing about the oneness of mankind. For the accomplishment of unity between the colored and whites will be an assurance of the world's peace. Then racial prejudice, national prejudice, limited patriotism and religious bias will pass away and remain no longer. I am pleased to see you at this gathering, white and dark, and I praise God that I have had this opportunity of seeing you loving each other, for this is the means of the glory of humanity. This is the means of the good-pleasure of God and of eternal bliss in His kingdom. Therefore I pray in your behalf that you may attain to the fullest degree of love and that the day may come when all differences between you may disappear.

Religion and Civilization

The greatest bestowal of God in the world of humanity is religion; for assuredly the divine teachings of religion are above all other sources of instruction and development to man. Religion confers upon man eternal life and guides his footsteps in the world of morality. It opens the doors of unending happiness and bestows everlasting honor upon the human kingdom. It has been the basis of all civilization and progress in the history of mankind.

We will therefore investigate religion, seeking from an unprejudiced standpoint to discover whether it is the source of illumination, the cause of development and the animating impulse of all human advancement. We will investigate independently, free from the restrictions of dogmatic beliefs, blind imitations of ancestral forms, and the influence of mere human opinion; for as we enter this question we will find some who declare that religion is a cause of uplift and betterment in the world, while others assert just as positively that it is a detriment and a source of degradation to mankind. We must give these questions thorough and impartial consideration so that no doubt or uncertainty may linger in our minds regarding them.

How shall we determine whether religion has been the cause of human advancement or retrogression?

We will first consider the founders of the religions—the prophets—review the story of their lives, compare the conditions preceding their appearance with those subsequent to their departure, following historical records and irrefutable facts instead of relying upon traditionary statements which are open to both acceptance and denial.

Among the great prophets was His Holiness Abraham who being an iconoclast and a herald of the oneness of God, was banished from His native land. He founded a family upon which the blessing of God descended; and it was owing to this religious basis and ordination that the Abrahamic house progressed and advanced. Through the divine benediction, noteworthy and luminous prophets issued from the lineage of His Holiness. There appeared Isaac, Ishmael, Jacob, Joseph, Moses, Aaron, David and Solomon. The Holy Land was conquered by the power of the Covenant of God with Abraham, and the glory of the Solomonic wisdom and sovereignty dawned. All this was due to the religion of God which this blessed lineage established and upheld. It is evident that throughout the history of Abraham and His posterity this was the source of their honor, advancement and civilization. Even today the descendants of His household and lineage are found throughout the world.

There is another and more significant aspect to this religious impulse and impetus. The children of Israel were in bondage and captivity in the land of Egypt four hundred years. They were in an extreme state of degradation and slavery under the tyranny and oppression of the Egyptians. While they were in the condition of abject poverty, in the lowest degree of abasement, ignorance and servility His Holiness Moses suddenly appeared among them. Although He was but a shepherd, such majesty, grandeur and efficiency became manifest in Him through the power of religion, that His influence continues to this day. His prophethood was established throughout the land and the law of His Word became the foundation of the laws of the nations. This unique personage, single and alone, rescued the children of Israel from bondage through the power of religious training and discipline. He led them to the Holy Land and founded there a great civilization which has become permanent and renowned and under which these people attained the highest degree of honor and glory. He freed them from bondage and captivity. He imbued them with qualities of progressiveness and capability. They proved to be a civilizing people with instincts toward education and scholastic attainment. Their philosophy became renowned; their industries were celebrated throughout the nations. In all lines of advancement which characterize a progressive people they achieved distinction. In the splendor of the reign of Solomon their sciences and arts advanced to such a degree that even the Greek philosophers journeyed to Jerusalem to sit at the feet of the Hebrew sages and acquire the basis of Israelitish law. According to eastern history this is an established fact. Even Socrates visited the Jewish doctors in the Holy Land, consorting with them and discussing the principles and basis of their religious belief. After his return to Greece he formulated his philosophical teaching of divine unity and advanced his belief in the immortality of the spirit beyond the dissolution of the body. Without doubt Socrates absorbed these verities from the wise men of the Jews with whom he came in contact. Hippocrates and other philosophers of the Greeks likewise visited Palestine and acquired wisdom from the Jewish prophets, studying the basis of ethics and morality, returning to their country with contributions which have made Greece famous.

When a movement fundamentally religious makes a weak nation strong, changes a nondescript tribal people into a mighty and powerful civilization, rescues them from captivity and elevates them to sovereignty, transforms their ignorance into knowledge and endows them with an impetus of advancement in all degrees of development—(this is not theory, but historical fact)—it becomes evident that religion is the cause of man's attainment to honor and sublimity.

But when we speak of religion we mean the essential foundation or reality of religion, not the dogmas and blind imitations which have gradually encrusted it and which are the cause of the decline and effacement of a nation. These are inevitably destructive and a menace and hindrance to a nation's life,—even as it is recorded in the Torah and confirmed in history that when the Jews became fettered by empty forms and imitations the wrath of God became manifest. When they forsook the foundations of the law of God, Nebuchadnezzar came and conquered the Holy Land. He killed and made captive the people of Israel, laid waste the country and populous cities and burned the villages. Seventy thousand Jews were carried away captive to Babylon. He destroyed Jerusalem, despoiled the great temple, desecrated the holy of holies and burned the Torah, the heavenly book of scriptures. Therefore we learn that allegiance to the essential foundation of the divine religions is ever the cause of development and progress, whereas the abandonment and beclouding of that essential reality through blind imitations and adherence to dogmatic beliefs is the cause of a nation's debasement and degradation. After their conquest by the Babylonians, the Jews were successively subjugated by the Greeks and Romans. Under the Roman general Titus, 70 A. D., the Holy Land was stripped and pillaged, Jerusalem razed to its foundations and the Israelites scattered broadcast throughout the world. So complete was their dispersion that they have continued without a country and government of their own to the present day.

From this review of the history of the Jewish people we learn that the foundation of the religion of God laid by His Holiness Moses was the cause of their eternal honor and national prestige, the animating impulse of their advancement and racial supremacy and the source of that excellence which will always command the respect and reverence of those who understand their peculiar destiny and outcome. The dogmas and blind imitations which gradually obscured the reality of the religion of God proved to be Israel's destructive influences causing the expulsion of these chosen people from the Holy Land of their Covenant and promise.

What then is the mission of the divine prophets? Their mission is the education and advancement of the world of humanity. They are the real teachers and educators, the universal instructors of mankind. If we wish to discover whether any one of these great souls or messengers was in reality a prophet of God we must investigate the facts surrounding His life and history; and the first point of our investigation will be the education He bestowed upon mankind. If He has been an educator, if He has really trained a nation or people, causing it to rise from the lowest depths of ignorance to the highest station of knowledge, then we are sure that He was a prophet. This is a plain and clear method of procedure, proof that is irrefutable. We do not need to seek after other proofs. We do not need to mention miracles, saying that out of rock water gushed forth, for such miracles and statements may be denied and refused by those who hear them. The deeds of Moses are conclusive evidences of His prophethood. If a man be fair, unbiased and willing to investigate reality he will undoubtedly testify to the fact that Moses was verily a man of God and a great personage.

In further consideration of this subject, I wish you to be fair and reasonable in your judgment, setting aside all religious prejudices. We should earnestly seek and thoroughly investigate realities, recognizing that the purpose of the religion of God is the education of humanity and the unity and fellowship of mankind. Furthermore we will establish the point that the foundations of the religions of God are one foundation. This foundation is not multiple for it is reality itself. Reality does not admit of multiplicity although each of the divine religions is separable into two divisions. One concerns the world of morality and the ethical training of human nature. It is directed to the advancement of the world of humanity in general; it reveals and inculcates the knowledge of God and makes possible the discovery of the verities of life. This is ideal and spiritual teaching, the essential quality of divine religion and not subject to change or transformation. It is the one foundation of all the religions of God. Therefore the religions are essentially one and the same.

The second classification or division comprises social laws and regulations applicable to human conduct. This is not the essential spiritual quality of religion. It is subject to change and transformation according to the exigencies and requirements of time and place. For instance in the time of Noah certain requirements made it necessary that all sea foods be allowable or lawful. During the time of the Abrahamic prophethood it was considered allowable because of a certain exigency that a man should marry his aunt, even as Sarah was the sister of Abraham's mother. During the cycle of Adam it was lawful and expedient for a man to marry his own sister, even as Abel, Cain and Seth the sons of Adam married their sisters. But in the law of the Pentateuch revealed by Moses these marriages were forbidden and their custom and sanction abrogated. Other laws formerly valid were annulled during the time of Moses. For example, it was lawful in Abraham's cycle to eat the flesh of the camel, but during the time of Jacob this was prohibited. Such changes and transformations in the teaching of religion are applicable to the ordinary conditions of life but they are not important or essential. His Holiness Moses lived in the wilderness of Sinai where crime necessitated direct punishment. There were no penitentiaries or penalties of imprisonment. Therefore according to the exigency of the time and place it was a law of God that an eye should be given for an eye and a tooth for a tooth. It would not be practicable to enforce this law at the present time; for instance to blind a man who accidentally blinded you. In the Torah there are many commands concerning the punishment of a murderer. It would not be allowable or possible to carry out these ordinances today. Human conditions and exigencies are such that even the question of capital punishment,—the one penalty which most nations have continued to enforce for murder,—is now under discussion by wise men who are debating its advisability. In fact, laws for the ordinary conditions of life are only valid temporarily. The exigencies of the time of Moses justified cutting off a man's hand for theft but such a penalty is not allowable now. Time changes conditions, and laws change to suit conditions. We must remember that these changing laws are not the essentials; they are the accidentals of religion. The essential ordinances established by a Manifestation of God are spiritual; they concern moralities, the ethical development of man and faith in God. They are ideal and necessarily permanent; expressions of the one foundation and not amenable to change or transformation. Therefore the fundamental basis of the revealed religion of God is immutable, unchanging throughout the centuries, not subject to the varying conditions of the human world.

Christ ratified and proclaimed the foundation of the law of Moses. Muḥammad and all the prophets have revoiced that same foundation of reality. Therefore the purposes and accomplishments of the divine messengers have been one and the same. They were the source of advancement to the body-politic and the cause of the honor and divine civilization of humanity the foundation of which is one and the same in every dispensation. It is evident then that the proofs of the validity and inspiration of a prophet of God are the deeds of beneficent accomplishment and greatness emanating from Him. If He proves to be instrumental in the elevation and betterment of mankind, He is undoubtedly a valid and heavenly messenger.

I wish you to be reasonable and just in your consideration of the following statements:

At the time when the Israelites had been dispersed by the power of the Roman empire and the national life of the Hebrew people had been effaced by their conquerors,—when the law of God had seemingly passed from them and the foundation of the religion of God was apparently destroyed,—Jesus Christ appeared. When His Holiness arose among the Jews, the first thing He did was to proclaim the validity of the Manifestation of Moses. He declared that the Torah, the Old Testament, was the Book of God and that all the prophets of Israel were valid and true. He extolled the mission of Moses and through His proclamation the name of Moses was spread throughout the world. Through Christianity the greatness of Moses became known among all nations. It is a fact that before the appearance of Christ, the name of Moses had not been heard in Írán. In India they had no knowledge of Judaism and it was only through the Christianizing of Europe that the teachings of the Old Testament became spread in that region. Throughout Europe there was not a copy of the Old Testament; but consider this carefully and judge it aright;—through the instrumentality of Christ, through the translation of the New Testament, the little volume of the Gospel, the Old Testament, the Torah, has been translated into six hundred languages and spread everywhere in the world. The names of the Hebrew prophets became household words among the nations, who believed that the children of Israel were verily the chosen people of God, a holy nation under the especial blessing and protection of God, and that therefore the prophets who had arisen in Israel were the day springs of revelation and brilliant stars in the heaven of the will of God.

Therefore His Holiness Christ really promulgated Judaism for He was a Jew and not opposed to the Jews. He did not deny the prophethood of Moses; on the contrary He proclaimed and ratified it. He did not invalidate the Torah; He spread its teachings. That portion of the ordinances of Moses which concerned transactions and unimportant conditions underwent transformation but the essential teachings of Moses were revoiced and confirmed by Christ without change. He left nothing unfinished or incomplete. Likewise through the supreme efficacy and power of the Word of God He united most of the nations of the east and the west. This was accomplished at a time when these nations were opposed to each other in hostility and strife. He led them beneath the overshadowing tent of the oneness of humanity. He educated them until they became united and agreed and through His spirit of conciliation the Roman, Greek, Chaldean and Egyptian were blended in a composite civilization. This wonderful power and extraordinary efficacy of the Word prove conclusively the validity of His Holiness Christ. Consider how His heavenly sovereignty is still permanent and lasting. Verily this is conclusive proof and manifest evidence.

From another horizon we see Muḥammad the prophet of Arabia appearing. You may not know that the first address of Muḥammad to His tribe was the statement, "Verily, Moses was a prophet of God and the Torah is a book of God. Verily, O ye people, ye must believe in the Torah, in Moses and the prophets. Ye must accept all the prophets of Israel as valid." In the Qur'án, the Muḥammadan Bible, there are seven statements or repetitions of the Mosaic narrative, and in all the historic accounts Moses is praised. Muḥammad announces that His Holiness Moses was the greatest prophet of God, that God guided Him in the wilderness of Sinai, that through the light of guidance Moses hearkened to the summons of God, that He was the interlocutor of God and the bearer of the tablet of the ten commandments, that all the contemporary nations of the world arose against Him and that eventually Moses conquered them, for falsehood and error are ever overcome by truth. There are many other instances of Muḥammad's confirmation of Moses. I am mentioning but a few. Consider that His Holiness Muḥammad was born among the savage and barbarous tribes of Arabia, lived among them and was outwardly illiterate and uninformed of the holy books of God. The Arabian people were in the utmost ignorance and barbarism. They buried their infant daughters alive, considering this to be an evidence of a valorous and lofty nature. They lived in bondage and serfdom under the Íránian and Roman governments and were scattered throughout the desert engaged in continual strife and bloodshed. When the light of Muḥammad dawned, the darkness of ignorance was dispelled from the deserts of Arabia. In a short period of time those barbarous peoples attained a superlative degree of civilization which with Baghdád as its center extended as far westward as Spain and afterward influenced the greater part of Europe. What proof of prophethood could be greater than this, unless we close our eyes to justice and remain obstinately opposed to reason.

Today the Christians are believers in Moses, accept Him as a prophet of God and praise Him most highly. The Muḥammadans are likewise believers in Moses, accept the validity of His prophethood, at the same time believing in Christ. Could it be said that the acceptance of Moses by the Christians and Muḥammadans has been harmful and detrimental to those people? On the contrary, it has been beneficial to them, proving that they have been fair-minded and just. What harm could result to the Jewish people then if they in return should accept His Holiness Christ and acknowledge the validity of the prophethood of His Holiness Muḥammad? By this acceptance and praiseworthy attitude the enmity and hatred which have afflicted mankind so many centuries would be dispelled, fanaticism and bloodshed pass away and the world be blessed by unity and agreement. Christians and Muḥammadans believe and admit that Moses was the interlocutor of God. Why do you not say that Christ was the Word of God? Why do you not speak these few words that will do away with all this difficulty? Then there will be no more hatred and fanaticism, no more warfare and bloodshed in the Land of Promise. Then there will be peace among you forever.

Verily, I now declare to you that Moses was the interlocutor of God and a most noteworthy prophet; that Moses revealed the fundamental law of God and founded the real ethical basis of the civilization and progress of humanity. What harm is there in this? Have I lost anything by saying this to you and believing it as a Bahá'í? On the contrary it benefits me, and His Holiness

Bahá'u'lláh, the founder of the Bahá'í Cause, confirms me, saying: "You have been fair and just in your judgment; you have impartially investigated the truth and arrived at a true conclusion; you have announced your belief in Moses a prophet of God and accepted the Torah the book of God." Inasmuch as it is possible for me to sweep away all evidences of prejudice by such a liberal and universal statement of belief why is it not possible for you to do likewise? Why not put an end to this religious strife and establish a bond of connection between the hearts of men? Why should not the followers of one religion praise the founder or teacher of another? The other religionists extol the greatness of His Holiness Moses and admit that He was the founder of Judaism. Why do the Hebrews refuse to praise and accept the other great messengers who have appeared in the world? What harm could there be in this? What rightful objection? None whatever. You would lose nothing by such action and statement. On the contrary you would contribute to the welfare of mankind. You would be instrumental in establishing the happiness of the world of humanity. The eternal honor of man depends upon the liberalism of this modern age. Inasmuch as our God is one God and the creator of all mankind, He provides for and protects all. We acknowledge him as a God of kindness, justice and mercy. Why then should we, His children and followers, war and fight, bringing sorrow and grief into the hearts of each other? God is loving and merciful. His intention in religion has ever been the bond of unity and affinity between humankind.

Praise be to God! the mediaeval ages of darkness have passed away and this century of radiance has dawned,—this century wherein the reality of things is becoming evident,—wherein science is penetrating the mysteries of the universe, the oneness of the world of humanity is being established and service to mankind is the paramount motive of all existence. Shall we remain steeped in our fanaticisms and cling to our prejudices? Is it fitting that we should still be bound and restricted by ancient fables and superstitions of the past; be handicapped by superannuated beliefs and the ignorances of dark ages, waging religious wars, fighting and shedding blood, shunning and anathematizing each other? Is this becoming? Is it not better for us to be loving and considerate toward each other? Is it not preferable to enjoy fellowship and unity; join in anthems of praise to the most high God and extol all His prophets in the spirit of acceptance and true vision? Then indeed this world will become a paradise and the promised Day of God will dawn. Then according to the prophecy of Isaiah the wolf and the lamb will drink from the same stream, the owl and the vulture will nest together in the same branches and the lion and the calf pasture in the same meadow. What does this mean? It means that fierce and contending religions, hostile creeds and divergent beliefs will reconcile and associate, notwithstanding their former hatreds and antagonism. Through the liberalism of human attitude demanded in this radiant century they will blend together in perfect fellowship and love. This is the spirit and meaning of Isaiah's words. There will never be a day when this prophecy will come to pass literally, for these animals by their natures cannot mingle and associate in kindness and love. Therefore this prophecy symbolizes the unity and agreement of races, nations and peoples who will come together in attitudes of intelligence, illumination and spirituality.

The age has dawned when human fellowship will become a reality.

The century has come when all religions shall be unified. . . .

Industrial Justice

You have questioned me about strikes. This question is and will be for a long time the subject of great difficulties. Strikes are due to two causes. One is the extreme sharpness and rapacity of the capitalists and manufacturers; the other, the excesses, the avidity and ill-will of the workmen and artisans. It is therefore necessary to remedy these two causes.

But the principal cause of these difficulties lies in the laws of the present civilization; for they lead to a small number of individuals accumulating incomparable fortunes, beyond their needs, whilst the greater number remains destitute, stripped and in the greatest misery. This is contrary to justice, to humanity, to equity; it is the height of iniquity, the opposite to what causes divine satisfaction.

This contrast is peculiar to the world of man: with other creatures, that is to say with nearly all animals, there is a kind of justice and equality. Thus in a shepherd's flock of sheep, in a troop of deer in the country, among the birds of the prairie, of the plain, of the hill or of the orchard, almost every animal receives a just share based on equality. With them such a difference in the means of existence is not to be found: so they live in the most complete peace and joy.

It is quite otherwise with the human species, which persists in the greatest error, and in absolute iniquity. Consider an individual who has amassed treasures by colonizing a country for his profit: he has obtained an incomparable fortune, and has secured profits and incomes which flow like a river, whilst a hundred thousand unfortunate people, weak and powerless, are in need of a mouthful of bread. There is neither equality nor brotherhood. So you see that general peace and joy are destroyed, the welfare of humanity is partially annihilated, and that collective life is fruitless. Indeed, fortune, honors, commerce, industry are in the hands of some industrials, whilst other people are submitted to quite a series of difficulties and to limitless troubles: they have neither advantages nor profits, nor comforts, nor peace.

Then rules and laws should be established to regulate the excessive fortunes of certain private individuals, and limit the misery of millions of the poor masses; thus a certain moderation would be obtained. However, absolute equality is just as impossible, for absolute equality in fortunes, honors, commerce, agriculture, industry, would end in a want of comfort, in discouragement, in disorganization of the means of existence, and in universal disappointment: the order of the community would be quite destroyed. Thus, there is a great wisdom in the fact that equality is not imposed by law: it is, therefore, preferable for moderation to do its work. The main point is, by means of laws and regulations to hinder the constitution of the excessive fortunes of certain individuals, and to protect the essential needs of the masses. For instance, the manufacturers and the industrials heap up a treasure each day, and the poor artisans do not gain their daily sustenance:

that is the height of iniquity, and no just man can accept it. Therefore, laws and regulations should be established which would permit the workmen to receive from the factory owner their wages and a share in the fourth or the fifth part of the profits, according to the wants of the factory; or in some other way the body of workmen and the manufacturers should share equitably the profits and advantages. Indeed, the direction and administration of affairs come from the owner of the factory, and the work and labor, from the body of the workmen. In other words, the workmen should receive wages which assure them an adequate support, and when they cease work, becoming feeble or helpless, they should receive from the owner of the factory a sufficient pension. The wages should be high enough to satisfy the workmen with the amount they receive, so that they may be able to put a little aside for days of want and helplessness.

When matters will be thus fixed, the owner of the factory will no longer put aside daily a treasure which he has absolutely no need of (without taking into consideration that if the fortune is disproportionate, the capitalist succumbs under a formidable burden, and gets into the greatest difficulties and troubles; the administration of an excessive fortune is very difficult, and exhausts man's natural strength). And, the workmen and artisans will no longer be in the greatest misery and want, they will no longer be submitted to the worst privations at the end of their life.

It is, then, clear and evident that the repartition of excessive fortunes amongst a small number of individuals, while the masses are in misery, is an iniquity and an injustice. In the same way, absolute equality would be an obstacle to life, to welfare, to order and to the peace of humanity. In such a question a just medium is preferable. It lies in the capitalists being moderate in the acquisition of their profits, and in their having a consideration for the welfare of the poor and needy; that is to say, that the workmen and artisans receive a fixed and established daily wage, and have a share in the general profits of the factory.

It would be well, with regard to the social rights of manufacturers, workmen and artisans, that laws be established, giving moderate profits to manufacturers, and to workmen the necessary means of existence and security for the future. Thus, when they become feeble and cease working, get old and helpless, and die leaving children under age, these children will not be annihilated by excess of poverty. And it is from the income of the factory itself, to which they have a right, that they will derive a little of the means of existence.

In the same way, the workmen should no longer rebel and revolt, nor demand beyond their rights; they should no longer go out on strike, they should be obedient and submissive, and not ask for impudent wages. But the mutual rights of both associated parties will be fixed and established according to custom by just and impartial laws. In case one of the two parties should transgress, the courts of justice would have to give judgment, and by an efficacious fine put an end to the transgression; thus order will be re-established, and the difficulties settled. The interference of courts of justice and of the Government in difficulties pending between manufacturers and workmen is legal, for the reason that current affairs between workmen and manufacturers cannot be compared with ordinary affairs between private persons, which do not concern the public, and with which the Government should not occupy itself. In reality, although they appear to be matters between private persons, these difficulties between patrons and workmen produce a general detriment; for commerce, industry, agriculture and the general affairs of the country are all intimately linked together. If one of these suffers an abuse, the detriment affects the mass. Thus the difficulties between workmen and manufacturers become a cause of general detriment.

The court of justice and the Government have therefore the right of interference. When a difficulty occurs between two individuals with reference to private rights, it is necessary for a third to settle the question: this is the part of the Government: then the question of strikes—which cause troubles in the country and are often connected with the excessive vexations of the workmen, as well as with the rapacity of manufacturers—how could it remain neglected?

Good God! is it possible that, seeing one of his fellow-creatures starving, destitute of everything, a man can rest and live comfortably in his luxurious mansion? He who meets another in the greatest misery, can he enjoy his fortune? That is why, in the religion of God, it is prescribed and established that wealthy men each year give over a certain part of their fortune for the maintenance of the poor and unfortunate. That is the foundation of the religion of God, and the most essential of the commandments.

As now man is not forced nor obliged by the Government, if by the natural tendency of his good heart, with the greatest spirituality, he goes to this expense for the poor, this will be a thing very much praised, approved and pleasing.

Such is the meaning of the good works in the Divine Books and Tablets.

Universal Peace

This recent war has proved to the world and the people that war is destruction while Universal Peace is construction; war is death while peace is life; war is rapacity and bloodthirstiness while peace is beneficence and humaneness; war is an appurtenance of the world of nature while peace is of the foundation of the religion of God; war is darkness upon darkness while peace is heavenly light; war is the destroyer of the edifice of mankind while peace is the everlasting life of the world of humanity; war is like a devouring wolf while peace is like the angels of heaven; war is the struggle for existence while peace is mutual aid and cooperation among the peoples of the world and the cause of the good-pleasure of the True One in the heavenly realm.

There is not one soul whose conscience does not testify that in this day there is no more important matter in the world than that of Universal Peace. Every just one bears witness to this and adores that esteemed Assembly because its aim is that this darkness may be changed into light, this bloodthirstiness into kindness, this torment into bliss, this hardship into ease and this enmity and hatred into fellowship and love. Therefore, the effort of those esteemed souls is worthy of praise and commendation.

But the wise souls who are aware of the essential relationships emanating from the realities of things consider that one single matter cannot, by itself, influence the human reality as it ought and should, for until the minds of men become united, no important matter can be accomplished. At present Universal Peace is a matter of great importance, but unity of conscience is essential, so that the foundation of this matter may become secure, its establishment firm and its edifice strong.

Therefore His Holiness Bahá'u'lláh, fifty years ago, expounded this question of Universal Peace at a time when He was confined in the fortress of 'Akká and was wronged and imprisoned. He wrote about this important matter of Universal Peace to all the great sovereigns of the world, and established it among His friends in the Orient. The horizon of the East was in utter darkness, nations displayed the utmost hatred and enmity towards each other, religions thirsted for each other's blood, and it was darkness upon darkness. At such a time His Holiness Bahá'u'lláh shone forth like the sun from the horizon of the East and illumined Írán with the lights of these teachings.

Among His teachings was the declaration of Universal Peace. People of different nations, religions and sects who followed Him came together to such an extent that remarkable gatherings were instituted consisting of the various nations and religions of the East. Every soul who entered these gatherings saw but one nation, one teaching, one pathway, one order, for the teachings of His Holiness Bahá'u'lláh were not limited to the establishment of Universal Peace. They embraced many teachings which supplemented and supported that of Universal Peace.

Among these teachings was the independent investigation of reality so that the world of humanity may be saved from the darkness of imitation and attain to the truth; may tear off and cast away this ragged and outgrown garment of 1,000 years ago and may put on the robe woven in the utmost purity and holiness in the loom of reality. As reality is one and cannot admit of multiplicity, therefore different opinions must ultimately become fused into one.

And among the teachings of His Holiness Bahá'u'lláh is the oneness of the world of humanity; that all human beings are the sheep of God and He is the kind Shepherd. This Shepherd is kind to all the sheep, because He created them all, trained them, provided for them and protected them. There is no doubt that the Shepherd is kind to all the sheep and should there be among these sheep ignorant ones, they must be educated; if there be children, they must be trained until they reach maturity; if there be sick ones, they must be cured. There must be no hatred and enmity, for as by a kind physician these ignorant, sick ones should be treated.

And among the teachings of His Holiness Bahá'u'lláh is, that religion must be the cause of fellowship and love. If it becomes the cause of estrangement then it is not needed, for religion is like a remedy; if it aggravates the disease then it becomes unnecessary.

And among the teachings of Bahá'u'lláh is, that religion must be in conformity with science and reason, so that it may influence the hearts of men. The foundation must be solid and must not consist of imitations.

And among the teachings of Bahá'u'lláh is, that religious, racial, political, economic and patriotic prejudices destroy the edifice of humanity. As long as these prejudices prevail, the world of humanity will not have rest. For a period of 6,000 years history informs us about the world of humanity. During these 6,000 years the world of humanity has not been free from war, strife, murder and bloodthirstiness. In every period war has been waged in one country or another and that war was due to either religious prejudice, racial prejudice, political prejudice or patriotic prejudice. It has therefore been ascertained and proved that all prejudices are destructive of the human edifice. As long as these prejudices persist, the struggle for existence must remain dominant, and bloodthirstiness and rapacity continue. Therefore, even as was the case in the past, the world of humanity cannot be saved from the darkness of nature and cannot attain illumination except through the abandonment of prejudices and the acquisition of the morals of the Kingdom.

If this prejudice and enmity are on account of religion (consider that), religion should be the cause of fellowship, otherwise it is fruitless. And if this prejudice be the prejudice of nationality (consider that) all mankind are of one nation; all have sprung from the tree of Adam, and Adam is the root of the tree. That tree is one and all these nations are like branches, while the individuals of humanity are like leaves, blossoms and fruits thereof. Then the establishment of various nations and the consequent shedding of blood and destruction of the edifice of humanity result from human ignorance and selfish motives.

As to the patriotic prejudice, this is also due to absolute ignorance, for the surface of the earth is one native land. Every one can live in any spot on the terrestrial globe. Therefore all the world is man's birthplace. These boundaries and outlets have been devised by man. In the creation, such boundaries and outlets were not assigned. Europe is one continent, Asia is one continent, Africa is one continent, Australia is one continent, but some of the souls, from personal motives and selfish interests, have divided each one of these continents and considered a certain part as their own country. God has set up no frontier between France and Germany; they are continuous. Yea, in the first centuries, selfish souls, for the promotion of their own interests, have assigned boundaries and outlets and have, day by day, attached more importance to these, until this led to intense enmity, bloodshed and rapacity in subsequent centuries. In the same way this will continue indefinitely, and if this conception of patriotism remains limited within a certain circle, it will be the primary cause of the world's destruction. No wise and just person will acknowledge these imaginary distinctions. Every limited area which we call our native country we regard as our mother-land, whereas the terrestrial globe is the mother-land of all, and not any restricted area. In short, for a few days we live on this earth and eventually we are buried in it, it is our eternal tomb. Is it worth while that we should engage in bloodshed and tear one another to pieces for this eternal tomb? Nay, far from it, neither is God pleased with such conduct nor would any sane man approve of it.

Consider! The blessed animals engage in no patriotic quarrels. They are in the utmost fellowship with one another and live together in harmony. For example, if a dove from the East and a dove from the West, a dove from the North and a dove from the South chance to arrive, at the same time, in one spot, they immediately associate in harmony. So is it with all the blessed animals and birds. But ferocious animals, as soon as they meet, attack and fight with each other, tear each other to pieces and it is impossible for them to live peaceably together in one spot. They are all unsociable and fierce, savage and combative fighters.

Regarding the economic prejudice, it is apparent that whenever the ties between nations become strengthened and the exchange of commodities accelerated, and any economic principle is established in one country, it will ultimately affect the other countries and universal benefits will result. Then why this prejudice?

As to the political prejudice, the policy of God must be followed and it is indisputable that the policy of God is greater than human policy. We must follow the Divine policy and that applies alike to all individuals. He treats all individuals alike: no distinction is made, and that is the foundation of the Divine Religions.

And among the teachings of His Holiness Bahá'u'lláh is the origination of one language that may be spread universally among the people. This teaching was revealed from the pen of His Holiness Bahá'u'lláh in order that this universal language may eliminate misunderstandings from among mankind.

And among the teachings of His Holiness Bahá'u'lláh is the equality of women and men. The world of humanity has two wings—one is women and the other men. Not until both wings are equally developed can the bird fly. Should one wing remain weak, flight is impossible. Not until the world of women becomes equal to the world of men in the acquisition of virtues and perfections, can success and prosperity be attained as they ought to be.

And among the teachings of Bahá'u'lláh is voluntary sharing of one's property with others among mankind. This voluntary sharing is greater than equality, and consists in this, that man should not prefer himself to others, but rather should sacrifice his life and property for others. But this should not be introduced by coercion so that it becomes a law and man is compelled to follow it. Nay, rather, man should voluntarily and of his own choice sacrifice his property and life for others, and spend willingly for the poor, just as is done in Írán among the Bahá'ís.

And among the teachings of His Holiness Bahá'u'lláh is man's freedom, that through the ideal Power he should be free and emancipated from the captivity of the world of nature; for as long as man is captive to nature he is a ferocious animal, as the struggle for existence is one of the exigencies of the world of nature. This matter of the struggle for existence is the fountain-head of all calamities and is the supreme affliction.

And among the teachings of Bahá'u'lláh is that religion is a mighty bulwark. If the edifice of religion shakes and totters, commotion and chaos will ensue and the order of things will be utterly upset, for in the world of mankind there are two safeguards that protect man from wrongdoing. One is the law which punishes the criminal; but the law prevents only the manifest crime and not the concealed sin; whereas the ideal safeguard, namely, the religion of God, prevents both the manifest and the concealed crime, trains man, educates morals, compels the adoption of virtues and is the all-inclusive power which guarantees the felicity of the world of mankind. But by religion is meant that which is ascertained by investigation and not that which is based on mere imitation, the foundation of Divine Religions and not human imitations.

And among the teachings of Bahá'u'lláh is that although material civilization is one of the means for the progress of the world of mankind, yet until it becomes combined with Divine civilization, the desired result, which is the felicity of mankind, will not be attained. Consider! These battleships that reduce a city to ruins within the space of an hour are the result of material civilization; likewise the Krupp guns, the Mauser rifles, dynamite, submarines, torpedo boats, armed aircraft and bombing aeroplanes—all these weapons of war are the malignant fruits of material civilization. Had material civilization been combined with Divine civilization, these fiery weapons would never have been invented. Nay, rather, human energy would have been wholly devoted to useful inventions and would have been concentrated on praiseworthy discoveries. Material civilization is like a lamp-glass. Divine civilization is the lamp itself and the glass without the light is dark. Material civilization is like the body. No matter how infinitely graceful, elegant and beautiful it may be, it is dead. Divine civilization is like the spirit, and the body gets its life from the spirit, otherwise it becomes a corpse. It has thus been made evident that the world of mankind is in need of the breaths of the Holy Spirit. Without the spirit the world of mankind is lifeless, and without this light the world of mankind is in utter darkness. For the world of nature is an animal world. Until man is born again from the world of nature, that is to say, becomes detached from the world of nature, he is essentially an animal, and it is the teachings of God which converts this animal into a human soul.

And among the teachings of Bahá'u'lláh is the promotion of education. Every child must be instructed in sciences as much as is necessary. If the parents are able to provide the expenses of this education, it is all right, otherwise the community must provide the means for the teaching of that child.

And among the teachings of His Holiness Bahá'u'lláh is justice and right. Until these are realized on the plane of existence, all things shall be in disorder and remain imperfect. The world of mankind is a world of oppression and cruelty, and a realm of aggression and error.

In fine, such teachings are numerous. These manifold principles, which constitute the greatest basis for the felicity of mankind and are of the bounties of the Merciful, must be added to the matter of Universal Peace and combined with it, so that results may accrue. Otherwise the realization of Universal Peace (by itself) in the world of mankind is difficult. As the teachings of His Holiness Bahá'u'lláh are combined with Universal Peace, they are like a table provided with every kind of fresh and delicious food. Every soul can find, at that table of infinite bounty, that which he desires. If the question is restricted to Universal Peace alone, the remarkable results which are expected and desired will not be attained. The scope of Universal Peace must be such that all the communities and religions may find their highest wish realized in it. At present the teachings of His Holiness Bahá'u'lláh are such that all the communities of the world, whether religious, political or ethical, ancient or modern, find in the teachings of Bahá'u'lláh the expression of their highest wish.

For example, the people of religions find, in the teaching of His

Holiness Bahá'u'lláh, the establishment of Universal Religion—a religion that perfectly conforms with present conditions, which in reality effects the immediate cure of the incurable disease, which relieves every pain, and bestows the infallible antidote for every deadly poison. For if we wish to arrange and organize the world of mankind in accordance with the present religious imitations and thereby to establish the felicity of the world of mankind, it is impossible and impracticable—for example, the enforcement of the laws of the Old Testament (Torah) and also of the other religions in accordance with present imitations. But the essential basis of all the Divine Religions which pertains to the virtues of the world of mankind and is the foundation of the welfare of the world of man, is found in the teachings of His Holiness Bahá'u'lláh in the most perfect presentation.

Similarly, with regard to the peoples who clamor for freedom: the moderate freedom which guarantees the welfare of the world of mankind and maintains and preserves the universal relationships, is found in its fullest power and extension in the teachings of His Holiness Bahá'u'lláh.

So with regard to political parties: that which is the greatest policy directing the world of mankind, nay, rather, the Divine policy, is found in the teachings of His Holiness Bahá'u'lláh.

Likewise with regard to the party of "equality" which seeks the solution of the economic problems: until now all proposed solutions have proved impracticable except the economic proposals in the teachings of His Holiness Bahá'u'lláh which are practicable and cause no distress to society.

So with the other parties: when ye look deeply into this matter, ye will discover that the highest aims of those parties are found in the teachings of Bahá'u'lláh. These teachings constitute the all-inclusive power among all men and are practicable. But there are some teachings of the past, such as those of the Torah, which cannot be carried out at the present day. It is the same with the other religions and the tenets of the various sects and the different parties.

For example, the question of Universal Peace, about which His Holiness Bahá'u'lláh says that the Supreme Tribunal must be established: although the League of Nations has been brought into existence, yet it is incapable of establishing Universal Peace. But the Supreme Tribunal which His Holiness Bahá'u'lláh has described will fulfil this sacred task with the utmost might and power. And His plan is this: that the national assemblies of each country and nation—that is to say parliaments—should elect two or three persons who are the choicest men of that nation, and are well informed concerning international laws and the relations between governments and aware of the essential needs of the world of humanity in this day. The number of these representatives should be in proportion to the number of inhabitants of that country. The election of these souls who are chosen by the national assembly, that is, the parliament, must be confirmed by the upper house, the congress and the cabinet and also by the president or monarch so these persons may be the elected ones of all the nation and the government. From among these people the members of the Supreme Tribunal will be elected, and all mankind will thus have a share therein, for every one of these delegates is fully representative of his nation. When the Supreme Tribunal gives a ruling on any international question, either unanimously or by majority-rule, there will no longer be any pretext for the plaintiff or ground of objection for the defendant. In case any of the governments or nations, in the execution of the irrefutable decision of the Supreme Tribunal, be negligent or dilatory, the rest of the nations will rise up against it, because all the governments and nations of the world are the supporters of this Supreme Tribunal. Consider what a firm foundation this is! But by a limited and restricted League the purpose will not be realized as it ought and should. This is the truth about the situation, which has been stated.

Consider how powerful are the teachings of His Holiness Bahá'u'lláh. At a time when His Holiness was in the prison of 'Akká and was under the restrictions and threats of two bloodthirsty kings, notwithstanding this fact, His teachings spread with all power in Írán and other countries. Should any teaching, or any principle, or any community fall under the threat of a powerful and bloodthirsty monarch it will be annihilated within a short space of time. At present for fifty years the Bahá'ís in Írán and most regions have been under severe restrictions and the threat of sword and spear. Thousands of souls have given their lives in the arena of sacrifice and have fallen as victims under the swords of oppression and cruelty. Thousands of esteemed families have been uprooted and destroyed. Thousands of children have been made fatherless. Thousands of fathers have been bereft of their sons. Thousands of mothers have wept and lamented for their boys who have been beheaded. All this oppression and cruelty, rapacity and bloodthirstiness did not hinder or prevent the spread of the teachings of Bahá'u'lláh. They spread more and more every day, and their power and might became more evident.

It may be that some foolish person among the Íránians will affix his name to the contents of the Tablets of His Holiness Bahá'u'lláh or to the explanations given in the letters of 'Abdu'l-Bahá and send it to that esteemed Assembly. Ye must be aware of this fact, for any Íránian who seeks fame or has some other intention will take the entire contents of the Tablets of His Holiness Bahá'u'lláh and publish them in his own name or in that of his community, just as happened at the Universal Races Congress in London before the war. An Íránian took the substance of the Epistles of His Holiness Bahá'u'lláh, entered that Congress, gave them forth in his own name and published them, whereas the wording was exactly that of His Holiness Bahá'u'lláh. Some such souls have gone to Europe and have caused confusion in the minds of the people of Europe and have disturbed the thoughts of some Orientalists. Ye must bear this fact in mind, for not a word of these teachings was heard in Írán before the appearance of Bahá'u'lláh. Investigate this matter so that it may become to you evident and manifest. Some souls are like parrots. They learn any note which they may hear, and sing it, but they themselves are unaware of what they utter. There is a sect in Írán at present made up of a few souls who are called Bábís, who claim to be followers of His Holiness the Báb, whereas they are utterly unaware of His Holiness. They have some secret teachings which are entirely opposed to the teachings of Bahá'u'lláh and in Írán people know this. But when these souls come to Europe, they conceal their own teachings and utter those of His Holiness Bahá'u'lláh, for they know that the teachings of His Holiness Bahá'u'lláh are powerful and they therefore declare publicly those teachings of Bahá'u'lláh in their own name. As to their secret teachings, they say that they are taken from the Book of Bayán, and the Book of Bayán is from His Holiness the Báb. When ye get hold of the translation of the Book of Bayán, which has been translated in Írán, ye will discover the truth that the teachings of Bahá'u'lláh are utterly opposed to the teachings of this sect. Beware lest ye disregard this fact. Should ye desire to investigate the matter further, inquire from Írán.

In fine, when traveling and journeying throughout the world, wherever one finds construction, it is the result of fellowship and love, while everything that is in ruin shows the effect of enmity and hatred. Notwithstanding this, the world of humanity has not become aware and has not awakened from the sleep of heedlessness. Again it engages in differences, in disputes and wrangling, that it may set up ranks of war and may run to and fro in the arena of battle and strife.

So is it with regard to the universe and its corruption, existence and non-existence. Every contingent being is made up of different and numerous elements and the existence of everything is a result of composition. That is to say, when between simple elements a composition takes place a being arises; the creation of beings comes about in this way. And when that composition is upset, it is followed by decomposition, the elements disintegrate, and that being becomes annihilated. That is to say, the annihilation of everything consists in the decomposition and the separation of elements. Therefore every union and color of leaves, of flowers and of fruits, each will contribute to the beauty and charm of the others and will make an admirable garden, and will appear in the utmost loveliness, freshness and sweetness. Likewise, when difference and variety of thoughts, forms, opinions, characters and morals of the world of mankind come under the control of one Supreme Power, that influence of composition among the elements is the cause of life, while dissociation and separation is the cause of death. In short, attraction and harmony of things are the cause of the production of fruits and useful results, while repulsion and inharmony of things are the cause of disturbance and annihilation. From harmony and attraction, all living contingent beings, such as plant, animal and man, are realized, and from inharmony and repulsion decay sets in and annihilation becomes manifest. Therefore whatever is the cause of harmony, attraction and union among men is the life of the world of humanity, and whatever is the cause of difference, of repulsion and of separation is the cause of the death of mankind. And when you pass by a garden wherein vegetable beds and plants, flowers and fragrant herbs are all combined so as to form a harmonious whole, this is an evidence that this plantation and this rose garden have been cultivated and arranged by the care of a perfect gardener, while when you see a garden in disorder, lacking arrangement and confused, this indicates that it has been deprived of the care of a skillful gardener, nay, rather, it is nothing but a mass of weeds. It has therefore been made evident that fellowship and harmony are indicative of the training by the real Educator, while separation and dispersion prove wildness and deprivation of Divine training.

Should any one object that, since the communities and nations and races and peoples of the world have different formalities, customs, tastes, temperaments, morals, varied thoughts, minds and opinions, it is therefore impossible for ideal unity to be made manifest and complete union among men to be realized, we say that differences are of two kinds: One leads to destruction, and that is like the difference between warring peoples and competing nations who destroy one another, uproot each other's families, do away with rest and comfort and engage in bloodshed and rapacity. That is blameworthy. But the other difference consists in variation. This is perfection itself and the cause of the appearance of Divine bounty. Consider the flowers of the rose garden. Although they are of different kinds, various colors and diverse forms and appearances, yet as they drink from one water, are swayed by one breeze and grow by the warmth and light of one sun, this variation and this difference cause each to enhance the beauty and splendor of the others. The differences in manners, in customs, in habits, in thoughts, opinions and in temperaments is the cause of the adornment of the world of mankind. This is praiseworthy. Likewise this difference and this variation, like the difference and variation of the parts and members of the human body, are the cause of the appearance of beauty and perfection. As these different parts and members are under the control of the dominant spirit, and the spirit permeates all the organs and members, and rules all the arteries and veins, this difference and this variation strengthen love and harmony and this multiplicity is the greatest aid to unity. If in a garden the flowers and fragrant herbs, the blossoms and fruits, the leaves, branches and trees are of one kind, of one form, of one color and of one arrangement, there is no beauty or sweetness, but when there is variety in the world of oneness, they will appear and be displayed in the most perfect glory, beauty, exaltation and perfection. Today nothing but the power of the Word of God which encompasses the realities of things can bring the thoughts, the minds, the hearts and the spirits under the shade of one Tree. He is the potent in all things, the vivifier of souls, the preserver and the controller of the world of mankind. Praise be to God, in this day the light of the Word of God has shone forth upon all regions, and from all sects, communities, nations, tribes, peoples, religions and denominations, souls have gathered under the shadow of the Word of Oneness and have in the most intimate fellowship united and harmonized!

CHAPTER SEVEN

SOUL, MIND AND SPIRIT

The Origin of Man

Know that it is one of the most abstruse spiritual truths that the world of existence, that is to say this endless universe, has no beginning.

We have already explained that the names and attributes of the Divinity themselves require the existence of beings. Although this subject has been explained in detail, we will speak of it again briefly. Know that an educator without pupils cannot be imagined, a monarch without subjects could not exist, a master without scholars cannot be appointed, a creator without a creature is impossible, a provider without those provided for cannot be conceived; for all the divine names and attributes demand the existence of beings. If we could imagine a time when no beings existed, this imagination would be the denial of the Divinity of God. Moreover, absolute non-existence cannot become existence. If the beings were absolutely non-existent, existence would not have come into being. Therefore, as the Essence of Unity, that is the existence of God, is everlasting and eternal—that is to say, it has neither beginning nor end—it is certain that this world of existence, this endless universe, has neither beginning nor end. Yes, it may be that one of the parts of the universe, one of the globes, for example, may come into existence, or may be disintegrated, but the other endless globes are still existing; the universe would not be disordered nor destroyed; on the contrary, existence is eternal and perpetual. As each globe has a beginning, necessarily it has an end, because every composition, collective or particular, must of necessity be decomposed; the only difference is that some are quickly decomposed, and others more slowly, but it is impossible that a composed thing should not eventually be decomposed.

It is necessary, therefore, that we should know what each of the important existences was in the beginning—for there is no doubt that in the beginning the origin was one: the origin of all numbers is one and not two. Then it is evident that in the beginning matter was one, and that one matter appeared in different aspects in each element; thus various forms were produced, and these various aspects as they were produced became permanent, and each element was specialized. But this permanence was not definite, and did not attain realization and perfect existence until after a very long time. Then these elements became composed, and organized and combined in infinite forms; or rather from the composition and combination of these elements innumerable beings appeared.

This composition and arrangement through the wisdom of God and His pre-existent might, were produced from one natural organization, which was composed and combined with the greatest strength, conformably to wisdom, and according to a universal law. From this it is evident that it is the creation of God, and is not a fortuitous composition and arrangement. This is why from every natural composition a being can come into existence, but from an accidental composition no being can come into existence. For example, if a man of his own mind and intelligence collects some elements and combines them, a living being will not be brought into existence, since the system is unnatural. This is the answer to the implied question, that, since beings are made by the composition and the combination of elements, why is it not possible for us to gather elements and mingle them together, and so create a living being. This is a false supposition, for the origin of this composition is from God; it is God who makes the combination, and as it is done according to the natural system, from each composition one being is produced, and an existence is realized. A composition made by man produces nothing, because man cannot create.

Briefly, we have said that from the composition and combination of elements, from their decomposition, from their measure, and from the effect of other beings upon them, resulted forms, endless realities, and innumerable beings. But it is clear that this terrestrial globe in its present form did not come into existence all at once; but that this universal existence gradually passed through different phases until it became adorned with its present perfection. Universal beings resemble and can be compared to particular beings, for both are subjected to one natural system, one universal law and divine organization. So you will find the smallest atoms in the universal system are similar to the greatest beings of the universe. It is clear that they come into existence from one laboratory of might under one natural system, and one universal law; therefore they may be compared to one another. Thus the embryo of man in the womb of the mother gradually grows and develops, and appears in different forms and conditions, until in the degree of perfect beauty it reaches maturity, and appears in a perfect form with the utmost grace. And in the same way, the seed of this flower which you see was in the beginning an insignificant thing, and very small; and it grew and developed in the womb of the earth, and after appearing in various forms, came forth in this condition with perfect freshness and grace. In the same manner it is evident that this terrestrial globe having once found existence, grew and developed in the matrix of the universe, and came forth in different forms and conditions, until gradually it attained this present perfection, and became adorned with innumerable beings, and appeared as a finished organization.

Then it is clear that original matter, which is in the embryonic state, and the mingled and composed elements which were its earliest forms, gradually grew and developed during many ages and cycles, passing from one shape and form to another, until they appeared in this perfection, this system, this organization and this establishment, through the supreme wisdom of God.

Let us return to our subject that man, in the beginning of his existence and in the womb of the earth, like the embryo in the womb of the mother, gradually grew and developed, and passed from one form to another, from one shape to another, until he appeared with this beauty and perfection, this force and this power. It is certain that in the beginning he had not this loveliness and grace and elegance, and that he only by degrees attained this shape, this form, this beauty, and this grace. There is no doubt that the human embryo did not at once appear in this form, neither did it then become the manifestation of the words: "Praise be unto God, the best of Creators." Gradually it passed through various conditions and different shapes, until it attained this form and beauty, this perfection; grace, and loveliness. Thus it is evident and confirmed that the development and growth of man on this earth, until he reached his present perfection, resembled the growth and development of the embryo in the womb of the mother: by degrees it passed from condition to condition, from form to form, from one shape to another, for this is according to the requirement of the universal system and divine law.

That is to say, the embryo passes through different states and traverses numerous degrees, until it reaches the form in which it manifests the words: "Praise be to God, the best of Creators," and until the signs of reason and maturity appear. And in the same way, man's existence on this earth, from the beginning until it reaches this state, form, and condition, necessarily lasts a long time, and goes through many degrees until it reaches this condition. But from the beginning of man's existence he is a distinct species. In the same way, the embryo of man in the womb of the mother was at first in a strange form; then this body passes from shape to shape, from state to state, from form to form, until it appears in utmost beauty and perfection. But even when in the womb of the mother and in this strange form, entirely different from his present form and figure, he is the embryo of the superior species, and not of the animal; his species and essence undergo no change. Now, admitting that the traces of organs which have disappeared actually exist, this is not a proof of the impermanence and the non-originality of the species. At the most it proves that the form, and fashion, and the organs of man have progressed. Man was always a distinct species, a man, not an animal. So, if the embryo of man in the womb of the mother passes from one form to another, so that the second form in no way resembles the first, is this a proof that the species has changed? that it was at first an animal, and that its organs progressed and developed until it became a man? No indeed! How puerile and unfounded is this idea and this thought! For the proof of the originality of the human species, and of the permanency of the nature of man, is clear and evident.

Modification of Species

We have now come to the question of the modification of species and of organic development: that is to say, to the point of inquiring whether man's descent is from the animal.

This theory has found credence in the minds of some European philosophers, and it is now very difficult to make its falseness understood, but in the future it will become evident and clear, and the European philosophers will themselves realize its untruth. For verily it is an evident error. When man looks at the beings with a penetrating regard, and attentively examines the condition of existences, and when he sees the state, the organization, and the perfection of the world, he will be convinced that in the possible world there is nothing more wonderful than that which already exists. For all existing beings, terrestrial and celestial, as well as this limitless space and all that is in it, have been created and organized, composed, arranged, and perfected as they ought to be; the universe has no imperfection; so that if all beings became pure intelligence and reflected for ever and ever, it is impossible that they could imagine anything better than that which exists.

If, however, the creation in the past had not been adorned with utmost perfection, then existence would have been imperfect and meaningless, and in this case creation would have been incomplete. This question needs to be considered with the greatest attention and thought. For example, imagine that the world of possibility—that is, the world of existence—resembles in a general way the body of man. If this composition, organization, perfection, beauty, and completeness which now exist in the human body were different, it would be absolute imperfection. Now, if we imagine a time when man belonged to the animal world, or when he was merely an animal, we shall find that existence would have been imperfect; that is to say, there would have been no man, and this chief member, which in the body of the world is like the brain and mind in man, would have been missing. The world would then have been quite imperfect. It is thus proved that if there had been a time when man was in the animal kingdom, the perfection of existence would have been destroyed; for man is the greatest member of this world, and if the body was without this chief member, surely it would be imperfect. We consider man as the greatest member because, among the creatures, he is the sum of all existing perfections. When we speak of man, we mean the perfect one, the foremost individual in the world, who is the sum of spiritual and apparent perfections, and who is like the sun among the beings. Then imagine that at one time the sun did not exist, but that it was a planet—surely at such a time the relations of existence would be disordered. How can such a thing be imagined? To a man who examines the world of existence, what we have said is sufficient.

There is another more subtle proof: all these endless beings which inhabit the world, whether man, animal, vegetable, mineral —whatever they may be—are surely, each one of them, composed of elements. There is no doubt that this perfection which is in all beings, is caused by the creation of God from the composing elements, by their appropriate mingling and proportionate quantities, the mode of their composition, and the influence of other beings. For all beings are connected together like a chain, and reciprocal help, assistance, and influence belonging to the properties of things, are the causes of the existence, development, and growth of created beings. It is confirmed through evidences and proofs that every being universally acts upon other beings, either absolutely or through association. Finally, the perfection of each individual being, that is to say the perfection which you now see in man or apart from him, with regard to their atoms, members, or powers, is due to the composition of the elements, to their measure, to their balance, to the mode of their combination, and to mutual influence. When all these are gathered together, then man exists.

As the perfection of man is entirely due to the composition of the atoms of the elements, to their measure, to the method of their combination, and to the mutual influence and action of the different beings—then, since man was produced ten or a hundred thousand years ago from these earthly elements with the same measure and balance, the same method of combination and mingling, and the same influence of the other beings, exactly the same man existed then as now. This is evident and not worth debating. A thousand million years hence, if these elements of man are gathered together and arranged in this special proportion, and if the elements are combined according to the same method, and if they are affected by the same influence of other beings, exactly the same man will exist. For example, if after a hundred thousand years there is oil, fire, a wick, a lamp, and the lighter of the lamp —briefly, if there are all the necessaries which now exist, exactly the same lamp will be obtained.

These are conclusive and evident facts. But the arguments which these European philosophers have used raise doubtful proofs and are not conclusive.

The Kingdom of Man

Know that people belong to two categories, that is to say, they constitute two parties. One party deny the spirit, and say that man also is a species of animal; for they say, do we not see that animals and men share the same powers and senses? These simple single elements which fill space are endlessly combined, and from each of these combinations one of the beings is produced. Among these beings is the possessor of spirit, of the powers and of the senses. The more perfect the combination, the nobler is the being. The combination of the elements in the body of man is more perfect than the composition of any other being; it is mingled in absolute equilibrium, therefore it is more noble and more perfect. "It is not," they say, "that he has a special power and spirit which the other animals lack: animals possess sensitive bodies, but man in some powers has more sensation—although, in what concerns the outer senses, such as hearing, sight, taste, smell, touch, and even in some interior powers like memory, the animal is more richly endowed than man." "The animal, too," they say, "has intelligence and perception": all that they concede is that man's intelligence is greater.

This is what the philosophers of the present state; this is their saying, this is their supposition, and thus their imagination decrees. So with powerful arguments and proofs, they make the descent of man go back to the animal, and say that there was once a time when man was an animal; that then the species changed, and progressed little by little until it reached the present status of man.

But the theologians say: No, this is not so. Though man has powers and outer senses in common with the animal, yet an extraordinary power exists in him of which the animal is bereft. The sciences, arts, inventions, trades, and discoveries of realities, are the results of this spiritual power. This is a power which encompasses all things, comprehends their realities, discovers all the hidden mysteries of beings, and through this knowledge controls them: it even perceives things which do not exist outwardly; that is to say, intellectual realities which are not sensible, and which have no outward existence, because they are invisible; so it comprehends the mind, the spirit, the qualities, the characters, the love and sorrow of man, which are intellectual realities. Moreover, these existing sciences, arts, laws, and endless inventions of man at one time were invisible, mysterious, and hidden secrets; it is only the all-encompassing human power which has discovered and brought them out from the plane of the invisible to the plane of the visible. So telegraphy, photography, phonography, and all such inventions and wonderful arts, were at one time hidden mysteries: the human reality discovered and brought them out from the plane of the invisible to the plane of the visible. There was even a time when the qualities of this iron which you see—indeed of all the metals—were hidden mysteries; men discovered this metal, and wrought it in this industrial form. It is the same with all the other discoveries and inventions of man, which are innumerable.

This we cannot deny. If we say that these are effects of powers which animals also have, and of the powers of the bodily senses, we see clearly and evidently that the animals are, in regard to these powers, superior to man. For example, the sight of animals is much more keen than the sight of man; so also is their power of smell and taste. Briefly, in the powers which animals and men have in common, the animal is often the more powerful. For example, let us take the power of memory: if you carry a pigeon from here to a distant country, and there set it free, it will return, for it remembers the way. Take a dog from here to the center of Asia, set him free, and he will come back here and never once lose the road. So it is with the other powers such as hearing, sight, smell, taste, and touch.

Thus it is clear that if there were not in man a power different from any of those of the animals, the latter would be superior to man in inventions and the comprehension of realities. Therefore it is evident that man has a gift which the animal does not possess. Now, the animal perceives sensible things, but does not perceive intellectual realities. For example, that which is within the range of its vision the animal sees, but that which is beyond the range of sight it is not possible for it to perceive, and it cannot imagine it. So it is not possible for the animal to understand that the earth has the form of a globe. But man from known things proves unknown things, and discovers unknown truths. For example, man sees the curve of the horizon, and from this he infers the roundness of the earth. The Pole Star at ‘Akká, for instance, is at 33°, that is to say, it is 33° above the horizon. When a man goes towards the North Pole, the Pole Star rises one degree above the horizon for each degree of distance that he travels, that is to say, the altitude of the Pole Star will be 34°, then 40°, then 50°, then 60°, then 70°. If he reaches the North Pole the altitude of the Pole Star will be 90° or have attained the zenith, that is to say, will be directly overhead. This Pole Star and its ascension are sensible things. The farther one goes towards the Pole, the higher the Pole Star rises; from these two known truths an unknown thing has been discovered, that is, that the horizon is curved: meaning that the horizon of each degree of the earth is a different horizon from that of another degree. Man perceives this, and proves from it an invisible thing which is the roundness of the earth. This it is impossible for the animal to perceive. In the same way it cannot understand that the sun is the center and that the earth revolves around it. The animal is the captive of the senses and bound by them; all that is beyond the senses, the things that they do not control, the animal can never understand; although in the outer senses it is greater than man. Hence it is proved and verified that in man there is a power of discovery by which he is distinguished from the animals, and this is the spirit of man.

Praise be to God! man is always turned towards the heights, and his aspiration is lofty; he always desires to reach a greater world than the world in which he is, and to mount to a higher sphere than that in which he is. The love of exaltation is one of the characteristics of man. I am astonished that certain philosophers of America and Europe are content to gradually approach the animal world, and so to go backwards; for the tendency of existence must be towards exaltation. Nevertheless, if you said to one of them, You are an animal—he would be extremely hurt and angry.

What a difference between the human world and the world of the animal; between the elevation of man and the abasement of the animal; between the perfection of man and the ignorance of the animal; between the light of man and the darkness of the animal; between the glory of man and the degradation of the animal! An Arab child of ten years can manage two or three hundred camels in the desert, and with his voice can lead them forward or turn them back. A weak Hindu can so control a huge elephant, that the elephant becomes the most obedient of servants. All things are subdued by the hand of man; he can resist nature, while all other creatures are captives of nature, none can depart from her requirements. Man alone can resist nature. Nature attracts bodies to the center of the earth; man through mechanical means goes far from it, and soars in the air. Nature prevents man from crossing the seas, man builds a ship, and he travels and voyages across the great ocean, and so on; the subject is endless. For example, man drives engines over the mountains and through the wildernesses, and gathers in one spot the news of the events of the East and West. All this is contrary to nature. The sea with its grandeur cannot deviate by an atom from the laws of nature; the sun in all its magnificence cannot deviate as much as a needle's point from the laws of nature, and can never comprehend the conditions, the state, the qualities, the movements, and the nature of man.

What, then, is the power in this small body of man which encompasses all this? What is this ruling power by which he subdues all things?

One more point remains: modern philosophers say: "We have never seen the spirit in man, and in spite of our researches into the secrets of the human body, we do not perceive a spiritual power. How can we imagine a power which is not sensible?" The theologians reply: "The spirit of the animal also is not sensible, and through its bodily powers it cannot be perceived. By what do you prove the existence of the spirit of the animal? There is no doubt that from its effects you prove that in the animal there is a power which is not in the plant, and this is the power of the senses; that is to say, sight, hearing, and also other powers; from these you infer that there is an animal spirit. In the same way, from the proofs and signs we have mentioned, we argue that there is a human spirit. Since in the animal there are signs which are not in the plant, you say this power of sensation is a property of the animal spirit; you also see in man signs, powers, and perfections which do not exist in the animal; therefore you infer that there is a power in him which the animal is without."

If we wish to deny everything that is not sensible, then we must deny the realities which unquestionably exist. For example, ethereal matter is not sensible, though it has an undoubted existence. The power of attraction is not sensible, though it certainly exists. From what do we affirm these existences? From their signs. Thus this light is the vibration of that ethereal matter, and from this vibration we infer the existence of ether.

Man and Evolution

Certain European philosophers agree that the species grows and develops, and that even change and alteration are also possible. One of the proofs that they give for this theory is that through the attentive study and verification of the science of geology it has become clear that the existence of the vegetable preceded that of the animal, and that of the animal preceded that of man. They admit that both the vegetable and the animal species have changed, for in some of the strata of the earth they have discovered plants which existed in the past and are now extinct; they have progressed, grown in strength, their form and appearance have changed, and so the species have altered. In the same way, in the strata of the earth there are some species of animals which have changed and are transformed. One of these animals is the serpent. There are indications that the serpent once had feet; but through the lapse of time those members have disappeared. In the same way, in the vertebral column of man there is an indication which amounts to a proof that, like other animals, he once had a tail. At one time that member was useful, but when man developed it was no longer of use, and therefore it gradually disappeared. As the serpent took refuge under the ground, and became a creeping animal, it was no longer in need of feet, so they disappeared; but their traces survive. The principal argument is this: that the existence of traces of members proves that they once existed; and as now they are no longer of service, they have gradually disappeared. Therefore while the perfect and necessary members have remained, those which are unnecessary have gradually disappeared by the modification of the species, but the traces of them continue.

The first answer to this argument is the fact that the animal having preceded man is not a proof of the evolution, change, and alteration of the species, nor that man was raised from the animal world to the human world. For while the individual appearance of these different beings is certain, it is possible that man came into existence after the animal. So when we examine the vegetable kingdom, we see that the fruits of the different trees do not arrive at maturity at one time; on the contrary, some come first and others afterwards. This priority does not prove that the later fruit of one tree was produced from the earlier fruit of another tree.

Secondly, these slight signs and traces of members have perhaps a great reason of which the mind is not yet cognizant. How many things exist of which we do not yet know the reason! So the science of physiology, that is to say the knowledge of the composition of the members, records that the reason and cause of the difference in the colors of animals, and of the hair of men, of the redness of the lips, and of the variety of the colors of birds, is still unknown; it is secret and hidden. But it is known that the pupil of the eye is black, so as to attract the rays of the sun; for if it were another color, that is, uniformly white, it would not attract the rays of the sun. Therefore, as the reason of the things we have mentioned is unknown, it is possible that the reason and the wisdom of these traces of members, whether they be in the animal or man, are equally unknown. Certainly there is a reason, even though it is not known.

Thirdly, let us suppose that there was a time when some animals, or even man, possessed some members which have now disappeared; this is not a sufficient proof of the change and evolution of the species. For man, from the beginning of the embryonic period till he reaches the degree of maturity, goes through different forms and appearances. His aspect, his form, his appearance, and color change; he passes from one form to another, and from one appearance to another. Nevertheless, from the beginning of the embryonic period he is of the species of man; that is to say, an embryo of a man, and not of an animal; but this is not at first apparent, but later it becomes visible and evident. For example, let us suppose that man once resembled the animal, and that now he has progressed and changed; supposing this to be true, it is still not a proof of the change of species; no, as before mentioned, it is merely like the change and alteration of the embryo of man until it reaches the degree of reason and perfection. We will state it more clearly: let us suppose that there was a time when man walked on his hands and feet, or had a tail; this change and alteration is like that of the fœtus in the womb of the mother; although it changes in all ways, and grows and develops until it reaches the perfect form, from the beginning it is a special species. We also see in the vegetable kingdom that the original species of the genus do not change and alter, but the form, color, and bulk will change and alter, or even progress.

To recapitulate: as man in the womb of the mother passes from form to form, from shape to shape, changes and develops, and is still the human species from the beginning of the embryonic period —in the same way man, from the beginning of his existence in the matrix of the world, is also a distinct species, that is, man, and has gradually evolved from one form to another. Therefore this change of appearance, this evolution of members, this development and growth, even though we admit the reality of growth and progress, does not prevent the species from being original. Man from the beginning was in this perfect form and composition, and possessed capacity and aptitude for acquiring material and spiritual perfections, and was the manifestation of these words, "We will make man in Our image and likeness." He has only become more pleasing, more beautiful, and more graceful. Civilization has brought him out of his wild state, just as the wild fruits which are cultivated by a gardener became finer, sweeter, and acquire more freshness and delicacy.

The gardeners of the world of humanity are the Prophets of God.

Spiritual Nature of Man

We have many times demonstrated and established that man is the noblest of beings, the sum of all perfections, and that all beings and all existences are the centers from which the glory of God is reflected, that is to say, the signs of the Divinity of God are apparent in the realities of things and of creatures. Just as the terrestrial globe is the place where the rays of the sun are reflected—as its light, its heat, and its influence are apparent and visible in all the atoms of the earth—so, in the same way, the atoms of beings, in this infinite space, proclaim and prove one of the divine perfections. Nothing is deprived of this benefit; it is either a sign of the mercy of God or it is a sign of His power, His greatness, His justice, His lordship which imparts education; or it is a sign of the generosity of God, His vision, His hearing, His knowledge, His grace, and so on.

Without doubt each being is the center of the shining forth of the glory of God: that is to say, the perfections of God appear from it and are resplendent in it. It is like the sun, which is resplendent in the desert, upon the sea, in the trees, in the fruits and blossoms, and in all earthly things. The world, indeed each existing being, proclaims to us one of the names of God, but the reality of man is the collective reality, the general reality, and is the center where the glory of all the perfections of God shine forth. That is to say, for each name, each attribute, each perfection which we affirm of God, there exists a sign in man; if it were otherwise, man could not imagine these perfections, and could not understand them. So we say that God is the seer, and the eye is the sign of His vision; if this sight were not in man, how could we imagine the vision of God? for the blind, that is one born blind, cannot imagine sight; and the deaf, that is one deaf from birth, cannot imagine hearing; and the dead cannot realize life. Consequently the Divinity of God, which is the sum of all perfections, reflects itself in the reality of man; that is to say, the Essence of Oneness is the gathering of all perfections, and from this unity He casts a reflection upon the human reality. Man then is the perfect mirror facing the Sun of Truth, and is the center of radiation: the Sun of Truth shines in this mirror. The reflection of the divine perfections appears in the reality of man, so he is the representative of God, the messenger of God. If man did not exist, the universe would be without result, for the object of existence is the appearance of the perfections of God.

Therefore it cannot be said there was a time when man was not. All that we can say is that this terrestrial globe at one time did not exist, and at its beginning man did not appear upon it. But from the beginning which has no beginning, to the end which has no end, a perfect manifestation always exists. This man of whom we speak is not every man; we mean the perfect man. For the noblest part of the tree is the fruit, which is the reason of its existence; if the tree had no fruit, it would have no meaning. Therefore it cannot be imagined that the worlds of existence, whether the stars or this earth, were once inhabited by the donkey, cow, mouse, and cat, and that they were without man! This supposition is false and meaningless. The word of God is clear as the sun. This is a spiritual proof, but one which we cannot at the beginning put forth for the benefit of the materialists; first we must speak of the logical proofs, afterwards the spiritual proofs.

MAN'S INNATE POWERS

The beginning of the existence of man on the terrestrial globe resembles his formation in the womb of the mother. The embryo in the womb of the mother gradually grows and develops until birth, after which it continues to grow and develop until it reaches the age of discretion and maturity. Though in infancy the signs of the mind and spirit appear in man, they do not reach the degree of perfection; they are imperfect. Only when man attains maturity do the mind and the spirit appear and become evident in utmost perfection.

So also the formation of man in the matrix of the world was in the beginning like the embryo; then gradually he made progress in perfection, and grew and developed until he reached the state of maturity, when the mind and spirit became visible in the greatest power. In the beginning of his formation the mind and spirit also existed, but they were hidden; later they were manifested. In the womb of the world mind and spirit also existed in the embryo, but they were concealed; afterwards they appeared. So it is that in the seed the tree exists, but it is hidden and concealed; when it develops and grows, the complete tree appears. In the same way the growth and development of all beings is gradual; this is the universal divine organization, and the natural system. The seed does not at once become a tree, the embryo does not at once become a man, the mineral does not suddenly become a stone. No, they grow and develop gradually, and attain the limit of perfection.

All beings, whether large or small, were created perfect and complete from the first, but their perfections appear in them by degrees. The organization of God is one: the evolution of existence is one: the divine system is one. Whether they be small or great beings, all are subject to one law and system. Each seed has in it from the first all the vegetable perfections. For example, in the seed all the vegetable perfections exist from the beginning, but not visibly; afterwards little by little they appear. So it is first the shoot which appears from the seed, then the branches, leaves, blossoms, and fruits; but from the beginning of its existence all these things are in the seed, potentially, though not apparently.

In the same way, the embryo possesses from the first all perfections, such as the spirit, the mind, the sight, the smell, the taste—in one word, all the powers—but they are not visible, and become so only by degrees.

Similarly, the terrestrial globe from the beginning was created with all its elements, substances, minerals, atoms, and organisms; but these only appeared by degrees: first the mineral, then the plant, afterward the animal, and finally man. But from the first these kinds and species existed, but were undeveloped in the terrestrial globe, and then appeared only gradually. For the supreme organization of God, and the universal natural system, surrounds all beings, and all are subject to this rule. When you consider this universal system, you see that there is not one of the beings, which at its coming into existence has reached the limit of perfection. No, they gradually grow and develop, and then attain the degree of perfection.

The Spirit in the Body

The wisdom of the appearance of the spirit in the body is this: the human spirit is a Divine Trust, and it must traverse all conditions; for its passage and movement through the conditions of existence will be the means of its acquiring perfections. So, when a man travels and passes through different regions and numerous countries with system and method, it is certainly a means of his acquiring perfection; for he will see places, scenes, and countries, from which he will discover the conditions and states of other nations. He will thus become acquainted with the geography of countries, and their wonders and arts; he will familiarize himself with the habits, customs, and usages of peoples; he will see the civilization and progress of the epoch; he will become aware of the policy of governments, and the power and capacity of each country. It is the same when the human spirit passes through the conditions of existence: it will become the possessor of each degree and station. Even in the condition of the body it will surely acquire perfections.

Besides this, it is necessary that the signs of the perfection of the spirit should be apparent in this world, so that the world of creation may bring forth endless results, and this body may receive life and manifest the divine bounties. So, for example, the rays of the sun must shine upon the earth, and the solar heat develop the earthly beings; if the rays and heat of the sun did not shine upon the earth, the earth would be uninhabited, without meaning, and its development would be retarded. In the same way, if the perfections of the spirit did not appear in this world, this world would be unenlightened and absolutely brutal. By the appearance of the spirit in the physical form, this world is enlightened. As the spirit of man is the cause of the life of the body, so the world is in the condition of the body, and man is in the condition of the spirit. If there were no man, the perfections of the spirit would not appear, and the light of the mind would not be resplendent in this world. This world would be like a body without a soul.

This world is also in the condition of a fruit-tree, and man is like the fruit; without fruit the tree would be useless.

Moreover, these members, these elements, this composition, which are found in the organism of man, are an attraction and magnet for the spirit; it is certain that the spirit will appear in it. So, a mirror which is clear will certainly attract the rays of the sun. It will become luminous, and wonderful images will appear in it. That is to say, when these existing elements are gathered together according to the natural order, and with perfect strength, they become a magnet for the spirit, and the spirit will become manifest in them with all its perfections.

Under these conditions it cannot be said "what is the necessity for the rays of the sun to descend upon the mirror?"—for the connection which exists between the reality of things, whether they be spiritual or material, requires that when the mirror is clear and faces the sun, the light of the sun must become apparent in it. In the same way, when the elements are arranged and combined in the most glorious system, organization and manner, the human spirit will appear and be manifest in them. This is the decree of the Powerful, the Wise.

Man's Relation to God

The connection between God and the creatures is that of the creator to the creation; it is like the connection between the sun and the dark bodies of contingent beings, and is the connection between the maker and the things that he has made. The sun in its own essence is independent of the bodies which it lights; for its light is in itself, and is free and independent of the terrestrial globe; so the earth is under the influence of the sun and receives its light, whereas the sun and its rays are entirely independent of the earth. But if there were no sun, the earth and all earthly beings could not exist.

The dependence through the creatures upon God is a dependence of emanation: that is to say, creatures emanate from God, they do not manifest Him. The relation is that of emanation and not that of manifestation. The light of the sun emanates from the sun, it does not manifest it. The appearance through emanation is like the appearance of the rays from the luminary of the horizons of the world: that is to say, the holy essence of the Sun of Truth is not divided, and does not descend to the condition of the creatures. In the same way, the globe of the sun does not become divided and does not descend to the earth: no, the rays of the sun, which are its bounty, emanate from it, and illumine the dark bodies.

But the appearance through manifestation is the manifestation of the branches, leaves, blossoms and fruit from the seed; for the seed in its own essence becomes branches and fruits, and its reality enters into the branches, the leaves, and fruits. This appearance through manifestation would be for God the Most High, simple imperfection, and this is quite impossible; for the implication would be that the Absolute Pre-existent is qualified with phenomenal attributes; but if this were so, pure independence would become mere poverty, and true existence would become non-existence, and this is impossible.

Therefore all creatures emanate from God; that is to say, it is by God that all things are realized, and by Him that all beings have attained to existence. The first thing which emanated from

God is that universal reality, which the ancient philosophers termed the "First Mind," and which the people of Bahá call the "First Will." This emanation, in that which concerns its action in the world of God, is not limited by time or place; it is without beginning or end; beginning and end in relation to God are one. The pre-existence of God is the pre-existence of essence, and also pre-existence of time, and the phenomenality of contingency is essential and not temporal. . . .

Though the "First Mind" is without beginning, it does not become a sharer in the pre-existence of God, for the existence of the universal reality in relation to the existence of God is nothingness, and it has not the power to become an associate of God and like unto Him in pre-existence. This subject has been before explained.

The existence of living things signifies composition, and their death decomposition. But universal matter and the elements do not become absolutely annihilated and destroyed: no, their non-existence is simply transformation. For instance, when man is annihilated he becomes dust, but he does not become absolutely non-existent; he still exists in the shape of dust; but transformation has taken place, and this composition is accidentally decomposed. The annihilation of the other beings is the same, for existence does not become absolute non-existence, and absolute non-existence does not become existence.

Soul, Mind and Spirit

It has been before explained that spirit is universally divided into five categories: the vegetable spirit, the animal spirit, the human spirit, the spirit of faith, and the Holy Spirit.

The vegetable spirit is the power of growth which is brought about in the seed through the influence of other existences.

The animal spirit is the power of all the senses, which is realized from the composition and mingling of elements; when this composition decomposes, the power also perishes and becomes annihilated. It may be likened to this lamp: when the oil, wick, and fire are combined it is lighted, and when this combination is dissolved, that is to say, when the combined parts are separated from one another, the lamp also is extinguished.

The human spirit which distinguishes man from the animal is the rational soul; and these two names—the human spirit and the rational soul—designate one thing. This spirit, which in the terminology of the philosophers is the rational soul, embraces all beings, and as far as human ability permits discovers the realities of things and becomes cognizant of their peculiarities and effects, and of the qualities and properties of beings. But the human spirit, unless assisted by the spirit of faith, does not become acquainted with the divine secrets and the heavenly realities. It is like a mirror which, although clear, polished, and brilliant, is still in need of light. Until a ray of the sun reflects upon it, it cannot discover the heavenly secrets.

But the mind is the power of the human spirit. Spirit is the lamp; mind is the light which shines from the lamp. Spirit is the tree, and the mind is the fruit. Mind is the perfection of the spirit, and is its essential quality, as the sun's rays are the essential necessity of the sun.

Five Physical and Five Spiritual Powers

In man five outer powers exist, which are the agents of perception, that is to say, through these five powers man perceives material beings. These are sight, which perceives visible forms; hearing, which perceives audible sounds; smell, which perceives odors; taste, which perceives foods; and feeling, which is in all parts of the body, and perceives tangible things. These five powers perceive outward existences.

Man has also spiritual powers: imagination, which conceives things; thought, which reflects upon realities; comprehension, which comprehends realities, memory, which retains whatever man imagines, thinks, and comprehends. The intermediary between the five outward powers and the inward powers, is the sense which they possess in common, that is to say, the sense which acts between the outer and inner powers, conveys to the inward powers whatever the outer powers discern. It is termed the common faculty, because it communicates between the outward and inward powers, and thus is common to the outward and inward powers.

For instance, sight is one of the outer powers; it sees and perceives this flower, and conveys this perception to the inner power—the common faculty—which transmits this perception to the power of imagination, which in its turn conceives and forms this image and transmits it to the power of thought; the power of thought reflects, and having grasped the reality, conveys it to the power of comprehension; the comprehension, when it has comprehended it, delivers the image of the object perceived to the memory, and the memory keeps it in its repository.

The outward powers are five: the power of sight, of hearing, of taste, of smell, and of feeling.

The inner powers are also five: the common faculty, and the powers of imagination, thought, comprehension, and memory.

Innate, Inherited and Acquired Character

With regard to the innate character, although the divine creation is purely good, yet the varieties of natural qualities in man come from the difference of degree; all are excellent, but they are more or less so, according to the degree. So all mankind possess intelligence and capacities, but the intelligence, the capacity, and the worthiness of men differ. This is evident.

For example, take a number of children of one family, of one place, of one school, instructed by one teacher, reared on the same food, in the same climate, with the same clothing, and studying the same lessons—it is certain that among these children some will be clever in the sciences, some will be of average ability, and some dull. Hence it is clear that in the original nature there exists a difference of degree, and varieties of worthiness and capacity. This difference does not imply good or evil, but is simply a difference of degree. One has the highest degree, another the medium degree, and another the lowest degree. So man exists, the animal, the plant, and the mineral exist also—but the degrees of these four existences vary. What a difference between the existence of man and of the animal! Yet both are existences. It is evident that in existence there are differences of degrees.

The variety of inherited qualities comes from strength and weakness of constitution; that is to say, when the two parents are weak, the children will be weak; if they are strong, the children will be robust. In the same way, purity of blood has a great effect; for the pure germ is like the superior stock which exists in plants and animals. For example, you see that children born from a weak and feeble father and mother will naturally have a feeble constitution and weak nerves; they will be afflicted, and will have neither patience, nor endurance, nor resolution, nor perseverance, and will be hasty; for the children inherit the weakness and debility of their parents.

Besides this, an especial blessing is conferred on some families and some generations. Thus it is an especial blessing that from among the descendants of Abraham should have come all the Prophets of the children of Israel. This is a blessing that God has granted to this descent: to Moses from His father and mother, to Christ from His mother's line; also to Muḥammad and the Báb, and to all the Prophets and the Holy Manifestations of Israel.

Hence it is evident that inherited character also exists, and to such a degree that if the characters are not in conformity with their origin, although they belong physically to that lineage, spiritually they are not considered members of the family; like Canaan, who is not reckoned as being of the race of Noah.

But the difference of the qualities with regard to culture is very great; for education has great influence. Through education the ignorant become learned, the cowardly become valiant; through cultivation the crooked branch becomes straight, the acid, bitter fruit of the mountains and woods becomes sweet and delicious, and the five-petalled flower becomes hundred-petalled. Through education savage nations become civilized, and even the animals become domesticated. Education must be considered as most important; for as diseases in the world of bodies are extremely contagious, so, in the same way, qualities of spirit and heart are extremely contagious. Education has a universal influence and the differences caused by it are very great.

Perhaps some one will say, that since the capacity and worthiness of men differ, therefore the difference of capacity certainly causes the difference of characters.

But this is not so; for capacity is of two kinds, natural capacity and acquired capacity. The first, which is the creation of God, is purely good—in the creation of God there is no evil; but the acquired capacity has become the cause of the appearance of evil. For example, God has created all men in such a manner, and has given them such a constitution and such capacities, that they are benefited by sugar and honey, and harmed and destroyed by poison. This nature and constitution is innate, and God has given it equally to all mankind. But man begins little by little to accustom himself to poison, by taking a small quantity each day, and gradually increasing it, until he reaches such a point that he cannot live without a gram of opium every day. The natural capacities are thus completely perverted. Observe how much the natural capacity and constitution can be changed, until by different habits and training they become entirely perverted. One does not criticize vicious people because of their innate capacities and nature, but rather for their acquired capacities and nature.

In creation there is no evil; all is good. Certain qualities and natures innate in some men and apparently blameworthy are not so in reality. For example, from the beginning of his life you can see in a nursing child the signs of desire, of anger, and of temper. Then, it may be said, good and evil are innate in the reality of man, and this is contrary to the pure goodness of nature and creation. The answer to this is that desire, which is to ask for something more, is a praiseworthy quality provided that it is used suitably. So, if a man has the desire to acquire science and knowledge, or to become compassionate, generous, and just, it is most praiseworthy. If he exercises his anger and wrath against the bloodthirsty tyrants who are like ferocious beasts, it is very praiseworthy; but if he does not use these qualities in a right way, they are blameworthy.

Then it is evident that in creation and nature evil does not exist at all; but when the natural qualities of man are used in an unlawful way, they are blameworthy. So, if a rich and generous person gives a sum of money to a poor man for his own necessities, and if the poor man spends that sum of money on unlawful things, that will be blameworthy. It is the same with all the natural qualities of man, which constitute the capital of life; if they be used and displayed in an unlawful way, they become blameworthy. Therefore it is clear that creation is purely good. Consider that the worst of qualities and most odious of attributes, which is the foundation of all evil, is lying. No worse or more blameworthy quality than this can be imagined to exist; it is the destroyer of all human perfections, and the cause of innumerable vices. There is no worse characteristic than this; it is the foundation of all evils. Notwithstanding all this, if a doctor consoles a sick man by saying: "Thank God you are better, and there is hope of your recovery," though these words are contrary to the truth, yet they may become the consolation of the patient and the turning-point of the illness. This is not blameworthy.

Man's Knowledge of God

Know that there are two kinds of knowledge: the knowledge of the essence of a thing, and the knowledge of its qualities. The essence of a thing is known through its qualities, otherwise it is unknown and hidden.

As our knowledge of things, even of created and limited things, is knowledge of their qualities and not of their essence, how is it possible to comprehend in its essence the Divine Reality, which is unlimited? For the substance of the essence of anything is not comprehended, but only its qualities. For example, the substance of the sun is unknown, but is understood by its qualities, which are heat and light. The substance of the essence of man is unknown and not evident, but by its qualities it is characterized and known. Thus everything is known by its qualities and not by its essence. Although the mind encompasses all things, and the outward beings are comprehended by it, nevertheless these beings with regard to their essence are unknown; they are only known with regard to their qualities.

Then how can the eternal everlasting Lord, who is held sanctified from comprehension and conception, be known by His essence? That is to say, as things can only be known by their qualities and not by their essence, it is certain that the Divine Reality is unknown with regard to its essence, and is known with regard to its attributes. Besides, how can the phenomenal reality embrace the Pre-existent Reality? For comprehension is the result of encompassing—embracing must be, so that comprehension may be—and the Essence of Unity surrounds all, and is not surrounded. Also the difference of condition in the world of beings is an obstacle to comprehension. For example: this mineral belongs to the mineral kingdom; however far it may rise, it can never comprehend the power of growth. The plants, the trees, whatever progress they may make, cannot conceive of the power of sight or the powers of the other senses; and the animal cannot imagine the condition of man, that is to say, his spiritual powers. Difference of condition is an obstacle to knowledge; the inferior degree cannot comprehend the superior degree. How then can the phenomenal reality comprehend the Pre-existent Reality? Knowing God, therefore, means the comprehension and the knowledge of His attributes, and not of His Reality. This knowledge of the attributes is also proportioned to the capacity and power of man; it is not absolute. Philosophy consists in comprehending the reality of things as they exist, according to the capacity and the power of man. For the phenomenal reality can comprehend the Pre-existent attributes only to the extent of the human capacity. The mystery of Divinity is sanctified and purified from the comprehension of the beings, for all that comes to the imagination is that which man understands, and the power of the understanding of man does not embrace the Reality of the Divine Essence. All that man is able to understand are the attributes of Divinity, the radiance of which appears and is visible in worlds and souls.

When we look at the worlds and the souls, we see wonderful signs of the divine perfections, which are clear and apparent; for the reality of things proves the Universal Reality. The Reality of Divinity may be compared to the sun, which from the height of its magnificence shines upon all the horizons and each horizon, and each soul, receives a share of its radiance. If this light and these rays did not exist, beings would not exist; all beings express something, and partake of some ray and portion of this light. The splendors of the perfections, bounties, and attributes of God shine forth and radiate from the reality of the Perfect Man, that is to say, the Unique One, the universal Manifestation of God. Other beings receive only one ray, but the universal Manifestation is the mirror for this Sun, which appears and becomes manifest in it, with all its perfections, attributes, signs, and wonders.

The knowledge of the Reality of the Divinity is impossible and unattainable, but the knowledge of the Manifestations of God is the knowledge of God, for the bounties, splendors, and divine attributes are apparent in them. Therefore if man attains to the knowledge of the Manifestations of God, he will attain to the knowledge of God; and if he be neglectful of the knowledge of the Holy Manifestation, he will be bereft of the knowledge of God. It is then ascertained and proved that the Holy Manifestations are the center of the bounty, signs, and perfections of God. Blessed are those who receive the light of the divine bounties from the enlightened Dawning-points!

We hope that the friends of God, like an attractive force, will draw these bounties from the source itself, and that they will arise with such illumination and signs that they will be evident proofs of the Sun of Reality.

The Immortality of the Spirit

The immortality of the spirit is mentioned in the Holy Books; it is the fundamental basis of the divine religions. Now punishments and rewards are said to be of two kinds. Firstly, the rewards and punishments of this life; secondly, those of the other world. But the paradise and hell of existence are found in all the worlds of God, whether in this world or in the spiritual heavenly worlds. Gaining these rewards is the gaining of eternal life. That is why Christ said, "Act in such a way that you may find eternal life, and that you may be born of water and the spirit, so that you may enter into the Kingdom."

The rewards of this life are the virtues and perfections which adorn the reality of man. For example, he was dark and becomes luminous, he was ignorant and becomes wise, he was neglectful and becomes vigilant, he was asleep and becomes awakened, he was dead and becomes living, he was blind and becomes a seer, he was deaf and becomes a hearer, he was earthly and becomes heavenly, he was material and becomes spiritual. Through these rewards he gains spiritual birth, and becomes a new creature. He becomes the manifestation of the verse in the Gospel where it is said of the disciples that they were born not of blood, nor of the will of the flesh, nor of the will of man, but of God; that is to say, they were delivered from the animal characteristics and qualities which are the characteristics of human nature, and they became qualified with the divine characteristics, which are the bounty of God; this is the meaning of the second birth. For such people there is no greater torture than being veiled from God, and no more severe punishment than sensual vices, dark qualities, lowness of nature, engrossment in carnal desires. When they are delivered through the light of faith from the darkness of these vices, and become illuminated with the radiance of the Sun of Reality, and ennobled with all the virtues, they esteem this the greatest reward, and they know it to be the true paradise. In the same way they consider that the spiritual punishment, that is to say the torture and punishment of existence, is to be subjected to the world of nature, to be veiled from God, to be brutal and ignorant, to fall into carnal lusts, to be absorbed in animal frailties; to be characterized with dark qualities, such as falsehood, tyranny, cruelty, attachment to the affairs of the world, and being immersed in satanic ideas; for them, these are the greatest punishments and tortures.

Likewise the rewards of the other world are the eternal life which is clearly mentioned in all the Holy Books, the divine perfections, the eternal bounties, and everlasting felicity. The rewards of the other world are the perfections and the peace obtained in the spiritual worlds after leaving this world; whilst the rewards of this life are the real luminous perfections which are realized in this world, and which are the cause of eternal life, for they are the very progress of existence. It is like the man who passes from the embryonic world to the state of maturity, and becomes the manifestation of these words: "Blessed be God, the best of creators." The rewards of the other world are peace, the spiritual graces, the various spiritual gifts in the Kingdom of God, the gaining of the desires of the heart and the soul, and the meeting of God in the world of eternity. In the same way the punishments of the other world, that is to say, the torments of the other world, consist in being deprived of the special divine blessings and the absolute bounties, and falling into the lowest degrees of existence. He who is deprived of these divine favors, although he continues after death, is considered as dead by the people of truth.

The logical proof of the immortality of the spirit is this, that no sign can come from a non-existing thing; that is to say, it is impossible that from absolute non-existence signs should appear, for the signs are the consequence of an existence, and the consequence depends upon the existence of the principle. So, from a non-existing sun no light can radiate, from a non-existing sea no waves appear, from a non-existing cloud no rain falls; a non-existing tree yields no fruit; a non-existing man neither manifests nor produces anything. Therefore as long as signs of existence appear, they are a proof that the possessor of the sign is existent.

Consider that today the Kingdom of Christ exists: from a non-existing king how could such a great kingdom be manifested? How, from a non-existing sea, can the waves mount so high? From a non-existing garden, how can such fragrant breezes be wafted? Reflect that no effect, no trace, no influence remains of any being after its members are dispersed and its elements are decomposed, whether it be a mineral, a vegetable, or an animal. There is only the human reality and the spirit of man which, after the disintegration of the members, dispersing of the particles, and the destruction of the composition, persists, and continues to act and to have power.

This question is extremely subtle: consider it attentively. This is a rational proof which we are giving, so that the wise may weigh it in the balance of reason and justice. But if the human spirit will rejoice and be attracted to the Kingdom of God, if the inner sight becomes opened, and the spiritual hearing strengthened, and the spiritual feelings predominant, he will see the immortality of the spirit as clearly as he sees the sun, and the glad tidings and signs of God will encompass him.

Know that the power and the comprehension of the human spirit are of two kinds: that is to say, they perceive and act in two different modes. One way is through instruments and organs: thus with this eye it sees, with this ear it hears, with this tongue it talks. Such is the action of the spirit, and the perception of the reality of man, by means of organs. That is to say, that the spirit is the seer, through the eyes; the spirit is the hearer, through the ear; the spirit is the speaker, through the tongue.

The other manifestation of the powers and actions of the spirit is without instruments and organs. For example, in the state of sleep without eyes it sees, without an ear it hears, without a tongue it speaks, without feet it runs. Briefly, these actions are beyond the means of instruments and organs. How often it happens that it sees a dream in the world of sleep, and its signification becomes apparent two years afterwards in corresponding events. In the same way, how many times it happens that a question which one cannot solve in the world of wakefulness, is solved in the world of dreams. In wakefulness the eye sees only for a short distance, but in dreams he who is in the East sees the West: awake he sees the present, in sleep he sees the future. In wakefulness, by means of rapid transit, at the most he can travel only twenty farsakha an hour; in sleep, in the twinkling of an eye, he traverses the East and West. For the spirit travels in two different ways: without means, which is spiritual traveling; and with means, which is material traveling: as birds which fly, and those which are carried.

In the time of sleep this body is as though dead; it does not see nor hear, it does not feel, it has no consciousness, no perception: that is to say, the powers of man have become inactive, but the spirit lives and subsists. Nay, its penetration is increased, its flight is higher, and its intelligence is greater. To consider that after the death of the body the spirit perishes, is like imagining that a bird in a cage will be destroyed if the cage is broken, though the bird has nothing to fear from the destruction of the cage. Our body is like the cage, and the spirit is like the bird. We see that without the cage this bird flies in the world of sleep; therefore if the cage becomes broken, the bird will continue and exist: its feelings will be even more powerful, its perceptions greater, and its happiness increased. In truth, from hell it reaches a paradise of delights, because for the thankful birds there is no paradise greater than freedom from the cage. That is why with utmost joy and happiness the martyrs hasten to the plain of sacrifice.

In wakefulness the eye of man sees at the utmost as far as one hour of distance, because through the instrumentality of the body the power of the spirit is thus determined; but with the inner sight and the mental eye it sees America, and it can perceive that which is there, and discover the conditions of things and organize affairs. If, then, the spirit were the same as the body, it would be necessary that the power of the inner sight should also be in the same proportion. Therefore it is evident that this spirit is different from the body, and that the bird is different from the cage, and that the power and penetration of the spirit is stronger without the intermediary of the body. Now, if the instrument is abandoned, the possessor of the instrument continues to act. For example, if the pen is abandoned or broken, the writer remains living and present; if a house is ruined, the owner is alive and existing. This is one of the logical evidences for the immortality of the soul.

There is another: this body becomes weak, or heavy, or sick, or it finds health; it becomes tired or rested; sometimes the hand or leg is amputated, or its physical power is crippled; it becomes blind or deaf or dumb; its limbs may become paralyzed; briefly, the body may have all the imperfections. Nevertheless, the spirit in its original state, in its own spiritual perception, will be eternal and perpetual; it neither finds any imperfection nor will it become crippled. But when the body is wholly subjected to disease and misfortune, it is deprived of the bounty of the spirit; like a mirror which, when it becomes broken, or dirty, or dusty, cannot reflect the rays of the sun, nor any longer show its bounties.

We have already explained that the spirit of man is not in the body, because it is freed and sanctified from entrance and exit, which are bodily conditions. The connection of the spirit with the body is like that of the sun with the mirror. Briefly, the human spirit is in one condition; it neither becomes ill from the diseases of the body, nor cured by its health; it does not become sick, nor weak, nor miserable, nor poor, nor light, nor small. That is to say, it will not be injured because of the infirmities of the body, and no effect will be visible even if the body becomes weak or if the hands and feet and tongue be cut off, or if it loses the power of hearing or sight. Therefore it is evident and certain that the spirit is different from the body, and that its duration is independent of that of the body; on the contrary, the spirit with the utmost greatness rules in the world of the body, and its power and influence, like the bounty of the sun in the mirror, are apparent and visible. But when the mirror becomes dusty or breaks, it will cease to reflect the rays of the sun.

Perfection Is Endless

Know that the conditions of existence are limited to the conditions of servitude, of prophethood, and of Deity, but the divine and the contingent perfections are unlimited. When you reflect deeply, you discover that also outwardly the perfections of existence are also unlimited, for you cannot find a being so perfect that you cannot imagine a superior one. For example, you cannot see a ruby in the mineral kingdom, a rose in the vegetable kingdom, or a nightingale in the animal kingdom, without imagining that there might be better specimens. As the divine bounties are endless, so human perfections are endless. If it were possible to reach a limit of perfection, then one of the realities of the beings might reach the condition of being independent of God, and the contingent might attain to the condition of the absolute. But for every being there is a point which it cannot overpass; that is to say, he who is in the condition of servitude, however far he may progress in gaining limitless perfections, will never reach the condition of Deity. It is the same with the other beings: a mineral, however far it may progress in the mineral kingdom, cannot gain the vegetable power; also in a flower, however far it may progress in the vegetable kingdom, no power of the senses will appear. So this silver mineral cannot gain hearing or sight; it can only improve in its own condition, and become a perfect mineral, but it cannot acquire the power of growth, or the power of sensation, or attain to life; it can only progress in its own condition.

For example, Peter cannot become Christ. All that he can do is, in the condition of servitude, to attain endless perfections; for every existing reality is capable of making progress. As the spirit of man after putting off this material form has an everlasting life, certainly any existing being is capable of making progress; therefore it is permitted to ask for advancement, forgiveness, mercy, beneficence, and blessings for a man after his death, because existence is capable of progression. That is why in the prayers of Bahá’u’lláh forgiveness and remission of sins are asked for those who have died. Moreover, as people in this world are in need of God, they will also need Him in the other world. The creatures are always in need, and God is absolutely independent, whether in this world or in the world to come.

The wealth of the other world is nearness to God. Consequently it is certain that those who are near the Divine Court are allowed to intercede, and this intercession is approved by God. But intercession in the other world is not like intercession in this world: it is another thing, another reality, which cannot be expressed in words.

If a wealthy man at the time of his death bequeaths a gift to the poor and miserable, and gives a part of his wealth to be spent for them, perhaps this action may be the cause of his pardon and forgiveness, and of his progress in the Divine Kingdom.

Also a father and mother endure the greatest troubles and hardships for their children; and often when the children have reached the age of maturity, the parents pass on to the other world. Rarely does it happen that a father and mother in this world see the reward of the care and trouble they have undergone for their children. Therefore children, in return for this care and trouble, must show forth charity and beneficence, and must implore pardon and forgiveness for their parents. So you ought, in return for the love and kindness shown you by your father, to give to the poor for his sake, with greatest submission and humility implore pardon and remission of sins, and ask for the supreme mercy.

It is even possible that the condition of those who have died in sin and unbelief may become changed; that is to say, they may become the object of pardon through the bounty of God, not through His justice; for bounty is giving without desert, and justice is giving what is deserved. As we have power to pray for these souls here, so likewise we shall possess the same power in the other world, which is the Kingdom of God. Are not all the people in that world the creatures of God? Therefore in that world also they can make progress. As here they can receive light by their supplication, there also they can plead for forgiveness, and receive light through entreaties and supplications. Thus as souls in this world, through the help of the supplications, the entreaties, and the prayers of the holy ones, can acquire development, so is it the same after death. Through their own prayers and supplications they can also progress; more especially when they are the object of the intercession of the Holy Manifestations.

The Evolution of Man in the Other World

Know that nothing which exists remains in a state of repose, that is to say, all things are in motion. Everything is either growing or declining, all things are either coming from non-existence into being, or going from existence into non-existence. So this flower, this hyacinth, during a certain period of time was coming from the world of non-existence into being, and now it is going from being into non-existence. This state of motion is said to be essential—that is, natural; it cannot be separated from beings because it is their essential requirement, as it is the essential requirement of fire to burn.

Thus it is established that this movement is necessary to existence, which is either growing or declining. Now, as the spirit continues to exist after death, it necessarily progresses or declines;

and in the other world, to cease to progress is the same as to decline; but it never leaves its own condition, in which it continues to develop. For example, the reality of the spirit of Peter, however far it may progress, will not reach to the condition of the Reality of Christ; it progresses only in its own environment.

Look at this mineral: however far it may evolve, it only evolves in its own condition; you cannot bring the crystal to a state where it can attain to sight: this is impossible. So the moon which is in the heavens, however far it might evolve, could never become a luminous sun; but in its own condition it has apogee and perigee. However far the disciples might progress, they could never become Christ. It is true that coal could become a diamond, but both are in the mineral condition and their component elements are the same.

Progress After Death

When we consider beings with the seeing eye, we observe that they are limited to three sorts: that is to say, as a whole, they are either mineral, vegetable, or animal; each of these three classes containing species. Man is the highest species because he is the possessor of the perfections of all the classes; that is, he has a body which grows and which feels. As well as having the perfections of the mineral, of the vegetable, and of the animal, he also possesses an especial excellence which the other beings are without; that is, the intellectual perfections. Therefore man is the most noble of beings.

Man is in the highest degree of materiality, and at the beginning of spirituality; that is to say, he is the end of imperfection and the beginning of perfection. He is at the last degree of darkness, and at the beginning of light; that is why it has been said that the condition of man is the end of the night and the beginning of day, meaning that he is the sum of all the degrees of imperfection, and that he possesses the degrees of perfection. He has the animal side as well as the angelic side; and the aim of an educator is to so train human souls, that their angelic aspect may overcome their animal side. Then, if the divine power in man which is his essential perfection, overcomes the satanic power, which is absolute imperfection, he becomes the most excellent among the creatures; but if the satanic power overcomes the divine power, he becomes the lowest of the creatures. That is why he is the end of imperfection and the beginning of perfection. Not in any other of the species in the world of existence is there such a difference, contrast, contradiction, and opposition, as in the species of man. Thus the reflection of the Divine Light was in man, as in Christ, and see how loved and honored He is! At the same time we see man worshipping a stone, a clod of earth, or a tree: how vile he is, in that his object of worship should be the lowest existence—that is a stone, or clay, without spirit; a mountain, a forest, or a tree. What shame is greater for man than to worship the lowest existence? In the same way, knowledge is a quality of man, and so is ignorance; truthfulness is a quality of man, so is falsehood; trustworthiness and treachery, justice and injustice, are qualities of man, and so forth. Briefly, all the perfections and virtues, and all the vices, are qualities of man.

Consider equally the differences between individual men. The Christ was in the form of man, and Caiaphas was in the form of man; Moses and Pharaoh, Abel and Cain, Bahá'u'lláh and Yaḥyá, were men.

Man is said to be the greatest representative of God, and he is the Book of Creation because all the mysteries of beings exist in him. If he comes under the shadow of the True Educator and is rightly trained, he becomes the essence of essences, the light of lights, the spirit of spirits; he becomes the center of the divine appearances, the source of spiritual qualities, the rising-place of heavenly lights, and the receptacle of divine inspirations. If he is deprived of this education he becomes the manifestation of satanic qualities, the sum of animal vices, and the source of all dark conditions.

The reason of the mission of the Prophets is to educate men; so that this piece of coal may become a diamond, and this fruitless tree may be engrafted, and yield the sweetest, most delicious fruits. When man reaches the noblest state in the world of humanity, then he can make further progress in the conditions of perfection, but not in state; for such states are limited, but the divine perfections are endless.

Both before and after putting off this material form, there is progress in perfection, but not in state. So beings are consummated in perfect man. There is no other being higher than a perfect man. But man when he has reached this state can still make progress in perfections but not in state, because there is no state higher than that of a perfect man to which he can transfer himself. He only progresses in the state of humanity, for the human perfections are infinite. Thus, however learned a man may be, we can imagine one more learned.

Hence, as the perfections of humanity are endless, man can also make progress in perfections after leaving this world.

Tablet on Purity

Cleanliness and sanctity in all conditions are characteristics of pure beings and necessities of free souls. The first perfection consists in cleanliness and sanctity and in purity from every defect. When man in all conditions is pure and immaculate, he will become the center of the reflection of the manifest Light. In all his actions and conduct there must first be purity, then beauty and independence. The channel must be cleansed before it is filled with sweet water. The pure eye comprehendeth the sight and the meeting of God; the pure nostril inhaleth the perfumes of the rose-garden of bounty; the pure heart becometh the mirror of the beauty of truth. This is why, in the heavenly Books, the divine counsels and commands have been compared to water. So, in the Qur'án it is said, "and we have caused a pure water to descend from heaven;" and in the Gospel, "Except a man hath received the baptism of water and of the spirit, he cannot enter into the Kingdom of God." Then it is evident that the divine teachings are the heavenly grace and the showers of the mercy of God, which purify the hearts of men.

The meaning is, in all conditions, cleanliness and sanctity, purity and delicacy exalt humanity and make the contingent beings progress. Even when applied to physical things, delicacy causeth the attainment of spirituality, as it is established in the Holy Scriptures.

External cleanliness, although it is but a physical thing, hath a great influence upon spirituality. For example, although sound is but the vibrations of the air which affect the tympanum of the ear, and vibrations of the air are but an accident among the accidents which depend upon the air, consider how much marvelous notes or a charming song influence the spirits! A wonderful song giveth wings to the spirit and filleth the heart with exaltation. To return to the subject, the fact of having a pure and spotless body likewise exerciseth an influence upon the spirit of man.

Now, see how much purity is approved in the Court of God, that it should be especially mentioned in the Holy Books of the Prophets. So the Holy Books forbid the eating of any unclean thing, or the use of anything which is not pure. Certain prohibitions are absolute and imperative for all: he who commits that which is forbidden is detested by God and excluded from the number of the elect. This applieth to the things forbidden by an absolute prohibition and of which the perpetration is a grave sin; they are so vile that even to mention them is shameful. There are other forbidden things which do not cause an immediate evil and of which the pernicious effect is only gradually produced. They are also abhorred, blamed and rejected by God, but their prohibition is not recorded in an absolute way, although cleanliness and sanctity, spotlessness and purity, the preservation of health and independence are required by these interdictions.

One of these last prohibitions is the smoking of tobacco, which is unclean, malodorous, disagreeable and vulgar and of which the gradual harmfulness is universally recognized. All clever physicians have judged, and have also shown by experiment, that one of the constituents of tobacco is a mortal poison and that smokers are exposed to different indispositions and maladies. That is why cleanly people have a marked aversion for its use.

His supreme Highness the Báb—may my soul be His sacrifice!—in the beginning of His Cause, openly forbade it and all the friends abandoned its use. But, as it was a time for caution and he who abstained from smoking was ill treated, persecuted and even killed, therefore the friends were obliged, as a matter of prudence, to smoke. Later, the Kitáb-i-Aqdas was revealed and as the prohibition of tobacco was not clearly stated in it, the friends did not renounce it. But the Blessed Perfection had always a marked aversion for its use. At the beginning of the Cause, for certain reasons, He smoked a little, but later He abandoned it completely, and the holy souls who obeyed Him in all circumstances, also entirely gave up smoking. I wish to say that, in the sight of God, the smoking of tobacco is a thing which is blamed and condemned, very unclean, and of which the result is by degrees injurious. Besides it is a cause of expense and of loss of time and it is a harmful habit. So, for those who are firm in the Covenant, it is a thing reprobated by the reason and by tradition, the renouncement of which giveth gradual repose and tranquility, permitteth one to have stainless hands and a clean mouth, and hair which is not pervaded by a bad odor.

Without any doubt, the friends of God on receiving this epistle will renounce this injurious habit by all means, even if it be necessary to do so by degrees. This is my hope.

As to the question of opium, disgusting and execrated, I resign myself to God for its punishment. The formal text of the Kitáb-i-Aqdas forbids and reproves it and, according to reason, its use leads to madness. Experience hath shown that he who giveth himself up to it is completely excluded from the world of humanity. Let us take refuge in God against the perpetration of so shameful a thing, which is the destruction of the foundations of humanity and which causeth a perpetual unhappiness. It taketh possession of the soul of man, killeth the reason, weakeneth the intelligence, maketh a living man dead and extinguisheth the natural heat. It is impossible to imagine anything more pernicious. Happy is he who never mentioneth the word opium! But what is the fate of those who make use of it!

O friends of God! Force and violence, constraint and oppression are condemned in this divine cycle, but to prevent the use of opium, all means must be employed, so that the human species may be delivered and freed from this great calamity. Otherwise, alas! for all the negligent before God.

O Lord! Give to the people of Bahá cleanliness and holiness in all conditions, purify and free them from all defilement, deliver them from the use of all that is execrated, liberate them from the chains of habits, so that they may be pure and free, clean and spotless, that they may be worthy servants of the Sacred Threshold and may deserve to enter into relation with God. Deliver them from alcohol and tobacco, and save them from opium, the purveyor of madness! Make them companions of the holy breezes, in order that they may know the pleasures of the wine of the love of God, and that they may attain to the joy and the happiness of attraction to the Kingdom of Abhá!

Hast Thou not said, "All that thou hast in thy cellar will not appease the thirst of my love—bring me, O cup-bearer of the wine of the spirit, a cup full as the sea!"

O friends of God! Experience hath shown how much the renouncing of tobacco, wine and opium, giveth health, strength and intellectual enjoyments, penetration of judgment and physical vigor. There exists today a tribe which refrains and abstains from tobacco, alcohol and opium and it completely excels all others in power, in bravery, in health, beauty and grace. A single one of these men can withstand ten men of other tribes, and this hath been universally proved; that is to say, generally, the individuals of this tribe are superior to the individuals of the other tribes.

Therefore strive that the greatest cleanliness and sanctity, which is the great desire of 'Abdu'l-Bahá, should be resplendent among the Bahá'ís, and that the companions of God should surpass the rest of mankind in all conditions and perfections; that they may be physically and morally superior to others; that through cleanliness and purity, refinement and health, they may be the chief of wise men, and that by their affranchisement, their prudence, and the control of their desires, they may be the princes of the pure, the free and the wise.

God and the Universe

. . . By materialists, whose belief with regard to Divinity hath been explained, is not meant philosophers in general, but rather that group of materialists of narrow vision that worship that which is sensed, that depend upon the five senses only, and whose criterion of knowledge is limited to that which can be perceived by the senses. All that can be sensed is to them real, whilst whatever falleth not under the power of the senses is either unreal or doubtful. The existence of the Deity they regard as wholly doubtful.

It is as thou hast written, not philosophers in general but narrow-minded materialists that are meant. As to deistic philosophers, such as Socrates, Plato and Aristotle, they are indeed worthy of esteem and of the highest praise, for they have rendered distinguished services to mankind. In like manner we regard the materialistic, accomplished, moderate philosophers, that have been of service (to mankind).

We regard knowledge and wisdom as the foundation of the progress of mankind, and extol philosophers that are endowed with broad vision. Peruse carefully the San Francisco University Journal that the truth may be revealed to thee.

Now concerning mental faculties, they are in truth of the inherent properties of the soul, even as the radiation of light is the essential property of the sun. The rays of the sun are renewed but the sun itself is ever the same and unchanged. Consider how the human intellect develops and weakens, and may at times come to naught, whereas the soul changeth not. For the mind to manifest itself, the human body must be whole; and a sound mind cannot be but in a sound body, whereas the soul dependeth not upon the body. It is through the power of the soul that the mind comprehendeth, imagineth and exerteth its influence, whilst the soul is a power that is free. The mind comprehendeth the abstract by the aid of the concrete, but the soul hath limitless manifestations of its own. The mind is circumscribed, the soul limitless. It is by the aid of such senses as those of sight, hearing, taste, smell and touch, that the mind comprehendeth, whereas, the soul is free from all agencies. The soul as thou observest, whether it be in sleep or waking, is in motion and ever active. Possibly it may, whilst in a dream, unravel an intricate problem, incapable of solution in the waking state. The mind, moreover, understandeth not whilst the senses have ceased to function, and in the embryonic stage and in early infancy the reasoning power is totally absent, whereas the soul is ever endowed with full strength. In short, the proofs are many that go to show that despite the loss of reason, the power of the soul would still continue to exist. The spirit however possesseth various grades and stations.

As to the existence of spirit in the mineral: it is indubitable that minerals are endowed with a spirit and life according to the requirements of that stage. This unknown secret, too, hath become known unto the materialists who now maintain that all beings are endowed with life, even as He saith in the Qur'án, "All things are living."

In the vegetable world, too, there is the power of growth, and that power of growth is the spirit. In the animal world there is the sense of feeling, but in the human world there is an all-embracing power. In all the preceding stages the power of reason is absent, but the soul existeth and revealeth itself. The sense of feeling understandeth not the soul, whereas the reasoning power of the mind proveth the existence thereof.

In like manner the mind proveth the existence of an unseen Reality that embraceth all beings, and that existeth and revealeth itself in all stages, the essence whereof is beyond the grasp of the mind. Thus the mineral world understandeth neither the nature nor the perfections of the vegetable world; the vegetable world understandeth not the nature of the animal world, neither the animal world the nature of the reality of man that discovereth and embraceth all things.

The animal is the captive of nature and cannot transgress the rules and laws thereof. In man, however, there is a discovering power that transcendeth the world of nature and controlleth and interfereth with the laws thereof. For instance, all minerals, plants and animals are captives of nature. The sun itself with all its majesty is so subservient to nature that it hath no will of its own and cannot deviate a hair's-breadth from the laws thereof. In like manner all other beings, whether of the mineral, the vegetable or the animal world, cannot deviate from the laws of nature, nay, all are the slaves thereof. Man, however, though in body the captive of nature is yet free in his mind and soul, and hath the mastery over nature.

Consider: according to the law of nature man liveth, moveth and hath his being on earth, yet his soul and mind interfere with the laws thereof, and, even as the bird he flieth in the air, saileth speedily upon the seas and as the fish soundeth the deep and discovereth the things therein. Verily this is a grievous defeat inflicted upon the laws of nature.

So is the power of electrical energy: this unruly violent force that cleaveth mountains is yet imprisoned by man within a globe! This is manifestly interfering with the laws of nature. Likewise man discovereth those hidden secrets of nature that in conformity with the laws thereof must remain concealed, and transfereth them from the invisible plane to the visible. This, too, is interfering with the law of nature. In the same manner he discovereth the inherent properties of things that are the secrets of nature. Also he bringeth to light the past events that have been lost to memory, and foreseeth by his power of induction future happenings that are as yet unknown. Furthermore, communication and discovery are limited by the laws of nature to short distances, whereas man, through that inner power of his that discovereth the reality of all things, connecteth the East with the West. This, too, is interfering with the laws of nature. Similarly, according to the law of nature all shadows are fleeting, whereas man fixeth them upon the plate, and this, too, is interference with a law of nature. Ponder and reflect: all sciences, arts, crafts, inventions and discoveries, have been once the secrets of nature and in conformity with the laws thereof must remain hidden; yet man through his discovering power interfereth with the laws of nature and transfereth these hidden secrets from the invisible to the visible plane. This again is interfering with the laws of nature.

In fine, that inner faculty in man, unseen of the eye, wresteth the sword from the hands of nature, and giveth it a grievous blow. All other beings, however great, are bereft of such perfections. Man hath the powers of will and understanding, but nature hath them not. Nature is constrained, man is free. Nature is bereft of understanding, man understandeth. Nature is unaware of past events, but man is aware of them. Nature forecasteth not the future; man by his discerning power seeth that which is to come.

Nature hath no consciousness of itself, man knoweth about all things.

Should any one suppose that man is but a part of the world of nature, and he being endowed with these perfections, these being but manifestations of the world of nature, and thus nature is the originator of these perfections and is not deprived therefrom, to him we make reply and say:—the part dependeth upon the whole; the part cannot possess perfections whereof the whole is deprived.

By nature is meant those inherent properties and necessary relations derived from the realities of things. And these realities of things, though in the utmost diversity, are yet intimately connected one with the other. For these diverse realities an all-unifying agency is needed that shall link them all one to the other. For instance, the various organs and members, the parts and elements, that constitute the body of man, though at variance, are yet all connected one with the other by that all-unifying agency known as the human soul, that causeth them to function in perfect harmony and with absolute regularity, thus making the continuation of life possible. The human body, however, is utterly unconscious of that all-unifying agency, and yet acteth with regularity and dischargeth its functions according to its will.

Now concerning philosophers, they are of two schools. Thus Socrates the wise believed in the unity of God and the existence of the soul after death; as his opinion was contrary to that of the narrow-minded people of his time, that divine sage was poisoned by them. All divine philosophers and men of wisdom and understanding, when observing these endless beings, have considered that in this great and infinite universe all things end in the mineral kingdom, that the outcome of the mineral kingdom is the vegetable kingdom, the outcome of the vegetable kingdom is the animal kingdom and the outcome of the animal kingdom the world of man. The consummation of this limitless universe with all its grandeur and glory hath been man himself, who in this world of being toileth and suffereth for a time, with diverse ills and pains, and ultimately disintegrates, leaving no trace and no fruit after him. Were it so, there is no doubt that this infinite universe with all its perfections has ended in shame and delusion with no result, no fruit, no permanence and no effect. It would be utterly without meaning. They were thus convinced that such is not the case, that this Great Workshop with all its power, its bewildering magnificence and endless perfections, cannot eventually come to naught. That still another life should exist is thus certain, and, just as the vegetable kingdom is unaware of the world of man, so we, too, know not of the Great Life hereafter that followeth the life of man here below. Our non-comprehension of that life, however, is no proof of its non-existence. The mineral world, for instance, is utterly unaware of the world of man and cannot comprehend it, but the ignorance of a thing is no proof of its non-existence. Numerous and conclusive proofs exist that go to show that this infinite world cannot end with this human life.

Now concerning the essence of Divinity: in truth it is on no account determined by anything apart from its own nature, and can in no wise be comprehended. For whatsoever can be conceived by man is a reality that hath limitations and is not unlimited; it is circumscribed, not all-embracing. It can be comprehended by man, and is controlled by him. Similarly it is certain that all human conceptions are contingent, not absolute; that they have a mental existence, not a material one. Moreover, differentiation of stages in the contingent world is an obstacle to understanding. How then can the contingent conceive the Reality of the absolute? As previously mentioned, differentiation of stages in the contingent plane is an obstacle to understanding. Minerals, plants and animals are bereft of the mental faculties of man that discover the realities of all things, but man himself comprehendeth all the stages beneath him. Every superior stage comprehendeth that which is inferior and discovereth the reality thereof, but the inferior one is unaware of that which is superior and cannot comprehend it. Thus man cannot grasp the Essence of Divinity, but can, by his reasoning power, by observation, by his intuitive faculties and the revealing power of his faith, believe in God, discover the bounties of His Grace. He becometh certain that though the Divine Essence is unseen of the eye, and the existence of the Deity is intangible, yet conclusive (spiritual) proofs assert the existence of that unseen Reality. The Divine Essence as it is in itself is however beyond all description. For instance, the nature of ether is unknown, but that it existeth is certain by the effects it produceth, heat, light and electricity being the waves hereof. By these waves the existence of ether is thus proven. And as we consider the outpourings of Divine Grace we are assured of the existence of God. For instance, we observe that the existence of beings is conditioned upon the coming together of various elements and their non-existence upon the decomposition of their constituent elements. For decomposition causes the dissociation of the various elements. Thus, as we observe the coming together of elements giveth rise to the existence of beings, and knowing that beings are infinite, they being the effect, how can the Cause be finite?

Now, formation is of three kinds and of three kinds only: accidental, necessary, and voluntary. The coming together of the various constituent elements of beings cannot be accidental, for unto every effect there must be a cause. It cannot be compulsory, for then the formation must be an inherent property of the constituent parts and the inherent property of a thing can in no wise be dissociated from it, such as light that is the revealer of things, heat that causeth the expansion of elements and the (solar) rays which are the essential property of the sun. Thus under such circumstances the decomposition of any formation is impossible, for the inherent properties of a thing cannot be separated from it. The third formation remaineth and that is the voluntary one, that is, an unseen force described as the Ancient Power, causeth these elements to come together, every formation giving rise to a distinct being.

As to the attributes and perfections such as will, knowledge, power and other ancient attributes that we ascribe to that Divine Reality, these are the signs that reflect the existence of beings in the visible plane and not the absolute perfections of the Divine Essence that cannot be comprehended. For instance, as we consider created things we observe infinite perfections, and the created things being in the utmost regularity and perfection we infer that the Ancient Power on whom dependeth the existence of these beings, cannot be ignorant; thus we say He is All-Knowing. It is certain that it is not impotent, it must be the All-Powerful;

it is not poor, it must be All-Possessing; it is not non-existent, it must be Ever-Living. The purpose is to show that these attributes and perfections that we recount for that Universal Reality are only in order to deny imperfections, rather than to assert the perfections that the human mind can conceive. Thus we say His attributes are unknowable.

In fine, that universal Reality with all its qualities and attributes that we recount is holy and exalted above all minds and understandings. As we, however, reflect with broad minds upon this infinite universe, we observe that motion without a motive force, and an effect without a cause are both impossible; that every being hath come to exist under numerous influences and continually undergoeth reaction. These influences, too, are formed under the action of still other influences. For instance, plants grow and flourish through the outpourings of vernal showers. whilst the cloud itself is formed under various other agencies and these agencies in their turn are reacted upon by still other agencies. For example, plants and animals grow and develop under the influence of what the philosophers of our day designate as hydrogen and oxygen and are reacted upon by the effects of these two elements; and these in turn are formed under still other influences. The same can be said of other beings whether they affect other things or be affected. Such process of causation goes on, and to maintain that this process goes on indefinitely is manifestely absurd. Thus such a chain of causation must of necessity lead eventually to Him who is the Ever-Living, the All-Powerful, who is Self-Dependent and the Ultimate Cause. This Universal Reality cannot be sensed, it cannot be seen. It must be so of necessity, for it is All-Embracing, not circumscribed, and such attributes qualify the effect and not the cause.

And as we reflect, we observe that man is like unto a tiny organism contained within a fruit; this fruit hath developed out of the blossom, the blossom hath grown out of the tree, the tree is sustained by the sap, and the sap formed out of earth and water. How then can this tiny organism comprehend the nature of the garden, conceive of the gardener and comprehend his being? That is manifestly impossible. Should that organism understand and reflect, it would observe that this garden, this tree, this blossom, this fruit would in nowise have come to exist by themselves in such order and perfection. Similarly the wise and reflecting soul will know of a certainty that this infinite universe with all its grandeur and order could not have come to exist by itself.

Similarly in the world of being there exist forces unseen of the eye, such as the force of ether previously mentioned, that cannot be sensed, that cannot be seen. However from the effects it produceth, that is from its waves and vibrations, light, heat, electricity appear and are made evident. In like manner is the power of growth, of feeling, of understanding, of thought, of memory, of imagination and of discernment; all these inner faculties are unseen of the eye and cannot be sensed, yet all are evident by the effects they produce.

Now as to the Power that knoweth no limitations; limitation itself proveth the existence of the unlimited, for the limited is known through the unlimited, just as weakness itself proveth the existence of power. Without wealth there would be no poverty, without knowledge no ignorance, without light no darkness. Darkness itself is a proof of the existence of light for darkness is the absence of light.

Now concerning nature, it is but the essential properties and the necessary relations inherent in the realities of things. And though these infinite realities are diverse in their character yet they are in the utmost harmony and closely connected together. As one's vision is broadened and the matter observed carefully, it will be made certain that every reality is but an essential requisite of other realities. Thus to connect and harmonize these diverse and infinite realities an all-unifying Power is necessary, that every part of existent being may in perfect order discharge its own function. Consider the body of man, and let the part be an indication of the whole. Consider how these diverse parts and members of the human body are closely connected and harmoniously united one with the other. Every part is the essential requisite of all other parts and has a function by itself. It is the mind that is the all-unifying agency that so uniteth all the component parts one with the other that each dischargeth its specific function in perfect order, and thereby cooperation and reaction are made possible. All parts function under certain laws that are essential to existence. Should that all-unifying agency that directeth all these parts be harmed in any way there is no doubt that the constituent parts and members will cease functioning properly; and though that all-unifying agency in the temple of man be not sensed or seen and the reality thereof be unknown, yet by its effects it manifesteth itself with the greatest power.

Thus it hath been proven and made evident that these infinite beings in this wondrous universe will discharge their functions properly only when directed and controlled by the Universal Reality, so that order may be established in the world. For example, interaction and cooperation between the constituent parts of the human body are evident and indisputable, yet this does not suffice; an all-unifying agency is necessary that shall direct and control the component parts, so that these through interaction and cooperation may discharge in perfect order their necessary and respective functions.

You are well aware, praised be the Lord, that both interaction and cooperation are evident and proven amongst all beings, whether large or small. In the case of large bodies interaction is as manifest as the sun, whilst in the case of small bodies, though interaction be unknown, yet the part is an indication of the whole. All these interactions therefore are connected with that all-embracing power which is their pivot, their center, their source and their motive power.

For instance, as we have observed, cooperation among the constituent parts of the human body is clearly established, and these parts and members render services unto all the component parts of the body. For instance, the hand, the foot, the eye, the ear, the mind, the imagination all help the various parts and members of the human body, but all these interactions are linked by an unseen, all-embracing power, that causeth these interactions to be produced with perfect regularity. This is the inner faculty of man, that is his spirit and his mind, both of which are invisible.

In like manner consider machinery and workshops and the interaction existing among the various component parts and sections, and how connected they are one with the other. All these relations and interactions, however, are connected with a central power which is their motive force, their pivot and their source. This central power is either the power of steam or the skill of the master-mind.

It hath therefore been made evident and proved that interaction, cooperation and interrelation amongst beings are under the direction and will of a motive Power which is the origin, the motive force and the pivot of all interactions in the universe.

Likewise every arrangement and formation that is not perfect in its order we designate as accidental, and that which is orderly, regular, perfect in its relations and every part of which is in its proper place and is the essential requisite of the other constituent parts, this we call a composition formed through will and knowledge. There is no doubt that these infinite beings and the association of these diverse elements arranged in countless forms must have proceeded from a Reality that could in no wise be bereft of will or understanding. This is clear and proven to the mind and no one can deny it. It is not meant, however, that that Universal Reality or the attributes thereof have beeen comprehended. Neither its Essence nor its true attributes hath any one comprehended. We maintain, however, that these infinite beings, these necessary relations, this perfect arrangement must of necessity have proceeded from a source that is not bereft of will and understanding, and this infinite composition cast into infinite forms must have been caused by an all-embracing Wisdom. This none can dispute save he that is obstinate and stubborn, and denieth the clear and unmistakable evidence, and becometh the object of the blessed Verse: "They are deaf, they are dumb, they are blind and shall return no more."

Now regarding the question whether the faculties of the mind and the human soul are one and the same. These faculties are but the inherent properties of the soul, such as the power of imagination, of thought, of understanding; powers that are the essential requisites of the reality of man, even as the solar ray is the inherent property of the sun. The temple of man is like unto a mirror, his soul is as the sun, and his mental faculties even as the rays that emanate from that source of light. The ray may cease to fall upon the mirror, but it can in no wise be dissociated from the sun.

In short, the point is this, that the world of man is supernatural in its relation to the vegetable kingdom, though in reality it is not so. Relatively to the plant, the reality of man, his power of hearing and sight, are all supernatural, and for the plant to comprehend that reality and the nature of the powers of man's mind is impossible. In like manner for man to comprehend the Divine Essence and the nature of the great Hereafter is in no wise possible. The merciful outpourings of that Divine Essence, however, are vouchsafed unto all beings and it is incumbent upon man to ponder in his heart upon the effusions of the Divine Grace, the soul being counted as one, rather than upon the Divine Essence itself. This is the utmost limit for human understanding. As it hath previously been mentioned, these attributes and perfections that we recount of the Divine Essence, these we have derived from the existence and observation of beings, and it is not that we have comprehended the essence and perfection of God. When we say that the Divine Essence understandeth and is free, we do not mean that we have discovered the Divine Will and Purpose, but rather that we have acquired knowledge of them through the Divine Grace revealed and manifested in the realities of things.

Now concerning our social principles, namely the teachings of His Holiness Bahá'u'lláh spread far and wide fifty years ago, they verily comprehend all other teachings. It is clear and evident that without these teachings progress and advancement for mankind are in no wise possible. Every community in the world findeth in these Divine Teachings the realization of its highest aspirations. These teachings are even as the tree that beareth the best fruits of all trees. Philosophers, for instance, find in these heavenly teachings the most perfect solution of their social problems, and similarly a true and noble exposition of matters that pertain to philosophical questions. In like manner men of faith behold the reality of religion manifestly revealed in these heavenly teachings, and clearly and conclusively prove them to be the real and true remedy for the ills and infirmities of all mankind. Should these sublime teachings be diffused, mankind shall be freed from all perils, from all chronic ills and sicknesses. In like manner are the Bahá'í economic principles the embodiment of the highest aspirations of all wage-earning classes and of economists of various schools.

In short, all sections and parties have their aspirations realized in the teachings of Bahá'u'lláh. As these teachings are declared in churches, in mosques and in other places of worship, whether those of the followers of Buddha or of Confucius, in political circles or amongst materialists, all shall bear witness that these teachings bestow a fresh life upon mankind and constitute the immediate remedy for all the ills of social life. None can find fault with any of these teachings, nay rather, once declared they will all be acclaimed, and all will confess their vital necessity, exclaiming, "Verily this is the truth and naught is there beside the truth but manifest error."

In conclusion, these few words are written, and unto everyone they will be a clear and conclusive evidence of the truth. Ponder them in thine heart. The will of every sovereign prevaileth during his reign, the will of every philosopher findeth expression in a handful of disciples during his lifetime, but the Power of the Holy Spirit shineth radiantly in the realities of the Messengers of God, and strengtheneth their will in such wise as to influence a great nation for thousands of years and to regenerate the human soul and revive mankind. Consider how great is this power! It is an extraordinary Power, an all-sufficient proof of the truth of the mission of the Prophets of God, and a conclusive evidence of the power of a Divine Inspiration.

CHAPTER EIGHT

THE LOOM OF REALITY

His Deathless Splendor

He is the All-Glorious.

The world's great Light, once resplendent upon all mankind, has set to shine everlastingly from the Abhá horizon, His Kingdom of fadeless glory, shedding splendor upon His loved ones from on high, and breathing into their hearts and souls the breath of eternal life.

Ponder in your hearts that which He hath foretold in His Tablet of "The Divine Vision" that hath been spread throughout the world. Therein He saith: "Thereupon she wailed and exclaimed 'May the world and all that is therein be a ransom for Thy woes, O Sovereign of heaven and earth! Wherefore hast Thou left Thyself in the hands of the dwellers of this prison-city of 'Akká? Hasten Thou to other realms, to Thy retreats above, unknown as yet to the mortal glance of the children of the world.' We smiled and spake not. Reflect upon these most exalted words, and comprehend the purpose of this hidden and sacred mystery."

O ye beloved of the Lord! Beware, beware lest ye hesitate and waver. Let not fear fall upon you, neither be troubled nor dismayed. Take ye good heed lest this calamitous day slacken the flames of your ardor, and quench your tender hopes. Today is the day for steadfastness and constancy. Blessed are they that stand firm and immovable as the rock, and brave the storm and stress of this tempestuous hour. They, verily, shall be the recipients of God's grace, verily shall receive His divine assistance, and shall be the truly victorious. They shall shine amidst mankind with a radiance which the dwellers of the Pavillion of Glory laud and magnify. To them is proclaimed this celestial call, revealed in His most holy Book: "O My people! Be not perplexed should the star of My presence disappear, and the ocean of My utterance be stilled. In My presence among you there was the wisdom of God, and in My absence from you there is yet another, inscrutable to all but the One, the All-Knowing. Verily, We behold you from Our realm of effulgent glory, and will graciously aid whosoever striveth for the triumph of Our Cause with the hosts of the celestial Concourse and a company of Our chosen angels."

The Sun of Truth, that most great Light, has set upon the horizon of the world to rise with deathless splendor over the Realm of the Limitless. In His most holy Book He calleth the firm and steadfast of His friends: "O peoples of the world! Should the radiance of My beauty be veiled, and the temple of My body be hidden, feel not perturbed, nay arise and bestir yourselves, that My Cause may triumph, and My Word be heard by all mankind."

The New Heaven, the New Earth

O ye beloved of God! O ye children of His Kingdom!

Verily, verily the new heaven and the new earth are come. The holy City, new Jerusalem, hath come down from on high in the form of a maid of heaven, veiled, beauteous, and unique, and prepared for reunion with her lovers on earth. The angelic company of the celestial Concourse have joined in a call that hath rung throughout the universe, all loudly and mightily acclaiming: "Hail, O City of God! Abide Thou, and make Thy habitation with the pure, virtuous and holy servants of Thine; for they are Thy people, and Thou art their Lord."

He hath wiped away their tears, kindled their light, rejoiced their hearts and enraptured their souls. Death shall no more overtake them, neither shall sorrow, crying and tribulation afflict them. The Lord God Omnipotent hath been enthroned in His Kingdom and hath made all things new. This is the truth, and what truth greater than the Revelation of St. John the divine? He is the Alpha and Omega. He is the One that will give unto him that is athirst of the fountain of the water of life, and bestow upon the sick the remedy of true salvation. He whom such grace aideth is verily he that receiveth the most glorious heritage from the prophets of God and His holy ones. The Lord will be his God, and he His dearly-beloved son.

Rejoice, then, O ye beloved of the Lord and His chosen ones, and ye the children of God and His people, raise your voice and laud and magnify the Lord, the Most High; for His light hath beamed forth, His signs have appeared, and the billows of His rising ocean have scattered on every shore many a precious pearl.

Spiritual Spring

Do ye know in what cycle ye are created and in what age ye exist? This is the age of the Blessed Perfection and this is the time of the Greatest Name! This is the century of the Manifestation, the age of the Sun of the Horizons and the beautiful springtime of His Holiness the Eternal One!

The earth is in motion and growth; the mountains, hills and prairies are green and pleasant; the bounty is overflowing; the mercy universal; the rain is descending from the cloud of mercy; the brilliant Sun is shining; the full moon is ornamenting the horizon of ether; the great ocean-tide is flooding every little stream; the gifts are successive; the favors consecutive; and the refreshing breeze is blowing, wafting the fragrant perfume of the blossoms. Boundless treasure is in the hand of the King of Kings! Lift the hem of thy garment in order to receive it.

If we are not happy and joyous at this season, for what other season shall we wait and for what other time shall we look?

This is the time for growing; the season for joyous gathering! Take the cup of the Testament in thy hand; leap and dance with ecstasy in the triumphal procession of the Covenant! Lay your confidence in the everlasting bounty, turn to the presence of the generous God; ask assistance from the Kingdom of Abhá; seek confirmation from the Supreme World; turn thy vision to the horizon of eternal wealth; and pray for help from the Source of Mercy!

Soon shall ye see the friends attaining their longed-for destination and pitching their tents, while we are but in the first day of our journey.

This period of time is the Promised Age, the assembling of the human race to the "Resurrection Day" and now is the great "Day of Judgment." Soon the whole world, as in springtime, will change its garb. The turning and falling of the autumn leaves is past; the bleakness of the winter time is over. The new year hath appeared and the spiritual springtime is at hand. The black earth is becoming a verdant garden; the deserts and mountains are teeming with red flowers; from the borders of the wilderness the tall grasses are standing like advance guards before the cypress and jessamine trees; while the birds are singing among the rose branches like the angels in the highest heavens, announcing the glad-tidings of the approach of that spiritual spring, and the sweet music of their voices is causing the real essence of all things to move and quiver.

Serve the Kingdom

When the darkness of ignorance and heedlessness concerning the realm of eternity and bereavement from the True One had encircled the universe, then the resplendent Luminary dawned and the brilliant Light illumined the horizon of the East. Hence, the Sun of Reality shone forth, scattering the sparkling lights of the Kingdom to the East and to the West. Those who had seeing eyes found the Most Great Glad-Tidings, began to cry the call, "O blessed are we! O blessed are we!"—and have beheld the reality of things in themselves, have discovered the mysteries of the Kingdom, were released from superstition and doubts, perceived the lights of Truth and became so intoxicated with the cup of the love of God, that, wholly forgetting themselves and the world while dancing, they ran with utmost joy and ecstasy to the city of Martyrdom, sacrificing their minds and their lives upon the altar of Love.

But those who were blinded became astonished and on account of these joyous acclamations were bewildered and beginning to cry, "Where is the light?" and said, "We do not behold any light, we do not see any rising sun! It is void of any truth! This is pure imagination!"

However, they have hastened bat-like in the darkness below the ground, and according to their own thoughts they have found a little comfort and tranquillity. Nevertheless, it is yet the early dawn and the strength of the heat and the rays of the Sun of Truth have not yet made their torrid and complete impression. When it reacheth the zenith, the heat will interpenetrate with such great intensity that it will move and spur to the greatest velocity even the insects below the earth. Although they are not able to behold the light, yet the penetration of the heat will move and agitate all of them.

Consequently, O ye friends of God, be ye thankful that in the Day of the Effulgence ye have turned your faces to the Orb of the regions and beheld the Lights! Ye have received a portion from the rays of Truth and are endowed with a share from the Everlasting Outpouring. Therefore, ye must not rest one minute, but thank Him for this bestowal.

Be ye not seated and silent! Diffuse the glad-tidings of the Kingdom far and wide to the ears, promulgate the Word of God, and put into practice the advices and covenants of God; that is, arise ye with such qualities and attributes that ye may continually bestow life to the body of the world, and nurse the infants of the universe up to the station of maturity and perfection. Enkindle with all your might in every meeting the light of the love of God, gladden and cheer every heart with the utmost loving-kindness, show forth your love to the strangers just as you show forth to your relations. If a soul is seeking to quarrel, ask ye for reconciliation; if he blame you, praise him; if he give you a deadly poison, bestow ye an all-healing antidote; if he createth death, administer ye eternal life; if he becometh a thorn, change ye into roses and hyacinths. Perchance, through such deeds and words, this darkened world will become illuminated, this terrestrial universe will become transformed into a heavenly realm, and this satanic prison become a divine court; warfare and bloodshed be annihilated, and love and faithfulness hoist the tent of unity upon the apex of the world.

These are the results of the divine advices and exhortations, and the epitome of the teachings of the Bahá'í Cycle.

Fulfillment of Prophecy

A fire from the Kingdom hath been kindled in the heart of the world, in the Blessed Tree, whose flame shall ere long set aglow the pillars of the earth and its rays illumine the horizons of the nations. All the signs have appeared, all the prophetic references have become clear, all that was revealed in the Books and Scriptures hath become fully manifest, and there is no ground for any one to hesitate in regard thereto.

Some people of former times and some sects avoided certain others as strangers, but now the glorious beloved One hath ridden upon His swift coursing steed, encircling about in the arena of truth and all that was hidden became manifest.

Let there be no more silence nor reticence, taciturnity nor negligence. The Candle is lighted—yet the moths continue motionless and melancholy behind the veils.

Now is the time to roar like unto a sea and seek to ascend heavenward! If we desire to reach the apex of the Supreme Kingdom, we must unfurl our wings; if we wish to dive into the depths of the ocean, we must teach our limbs swimming. The time is short and the Divine Courser moves swiftly on; let us keep up and compete with each other and let us light a brilliant candle!

Heralds of His Name

O phoenix of that immortal flame kindled in the sacred Tree!

Bahá'u'lláh (may my life, my soul, my spirit, be offered up as a sacrifice unto His lowly servants) hath, during His last days on earth, given the most emphatic promise that, through the outpourings of the grace of God and the aid and assistance vouchsafed from His Kingdom on high, souls will arise and holy beings appear who, as stars, would adorn the firmament of divine Guidance; illumine the dayspring of loving kindness and bounty; manifest the signs of the unity of God; shine with the light of sanctity and purity; receive their full measure of divine inspiration; raise high the sacred torch of faith; stand firm as the rock and immovable as the mountain; and grow to become luminaries in the heavens of His Revelation, mighty channels of His grace, means for the bestowals of God's bountiful care, heralds calling forth the name of the one true God, and establishers of the world's supreme foundation.

These shall labor ceaselessly by day and by night, shall heed neither trial nor woe, shall suffer no respite in their efforts, shall seek no repose, shall disregard all ease and comfort and, detached and unsullied, shall consecrate every fleeting moment of their life to the diffusion of the divine fragrance and the exaltation of God's holy Word. Their face will radiate heavenly gladness, and their hearts be filled with joy. Their souls will be inspired, and their foundation stand secure. They shall scatter in the world, and travel throughout all regions. They shall raise their voice in every assembly, and adorn and revive every gathering. They shall speak in every tongue, and interpret every hidden meaning. They shall reveal the mysteries of the Kingdom, and manifest unto every one the signs of God. They shall burn brightly even as a candle in the heart of every assembly, and beam forth as a star upon every horizon. The gentle breeze wafted from the garden of their hearts shall perfume and revive the souls of men, and the revelations of their minds, even as showers, reinvigorate the peoples and nations of the world.

I am waiting, eagerly waiting for these holy ones to appear; and yet, how long will they delay their coming? My prayer and ardent supplication, at eventide and at dawn, is that these shining stars may soon shed their radiance upon the world, that their sacred countenance may be unveiled to mortal eyes, and the billows of grace, rising from His oceans above, may flow upon all mankind. Pray ye also and supplicate unto Him that through the bountiful aid of the Ancient Beauty these souls may be unveiled to the eyes of the world.

The glory of God rest upon thee, and upon him whose face is illumined with that everlasting light that shineth from His Kingdom of Glory.

The World Is Infirm

O ye friends of God! The world is like the body of man—it hath become sick, feeble and infirm. Its eye is devoid of sight, its ear hath become destitute of hearing and its faculties of sense are entirely dissolved. The friends of God must become as wise physicians and care for and heal this sick person, in accord with the divine teachings, in order that—God willing—it may perchance gain health, find eternal healing and that its lost powers may be restored; and that the person of the world may find such health, freshness and purity that it will appear in the utmost beauty and charm.

The first remedy is to guide the people, so that they may turn unto God, hearken unto the divine commandments and go forth with a hearing ear and seeing eye. After this swift and certain remedy hath been applied, then according to the divine teachings, they ought to be trained in the conduct, morals and deeds of the Supreme Concourse, encouraged and inspired with the gifts of the Kingdom of Abhá. The hearts should be purified and cleansed from every trace of hatred and rancor and enabled to engage in truthfulness, conciliation, uprightness and love toward the world of humanity; so that the East and the West may embrace each other like unto two lovers, enmity and animosity may vanish from the human world and the universal peace be established!

O ye friends of God! Be kind to all peoples and nations, have love for all of them, exert yourselves to purify the hearts as much as you can, and bestow abundant effort in rejoicing the souls. Be ye a sprinkling of rain to every meadow and a water of life to every tree. Be ye as fragrant musk to every nostril and a soul-refreshing breeze to every invalid. Be ye salutary water to every thirsty one, a wise guide to every one led astray, an affectionate father or mother to every orphan, and, in the utmost joy and fragrance, a son or daughter to every one bent with age. Be ye a rich treasure to every indigent one; consider love and union as a delectable paradise, and count annoyance and hostility as the torment of hell-fire. Exert with your soul; seek no rest in body; supplicate and beseech with your heart and search for divine assistance and favor, in order that ye may make this world the Paradise of Abhá and this terrestrial globe the arena of the Supreme Kingdom. If ye make an effort, it is certain that these lights will shine, this cloud of mercy shall rain, this soul-nourishing breeze shall waft, and the scent of this most fragrant musk be diffused.

The Covenant

O ye beloved of God, know that steadfastness and firmness in this new and wonderful Covenant is indeed the spirit that quickeneth the hearts which are overflowing with the love of the Glorious Lord; verily, it is the power which penetrates into the hearts of the people of the world! Your Lord hath assuredly promised His servants who are firm and steadfast to render them victorious at all times, to exalt their word, propagate their power, diffuse their lights, strengthen their hearts, elevate their banners, assist their hosts, brighten their stars, increase the abundance of the showers of mercy upon them, and enable the brave lions to conquer.

Hasten, hasten, O ye firm believers! Hasten, hasten, O ye steadfast! Abandon the heedless, set aside every ignorant, take hold of the strong rope, be firm in this Great Cause, draw light from this Evident Light, be patient and be steadfast in this wise Religion! Ye shall see the hosts of inspiration descending successively from the Supreme World, the procession of attraction falling incessantly from the heights of heaven, the abundance of the Kingdom of El-Abhá outpouring continually and the teachings of God penetrating with the utmost power, while the heedless are indeed in evident loss.

Iscariot must not be forgotten; the Divine sheep must constantly be guarded against devouring wolves; the light of the Cause of God must be protected from contrary winds by means of a chimney; the oppressed fowls must be shielded against the birds of prey; blooming roses should be saved from the outstretched hands of injustice and the lambs of God must be fortified against the fierce claws of ravenous animals.

Were it not for the protecting power of the Covenant to guard the impregnable fort of the Cause of God, there would arise among the Bahá'ís, in one day, a thousand different sects as was the case in former ages. But in this Blessed Dispensation, for the sake of the permanency of the Cause of God and the avoidance of dissension amongst the people of God, the Blessed Beauty (may my soul be a sacrifice unto Him), has through the Supreme Pen written the Covenant and the Testament; He appointed a Center, the Exponent of the Book and the annuller of disputes. Whatever is written or said by Him is conformable to the truth and under the protection of the Blessed Beauty. He is infallible. The express purpose of this last Will and Testament is to set aside disputes from the world.

Suffer the friends to become firm in the Covenant and give the message of the Kingdom of Abhá to other souls.

Praise be to God that the believers in America are steadfast but the firmer they are the better that no one might be able to intrude and introduce disputes, for disputes destroy the foundation of God's Institution.

His Holiness Abraham, on Him be peace, made a covenant concerning His Holiness Moses and gave the glad-tidings of His coming. His Holiness Moses made a covenant concerning the Promised One, i.e. His Holiness Christ, and announced the good news of His Manifestation to the world. His Holiness Christ made a covenant concerning the Paraclete and gave the tidings of His coming. His Holiness the Prophet Muḥammad made a covenant concerning His Holiness the Báb and the Báb was the One promised by Muḥammad, for Muḥammad gave the tidings of His coming. The Báb made a Covenant concerning the Blessed Beauty of Bahá'u'lláh and gave the glad-tidings of His coming for the Blessed Beauty was the One promised by His Holiness the Báb. Bahá'u'lláh made a covenant concerning a promised One who will become manifest after one thousand or thousands of years. He likewise, with His Supreme Pen, entered into a great Covenant and Testament with all the Bahá'ís whereby they were all commanded to follow the Center of the Covenant after His departure, and turn not away even to a hair's breadth from obeying Him.

In the Book of Aqdas, He has given positive command in two

clear instances and has explicitly appointed the Interpreter of the Book. Also in all the Divine Tablets, especially in the Chapter of The Branch—all the meanings of which mean the Servitude of 'Abdu'l-Bahá, that is 'Abdu'l-Bahá—all that was needed to explain the Center of the Covenant and the Interpreter of the Book has been revealed from the Supreme Pen. Now as 'Abdu'l-Bahá is the Interpreter of the Book He says that the "Chapter of The Branch" means 'Abdu'l-Bahá, that is, the Servitude of 'Abdu'l-Bahá, and none other.

Race Unity

You have written that there were several meetings of joy and happiness, one for white and another for colored people. Praise be to God! As both races are under the protection of the All-Knowing God, therefore the lamps of unity must be lighted in such a manner in these meetings that no distinction be perceived between the white and colored. Colors are phenomenal, but the realities of men are essence. When there exists unity of the essence what power has the phenomenal? When the light of reality is shining what power has the darkness of the unreal? If it be possible, gather together these two races, black and white, into one Assembly, and put such love into their hearts that they shall not only unite but even intermarry. Be sure that the result of this will abolish differences and disputes between black and white. Moreover, by the Will of God, may it be so. This is a great service to humanity.

The Fire of the Love of God

O friend! Be set aglow with the fire of the love of God, so that the hearts of the people will become enlightened by the light of thy love.

Supplicate to God, pray to Him and invoke Him at midnight and at dawn. Be humble and submissive to God and chant the verses of thanksgiving at morn and eve, for that He guided thee unto the Manifest Light and showed to thee the straight Path and destined to thee the station of nearness in His wonderful Kingdom.

Verily I ask God to augment for thee, every day, the light of guidance and His gift of virtue, comfort and ease. Thus thou mayest set a good example in that region; that He may lift up the veil from before the eyes of thy mother and father, so that they may witness the lights of the Kingdom of God, which have encompassed all regions.

Ye Are the Angels

Verily, I, from this brilliant and Blessed Spot, speak to you face to face, while ye are in that far distant country, saying:

"O people of loyalty, O people of faithfulness, O people who are awakened by the Breath of God, O people who are inhaling the scent of life from the Spirit of God! The path hath become smooth, the way straightened, the carpet of the Kingdom is spread, the Tabernacle hath been elevated upon the Hill of Might, the powers of heaven have been shaken, the corners of the earth have quaked, the sun has been darkened, the moon ceased to give light, the stars have fallen, the nations of the earth have lamented, and the Son of Man hath come upon the clouds of heaven with power and great glory, and He hath sent His angels with the sound of the great trumpet, and no one knows the meaning of these emblems save the wise and informed.

"Ye are the angels, if your feet be firm, your spirits rejoiced, your secret thoughts pure, your eyes consoled, your ears opened, your breasts dilated with joy, and your souls gladdened, and if you arise to assist the Covenant, to resist dissension and to be attracted to the Effulgence! Verily, I say unto you that the Word of God has assuredly been explained and has become an evident sign and a strong and solid proof, and its traces shall be spread in the East and West, and to these all heads shall bow and all souls shall submit and kneel down with their faces to the ground."

Reality of Thanksgiving

In these times thanksgiving for the bounty of the Merciful One consists in the illumination of the heart and the feeling of the soul.

This is the reality of thanksgiving. But, although offering thanks through speech or writings is approvable, yet, in comparison with that, it is but unreal, for the foundation is spiritual feelings and merciful sentiments. I hope that you may be favored therewith. But the lack of capacity and merit in the Day of Judgment does not prevent one from bounty and generosity, for it is the day of grace and not justice, and to give every one his due is justice. Consequently, do not look upon thy capacity, nay, rather, look upon the infinite grace of the Bounty of Abhá whose grace is comprehending and whose bounty is perfect.

The Straight Path

Thank God for guiding thee unto the Straight Path, manifesting unto thee the Evident Light. He shall give thee a draught of the cup whereby thy spiritual power will be increased. Thou shalt advance unto the Lofty Station, acquire heavenly qualities and attain knowledge of the significances of the words of God in this glorious day.

It is incumbent upon thee to turn wholly unto the Kingdom of God, to enter entirely into this wonderful Cause, and to make thy thought, remembrance and effort confined to the education of thy character, the enlightenment through the light of Abhá, and to guide the people to the source of the mercy of thy Lord, the Clement, the Merciful.

Comfort thy mother and endeavor to do what is conducive to the happiness of her heart. Approach not those who are drowned in the sea of this world, but rather be enkindled by the fire of the love of God. Be thou such a flame whereby the hearts may be set aglow.

It is incumbent upon thee to assemble continuously with the beloved of God and to meet with those whose faces are illumined with the light of the love of God. Verily, I supplicate to God to make thee sincere in this love, to illumine thee with the light of His Kingdom, and to destine unto thee the illumination by the light of His attributes, to make thee a sign of mercy, a bird warbling the verses of unity; that thou mayest be nurtured in the bosom of His providence, and become a growing tree bearing fruit in the Paradise of El-Abhá.

Verily, thy Lord confirmeth him whom He willeth, and He is the Forgiving, the Merciful.

Cut Thyself from the World

If thou seekest to be intoxicated with the cup of the Most Mighty Gift, cut thyself from the world and be quit of self and desire. Exert thyself night and day until spiritual powers may penetrate thy heart and soul. Abandon the body and the material, until the merciful powers may become manifest; because not until the soil is become pure will it develop through the heavenly bounty; not until the heart is purified, will the radiance of the Sun of Truth shine therein. I beg of God that thou wilt day by day increase the purity of thy heart, the cheerfulness of thy soul, the light of thy insight and the search for Truth.

Arise With Great Power

Arise with every power to assist the Covenant of God and serve in His vineyard. Be confident that a confirmation will be granted unto you and a success on His part is given unto you. Verily, He shall support you by the angels of His holiness and reinforce you with the breaths of the Spirit that ye may mount the Ark of Safety, set forth the evident signs, impart the spirit of life, declare the essence of His commands and precepts, guide the sheep who are straying from the fold in all directions, and give the blessings. Ye have to use every effort in your power and strive earnestly and wisely in this new century. By God, verily the Lord of Hosts is your support, the angels of heaven your assistance, the Holy Spirit your companion and the Center of the Covenant your helper. Be not idle, but active and fear not. Look unto those who have been in the former ages—how they have resisted all nations and suffered all persecutions and afflictions, and how their stars shone, their attacks proved successful, their teachings established, their regions expanded, their hearts gladdened, their ideas cleared and their motives effective. Ye are now in a great station and noble rank and ye shall find yourselves in evident success and prosperity, the like of which the eye of existence never saw in former ages.

Divine Assistance

O thou who warmest thyself by the fire of the love of God, spreading from the Tree of the Covenant! Let thy soul be at ease and thy heart in peace concerning the perfect success and progress which the pen is not able to express, for in a short time thou shalt see the flag of the Kingdom waving in those far and wide regions, and the lights of the Truth shining brilliantly in its dawn above those horizons, and thou shalt know that thou art the center of the circle of the love of God, the axis around which souls revolve in their way and supplication to God. Therefore, thou must widen thy heart, dilate thy breast, have patience in plenty, calmness of soul and cut thyself from everything but God! By God, the truth is, if thou goest according to the teachings of El-Abd and followest the steps of Him who is annihilated in God, thou shalt see that the cohorts of the Kingdom of God will come to thy help, one after another, and that the hosts of the Might of God will be in thy presence in steady succession, the gates of the great victory opened and the rays of the brilliant morning diffused! By thy life, O my beloved! if thou didst know what God had ordained for thee, thou wouldst fly with delight and thy happiness, gladness and joy would increase every hour. El-Bahá be upon thee!

Proof of Nobility

The necessity and the particularity of the assured and believing ones is to be firm in the Cause of God and withstand the hidden and evident tests. Thanks be to God that you are distinguished and made eminent by this blessing. Anybody can be happy in the state of comfort, ease, health, success, pleasure and joy; but if one will be happy and contented in the time of trouble, hardship and prevailing disease, it is the proof of nobility. Thanks be to God that that dear servant of God is extremely patient under the disastrous circumstances, and in the place of complaining gives thanks.

The Source of Love

The advent of the prophets and the revelation of the Holy Books is intended to create love between souls and friendship between the inhabitants of the earth. Real love is impossible unless one turn his face towards God and be attracted to His Beauty.

Objective and Subjective Faith

Thou hast written of a verse in the Gospels, asking if at the time of Christ all souls did hear His call. Know that faith is of two kinds. The first is objective faith that is expressed by the outer man, obedience of the limbs and senses. The other faith is subjective, and unconscious obedience to the will of God. There is no doubt that, in the day of a Manifestation such as Christ, all contingent beings possessed subjective faith and had unconscious obedience to His Holiness Christ.

For all parts of the creational world are of one whole. Christ the Manifestor reflecting the divine Sun represented the whole. All the parts are subordinate and obedient to the whole. The contingent beings are the branches of the tree of life while the Messenger of God is the root of that tree. The branches, leaves and fruit are dependent for their existence upon the root of the tree of life. This condition of unconscious obedience constitutes subjective faith. But the discerning faith that consists of true knowledge of God and the comprehension of divine words, of such faith there is very little in any age. That is why His Holiness Christ said to His followers, "Many are called but few are chosen."

Spiritual Capacity

Those souls who have the capacity and ability to receive the outpourings of the Kingdom and the confirmation of the Holy Spirit, they become attracted through one word. But people who have not the capacity, no matter how much one explain the divine behests and advices or breathe the breath of the Holy Spirit, it will not make an effect; nay, rather they add to their hardness and heedlessness.

No sooner is the oil touched by fire than it is ignited, but the heat of the fire will not make any effect upon the black stone.

Now praise be to God that thou didst have a pure aim and great capacity so that as soon as thou didst hear the "Word" thou didst become attracted. Indeed this is one of the most great gifts of God.

The Beloved of God

The spiritual love of God maketh man pure and holy and clotheth him with the garment of virtue and purity. And when man attacheth his heart wholly to God and becometh related to the Blessed Perfection, the divine bounty will dawn. This love is not physical, nay, rather, it is absolutely spiritual.

The souls whose consciences are enlightened through the light of the love of God, they are like unto shining lights and resemble stars of holiness in the heaven of purity.

The real and great love is the love of God. That is holy above the imaginations and thoughts of men.

The beloved of God must each be the essence of purity and holiness; so may they be known by their purity, freedom and meekness in every land; they may drink from the eternal chalice of the love of God, enjoy its ecstasy, and through meeting the Beauty of Abhá, they should be joyful, active, aglow with zeal and wonderful. This is the station of the sincere. This is the quality of those who are firm. This is the illumination of the faces of those who are near.

Therefore, O ye friends of God, ye must in perfect purity attain spiritual unity and agreement to a degree that ye may express one spirit and one life.

In this condition physical bodies play no part; the command and authority are in the hand of the spirit. When the spirit becometh all inclusive, the spiritual union shall be attained. Night and day endeavor to attain perfect harmony; be thoughtful concerning your own spiritual developments and close your eyes to the shortcomings of one another.

By good deeds, pure lives, humility and meekness be a lesson for others.

If One Possesses the Love of God

O thou son of the Kingdom! If one possesses the love of God, everything that he undertakes is useful, but if the undertaking is without the love of God, then it is hurtful and the cause of veiling one's self from the Lord of the Kingdom. But with the love of God every bitterness is changed into sweetness and every gift becometh precious. For instance, a musical and melodious voice imparteth life to an attracted heart but lureth toward lust those souls who are engulfed in passion and desire.

With the love of God all sciences are accepted and beloved, but without it, are fruitless; nay, rather the cause of insanity. Every science is like unto a tree; if the fruit of it is the love of God, that is a blessed tree. Otherwise it is dried wood and finally a food for fire.

O thou sincere servant of the True One and the spiritual physician of the people! Whenever thou presentest thyself at the bed of a patient turn thy face toward the Lord of the Kingdom and supplicate assistance from the Holy Spirit and heal the ailments of the sick one. I beg of God to bestow upon thee an eloquent tongue.

The Magnet of the Kingdom

Note that thy Lord hath manifested the Magnet of the souls and hearts in the Pole of the existing world, to which all the sacred hearts are attracted from the far distant lands and countries.

The iron body is attractable although at long distances away; but the earthen one is not although in contact and very close.

Therefore, thank thou God for being an attractable body, to be drawn to the Magnet of the Kingdom of God.

The Encompassing Spirit

Verily, I say unto thee that the gifts of thy Lord are encircling thee in a similar way as the spirit encircles the body at the beginning of the amalgamation of the elements and natures in the womb; the power of the spirit begins then to appear in the body gradually and successively according to the preparation and capacity to receive that everlasting abundance.

Souls Are Like Mirrors

Souls are like unto mirrors, and the bounty of God is like unto the sun. When the mirrors pass beyond all coloring and attain purity and polish, and are confronted with the sun, they will reflect in full perfection its light and glory. In this condition one should not consider the mirror, but the power of the light of the sun, which hath penetrated the mirror, making it a reflector of the heavenly glory.

The World of Vision

As to the question whether the souls will recognize each other in the spiritual world: This fact is certain; for the Kingdom is the world of vision where all the concealed realities will become disclosed. How much more the well-known souls will become manifest. The mysteries of which man is heedless in this earthly world, those he will discover in the heavenly world, and there will he be informed of the secret of truth; how much more will he recognize or discover persons with whom he hath been associated. Undoubtedly, the holy souls who find a pure eye and are favored with insight will, in the kingdom of lights, be acquainted with all mysteries, and will seek the bounty of witnessing the reality of every great soul. Even they will manifestly behold the Beauty of God in that world. Likewise will they find all the friends of God, both those of the former and recent times, present in the heavenly assemblage.

Prayer Is Indispensable

O thou spiritual friend! Thou hast asked the wisdom of prayer. Know thou that prayer is indispensable and obligatory, and man under no pretext whatsoever is excused from performing the prayer unless he be mentally unsound, or an insurmountable obstacle prevent him. The wisdom of prayer is this: That it causeth a connection between the servant and the True One, because in that state man with all heart and soul turneth his face towards His Highness the Almighty, seeking His association and desiring His love and compassion. The greatest happiness for a lover is to converse with his beloved, and the greatest gift for a seeker is to become familiar with the object of his longing; that is why with every soul who is attracted to the Kingdom of God, his greatest hope is to find an opportunity to entreat and supplicate before his Beloved, appeal for His mercy and grace and be immersed in the ocean of His utterance, goodness and generosity.

Besides all this, prayer and fasting is the cause of awakening and mindfulness and conducive to protection and preservation from tests. . . .

Turn to the Holy Spirit

Know thou, that letter sent to thee by me, was only because of my perfect love for thee and my pity upon thee, for I had the desire that the fragrance of the Holy Spirit, which hath perfumed all regions and imbued the entire body of the world with the Spirit of Life, should pass over thee and abide with thee. Notwithstanding the high position it occupieth, still, with an eloquent tongue, through which the Spirit moveth, hearts are attracted and bosoms burn, it speaketh to the pure hearts and to the good and righteous souls in every spot of the earth. This is the powerful Spirit, the dazzling light, the brilliant star and the overwhelming and universal abundance. And, from its traces, spread and divulged everywhere, thou wilt know and realize its influence and comprehend its radiance. I ask God to expose thee to its fragrance, move thee by its breeze, enkindle thee by its coals of fire and illuminate thee by its brightness. Turn thyself wholly to it—thus thou shalt be enabled to ascertain its influence and power, the strength of its life and the greatness of its confirmation. Verily, I say unto thee, that if for the appearance of that Divine Essence thou desirest to have a definite proof, an indisputable testimony and a strong, convincing evidence, thou must prepare thyself to make thy heart empty and thine eye ready to look only toward the Kingdom of God. Then, at that time, the radiance of that widespread effulgence will descend upon thee successively, and that motion rendered thee by the Holy Spirit will make thee dispense with any other strong evidence that leadeth to the appearance of this Light, because the greatest and strongest proof for showing the abundance of the Spirit to the bodies is the very appearance of its power and influence in those bodies.

Inspiration of the Holy Spirit

I now assure thee, O servant of God, that, if thy mind become empty and pure from every mention and thought and thy heart attracted wholly to the Kingdom of God, forget all else besides God and come in communion with the Spirit of God, then the Holy Spirit will assist thee with a power which will enable thee to penetrate all things, and a Dazzling Spark which enlightens all sides, a Brilliant Flame in the zenith of the heavens, will teach thee that which thou dost not know of the facts of the universe and of the divine doctrine. Verily, I say unto thee, every soul which ariseth today to guide others to the path of safety and infuse in them the Spirit of Life, the Holy Spirit will inspire that soul with evidences, proofs and facts and the lights will shine upon it from the Kingdom of God. Do not forget what I have conveyed unto thee from the breath of the Spirit. Verily, it is the shining morning and the rosy dawn which will impart unto thee the lights, reveal the mysteries and make thee competent in science, and through it the pictures of the Supreme World will be printed in thy heart and the facts of the secrets of the Kingdom of God will shine before thee.

The Intermediary

Unless the Holy Spirit become intermediary, one cannot attain directly to the bounties of God. Do not overlook the obvious truths, for it is a self-evident fact that a child cannot be instructed without a teacher, and knowledge is a bounty from the bounties of God. The soil is not covered with grass and green without the rain of the cloud; therefore the cloud is the intermediary between the divine bounties and the soil. A body doth not develop and grow without the soul; therefore the soul is the medium of the spiritual life.

The Spirit of Faith

Now as to what thou askest concerning the spirit and its "return" to this world of humanity and this elemental space: Know that spirit in general is divided into five sorts—the vegetable spirit, the animal spirit, the human spirit, the spirit of faith, and the divine spirit of sanctity.

The vegetable spirit is the virtue augmentative, or growing or vegetative faculty, which results from the admixture of the simple elements, with the cooperation of water, air and heat.

The animal spirit is the virtue perceptive resulting from the admixture and absorption of the vital elements generated in the heart, which apprehend sense-impressions.

The human spirit consists of the rational, or logical, reasoning faculty, which apprehends general ideas and things intelligible and perceptible.

Now these "spirits" are not reckoned as Spirit in the terminology of the Scriptures and the usage of the people of the Truth, inasmuch as the laws governing them are as the laws which govern all phenomenal being in respect to generation, corruption, production, change and reversion, as is clearly indicated in the Gospel where it says: "Let the dead bury their dead;" "That which is born of the flesh is flesh, and that which is born of the Spirit is Spirit"; inasmuch as he who would bury these dead was alive with the vegetative, animal and rational human soul, yet did Christ—to whom be glory!—declare such dead and devoid of life, in that this person was devoid of the spirit of faith, which is of the Kingdom of God.

In brief, for these three spirits there is no restitution or "return," but they are subordinate to reversions and production and corruption.

But the spirit of faith which is of the Kingdom consists of the all-comprehending grace and the perfect attainment and the power of sanctity and the divine effulgence from the Sun of Truth on luminous light-seeking essences from the presence of the divine Unity. And by this Spirit is the life of the spirit of man, when it is fortified thereby, as Christ saith: "That which is born of the Spirit is Spirit." And this Spirit hath both restitution and return, inasmuch as it consists of the Light of God and the unconditioned grace. So, having regard to this state and station, Christ announced that John the Baptist was Elias, who was to come before Christ. And the likeness of this station is as that of lamps kindled: for these in respect to their glasses and oil-holders, are different, but in respect to their light, One, and in respect to their illumination, One; nay, each one is identical with the other, without imputation of plurality, or diversity or multiplicity or separateness. This is the Truth and beyond the Truth there is only error.

Trials a Gift from God

Thou hast written concerning the tests that have come upon thee. To the sincere ones, tests are as a gift from God, the Exalted, for a heroic person hasteneth, with the utmost joy and gladness, to the tests of a violent battlefield, but the coward is afraid and trembles and utters moaning and lamentation. Likewise, an expert student prepareth and memorizeth his lessons and exercises with the utmost effort, and in the day of examination he appeareth with infinite joy before the master. Likewise, the pure gold shineth radiantly in the fire of test. Consequently, it is made clear that for holy souls, trials are as the gift of God, the Exalted; but for weak souls they are an unexpected calamity. This test is just as thou hast written: it removeth the rust of egotism from the mirror of the heart until the Sun of Truth may shine therein. For, no veil is greater than egotism and no matter how thin that covering may be, yet it will finally veil man entirely and prevent him from receiving a portion from the eternal bounty.

The Mystery of Suffering

As to the subject of babes and infants and weak ones who are afflicted by the hands of oppressors: This contains great wisdom and this subject is of paramount importance. In brief, for those souls there is a recompense in another world and many details are connected with this matter. For those souls that suffering is the greatest mercy of God. Verily that mercy of the Lord is far better and preferable to all the comfort of this world and the growth and development of this place of mortality. If it be the will of God, when thou shalt be present this will be explained in detail by word of mouth.

Bahá'í Marriage

She must not rest until she makes him her spiritual as well as physical partner in life. But the Bahá'í engagement is the perfect communication and the entire consent of both parties. However, they must show forth the utmost attention and become informed of one another's character and the firm covenant made between each other must become an eternal binding, and their intentions must be everlasting affinity, friendship, unity and life. The bridegroom must, before the bridesman and a few others, say: "Verily, we are content with the will of God." And the bride must rejoin: "Verily, we are satisfied with the desire of God." This is Bahá'í matrimony.

The marriage of the Bahá'ís means that both man and woman must become spiritually and physically united, so that they may have eternal unity throughout all the divine worlds and improve the spiritual life of each other. This is Bahá'í matrimony.

Among the majority of the people marriage consists of physical relationship and this union and relationship is temporary for at the end physical separation is destined and ordained. But the marriage of the people of Bahá must consist of both physical and spiritual relationship for both of them are intoxicated with the wine of one cup, are attracted by one Peerless Countenance, are quickened with one Life and are illumined with one Light. This is the spiritual relationship and everlasting union. Likewise in the physical world they are bound together with strong and unbreakable ties.

When relationship, union and concord exist between the two from a physical and spiritual standpoint, that is the real union, therefore everlasting. But if the union is merely from the physical point of view, unquestionably it is temporal and at the end separation is inevitable.

Consequently when the people of Bahá desire to enter the sacred union of marriage, eternal connection and ideal relationship, spiritual and physical association of thoughts and conceptions of life must exist between them, so that in all the grades of existence and all the worlds of God this union may continue forever and ever for this real union is a splendor of the light of the love of God.

Likewise if the souls become real believers they will find themselves ushered into this exalted state of relationship, becoming the manifestors of the love of the Merciful and exhilarated with the cup of the love of God. Undoubtedly that union and relationship is eternal.

The souls who sacrifice self, become detached from the perfections of the realm of man and free from the shackles of this ephemeral world, assuredly the splendors of the rays of divine union shall shine in their hearts and in the eternal paradise they shall find ideal relationship, union and happiness.

Kindness to Animals

Then, O ye friends of God! Ye must not only have kind and merciful feelings for mankind, but ye should also exercise the utmost kindness towards every living creature. The physical sensibilities and instincts are common to animal and man. Man is, however, negligent of this reality and imagines that sensibility is peculiar to mankind, therefore he practices cruelty to the animal. In reality what difference is there in physical sensations! Sensibility is the same whether you harm man or animal: there is no difference. Nay, rather, cruelty to the animal is more painful because man has a tongue and he sighs, complains and groans when he receives an injury and complains to the government and the government protects him from cruelty; but the poor animal cannot speak, it can neither show its suffering nor is it able to appeal to the government. If it is harmed a thousand times by man it is not able to defend itself in words nor can it seek justice or retaliate. Therefore one must be very considerate towards animals and show greater kindness to them than to man. Educate the children in their infancy in such a way that they may become exceedingly kind and merciful to the animals. If an animal is sick they should endeavor to cure it; if it is hungry, they should feed it; if it is thirsty, they should satisfy its thirst; if it is tired, they should give it rest.

Man is generally sinful and the animal is innocent; unquestionably one must be more kind and merciful to the innocent. The harmful animals, such as the bloodthirsty wolf, the poisonous snake and other injurious animals are excepted, because mercy towards these is cruelty to man, and other animals. For instance, if you show kindness to a wolf this becomes a tyranny to the sheep, for it may destroy an entire flock of sheep. If you give the opportunity to a mad dog it may be the cause of the destruction of a thousand animals and men. Therefore, sympathy to the ferocious animal is cruelty to the peaceful animal, so they should be done away with. To the blessed animals, however, the utmost kindness should be exercised: the more the better it will be.

This sympathy and kindness is one of the fundamental principles of the divine kingdom. Ye should pay great attention to this question.

Economy a Great Treasure

It behoveth thee to sever thyself from all desires save thy Lord, the Supreme, expecting no help or aid from anyone in the universe, not even from thy father or children. Resign thyself to God! Content thyself with but little of this world's goods! Verily, economy is a great treasure. If one of thy relations oppress thee, complain not against him before the magistrate; rather manifest magnificent patience during every calamity and hardship. Verily thy Master is the Lord of Faithfulness! Forgive and overlook the shortcomings which have appeared in that one, for the sake of love and affection. Know that nothing will benefit thee in this life save supplication and invocation unto God, service in His vineyard, and, with a heart full of love, be in constant servitude unto Him.

If thy daily living become difficult, soon thy Lord will bestow upon thee that which shall satisfy thee. Be patient in the time of affliction and trial, endure every difficulty and hardship with a dilated heart, attracted spirit and eloquent tongue in remembrance of the Merciful. Verily this is the life of satisfaction, the spiritual existence, heavenly repose, divine benediction and the celestial table! Soon thy Lord will extenuate thy straitened circumstances even in this world.

Means of Livelihood

Thou hast asked regarding the means of livelihood. Trust in God and engage in your work and practice economy; the confirmations of God shall descend and you will be enabled to pay off your debts. Be ye occupied always with the mention of Bahá'u'lláh and seek ye no other hope and desire save Him.

Socialism

Thou hast asked whether to enlist in the Socialist party. The Bahá'ís must be in the Bahá'í Cause which comprehends all the degrees and is perfect from every standpoint.

Two Methods of Healing

There are two ways of healing sickness, material means and spiritual means. The first is by the use of remedies, of medicines;

the second consists in praying to God and in turning to Him. Both means should be used and practiced.

Illness caused by physical accident should be treated with medical remedies; those which are due to spiritual causes disappear through spiritual means. Thus an illness caused by affliction, fear, nervous impressions, will be healed by spiritual rather than by physical treatment. Hence, both kinds of remedies should be considered. Moreover, they are not contradictory, and thou shouldst accept the physical remedies as coming from the mercy and favor of God, who hath revealed and made manifest medical science so that His servants may profit from this kind of treatment also. Thou shouldst give equal attention to spiritual treatments, for they produce marvelous effects.

Now, if thou wishest to know the divine remedy which will heal man from all sickness and will give him the health of the divine kingdom, know that it is the precepts and teachings of God. Guard them sacredly.

If Thou Desirest Health

If the health and well-being of the body be expended in the path of the Kingdom, this is very acceptable and praiseworthy; and if it is expended to the benefit of the human world in general —even though it be to their material benefit and be a means of doing good—that is also acceptable. But if the health and welfare of man be spent in sensual desires, in a life on the animal plane, and in devilish pursuits—then disease is better than such health; nay, death itself is preferable to such a life. If thou art desirous of health, wish thou health for serving the Kingdom. I hope thou mayest attain a perfect insight, an inflexible resolution, a complete health and spiritual and physical strength in order that thou mayest drink from the fountain of eternal life and be assisted by the spirit of divine confirmation.

Duty to Attain Science

Now as to what thou askest concerning giving up the scientific attainment in Paris for the sake of confining thy days to the delivery of this Truth, it is indeed acceptable and beloved, but if thou acquire both it would be better and more perfect, because in this new century the attainment of science, arts and *belles lettres,* whether divine or worldly, material or spiritual, is a matter which is acceptable before God and a duty which is incumbent upon us to accomplish. Therefore, never deny the spiritual things to the material, rather both are incumbent upon thee. Nevertheless, at the time when thou art working for such a scientific attainment, thou must be controlled by the attraction of the love of thy Glorious Lord and mindful of mentioning His splendid Name. This being the case, thou must attain the art thou art studying to its perfection.

Work Is Worship

In this great dispensation, art (or a profession) is identical with an act of worship and this is a clear text of the Blessed Perfection. Therefore, extreme effort should be made in art and this will not prevent the teaching of the people in that region. Nay, rather, each should assist the other in art and guidance. For instance, when the studying of art is with the intention of obeying the command of God this study will certainly be done easily and great progress will soon be made therein; and when others discover this fragrance of spirituality in the action itself, this same will cause their awakening. Likewise, managing art with propriety will become the means of sociability and affinity; and sociability and affinity themselves tend to guide others to the Truth.

Science As Worship

Thy letter was received. Praise be to God it imparted the good news of thy health and safety and indicated that thou art ready to enter into an agricultural school. This is highly suitable. Strive as much as possible to become proficient in the science of agriculture for in accordance with the Divine Teachings, the acquisition of sciences and the perfection of arts is considered as acts of worship. If a man engages with all his power in the acquisition of a science or in the perfection of an art, it is as if he has been worshipping God in the churches and temples. Thus as thou enterest a school of agriculture and strivest in the acquisition of that science thou art day and night engaged in acts of worship—acts that are accepted at the threshold of the Almighty. What bounty greater than this that science should be considered as an act of worship and art as service to the Kingdom of God.

Music

This wonderful age has rent asunder the veils of superstition and has condemned the prejudice of the people of the East.

Among some of the nations of the Orient, music and harmony was not approved of, but the Manifested Light, Bahá'u'lláh, in this glorious period has revealed in Holy Tablets that singing and music are the spiritual food of the hearts and souls. In this dispensation, music is one of the arts that is highly approved and is considered to be the cause of the exaltation of sad and desponding hearts.

Therefore . . . . set to music the verses and the divine words so that they may be sung with soul-stirring melody in the Assemblies and gatherings, and that the hearts of the listeners may become tumultuous and rise towards the Kingdom of Abhá in supplication and prayer.

Severance from This World

Thou hast written of the severe calamity that has befallen thee—the death of thy respected husband. That honorable personage has been so much subjected to the stress and pain of this world that his highest wish became deliverance from it. Such is this mortal abode—a storehouse of afflictions and suffering. It is negligence that binds man to it for no comfort can be secured by any soul in this world, from monarch down to the least subject. If once it should offer man a sweet cup, a hundred bitter ones will follow it and such is the condition of this world. The wise man therefore does not attach himself to this mortal life and does not depend upon it; even at some moments he eagerly wishes death that he may thereby be freed from these sorrows and afflictions. Thus it is seen that some, under extreme pressure of anguish, have committed suicide.

As to him rest assured; he will be immersed in the ocean of pardon and forgiveness and will become the recipient of bounty and favor.

Consolation of Our Hearts

From the death of that beloved youth due to his separation from you the utmost sorrow and grief has been occasioned, for he flew away in the flower of his age and the bloom of his youth, to the heavenly nest.

But as he has been freed from this sorrow-stricken shelter and has turned his face toward the everlasting nest of the Kingdom and has been delivered from a dark and narrow world and has hastened to the sanctified realm of Light, therein lies the consolation of our hearts.

The inscrutable divine wisdom underlies such heart-rending occurrences. It is as if a kind gardener transfers a fresh and tender shrub from a narrow place to a vast region. This transference is not the cause of the withering, the waning or the destruction of that shrub, nay rather it makes it grow and thrive, acquire freshness and delicacy and attain verdure and fruition. This hidden secret is well-known to the gardener, while those souls who are unaware of this bounty suppose that the gardener in his anger and wrath has uprooted the shrub. But to those who are aware this concealed fact is manifest and this predestined decree considered a favor. Do not feel grieved and disconsolate therefore at the ascension of that bird of faithfulness, nay under all circumstances pray and beg for that youth forgiveness and elevation of station.

I hope that you will attain to the utmost patience, composure and resignation, and I supplicate and entreat at the Threshold of Oneness and beg pardon and forgiveness. My hope from the infinite bounties of God is that He may cause this dove of the garden of faith to abide on the branch of the Supreme Concourse that it may sing in the best of tunes the praises and the excellencies of the Lord of names and attributes.

The University of the Kingdom

Thou hast written that thou art a student in the progressive spiritual school. Happy is thy condition! If the various progressive schools join themselves to the universal university of the Kingdom, such knowledge and sciences will be brought into light that man will see that the potentialities of the "Open Tablet" of existence are infinite; will realize that all the created things are as letters and words; will be instructed in the lessons of the degrees of significances; will perceive the signs of oneness in the primordial atoms of the earth; will hear the voice of the Lord of the Kingdom; will behold the confirmations of the Holy Spirit and will find such ecstasy and joy that, being unable to contain himself in the vast area of existence, he will prepare himself for the journey toward the Kingdom and will hasten to the immensity of the Realm of Might. As soon as a bird is fledged, it cannot keep itself on the ground; nay, rather it soareth up toward the Supreme Apex—except the birds whose feet are tied, whose wings are clipped and feathers broken and who are soiled with water and clay.

O thou seeker of Truth! The realm of the Kingdom is a unit. The only difference lies in this: That when the season of spring dawneth, a new and wonderful motion and rejuvenation is witnessed in all the existing things; the mountains and meadows are revived; the trees find freshness and delicacy and are clothed with radiant and bright leaves, blossoms and fruits. In a like manner the preceding Manifestations form an inseparable link with the subsequent dispensations; nay, rather they are identical with each other. Since the world is constantly developing itself, the rays become stronger, the outpouring becometh greater and the sun appeareth in the meridian orbit.

O thou yearner after the Kingdom! Each Manifestation is the heart of the world and the proficient Physician of every patient.

The world of humanity is sick, but that skilled Physician hath the healing remedy and He bestoweth divine teachings, exhortations and advices which are the remedy of every ailment and the dressing for every wound. Undoubtedly, the wise physician discovereth the needs of the patient at every season and prescribeth medicine. Therefore, when thou wilt compare the teachings of the Beauty of Abhá with the requisitions and necessities of the present time, thou wilt conclude that they are to the sick body of the world the swift healing antidote; nay, rather they are the remedy of everlasting health. The prescription of the proficient physicians of the past and the future will not be the same; nay, rather they will be in accord with the ailment of the patient. Although the medicine is changed, yet all of these are for the sole purpose of the healing of the sick. In former dispensations the sick body of the world could not bear the strong and overpowering remedies. That is why His Highness the Christ said: "I have yet many things to say unto you, but ye cannot bear them now. Howbeit, when He, the Spirit of the Comforter, who is sent by the Father, is come, He will guide you into all truth." Therefore, in this age of lights, specific teachings have become universal, in order that the outpouring of the Merciful One environ both the East and the West, the oneness of the kingdom of humanity become visible and the luminosity of truth enlighten the world of consciousness. The descent of the New Jerusalem is the heavenly religion which secures the prosperity of the human world and is the effulgence of the illumination of the realm of God.

The Unknowable Essence

All the people have formed a god in the world of thought, and that form of their own imagination they worship; when the fact is that the imagined form is finite and the human mind is infinite. Surely the infinite is greater than the finite, for imagination is accidental while the mind is essential; surely the essential is greater than the accidental.

Therefore consider: All the sects and peoples worship their own thought; they create a god in their own minds and acknowledge him to be the creator of all things, when that form is a superstition—thus people adore and worship imagination.

That Essence of the Divine Entity and the Unseen of the unseen is holy above imagination and is beyond thought. Consciousness doth not reach It. Within the capacity of comprehension of a produced reality that Ancient Reality cannot be contained. It is a different world; from it there is no information; arrival thereat is impossible; attainment thereto is prohibited and inaccesible. This much is known: It exists and Its existence is certain and proven—but the condition is unknown.

All the philosophers and the doctors knew that It *is*, but they were perplexed in the comprehension of Its existence and were at last discouraged, and in great despair they left this world. For the comprehension of the condition and mysteries of that Reality of realities and Mystery of mysteries there is need for another power and another sense. That power and sense is not possessed by mankind, therefore they have not found any information. For example: If a man possess the power of hearing, the power of tasting, the power of smelling and the power of feeling, but no power of seeing, he cannot see. Hence, through the powers and senses present in man the realization of the Unseen Reality, which is pure and holy above the reach of doubts, is impossible. Other powers are needed and other senses required. If those powers and senses are obtained, then information can be had; otherwise, not.

Faith and Knowledge

Regarding the "two wings" of the soul: These signify wings of ascent. One is the wing of knowledge, the other of faith, as this is the means of the ascent of the human soul to the lofty station of divine perfections.

Knowledge and Deeds

Although a person of good deeds is acceptable at the Threshold of the Almighty, yet it is first "to know," and then "to do." Although a blind man produceth a most wonderful and exquisite art, yet he is deprived of seeing it. Consider how most animals labor for man, draw loads and facilitate travel; yet, as they are ignorant, they receive no reward for this toil and labor. The cloud raineth, roses and hyacinths grow; the plain and meadow, the garden and trees become green and blossom; yet they do not realize the results and outcome of all these. The lamp is lighted, but as it hath not a conscious knowledge of itself, no one hath become glad because of it. Moreover, a soul of excellent deeds and good manners will undoubtedly advance from whatever horizon he beholdeth the lights radiating. Herein lies the difference: By faith is meant, first, conscious knowledge, and second, the practice of good deeds.

Training of Children

As to thy question concerning training children: It is incumbent upon thee to nurture them from the breast of the love of God, to urge them towards spiritual matters, to turn unto God and to acquire good manners, best characteristics and praiseworthy virtues and qualities in the world of humanity, and to study sciences with the utmost diligence; so that they may become spiritual, heavenly and attracted to the fragrances of sanctity from their childhood and be reared in a religious, spiritual and heavenly training. Verily, I beg of God to confirm them therein.

Spiritual Knowledge

If thou wishest the divine knowledge and recognition, purify thy heart from all beside God, be wholly attracted to the ideal, beloved One; search for and choose Him and apply thyself to rational and authoritative arguments. For arguments are a guide to the path and by this the heart will be turned unto the Sun of Truth. And when the heart is turned unto the Sun, then the eye will be opened and will recognize the Sun through the Sun itself. Then man will be in no need of arguments (or proofs), for the Sun is altogether independent, and absolute independence is in need of nothing, and proofs are one of the things of which absolute independence has no need. Be not like Thomas; be thou like Peter. I hope you will be healed physically, mentallv and spiritually.

Qualifications of the Enlightened Soul

As to the seven qualifications (of the divinely enlightened soul) of which thou hast asked an explanation, it is as follows:

Knowledge. Man must attain the knowledge of God.

Faith.

Steadfastness.

Truthfulness. Truthfulness is the foundation of all the virtues of the world of humanity. Without truthfulness, progress and success in all of the worlds of God are impossible for a soul. When this holy attribute is established in man, all the divine qualities will also become realized.

Uprightness. And this is one of the greatest divine attainments.

Fidelity. This is also a beautiful trait of the heavenly man.

Evanescence or Humility. That is to say, man must become evanescent in God. Must forget his own selfish conditions that he may thus arise to the station of sacrifice. It should be to such a degree that if he sleep, it should not be for pleasure, but to rest the body in order to do better, to speak better, to explain more beautifully, to serve the servants of God and to prove the truths. When he remains awake, he should seek to be attentive, serve the Cause of God and sacrifice his own stations for those of God. When he attains to this station, the confirmations of the Holy Spirit will surely reach him, and man with this power can withstand all who inhabit the earth.

Eternal Sovereignty

All the people of the world are, as thou dost observe, in the sleep of negligence. They have forgotten God altogether. They are all busy in war and strife. They are undergoing misery and destruction. They are, like unto the loathsome worms, trying to lodge in the depth of the ground, while a single flood of rain sweeps all their nests and lodging away. Nevertheless, they do not come to their senses. Where is the majesty of the Emperor of Russia? Where is the might of the German Emperor? Where is the greatness of the Emperor of Austria? In a short time all these palaces were turned into ruins and all these pretentious edifices underwent destruction. They left no fruit and no trace, save eternal ruin.

The souls who have been enlightened with the light of the Kingdom, however, have founded eternal sovereignty. They shine, like unto the stars, upon the horizon of everlasting glory. The Apostles were fishers. Consider thou to what a high station they did rise; and to what great sovereignty they did attain, whose duration and permanence runs to eternity! Mary Magdalen was a peasant woman. She was without any name and fame or consequence. But her candle is, in the assemblage of the world, lighted till eternity.

Confirmation and Assistance

It is known and clear that today the unseen divine assistance encompasseth those who deliver the Message. And if the work of delivering the Message be neglected, the assistance shall be entirely cut off, for it is impossible that the friends of God could receive assistance unless they be engaged in delivering the Message. Under all conditions the Message must be delivered, but with wisdom. If it be not possible openly, it must be done quietly. The friends should be engaged in educating the souls and should become instruments in aiding the world of humanity to acquire spiritual joy and fragrance. For example: If every one of the friends (believers) were to establish relations of friendship and right dealings with one of the negligent souls, associate and live with him with perfect kindliness, and meanwhile through good conduct and moral behavior lead him to divine instruction, to heavenly advice and teachings, surely he would gradually arouse that negligent person and would change his ignorance into knowledge.

Souls are liable to estrangement. Such methods should be adopted that the estrangement should be first removed, then the Word will have effect.

If one of the believers be kind to one of the negligent ones and with perfect love should gradually make him understand the reality of the Cause of God in such a way that the latter should know in what manner the Religion of God hath been founded and what its object is, doubtless he will become changed; excepting abnormal souls who are reduced to the state of ashes and whose hearts are like stones, yea, even harder.

If by this method every one of the friends of God were to try to lead one soul to the right path, the number of the believers would be doubled every year. But this should be carried out with perfect wisdom and in such a manner that no harm would ever result therefrom.

This World a Mirage

O beloved of God! Know ye that the world is like unto a mirage which the thirsty one thinks to be water; its water is a vapor; its mercy a difficulty; its repose hardship and ordeal; leave it to its people and turn unto the Kingdom of your Lord the Merciful. Thus the lights of mercy and beneficence may shine upon you, the heavenly table descend for you, your Lord may bestow upon you the greatest gifts and favors, whereby your breasts may become dilated, your hearts gladdened, your souls purified, and your eyes enlightened.

O beloved of God! Is there any giver save God? He chooseth for His mercy whomsoever He desireth.

He shall open unto you the doors of His knowledge, fill your hearts with His love, rejoice your spirits by the wafting of His holy fragrances, illumine your faces by the Manifest Light and elevate your names among the people.

Protection of the Bahá'ís

Throughout these years of disturbance and commotion when

the world of humanity was physically and spiritually afflicted, the friends of God passed the day in rest, ease and comfort. In the western countries only a few shared in the hardship and affliction of other souls while the mass of the friends and the maid-servants of the Merciful . . . . have been living quietly and peacefully. In the Orient every nation became distracted and every gathering dispersed save the friends of God who remained all protected and sheltered from every trouble and calamity in the Fort of Bahá'u'lláh's protection. Verily this is a divine miracle—that we helpless, friendless, unprotected, unsupported wanderers in these regions should be saved amidst the fire of oppression and tyranny. This is God's miracle.

The Return of Christ

In the day of Christ all nations were expecting that His Holiness Christ should come from heaven, and He came from heaven, though outwardly He came from the womb of Mary. Hence, He hath said in the Gospels: "No one shall ascend to heaven except the one who hath come from heaven." Now all the people expect Him to come from heaven.

If thou wishest to find the truth, compare the days of the Manifestation of the Beauty of Abhá with the days of Christ; consider this is identically like that and the same doubts and oppositions are put forth.

As to the proofs and arguments of the Beauty of Abhá, these are manifest like the sun. If thou wishest a discerning eye and seekest for a hearing ear, set thou aside that which thou hast heard from fathers and ancestors, for such things are imitation—and then seek for the truth with the utmost attention until the divine confirmation may reach thee and the matter may be properly disclosed unto thee.

Eternal Life

Concerning thy question whether all the souls enjoy eternal life: Know thou those souls partake of the eternal life in whom the spirit of life is breathed from the Presence of God and all beside them are dead—without life, as Christ hath explained in the texts of the Gospel. Any person whose insight is opened by God seeth the souls in their stations after the disintegration of the bodies. Verily they are living and are subsisting before their Lord and he seeth also the dead souls submerged in the gulfs of mortality. Then know thou verily all the souls are created according to the nature of God and all are in the state of purity at the time of their births. But afterward they differ from one another insofar as they acquire excellencies or defects. Nevertheless, the creatures have different degrees in existence insofar as the creation goes, for capacities are different, but all of them are good and pure, then afterward they are polluted and defiled. Although there are different states of creation, yet all of them are beneficial. Glance thou over the temple of man, its members and its parts. Among them there are the eye, ear, nose, mouth, hands and fingers. Notwithstanding the differences between these organs, all of them are useful in their proper spheres. But if one of them is out of order, there is need of a remedy and if the medicine does not heal, then the amputation of that member becomes necessary.

Spreaders of Calumny

In sooth, there will be found in those regions certain persons like the Pharisees of the time of Christ, who, night and day, will exert themselves with all heart and soul to cast forth doubts, in order that they may deprive the souls of the glad-tidings of the Holy Spirit. They will disseminate false rumors and utter many a calumny and will publish and announce stories. They will undertake all these only for the sake of earthly vanities.

And some Pharisees among the missionaries of the Gospel will hasten thither from Írán and say, "We are aware of the secret of the matter." All they may say is sheer slander.

Now know you these things, that in its time you may dispel and annihilate the darkness of those suspicions, like unto a manifest light. I beg of God that He may grant thee a power that thou mayest resist all in the earth—how much more these weak, hired individuals who receive salary and bribe for spreading such calumnies!

Be ye admonished, O possessors of understanding!

THE SPIRIT OF CHRIST

The body is composed, in truth, of corporeal elements and every composition is necessarily subject to decomposition; but the spirit is an essence, simple, pure, spiritual, eternal, perpetual and divine. He who seeketh Christ from the point of view of His body hath, in truth, debased Him and hath gone astray from Him; but he who seeketh Christ from the point of view of His Spirit will grow from day to day in joy, attraction, zeal, proximity, perception and vision.

Thou hast then to seek the Spirit of Christ in this marvelous day. The heaven whither Christ ascended is not an infinite space. His heaven is much rather the kingdom of His Lord, the Munificent. As He said, "The Son of Man is in heaven." It is known then that His heaven is beyond the boundaries that surround existence and that He is elevated for the people who adore.

Pray God to ascend to this heaven, to taste of its food—and know thou that the people have not understood to this day the mystery of the Holy Scriptures. They believe that Christ was deprived of His heaven when He was in this world, that He had fallen from the heights of His elevation and that later He ascended to this elevated pinnacle—that is to say, towards the heaven which doth not exist, for there is only space. They expect that He will descend from this heaven seated upon a cloud. They believe that there is in the heavens a cloud upon which He will be seated and by which He will descend; while, in reality, the clouds are vapors which rise from the earth and which do not descend from the heavens. The cloud mentioned in the Holy Scriptures is the human body, because it is a veil for them, like a cloud, which prevents them from seeing the Sun of Truth which is shining in the horizon of Christ.

SALVATION

You ask if, through the appearance of the kingdom of God, every soul hath been saved. The Sun of Reality hath appeared to all the world. This luminous appearance is salvation and life; but only he who hath opened the eye of reality and who hath seen these lights will be saved.

THE SPIRITUAL CHURCH

Thou hast questioned how thou canst accept this divine Cause, for thou art a member of the church. In the day of the Manifestation of Christ, many souls became portionless and deprived because they were members of the Holy of Holies in Jerusalem. According to that membership, they became veiled from that brilliant Beauty. Therefore, turn thou thy face to the Church of God which consists in divine instructions and merciful exhortations. For what similarity is there between the church of stone and cement and the celestial Holy of Holies!

Endeavor that thou mayest enter in this Church of God. Although thou has given oath to attend the church, yet thy spirit is under the Covenant and Testament of the spiritual Divine Church. Thou shouldst protect this. Although they consider the wine and the bread in the church as the blood and body of Christ, yet this is but the appearance and not the reality. But the reality of Christ is the words of the Holy Spirit. If thou art able, take a portion thereof.

The performance of baptismal celebration would cleanse the body, but the spirit hath no share; but the divine teachings and the exhortations of the Beauty of Abhá will baptize the soul. This is the real baptism. I hope that thou wilt receive this baptism.

THE SUPPER OF THE LORD

The Supper of the Lord which His Highness the Spirit ate with the apostles was a heavenly supper and not one of material bread and water, for material objects have no connection with spiritual objects. As at that time material food was also present, therefore the leaders of the religion of Christ thought that it was material food which was changed into spiritual food.

The proof that it was not material food is this: The apostles upon many occasions partook of material food with His Highness Christ, yet the supper of that night became designated as the "Lord's Supper." From this designation it is plain and evident that they ate heavenly food at that supper. That heavenly food consisted of the love of God, the knowledge of God, the mysteries of God and the bestowal of God.

Understanding the Mysteries

Shouldst thou come with the whole of thy being to God and be attracted to the lights of the Kingdom of God and be enkindled by the fire of the love of God, then wilt thou see that which thou canst not see today, wilt comprehend the inner significance of the Word of God and thoroughly understand the mysteries contained in the holy Books.

But as to the Jewish doctors, Christian priests and monks who read those Books, verily, they know the letter only and they utter the words, as parrots, without understanding their inner meanings. They comprehend them not, because they are engrossed in worldly desires and lusts and their hearts are attached to mundane allurements. Verily, are they not heedless of God and understand nothing and find not the right path?

Reincarnation

As to what thou hast written concerning "Reincarnation": Believing in reincarnation is one of the old tenets held by most nations and creeds, as well as by the Greek and Roman philosophers and wise men, the old Egyptians and the chief Assyrians. But all these sayings and superstitions are vanity in the sight of God.

The greatest argument produced by those who held to reincarnation has been this: "That it is necessary to the justice of God to give every one his due. Now everybody who is afflicted by any calamity is said to have sinned; but when a little child, which is still in the womb of its mother and hath just been formed, is found to be blind, deaf or imperfect, how could it have committed any sin that we might say this imperfection is given to it as a punishment therefor—so, though such a child hath not done outwardly any sin in the womb of its mother, yet they say it must have sinned when it was in its former body, which hath caused it to suffer this punishment."

Indeed, these people have been negligent of the fact that had the creation been carried out in a uniform fashion, how could the statement be true, that "God doeth whatever He wisheth and God doeth whatever he desireth!"

Though the fact of "Return" is mentioned in the Divine Books, by this is intended the return of the qualities, characters, perfections, truths and lights, which re-appear in every age, and not of certain persons and souls. For example: If we say this lamp is the return of that of last night, or that the last year's flower hath returned in the garden, in this sense the return of the individual, or identity, or personality is not meant; nay, rather, it is intended that the same qualities and states existing in that lamp or flower, which are now seen in this lamp or flower, have returned. That is, the same perfections and virtues and properties which existed in the past springtime have returned during this present springtime. For instance: When one says, these fruits are the same as those of last year; in this sense, he hath reference to the freshness and delicacy of the fruit, which hath returned, although there is no doubt that the identical fruit of last year hath not returned.

Have the friends of God found such enjoyments and repose during their existence on this visible earth, that they might wish to have their return renewed and repeated constantly? Are all these calamities, injuries, trials and difficulties of the once coming not sufficient for them that they should wish a repeated life in this world? Hath this cup been of such sweetness that they should long for it successively and repeatedly? No! the friends of the Beauty of El-Bahá never seek any recompense or reward except the meeting and the visit in the Kingdom of El-Bahá; and they never walk but in the valley of desire to attain the Supreme Height. They only wish the immortal blessing and the eternal gift, which are sanctified above the worldly understanding.

Because, when thou lookest with the iron sight, thou wilt find that all mankind is suffering in this earthly world; there is no one in such tranquillity that this state might have been a reward for his good deeds in a former life and there is no soul so happy that this might be the fruit of his past pain! Had the life of a man in his spiritual being been only confined to his life in this world, the creation would have proved useless; the divine qualities would have no result and effect; nay, all things, created beings and the world of creation would have proved abortive. I ask pardon of God for such false imaginations and for such errors!

As the usefulness and powers of the life were not seen in that dark and narrow world, but when it is brought into this vast world, all the use of its growth and development becometh manifest and obvious in it, so likewise, reward and punishment, paradise and hell, and the requital of deeds and actions done by it in the present life become manifest and evident when it is transferred to the world to come—which is far from this world! Had the life and growth of the child in the womb been confined to that condition, then the existence of the child in the womb would have proved utterly abortive and unintelligible; as would the life of this world, were its deeds, actions and their results not to appear in the world to come.

Therefore, know thou that the True One possesseth invisible worlds which human meditation is unable to comprehend and the intellect of man hath no power to imagine. When thou wilt purify and clarify thy spiritual nostrils from every worldly moisture, then thou wilt inhale the holy fragrances diffusing from the merciful gardens of these worlds.

This Glad-Tidings

O my friend, verily the Cause is great and great, and the penetration of the Word of God in the temple of all the regions is similar to the pervasion of the soul in a sound body.

By the life of Bahá, verily, the power of the Kingdom of God hath taken hold of the pillars of the world, and hath possessed all the nations. Thou wilt surely find the standards of the Testament waving in all regions, the chanting of the verses of unity raised in exalted assemblies, and the lights of the Sun of Truth and its heat dispersing the thick clouds massed on the horizon. Be rejoiced at this glad-tidings, whereby the hearts of the sincere among the beloved are cheered.

Consider the Past

Consider the past, so that thou mayest become informed of the mysteries which shall be disclosed in the future. When the disciples were calling in the name of Christ, the Jews scoffed, scorned and laughed at them. They were saying, "They are taken with madness, and madness is made an art." They even beat them with whips, threw stones at them, prevented the people from approaching them, and were saying, "This man is naught but a sorcerer, blasphemeth God and is possessed of a devil."

Then observe how that persecution and scorn were changed to glory, honor and reverence. Ultimately, they honored their sublime stations and acknowledged their loftiness, which was exalted, promoted and glorified in the center of the horizons until it reached the degree of exaggeration in deeds. They made for them likenesses and pictures, decorated with jewels shining in the eyes; they placed these likenesses or pictures in the temples, churches and monasteries built on the tops of the mountains, and worshipped them with respect, glory, majesty and reverence. This is the condition of the neglectful ones who are deprived of the Truth at the day of their existence among them. After the ascension of their spirits unto the center of purity and piety, then the negligent ones repent and return, making likenesses and pictures according to their own ideas, which do not bear resemblance, and worship the same. This is the station of the ignorant ones who are as animals, following every croaker and shaken by every wind. "Forsake them to play in their shallow waters."

This Branch Will Ascend

O maid-servant of God! This prison is indeed more precious and sweet than a garden to me, this fetter is greater than any liberty and the confinement is broader than the most spacious wilderness. Therefore, grieve not on this account. Verily, if my Lord destine unto me and causes me to taste the sweetness of the cup of the great martyrdom, my greatest desire will be fulfilled. Fear not if this Branch be severed from the material earth and cast aside the leaves—nay, rather, its leaves will flourish, for this Branch will grow after it is cut from the earth, will ascend until it shelters the universe, its foliage will reach the supreme Apex and bear fruits, imparting fragrant perfume unto the world.

After This Storm

O ye beloved of God! When the winds blow severely, rains fall fiercely, the lightning flashes, the thunder roars, the bolt descends and storms of trial become severe, grieve not; for after this storm, verily, the divine spring will arrive, the hills and fields will become verdant, the expanses of grain will joyfully wave, the earth will become covered with blossoms, the trees will be clothed with green garments and adorned with blossoms and fruits. Thus blessings become manifest in all countries. These favors are results of those storms and hurricanes.

The discerning man rejoiceth at the day of trials, his breast becometh dilated at the time of severe storms, his eyes become brightened when seeing the showers of rain and gusts of wind, whereby trees are uprooted; because he foreseeth the result and the end, the leaves, blossoms and fruits; while the ignorant person becometh troubled when he seeth a storm, is saddened when it raineth severely, is terrified by the thunder and trembleth at the surging of the waves which storm the shores.

As ye have heard of the former times, when Christ—glory be to Him!—appeared, a storm of trials arose, afflictions appeared, the winds of tests blew, the thunder of temptation descended and hosts of people surrounded the houses of the friends; then the weak ones were shaken and were misled after once being guided; but the disciples withstood the hardships and endured the storms of ordeals, remaining firm in the Religion of God. Then observe that which occurred after the storm and what appeared subsequent to that severity, whereby the members trembled.

God changed the sorrow to joy, the destructive darkness of

calamity into the shining light from the Supreme Concourse. The people at the beginning persecuted and reviled the believers in God and said of them: "These are the people of aberration." Then, when their light appeared, their stars shone and their lamps illuminated, the people returned into love and affinity; they prayed to them, offered words of glory night and day and remembered them in eulogy, reverence, honor and majesty.

Therefore, O ye beloved of God, be not grieved when people stand against you, persecute you, afflict and trouble you and say all manner of evil against you. The darkness will pass away and the light of the manifest signs will appear, the veil will be withdrawn and the Light of Reality will shine forth from the unseen Kingdom of El-Abhá. This we inform you before it occurs, so that when the hosts of people arise against you for my love, be not disturbed or troubled; nay, rather, be firm as a mountain, for this persecution and reviling of the people upon you is a pre-ordained matter. Blessed is the soul who is firm in the path!

The Center

The light hath a center and if one desire to seek it otherwise but from the center, he can never attain to it. In this solar system the source of light is the sun and every light is acquired from it; even the lamps of the night are ignited through the sun, for if there were no sun the trees would not grow nor the mines develop, so that the oil be extracted from those trees and mines, and the lamps of the night be lit by it. Is it possible that one attain to the light in this globular sphere without the mediation of the sun? No, by the life of God! To suppose it, is pure imagination. But the truth is this: The main source of the lights is the sun and the rays are shed from it upon all the regions.

Mental and Spiritual Education

The republic of wise men believes that the difference in minds and opinions is due to the difference of education and the acquisition of ethics. That is, that minds are equal in origin, but education and the acquisition of ethics cause minds to differ and comprehensions to be at variance; that this difference is not in entity but in education and teaching; that there is no individual distinction for any soul. Hence, the members of the human race all possess the capacity of attaining to the highest station, and the proof they adduce therefor is this: "The inhabitants of a country like Africa are all as wandering savages and wild animals; they lack intelligence and knowledge; all are uncivilized; not one civilized and wise man is to be found among them. On the contrary, consider the civilized countries, the inhabitants of which are living in the highest state of culture and ethics, solidarity and inter-dependence; possessing, with few exceptions, acute power of comprehension and sound mind. Therefore, it is made clear and evident that the superiority and inferiority of minds and comprehensions arises from education and cultivation, or from their lack and absence. A bent branch is straightened by training and the wild fruit of the jungle is made the product of the orchard. An ignorant man by learning becomes knowing, and the world of savagery, through the bounty of a wise educator, is changed into a civilized kingdom. The sick is healed by medication, and the poor man, by learning the arts of commerce, is made rich. The follower, by attaining the virtues of the leader, becomes great, and the lowly man, by the education of the teacher, rises from the nadir of oblivion to the zenith of celebrity." These are the proofs of the wise men.

The prophets also acknowledge this opinion, towit: That education hath a great effect upon the human race, but they declare that minds and comprehensions are originally different. And this matter is self-evident; it cannot be refuted. We see that certain children of the same age, nativity and race, nay, from the same household, under the tutorship of one teacher, differ in their minds and comprehensions. One advanceth rapidly, another is slow in catching the rays of culture, still another remaineth in the lowest degree of stupidity.

No matter how much the shell is educated, it can never become the radiant pearl. The black stone will not become the world illuming gem. The calocynth and the thorny cactus can never by training and development become the blessed tree. That is to say, training doth not change the human gem, but it produceth a marvelous effect. By this effective power all that is registered latent of virtues and capacities in the human reality will be revealed.

Cultivation by the farmer maketh of the grain the harvest, and the effort of the gardener maketh of the seed a noble tree. The gentle teacher promoteth the children of the school to the lofty altitude and the bestowal of the trainer placeth the little child upon the throne of ether. Therefore, it is demonstrated and proven that minds are different in the original entity or nature, and that education commandeth a decided and great influence. Were there no educator, all souls would remain savage, and were it not for the teacher, the children would be ignorant creatures.

It is for this reason that, in this New Cycle, education and training are recorded in the Book of God as obligatory and not voluntary. That is, it is enjoined upon the father and mother, as a duty, to strive with all effort to train the daughter and the son, to nurse them from the breast of knowledge and to rear them in the bosom of sciences and arts. Should they neglect this matter, they shall be held responsible and worthy of reproach in the presence of the stern Lord.

This is a sin unpardonable, for they have made that poor babe a wanderer in the Sahara of ignorance, unfortunate and tormented; to remain during a lifetime a captive of ignorance and pride, negligent and without discernment. Verily, if that babe depart from this world at the age of infancy, it is sweeter and better. In this sense, death is better than life; deprivation than salvation; non-existence lovelier than existence; the grave better than the palace; and the narrow, dingy tomb better than the spacious, regal home; for in the sight of mankind that child is abased and degraded and in the sight of God weak and defective. In gatherings it is ashamed and humiliated and in the arena of examination subdued and defeated by young and old. What a mistake is this! What an everlasting humiliation!

Therefore, the beloved of God and the maid-servants of the Merciful must train their children with life and heart and teach them in the school of virtue and perfection. They must not be lax in this matter; they must not be inefficient. Truly, if a babe did not live at all it were better than to let it grow ignorant, for that innocent babe, in later life, would become afflicted with innumerable defects, responsible to and questioned by God, reproached and rejected by the people. What a sin this would be and what an omission!

The first duty of the beloved of God and the maid-servants of the Merciful is this: They must strive by all possible means to educate both sexes, male and female; girls like boys; there is no difference whatsoever between them. The ignorance of both is blameworthy, and negligence in both cases is reprovable. "Are they who know and they who do not know equal?"

The command is decisive concerning both. If it be considered through the eye of reality, the training and culture of daughters is more necessary than that of sons, for these girls will come to the station of motherhood and will mold the lives of the children. The first trainer of the child is the mother. The babe, like unto a green and tender branch, will grow according to the way it is trained. If the training be right, it will grow right, and if crooked, the growth likewise, and unto the end of life it will conduct itself accordingly.

Hence, it is firmly established that an untrained and uneducated daughter, on becoming a mother, will be the prime factor in the deprivation, ignorance, negligence and the lack of training of many children.

O ye beloved of God and the maid-servants of the Merciful! Teaching and learning, according to the decisive texts of the Blessed Beauty, is a duty. Whosoever is indifferent therein depriveth himself of the great bounty.

Beware! Beware! that ye fail not in this matter. Endeavor with heart, with life, to train your children, especially the daughters. No excuse is acceptable in this matter.

Thus may eternal glory and everlasting supremacy, like unto the mid-day sun, shine forth in the assemblage of the people of Bahá, and the heart of 'Abdu'l-Bahá become happy and thankful.

CHAPTER NINE

THE DIVINE PLAN

The Cause of Bahá'u'lláh

The Cause of Bahá'u'lláh is the same as the Cause of Christ. It is the same Temple and the same Foundation. Both of these are spiritual springtimes and seasons of the soul-refreshing awakening and the cause of the renovation of the life of mankind. The spring of this year is the same as the spring of last year. The origins and ends are the same. The sun of today is the sun of yesterday. In the coming of Christ, the divine teachings were given in accordance with the infancy of the human race. The teachings of Bahá'u'lláh have the same basic principles, but are according to the stage of the maturity of the world and the requirements of this illumined age

The Community of the Greatest Name

O ye Cohorts of God! Today in the present world each community is wandering in a wilderness, moving in accord with some passion and desire, and running to and fro in pursuance of his own imagination. Among the communities of the world, this community of the "Most Great Name" is free from every thought, keeping aloof from every project and scheme, arising with the purest designs and intentions, and striving and endeavoring with the utmost hope to live in accordance with the divine teachings in order that the surface of the earth become the delectable paradise, the nether world become the mirror of the Kingdom, the universe become another universe, and the human race attain to higher morals, conduct and manners.

O ye Cohorts of God! Through the protection and help of the Blessed Perfection—may my life be a sacrifice to His beloved ones! —you must conduct and deport yourselves in such a manner that you may stand out among other souls distinguished by a brilliancy like unto the sun. If any one of you enters a city he must become the center of attraction because of the sincerity, faithfulness, love, honesty, fidelity, truthfulness and loving-kindness of his disposition and nature toward all the inhabitants of the world, that the people of the city may all cry out: "This person is unquestionably a Bahá'í; for his manners, his behavior, his conduct, his morals, his nature and his disposition are of the attributes of the Bahá'ís." Until you do attain to this station, you have not fulfilled the Covenant and the Testament of God. For according to the irrefutable texts, He has taken from us a firm covenant that we may live and act in accord with the divine exhortations, commands and lordly teachings.

O ye Cohorts of God! Now is the time when the signs and the perfections of the "Most Great Name" become manifest and clear in this golden cycle in order that it may become demonstrated and established beyond doubt that this period is the period of the Blessed Perfection, and this cycle is distinguished from all other cycles and epochs.

God Loveth Those Who Work in Groups

O ye friends of God! Today is the day of union and this age is the age of harmony in the world of existence. "Verily, God loveth those who are working in His path in groups, for they are a solid foundation." Consider ye that he says "in groups," united and bound together, supporting one another. "To work," mentioned in this holy verse, does not mean, in this greatest age, to perform it with swords, spears, shafts and arrows, but rather with sincere intentions, good designs, useful advices, divine moralities, beautiful actions, spiritual qualities, educating the public, guiding the souls of mankind, diffusing spiritual fragrances, explaining divine illustrations, showing convincing proofs and doing charitable deeds. When the holy souls, through the angelic power, will arise to show forth these celestial characteristics, establishing a band of harmony, each of these souls shall be regarded as one thousand persons and the waves of this greatest ocean shall be considered as the army of the hosts of the Supreme Concourse.

What a great blessing it is when the torrents, streams, currents, tides, and drops are all gathered in one place! They will form a great ocean and the real harmony shall overcome and reign in such a manner that all the rules, laws, distinctions and differences of the imaginations of these souls shall disappear and vanish like little drops and shall be submerged in the ocean of spiritual unity. By the Ancient Beauty, in this case and condition, the blessings of the great ocean will overflow and canals shall become as spacious as an endless ocean and each drop shall become as a boundless sea!

O ye friends of God! Strive to attain to this high and sublime station and show forth such a brightness in these days that its radiance may appear from the eternal horizons. This is the real foundation of the Cause of God; this is the essence of the divine doctrine; this is the cause of the revelation of the heavenly Scriptures; this is the means of the appearance of the Sun of the divine world; this is the way of the establishment of God upon the bodily throne.

The Divine Shepherd

Every flock of the sheep of God which is protected under the shadow of the Divine Shepherd will not be scattered, but when the sheep are dispersed from the flock, they will necessarily be caught and torn by the wolf.

Therefore, it is incumbent upon you to flock together! It is incumbent upon you to be united! It is incumbent upon you to expose yourselves to the fragrances of God at every time and moment!

The Fundamental Aim

The aim of the appearance of the Blessed Perfection—may my life be a sacrifice for His beloved ones!—was the unity and agreement of all the people of the world. Therefore, my utmost desire, firstly, is the accord and union and love of the believers and after that of all the people of the world. Now, if unity and agreement is not established among the believers, I will become heartbroken and the afflictions will leave a greater imprint upon me. But if the fragrance of love and unity among the believers is wafted to my nostrils, every trial will become a mercy, every unhappiness a joy, every difficulty an expansion, every misery a treasure and every hardship a felicity.

This Meeting Is Blessed

Praise be to God! that ye are gathered in one assembly like unto the stars of the Pleiades, are illumined with the light of the knowledge of God and through the outpouring of the cloud of the love of God, ye are the fresh flowers of the meadow and plain; ye are intimate and familiar with infinite unity and love.

Therefore, this meeting is blessed. But if it is firmly established and become constant, it will bring forth great results and most weighty developments will be attained. Consequently, persevere ye in renewing your meetings and display utmost magnanimity in firmness and steadfastness. When the root of the tree of the garden is well established and its protection is safeguarded, it will bring forth luscious fruits.

Likewise, when the regiment of an army and the individuals of a cohort are united and related with ease, untold triumphs will be acquired. But if they come together one day and disperse another day, no fruits will be produced.

Therefore, as ye have prepared an army of heaven and become the host of life, ye must continue to hold meetings, have spiritual communications, be firm in resolution, steadfast in purpose and be constant and persevering so that ye may win celestial conquests.

The Spiritual Election

The blessed letter indicating the election of the Spiritual Meeting was received and proved a source of joy. Thank God, the beloved of that city, in perfect unity, love and oneness, held the new election and were confirmed and strengthened to elect such holy souls as are near the divine Threshold and known by the republic of the beloved to be firm and steadfast in the Covenant.

Now they (the members) must, in perfect spirit and fragrance, in sincerity of heart, in attraction by the fragrances of God and by the confirmations of the Holy Spirit, engage in service; in the promotion of the Word of God; the diffusion of the fragrances of God; the training of souls; the promulgation of the Most Great Peace. They must raise the Banner of Guidance and become the host of the Supreme Concourse.

Indeed, blessed souls have been elected. When I read their names, spiritual joy was immediately realized, for, praise be to God! certain souls have appeared in that continent who are servants of the Kingdom, self-sacrificing ones of the Peerless Majesty.

O ye friends of mine! Illuminate the meeting with the light of the love of God, make it joyful and happy through the melody of the Kingdom of Holiness, and with heavenly food and through the "Lord's Supper" confer life.

The House of Justice

O thou party who art assisted by the hosts of the Kingdom of El-Abhá!

Blessed are ye who are assembled in the shadow of the Word of God, who are abiding in the cave of the Covenant of God, who are comforted by dwelling in the Paradise of El-Abhá, who are cheerfully moved with the breezes which blow from the point of the providence of God, and who have arisen to render service to the Cause of God, to promulgate the Religion of God, to promote the Word of God and to hoist the standards of sanctity in those regions and climes.

By the life of El-Bahá! Verily, the perfect and divine power will breathe in you with bounties from the Holy Spirit and enable you to accomplish a thing the like of which hath never been seen by the eye of existence.

O party of the Covenant! Verily, the Beauty of El-Bahá hath promised the most great assistance to the beloved who are firm in the Covenant and to confirm them through the mightiest power. Ye will surely find in your luminous assembly such signs as will shine within hearts and souls. Adhere to the hem of the robe of the Lofty

One and do your best to spread the Covenant of God and to be kindled with the fire of the love of God, so that your hearts may move with joy through the fragrances of humbleness which are being diffused from the heart of 'Abdu'l-Bahá. Make feet firm, strengthen hearts and rely upon the everlasting bounties which will successively pour on you from the Kingdom of El-Abhá. Know, verily, the lights of Bahá will shine forth unto you during your gathering together in the brilliant Paradise.

It is incumbent on you to have union and harmony. It is incumbent upon you to have affinity and accord, so that ye may become united in body and soul as the Pleiades, and as strings of brilliant pearls. Thereby your foundation will be laid, your argument will become manifest, your stars will beam forth and your souls will be comforted.

Whenever ye enter the council-chamber, recite this prayer with a heart throbbing with the love of God and a tongue purified from all but His remembrance, that the All-Powerful may graciously aid you to achieve supreme victory:—

"O God, my God! We are servants of Thine that have turned with devotion to Thy Holy Face, that have detached ourselves from all beside Thee in this glorious Day. We have gathered in this spiritual assembly, united in our views and thoughts, with our purposes harmonized to exalt Thy Word amidst mankind. O Lord, our God! Make us the signs of Thy Divine Guidance, the Standards of Thy exalted Faith amongst men, servants to Thy mighty Covenant. O Thou our Lord Most High! Manifestations of Thy Divine Unity in Thine Abhá Kingdom, and resplendent stars shining upon all regions. Lord! Aid us to become seas surging with the billows of Thy wondrous Grace, streams flowing from Thy all-glorious Heights, goodly fruits upon the Tree of Thy heavenly Cause, trees waving through the breezes of Thy Bounty in Thy celestial Vineyard. O God! Make our souls dependent upon the Verses of Thy Divine Unity, our hearts cheered with the outpourings of Thy Grace, that we may unite even as the waves of one sea and become merged together as the rays of Thine effulgent Light; that our thoughts, our views, our feelings may become as one reality, manifesting the spirit of union throughout the world. Thou art the

Gracious, the Bountiful, the Bestower, the Almighty, the Merciful, the Compassionate."

The signature of that meeting should be the Spiritual Gathering (House of Spirituality) and the wisdom is that hereafter the government should not infer by the term "House of Justice" that a court is signified, that it is connected with political affairs, or that at any time it will interfere with governmental affairs.

Hereafter, enemies will be many. They would use this subject as a cause for disturbing the mind of the government and confusing the thoughts of the public. The intention was to make known that by the term Spiritual Gathering (House of Spirituality), that Gathering has not the least connection with material affairs, and that its whole aim and consultation is confined to matters connected with spiritual affairs.

Obedience to the Assembly

In this day, the gathering of a board for consultation is of great importance and a great necessity. For all, obedience to it is a necessity, especially because the members (of it) are the hands of the Cause.

So they (members) must confer and consult in such a way that neither disagreement nor abhorrence may occur. When meeting for consultation, each must use perfect liberty in stating his views and unveiling the proof of his demonstration. If another contradicts him, he must not become excited because if there be no investigation or verification of questions and matters, the agreeable view will not be discovered neither understood. The brilliant light which comes from the collision of thoughts is the "lightener" of facts.

If all views are in harmony at the end of a conference, it will be excellent; but if, God forbid! disagreement occurs, then the decision must be according to the greater number in harmony. If, after reaching the result, one or other of the members does not agree with it, neither of the other members nor any one must argue with or reproach him, but keep silence; then they will write to this Servant.

None (of the members of the board) must spread the matters or methods pertaining to the conference. At the opening of the conference they are to ask God for special assistance and help and for their Ruler and his assistants and for the Governors of the country.

During the conference no hint must be entertained regarding political affairs. All conferences must be regarding the matters of benefit, both as a whole and individually, such as the guarding of all in all cases, their protection and preservation, the improvement of character, the training of children, etc.

If any person wishes to speak of government affairs, or to interfere with the order of Governors, the others must not combine with him because the Cause of God is withdrawn entirely from political affairs; the political realm pertains only to the Rulers of those matters: it has nothing to do with the souls who are exerting their utmost energy to harmonizing affairs, helping character and inciting (the people) to strive for perfections. Therefore no soul is allowed to interfere with (political) matters, but only in that which is commanded.

'Abdu'l-Bahá Is Present

Thou hast written concerning the meetings and the gathering places of the believers of God. Such assemblies and congregations will greatly aid the promotion of the Word—and all the audience, whether friends or not friends, become affected. But when the friends have the intention of entering in these meetings and assemblies, they must first make the purpose pure, disengage the heart from all other reflections, ask the inexhaustible divine confirmation and with the utmost devotion and humility set their feet in the gathering-place. Let them not introduce any topic in the meeting except the mentioning of the True One, neither must they confuse that merciful assembly with perplexed outside questions. They must either teach or open their tongues in propounding argument, either commune or supplicate and pray to God, either read Tablets or give out advices or exhortations.

Make ye an effort in every meeting that the Lord's Supper may become realized and the heavenly food descend. This heavenly food is knowledge, understanding, faith, assurance, love, affinity, kindness, purity of purpose, attraction of hearts and the union of souls. It was this manner of the Lord's Supper which descended from the heavenly kingdom in the day of Christ. When the meeting is conducted after this manner, then 'Abdu'l-Bahá also is present in heart and soul, though His body may not be with you.

The Center of Decision

If any differences of opinion may arise in those regions you must keep yourself entirely aloof and show forth love and kindness to all, saying it is better to refer to the ordained Center all the affairs. Whatever He commands that very thing is acceptable and beloved. You must be satisfied with this. Strife is the cause of the dispersion of the Word of God. Whatever I say and write, that is the duty of all to comply with. Beside that no other word is permitted.

Regarding the establishment of the board of translation. This matter is yet a theory, but its realization depends upon many affairs which are far from attainment at present. Until these affairs are realized, the board of translation will not find an outward expression.

The most great work to accomplish is this:—that ye must strive so that the believers of God in America may arise to union and concord. The most important feat in this day is harmony and agreement. No soul must interfere with another and no one must find fault with the rest. Praise be to God that all of them are believers in the Beauty of Abhá, and 'Abdu'l-Bahá is glad and happy on that account. But they must arise to perform good deeds according to divine instructions, so that they may guide the people with heavenly actions and manners:—to such an extent that all the inhabitants of the world may draw conclusions from their behavior and deeds, that these persons are Bahá'ís. For the manifestation of such deeds and actions from anybody else except Bahá'ís is impossible and impracticable.

This is the foundation of the religion of God and the law of God! Blessed is the one who practices them!

The Basis of Union

Organize ye Spiritual Assemblies; lay ye the foundation of union and concord in this world; destroy ye the fabric of strife and war from the face of the earth; construct ye the temple of harmony and agreement; enkindle ye the light of the realm of the oneness of humanity; open ye your eyes; gaze and behold ye the other world! The kingdom of peace, salvation, uprightness and reconciliation is founded in the invisible world, and it will by degrees become manifest and apparent through the power of the Word of God!

I supplicate God that ye may become the army of that kingdom, in order that by the power of the Most Great Name, the friends of God may conquer this world through love, friendship and the strength of the Kingdom of peace; the human race become compassionate, and bloodshed and carnage be completely effaced from the universe.

The spirit of truth is soaring on the supreme apex, like unto a bird, in order that it may discover a severed heart and alight therein and make its nest.

I hope that all the friends become manifestors of knowledge and the centers of merciful feelings. Each of them become like unto an angel and radiate heavenly deeds, thoughts and actions.

The Spiritual Assembly

Thy letter was received. Thou hast written of the organization of an assembly in that city. Look not at the small number; nay, rather seek the pure hearts. One holy soul is better than one thousand other souls. If a few souls gather together in a beloved meeting with the feelings of the Kingdom, with the divine attractions, with pure hearts and with absolute purity and holiness, to consort in spirit and fragrance, that gathering will have its effect upon all the world. The conditions, the words and the deeds of that gathering will lead a world to eternal happiness and will be an evidence of the favors of the Kingdom. The Holy Spirit will strengthen them and the hosts of the Supreme Concourse will render them victorious and the angels of Abhá will come in succession. By angels is meant the divine confirmations and heavenly powers. Angels are also those holy souls who have severed attachment to the earthly world, who are free from the fetters of self and passion and who have attached their hearts to the divine realm and the merciful kingdom. They are of the kingdom, heavenly; they are of the merciful One, divine. They are the manifestations of the divine grace and the dawns of spiritual bounty.

The spiritual meetings, which are organized in this cycle of God and this divine century, have never had their simile or likeness in bygone cycles. For the great meetings were under the protection of aristocratic men, while these meetings are under the protection of the bounty of El-Abhá. The helper or supporter of those was either a prince or a king; either a priest was the principal, or a great republic; but the helper, the assistant, the confirmer and the inspirer of these spiritual meetings is His Majesty the everlasting God.

Consider not the present condition, but rather foresee the future and the end. A seed in the beginning is very small, but in the end a great tree. One should not consider the seed, but the tree and its abundance of blossoms, leaves and fruits.

Consider the days of Jesus, when there was only a small body of people, and then observe the great tree which grew from that seed and what an abundant fruit it produced. This is greater than that, forasmuch as it is the calling of the Lord of Hosts and the voice of the trumpet of the living God; it is the summons unto the harmony and unison of the world, and it is the banner of faithfulness, trustworthiness and friendship among the different nations and sects of the universe; it is the light of the Sun of Truth and the spirituality of the Majestic One. Verily this great cycle will encompass all the horizons and ultimately all the nations will gather together under this standard.

O ye who are firm in the Covenant!

'Abdu'l-Bahá is constantly engaged in ideal communication with any Spiritual Assembly which is instituted through the divine bounty, and the members of which are in the utmost devotion turning to the divine kingdom and are firm in the Covenant. To them He is heartily attached and with them He is linked by everlasting ties. Thus correspondence with them is sincere, constant and uninterrupted.

The Spiritual Assemblies which are organized for the sake of teaching the truth, whether Assemblies for men, Assemblies for women or mixed Assemblies are all accepted and are conducive to the spreading of the fragrances of God. This is essential. Likewise the public meetings in which one day during the week the believers gather to be engaged in the commemoration of God, to read Communes and deliver effective speeches is acceptable and beloved. But now is not the time—it is utterly impossible to establish the House of Justice which is mentioned in the Book of Aqdas, nay rather it is impracticable and not to be thought of, that is for the time when the Cause is proclaimed and the Commands have become effective. Therefore now is not the time for the House of Justice, which must be established by general election. Its mention is not permissible and its realization impossible.

Endeavor ye as much as possible that differences may not arise in the affairs; let not every insignificant matter become the cause of disagreement. If such conditions exist the end will be complete dispersion. The believers and maid-servants of the Merciful must all consider how to produce harmony, so that the unity of the human world may be realized, not that every wholly unimportant subject become conducive to differences of opinion.

It is my hope that the friends and the maid-servants of America become united on all subjects and not disagree at all. If they agree upon a subject, even though it be wrong, it is better than to disagree and be in the right, for this difference will produce the demolition of the divine foundation. Though one of the parties may be in the right and they disagree that will be the cause of a thousand wrongs, but if they agree and both parties are in the wrong, as it is in unity the truth will be revealed and the wrong made right.

The members of the Spiritual Meeting must endeavor, by the power of the Holy Spirit, to make the souls real Bahá'ís. If they attain this glorious purpose, that country will be illumined and that land will become a veritable paradise, all nations will look to that assembly and from the explanation and exposition thereof receive realities and meanings.

Trust no man save him whose breast hath been dilated by God through the light of faith, whom God hath confirmed in His religion, and who is severed from all else save God and attracted by His fragrances.

In future, of course, certain people will come to you claiming faith; do not believe them nor trust them, unless after critical examination, search and investigation, and a long period of waiting, they shall appear to be faithful and truthful in word, confident in heart, attracted in spirit, pure in intention, patient in hardship, enduring the most severe tests; then associate with them. Because some sects will send certain men to mingle with you in order to throw suspicion upon those who are weak, therefore avoid them carefully. But let such be hidden that you may not become a cause of hindrance.

Thou hast written regarding the articles and papers which are written by the believers of God and the forwarding of them to this land for correction. This servant, on account of the multitude of works and occupations, hath no time whatever to attend to this matter. If these articles are read in the spiritual assembly of each city in America and the printing and spreading of them is advised and approved by the assembly, it is acceptable. This permission is granted so that those souls do not become disappointed and may be engaged in the composition and printing of instructive papers.

Mercy and Justice

The foundation of the Kingdom of God is laid upon justice, fairness, mercy, sympathy and kindness to every soul. Then strive ye with heart and soul to practice love and kindness to the world of humanity at large, except to those souls who are selfish and insincere. It is not advisable to show kindness to a person who is a tyrant, a traitor or a thief because kindness encourages him to become worse and does not awaken him. The more kindness you show to a liar the more he is apt to lie, for he thinks that you know not, while you do know, but extreme kindness keeps you from revealing your knowledge.

INTER-ASSEMBLY UNION

The Spiritual Meeting of men and the Spiritual Meeting of women in Chicago are indeed endeavoring to serve. If they unite, as they should, they will produce great results. Especially, if the Spiritual Meetings of Chicago unite with those of New York and become bound together, in a short while the fragrance of the divine garden, which giveth life, will perfume all regions.

The Spiritual Meeting of Consultation of New York must be in the utmost union and harmony with the Spiritual Meeting of Consultation of Chicago, and that which they deem advisable to publish, these two Meetings of Consultation must unitedly approve of it and deem its publication advisable. Then the Meeting of Consultation must send one copy thereof to 'Akká, in order that it may be also approved of here and then returned, and that then it may be printed and published.

That the two Spiritual Meetings of Chicago and New York must be in unity and harmony is very important, and when a Spiritual Meeting may be also organized in Washington in a befitting manner, these two meetings must be also in unity and harmony with that meeting.

To be brief, it hath been decided by the desire of God that union and harmony may day by day increase among the friends of God and the maid-servants of the Merciful One, in the West. Not until this is realized will the affairs advance by any means whatever! And the greatest means for the union and harmony of all is Spiritual Meetings. This matter is very important and is as a magnet for divine confirmation. If the beauty of this Divine Beloved One—that is, unity of believers—does appear in the ornament of the Kingdom of Abhá, it is certain that those countries will, in a short time, become the Paradise of Abhá and the light of unity and singleness will shine upon the whole world from the West. We are endeavoring with all heart and soul, have no rest night and day, nor a moment of tranquillity, so that we may make the world of humanity the mirror of the divine unity; how much more the beloved of God! And this wish and hope shall appear and shine forth at that time when the true friends of God may arise and act in accord with the teachings of the Beauty of Abhá—may my life be a sacrifice to His beloved ones! One of the teachings is that love and faithfulness must so prevail in the hearts that men may see the stranger as a friend, the sinner as an intimate fellow, may count enemies as allies, regard foes as loving comrades, call their executioner the giver of life, consider the denier as a believer and the unbeliever as a faithful one—that is, men must behave in such a manner as may befit the believers, the faithful, the friend and the confidant. If this lamp may shine in a befitting manner in the assemblage of the world you will find that the regions will become fragrant and the world become a delectable paradise, the surface of the earth will become an excellent garden, the world will become as one home, the different nations will become as one kind, and the peoples and nationalities of the East and West will become as one household. I hope such a day may come and such lights may dawn and such a Countenance may appear in the utmost beauty.

O ye dear friends of mine! The Assemblies of those regions must be connected with one another and must communicate with each other. Even communicate with the Assemblies of the East, so that this may become the means of the great unity and concord.

The Mashriqu'l-Adhkár

Ye have written regarding the erection of the Temple and the purchase of the ground, or the finding of a place to be as a home for the gathering of the believers. At this moment that 'Abdu'l-Bahá is immersed in the ocean of calamities, this news caused him joy and happiness, that—praise be to God!—the friends and the maid-servants of the Merciful are thinking to serve the Kingdom of God.

Concerning the erection of the Temple: Now all the believers must become united, so that the Temple may be built soon in one place. For should the believers undertake the erection of the Temple in many places, it will not become completed anywhere; and as in Chicago they have preceded every other place to plan the erection of the Temple, undoubtedly to cooperate and help them is nobler and a necessity. Then, when it is built in one place, it will become erected in many other places. If, for the present, you prepare or establish a home in New York, though by renting it, to become a center for the gathering of the believers of God, it is very acceptable. God willing, in all the states of America in the future there will be erected Temples with infinite architectural beauty, art, with pleasing proportion and handsome and attractive appearances; especially in New York. But for the present, be ye satisfied with a rented place.

O friends of 'Abdu'l-Bahá and His co-sharers and partners in the servitude of the Lord of Hosts! Verily the greatest affair and the most important matter today is to establish a Mas͟hriqu'l-Ad͟hkár and to found a Temple from which the voice of praisings may rise to the Kingdom of the majestic Lord. Blessings be upon you for having thought to do so and intending to erect such an edifice, advancing all in devoting your wealth in this great purpose and in this splendid work. You will soon see the angels of confirmation following after you and the hosts of reinforcement crowding before you.

When the Mas͟hriqu'l-Ad͟hkár is accomplished, when the lights are emanating therefrom, the righteous ones are presenting themselves therein, the prayers are performed with supplication towards the mysterious Kingdom, the voice of glorification is raised to the Lord, the Supreme, then the believers shall rejoice, the hearts shall be dilated and overflow with the love of the All-living and Self-existent God. The people shall hasten to worship in that heavenly Temple, the fragrances of God will be elevated, the divine teachings will be established in the hearts like the establishment of the Spirit in mankind; the people will then stand firm in the Cause of your Lord, the Merciful. Praise and greetings be upon you.

Now the day has arrived in which the edifice of God, the divine sanctuary, the spiritual temple, shall be erected in America! I entreat God to assist the confirmed believers in accomplishing this great service and with entire zeal to rear this mighty structure which shall be renowned throughout the world. The support of God will be with those believers in that district that they may be successful in their undertaking, for the Cause is great and great; because this is the first Mas͟hriqu'l-Ad͟hkár in that country and from it the praise of God shall ascend to the Kingdom of Mystery and the tumult of His exaltation and greetings from the whole world shall be heard!

Whosoever arises for the service of this building shall be assisted with a great power from His Supreme Kingdom and upon him spiritual and heavenly blessings shall descend, which shall fill his heart with wonderful consolation and enlighten his eyes by beholding the glorious and eternal God!

The contribution that thou hast made to the Temple is beloved. The Temple is the most great foundation of the world of humanity and it hath many branches. Although the Temple is the place of worship, with it is connected a hospital, pharmacy, pilgrims' house, school for the orphans, and a university for the study of high sciences. Every Temple is connected with these five things. I hope that now in America they will build a Temple and gradually add to it the hospital, school, university, pharmacy and pilgrims' house with the utmost efficiency and thoroughness. Thou shouldst make known to the believers these details, so that they may realize how important the Temple is. The Temple is not only a place for worship; nay, it is perfect in every way.

Thy letter hath arrived and the contents have given glad-tidings that the ground for the Temple hath been bought and also told about the meeting which was held concerning the needs for the Temple. From this news great fragrance and joy were produced. Thanks be to God that thou hast helped to establish a meeting for this purpose. I hope that the members of this meeting will become the receivers of the divine benevolence and be aided by the heavenly assistances. But consult with the House of Spirituality of Chicago. Ye must all be perfectly united and harmonious until, through this harmony, ye may perpetually receive help from the Kingdom of God.

Concerning the members of this spiritual meeting, you suggested that they be selected from all the spiritual meetings of the other cities of America. I quite approve and am very much pleased with this plan. This will become the cause of harmony in the Word in all America. Therefore, ask every spiritual meeting in the other cities that they will each select one and send him, and from these selected ones and with those who are selected from the Chicago meeting, establish a new meeting for the provision of the needs of the Temple. If this be established with perfect fragrance and joy, it will produce great results. In this new meeting, especially for the establishment of the Temple, women are also to be members.

Give to all the divine friends the glad-tidings of the boundless heavenly blessings and tell them that the glances of the eyes of Providence are upon them and the perfect favor and bounty are descending upon them.

Thy detailed letter was received. Its contents indicated that thou didst travel in the cities of America and visited the friends of God until thou didst reach the general Convention held in Chicago for the building of the Mas͟hriqu'l-Ad͟hkár. In thy letter thou hast written in praise and commendation of the illumination of that Convention. Truly I say, the Convention of the Bahá'í delegates in Chicago was a heavenly gathering and confirmed by Divine Assistance.

The splendor of the Kingdom of Abhá shone forth and the soul-refreshing breeze wafted from the direction of Providence.

It was an effulgence from the rays of the Sun of Truth that the friends of God gathered in that illumined Assembly with the utmost love, unity and concord. The intentions of every one were reinforced by divine confirmation, the aim of every one was service in the Cause of God, servitude in the Threshold of the Almighty and the erection of the Mas͟hriqu'l-Ad͟hkár. The results of that

Convention in the future will be far-reaching and most important, and evident signs shall become manifest. As it was the first general Convention in America, it displayed wonderful influence. The gathering of that illumined Assembly in such a short space of time would have been impossible without the power of the divine Covenant and Testament. But the Covenant has such a great sway that it astonishes the minds. In every region the sign of the power of the Convention is apparent and manifest.

For instance, in Írán the fire of revolution blazed in such wise that all communities, government and nations, became afflicted with the most severe trials; but the power of the Covenant protected the Bahá'í friends to such a degree that in this turbulent storm no dust fell upon them, except in one locality, which became the cause of the spreading of the Religion of God and the diffusion of the Word of God. Now all the parties in Írán are wondering how the people of Bahá were guarded and protected. Praise be to God that in Ṭihrán and all the provinces of Írán the Call of God has been raised, the Ensign of the Covenant has been unfurled, the cry of "Yá-Bahá'u'l-Abhá!" has been heard and the melody of the Kingdom of Abhá has been promulgated among the people of intelligence. . . .

Thou hast written concerning the organization of a council for the building of the Mas͟hriqu'l-Ad͟hkár. This news brought much spirit and fragrance, for the nine delegates, sent by the various assemblies, gathered in that meeting and consulted concerning the building of the Mas͟hriqu'l-Ad͟hkár.

The Mas͟hriqu'l-Ad͟hkár is the most important matter and the greatest divine institute. Consider how the first institute of His Holiness Moses, after His exodus from Egypt, was the "Tent of Martyrdom" which He raised and which was the traveling Temple. It was a tent which they pitched in the desert, wherever they abode, and worshipped in it. Likewise, after His Holiness Christ—may the spirit of the world be a sacrifice to Him!—the first institute by the disciples was a Temple. They planned a church in every country. Consider the Gospel and the importance of the Mas͟hriqu'l-Ad͟hkár will become evident.

In fine, I hope that all the beloved of God, collectively, in the continent of America, men and women, will strive night and day until the Mas͟hriqu'l-Ad͟hkár be erected in the utmost solidity and beauty.

The Collective Center of the Kingdom

To the Assemblies and Meetings of the believers of God and the maid-servants of the Merciful in the United States and Canada:
Upon them be Bahá'u'lláh El-Abhá!

HE IS GOD!

O ye heavenly souls, sons and daughters of the Kingdom!

God says in the Qur'án: "Take ye hold of the Cord of God, all of you, and become ye not disunited."

In the contingent world there are many collective centers which are conducive to association and unity between the children of men. For example, patriotism is a collective center; nationalism is a collective center; identity of interests is a collective center; political alliance is a collective center; the union of ideals is a collective center, and the prosperity of the world of humanity is dependent upon the organization and promotion of the collective centers. Nevertheless, all the above institutions are in reality, the matter and not the substance, accidental and not eternal—temporary and not everlasting. With the appearance of great revolutions and upheavals, all these collective centers are swept away. But the Collective Center of the Kingdom, embodying the Institutes and Divine Teachings, is the eternal Collective Center. It establishes relationship between the East and the West, organizes the oneness of the world of humanity, and destroys the foundation of differences. It overcomes and includes all the other collective centers. Like unto the ray of the sun, it dispels entirely the darkness, encompassing all the regions, bestows ideal life, and causes the effulgence of divine illumination. Through the breaths of the Holy Spirit it performs miracles; the Orient and the Occident embrace each other, the North and South become intimates and associates; conflicting and contending opinions disappear; antagonistic aims are brushed aside, the law of the struggle for existence is abrogated, and the canopy of the oneness of the world of humanity is raised on the apex of the globe, casting its shade over all the races of men. Consequently, the real Collective Center is the body of the divine teachings, which include all the degrees and embrace all the universal relations and necessary laws of humanity.

Consider! The people of the East and the West were in the utmost strangeness. Now to what a high degree they are acquainted with each other and united together! How far are the inhabitants of Írán from the remotest countries of America! And now observe how great has been the influence of the heavenly power, for the distance of thousands of miles has become identical with one step! How various nations that have had no relations or similarity with each other are now united and agreed through this divine potency! Indeed to God belongs power in the past and in the future! And verily God is powerful over all things!

Consider! When the rain, the heat, the sun and the gentle zephyrs cooperate with each other, what beautiful gardens are produced! How the various kinds of hyacinths, flowers, trees and plants associate with each other and are conducive to the adornment and charm of one another! Hence the oneness of the bounty of the sun, the oneness of rain and the oneness of the breeze have so overcome all other considerations, that the variety of hues, fragrances and tastes have increased the adornment, the attraction and sweetness of the whole. In a similar manner, when the divine Collective Center and the outpouring of the Sun of Reality and the breaths of the Holy Spirit are brought together, the variety of races and the differences existing between countries will become the cause of the embellishment, decoration and elegance of the world of humanity.

Therefore, the believers of God throughout all the Republics of America, through the divine power, must become the cause of the promotion of heavenly teachings and the establishment of the oneness of humanity. Every one of the important souls must arise, blowing over all parts of America the breath of life conferring upon the people a new spirit, baptizing them with the fire of the love of God, the water of life, and the breaths of the Holy Spirit —so that the second birth may become realized. For it is written in the Gospel: "That which is born of the flesh is flesh; and that which is born of the spirit is spirit."

Therefore, O ye believers of God in the United States and Canada! Select ye important personages, or that they by themselves, becoming severed from rest and composure of the world, may arise and travel throughout Alaska, the Republic of Mexico, and south of Mexico, in the Central American Republics, such as Guatemala, Honduras, Salvador, Nicaragua, Costa Rica, Panama and Belize; and through the great South American Republics, such as Argentine, Uruguay, Paraguay, Brazil, French Guiana, Dutch Guiana, British Guiana, Venezuela, Ecuador, Peru, Bolivia and Chile; also in the group of the West Indies Islands such as Cuba, Haiti, Porto Rico, Jamaica and Santo Domingo, and the group of Islands of the Lesser Antilles, the Islands of Bahama and the Islands of Bermuda; likewise to the Islands of the east, west and south of South America, such as Trinidad, Falkland Islands, Galapago Islands, Juan Fernandez and Tobago. Visit ye especially the city of Bahia, on the eastern shore of Brazil. Because in the past years this city was christened with the name, Bahia, there is no doubt that it has been through the inspiration of the Holy Spirit.

Consequently, the believers of God must display the utmost effort, upraise the divine melody throughout those regions, promulgate the heavenly teachings and waft over all, the spirit of eternal life; so that those Republics may become so illumined with the splendors and the effulgences of the Sun of Reality that they may become the objects of the praise and commendation of all other countries. Likewise, ye must give great attention to the Republic of Panama, for in that point the Occident and the Orient find each other united through the Panama Canal, and it is also situated between the two great oceans. That place will become very important in the future. The Teachings once established there, they will unite the East and the West, the North and the South.

Hence the intention must be purified, the effort ennobled and exalted, so that ye may establish affinity between the hearts of the world of humanity. This glorious aim will not become realized save through the promotion of divine teachings which are the foundations of the holy religions.

Consider how the religions of God served the world of humanity! How the religion of Torah became conducive to the glory and honor and progress of the Israelitish nation! How the breaths of the Holy Spirit of His Holiness Christ created affinity and unity between divergent communities and quarreling families! How the sacred power of His Holiness Muḥammad became the means of uniting and harmonizing the contentious tribes and the different clans of Peninsular Arabia—to such an extent that one thousand tribes were welded into one tribe, strife and discord was done away with, all of them unitedly and with one accord strove in advancing the cause of culture and civilization, and thus were freed from the lowest degree of degradation, soaring toward the height of everlasting glory! Is it possible to find a greater Collective Center in the phenomenal world than this? In comparison to this Divine Collective Center, the national collective center, the patriotic collective center, the political collective center, and the cultural and intellectual collective center are like child's play!

Now strive ye that the Collective Center of the sacred religions, for the inculcation of which all the Prophets were manifested and which is no other than the spirit of the Divine Teachings,—be spread in all parts of America—so that each one of you may shine forth from the horizon of Reality like unto the morning star, divine illumination may overcome the darkness of nature, and the world of humanity may become enlightened. This is the most great work! Should ye become confirmed therein, this world will become another world, the surface of the earth will become the delectable Paradise, and eternal Institutions be founded.

Let whosoever travels to different parts to teach, peruse over mountain, desert, land and sea this supplication!

O God! O God! Thou seest my weakness, lowliness and humility amongst Thy creatures; nevertheless I have trusted on Thee and have arisen in the promotion of Thy Teachings amongst Thy strong servants, relying on Thy power and might!

O Lord! I am a broken-winged bird and desire to soar in this Thy space to which there is no limit. How is it possible for me to do this save through Thy providence and grace, Thy confirmation and assistance!

O Lord! Have pity on my weakness and strengthen me with Thy power!

O Lord! Have pity on my impotency and assist me with Thy might and majesty!

O Lord! Should the breaths of the Holy Spirit confirm the weakest of creatures, he shall attain to the highest station of greatness and shall possess anything he desireth. Indeed Thou hast assisted Thy servants in the past, and they were the weakest of Thy creatures, the lowliest of Thy servants and the most insignificant of those who lived upon the earth; but through Thy sanction and potency they took precedence over the most glorious of Thy people and the most noble of Thy mankind. Whereas formerly they were as moths, they became royal falcons and whereas before they were as bubbles they became seas. Through Thy bestowal, Thy mercy and Thy most great favor, they became stars shining in the horizon of guidance, birds singing in the rose garden of immortality, lions roaring in the forest of knowledge and wisdom, and whales swimming in the oceans of life.

Verily, Thou art the clement, the powerful, the mighty, and the most merciful of the merciful!

BAHÁ'U'LLÁH THE LORD OF HOSTS

TO THE BELIEVERS OF GOD AND THE MAID-SERVANTS OF THE MERCIFUL OF THE BAHÁ'Í ASSEMBLIES IN THE UNITED STATES AND CANADA:

Upon them be Bahá'u'lláh El-Abhá!

HE IS GOD!

O ye apostles of Bahá'u'lláh,—May my life be a ransom to you!

The blessed Person of the Promised One is interpreted in the Holy Book as the Lord of Hosts, i. e., the heavenly armies. By heavenly armies those souls are intended who are entirely freed from the human world, transformed into celestial spirits and have become divine angels. Such souls are the rays of the Sun of Reality who will illumine all the continents. Each one is holding in his hand a trumpet, blowing the breath of life over all the regions. They are delivered from human qualities and the defects of the world of nature, are characterized with the characteristics of God, and are attracted with the fragrances of the Merciful. Like unto the apostles of Christ, who were filled with Him, these souls also have become filled with His Holiness Bahá'u'lláh, i. e., the love of Bahá'u'lláh has so mastered every organ, part and limb of their bodies, as to leave no effect by the promptings of the human world.

These souls are the armies of God and the conquerors of the East and the West. Should one of them turn his face toward some direction and summon the people to the Kingdom of God, all the ideal forces and lordly confirmations will rush to his support and reinforcement. He will behold all the doors open and all the strong fortifications and impregnable castles razed to the ground. Singly and alone he will attack the armies of the world, defeat the right and left wings of the hosts of all the countries, break through the lines of the legions of all the nations and carry his attack to the very center of the powers of the earth. This is the meaning of the Hosts of God.

Any soul from among the believers of Bahá'u'lláh who attains to this station, will become known as the Apostle of Bahá'u'lláh. Therefore strive ye with heart and soul—so that ye may reach this lofty and exalted position, be established on the throne of everlasting glory, and crown your heads with the shining diadem of the Kingdom, whose brilliant jewels may irradiate upon centuries and cycles.

O ye kind friends! Uplift your magnanimity and soar high toward the apex of heaven—so that your blessed hearts may become illumined more and more, day by day, through the Rays of the Sun of Reality, i. e., His Holiness Bahá'u'lláh; at every moment the spirits may obtain a new life, and the darkness of the world of nature may be entirely dispelled—thus ye may become incarnate light and personified spirit, become entirely unaware of the sordid matters of this world and in touch with the affairs of the divine world.

Consider ye what doors His Holiness Bahá'u'lláh has opened before you, and what a high and exalted station He has destined for you, and what bounties He has prepared for you! Should we become intoxicated with this cup, the sovereignty of this globe of earth will become lower in our estimation than the children's plays. Should they place in the arena the crown of the government of the whole world, and invite each one of us to accept it, undoubtedly we shall not condescend, and shall refuse to accept it.

To attain to this supreme station is, however, dependent on the realization of certain conditions.

The first condition is firmness in the Covenant of God. For the power of the Covenant will protect the Cause of Bahá'u'lláh from the doubts of the people of error. It is the fortified fortress of the Cause of God and the firm pillar of the religion of God. Today no power can conserve the oneness of the Bahá'í world save the Covenant of God; otherwise differences like unto a most great tempest will encompass the Bahá'í world. It is evident that the axis of the oneness of the world of humanity is the power of the Covenant and nothing else. Had the Covenant not come to pass, had it not been revealed from the Supreme Pen and had not the Book of the Covenant, like unto the ray of the Sun of Reality, illuminated the world, the forces of the Cause of God would have been utterly scattered and certain souls who were the prisoners of their own passions and lusts would have taken into their hands an axe, cutting the root of this Blessed Tree. Every person would have pushed forward his own desire and every individual aired his own opinion! Notwithstanding this great Covenant, a few negligent souls galloped with their chargers into the battlefield, thinking perchance they might be able to weaken the foundation of the Cause of God: but praise be to God, all of them were afflicted with regret and loss, and ere long they shall see themselves in poignant despair. Therefore, in the beginning one must make his steps firm in the Covenant—so that the confirmations of Bahá'u'lláh may encircle from all sides, the cohorts of the Supreme Concourse may become the supporters and the helpers, and the exhortations and advices of 'Abdu'l-Bahá, like unto the pictures engraved on stone, may remain permanent and ineffaceable in the tablets of the hearts.

The second condition: Fellowship and love amongst the believers. The divine friends must be attracted to and enamored of each other and ever be ready and willing to sacrifice their own lives for each other. Should one soul from amongst the believers meet another, it must be as though a thirsty one with parched lips has reached to the fountain of the water of life, or a lover has met his true beloved. For one of the greatest divine wisdoms regarding the appearance of the Holy Manifestations is this: The souls may come to know each other and become intimate with each other; the power of the love of God may make all of them the waves of one sea, the flowers of one rose garden and the stars of one heaven. This is the wisdom for the appearance of the Holy Manifestations! When the most great bestowal reveals itself in the hearts of the believers, the world of nature will be transformed, the darkness of the contingent being will vanish, and heavenly illumination will be obtained. Then the whole world will become the Paradise of Abhá, every one of the believers of God will become a blessed tree, producing wonderful fruits.

O ye friends! Fellowship, fellowship! Love, love! Unity, unity! —So that the power of the Bahá'í Cause may appear and become manifest in the world of existence. Just at this moment I am engaged in your commemoration and this heart is in the utmost glow and excitement! Were ye to realize how this conscience is attracted with the love of the friends, unquestionably ye would obtain such a degree of joy and fragrance that ye would all become enamored with each other!

The third condition: Teachers must continually travel to all parts of the continent, nay, rather, to all parts of the world, but they must travel like 'Abdu'l-Bahá, who journeyed throughout the cities of America. He was sanctified and free from every attachment and in the utmost severance. Just as His Holiness Christ says: "Shake off the very dust from your feet."

Ye have observed that while in America many souls in the utmost of supplication and entreaty desired to offer some gifts, but this servant, in accord with the exhortations and behests of the Blessed Perfection, never accepted a thing, although on certain occasions we were in most straitened circumstances. But on the other hand, if a soul for the sake of God, voluntarily and out of his pure desire, wishes to offer a contribution (toward the expenses of a teacher) in order to make the contributor happy, the teacher may accept a small sum, but must live with utmost contentment.

The aim is this: The intention of the teacher must be pure, his heart independent, his spirit attracted, his thought at peace, his resolution firm, his magnanimity exalted and in the love of God a shining torch. Should he become as such, his sanctified breath will even affect the rock; otherwise there will be no result whatsoever. As long as a soul is not perfected, how can he efface the defects of others! Unless he is detached from aught else save God, how can he teach the severance to others!

In short, O ye believers of God! Endeavor ye; so that ye may take hold of every means in the promulgation of the religion of God and the diffusion of the fragrances of God.

Amongst other things is the holding of the meetings for teaching—so that blessed souls and the old ones from amongst the believers may gather together the youths of the love of God in schools of instruction and teach them all the divine proofs and irrefragable arguments, explain and elucidate the history of the Cause, and interpret also the prophecies and proofs which are recorded and are extant in the divine Books and Epistles regarding the Manifestation of the Promised One, so that the young ones may go in perfect knowledge in all these degrees.

Likewise, whenever it is possible a committee must be organized for the translation of the Tablets. Wise souls who have mastered and studied perfectly the Íránian, Arabic and foreign languages, or know one of the foreign languages—must commence translating Tablets and books containing the proofs of this Revelation, and publishing those books, circulate them throughout the five continents of the globe.

Similarly, the Magazine, the Star of the West, must be edited in the utmost regularity, but its contents must be the promulgator of the Cause of God—so that both in the East and the West, they may become informed of the most important events.

In short, in all the meetings, whether public or private, nothing should be discussed save that which is under consideration, and all the articles be centered around the Cause of God. Promiscuous talks must not be dragged in and contention is absolutely forbidden.

The teachers traveling in different directions must know the language of the country in which they will enter. For example, a person being proficient in the Japanese language may travel in Japan, or a person knowing the Chinese language may hasten to China, and so forth.

In short, after this universal war, the people have obtained extraordinary capacity to hearken to the divine teachings, for the wisdom of this war is this: That it may become proven to all that the fire of war is world-consuming, whereas the rays of peace are world-enlightening. One is death, the other is life; this is extinction, that is immortality; one is the most great calamity, the other is the most great bounty; this is darkness, that is light; this is eternal humiliation and that is everlasting glory; one is the destroyer of the foundation of man, the other is the founder of the prosperity of the human race.

Consequently, a number of souls may arise and act in accordance with the aforesaid conditions, and hasten to all parts of the world, especially from America to Europe, Africa, Asia and Australia, and travel through Japan and China. Likewise, from Germany teachers and believers may travel to the continents of America, Africa, Japan and China; in brief, they may travel through all the continents and islands of the globe. Thus in a short space of time, most wonderful results will be produced, the banner of Universal Peace will be waving on the apex of the world and the lights of the oneness of the world of humanity may illumine the universe.

In brief, O ye believers of God! The text of the Divine Book is this: If two souls quarrel and contend about a question of the Divine questions, differing and disputing, *both are wrong*. The wisdom of this incontrovertible law of God is this: That between two souls from amongst the believers of God, no contention and dispute might arise; that they may speak with each other with infinite amity and love. Should there appear the least trace of controversy, they must remain silent, and both parties must continue their discussions no longer, but ask the reality of the question from the Interpreter. This is the irrefutable command!

The Master's Last Tablet to America

O ye friends of God!

'Abdu'l-Bahá is day and night thinking of you and mentioning you, for the friends of God are dear to Him. Every morning at dawn I supplicate the Kingdom of God and ask that you may be filled with the breath of the Holy Spirit, so that you may become brilliant candles, shine with the light of guidance and dispel the darkness of error. Rest assured that the confirmations of the Abhá Kingdom will continuously reach you.

Through the power of the divine springtime, the downpour of the celestial clouds and the heat of the Sun of Reality, the tree of life is just beginning to grow. Before long, it will produce buds, bring forth leaves and fruits, and cast its shade over the East and the West. This Tree of Life is the Book of the Covenant.

In America, in these days, severe winds have surrounded the Lamp of the Covenant, hoping that this brilliant Light may be extinguished, and this Tree of Life may be uprooted. Certain weak, capricious, malicious and ignorant souls have been shaken by the earthquake of hatred, of animosity, have striven to efface the Divine Covenant and Testament, and render the clear water muddy so that in it they might fish. They have arisen against the Center of the Covenant like the people of Bayán who attacked the Blessed Beauty and every moment uttered a calumny. Every day they seek a pretext and secretly arouse doubts, so that the Covenant of Bahá'u'lláh may be completely annihilated in America.

O friends of God! Be awake, be awake; be vigilant, be vigilant! His Holiness, the Báb, made a Covenant for Bahá'u'lláh with all the people of the Bayán, so that on the day of appearance of

"Him Whom God shall manifest"—and of the radiation of the Light of Bahá'u'lláh, they might believe and be assured, arise in service and promulgate the Word of God. Later the people of the Bayán, like Mírzá Yaḥyá and many others, arose against the Blessed Beauty, invented every sort of calumny, aroused doubt in the minds of the people, and from the Books of His Holiness the Báb—that were full of references to "Him Whom God shall manifest"—tried to prove Bahá'u'lláh false. Every day they wrote and spread a pamphlet opposing Bahá'u'lláh, caused trouble and perplexity among the people; they inflicted the greatest injury and cruelty, yet counted themselves firm in the Covenant of His Holiness, the Báb. However, when the light of the Covenant of His Holiness, the Báb, lighted the universe, then all the faithful and sincere souls were freed from the darkness of the violation of the people of the Bayán and shone like brilliant candles.

Bahá'u'lláh, in all the Tablets and Epistles, forbade the true and firm friends from associating and meeting the violators of the Covenant of His Holiness, the Báb, saying that no one should go near them because their breath is like the poison of the snake that kills instantly.

In the Hidden Words, He says: "Esteem the friendship of the just, but withhold both mind and hand from the company of the wicked."

Addressing one of the friends, He says: "It is clear to your honor that before long Satan, in the garb of man, will reach that land and will try to mislead the friends of the Divine Beauty through temptations which arouse the desires of self, and will cause them to follow the footsteps of Satan away from the right and glorious path, and prevent them from attaining the Blessed Shore of the King of Oneness. This is a hidden information of which we have informed the chosen ones lest they may be deprived of their praiseworthy station by associating with the embodiments of hatred. Therefore, it is incumbent upon all the friends of God to shun any person in whom they perceive the emanation of hatred for the Glorious Beauty of Abhá, though he may quote all the Heavenly Utterances and cling to all the Books." He continues—

Glorious be His Name!—"Protect yourselves with utmost vigilance, lest you be entrapped in the snare of deception and fraud." This is the advice of the Pen of Destiny.

In another address, He says: "Therefore, to avoid these people will be the nearest path by which to attain the divine good pleasure; because their breath is infectious, like unto poison."

In another Tablet, He says: "O Káẓim, close thine eye to the people of the world; drink the water of knowledge from the heavenly cup bearers, and listen not to the nonsensical utterances of the manifestations of Satan, because the manifestations of Satan are occupying today the observation posts of the glorious path of God, and preventing the people by every means of deception and ruse. Before long you will witness the turning away of the people of Bayán from the Manifestation of the Merciful."

In another Tablet, He says: "Endeavor to your utmost to protect yourselves, because Satan appears in different robes and appeals to everyone according to each person's own way, until he becomes like unto him—then he will leave him alone."

In another Tablet, He says: "Shun any man in whom you perceive enmity for this Servant, though he may appear in the garb of piety of the former and later people, or may arise to the worship of the two worlds."

In another Tablet, He says: "O Mahdi! Be informed by these utterances and shun the manifestations of the people of hell, the rising place of Nimrods, the rising place of Pharees, the fountain of Tagut, and the soothsayers."

Again He says: "Say, O my friend and my pure ones! Listen to the Voice of this Beloved Prisoner in this Great Prison. If you detect in any man the least perceptible breath of violation, shun him and keep away from him." Then He says: "Verily, they are manifestations of Satan."

In another Tablet, He says: "And turn your faces to the Great Countenance for before long the foul odors of the wicked persons will pass over these regions. God willing, you may remain protected during these days."

In the 18th chapter of the Gospel of Matthew, 6th to 9th verses,

His Holiness Christ says: "But whosoever shall offend one of these little ones which believe in Me, it were better for him that a millstone were hanged about his neck and that he were drowned in the depth of the sea. Woe unto the world because of offenses, for it must needs be that offenses come, but woe to that man by whom the offense cometh. Wherefore if thy hand or thy feet offend thee, cut them off and cast them from thee; it is better for thee to enter into life halt or maimed, rather than having two hands or two feet, to be cast into everlasting fire. And if thine eye offend thee, pluck it out and cast it from thee."

And in the 21st chapter and 38th verse of the Gospel of Matthew, He says: "But when the husbandmen saw the son, they said among themselves, this is the heir, come let us kill him and let us seize on his inheritance. And they caught him and cast him out of the vineyard and slew him."

Also in the 22nd chapter and the 14th verse of the Gospel of Matthew, He says "But many are called and few are chosen."

In the Holy Writings of His Holiness, Bahá'u'lláh, in a thousand places at least, the violators of the Covenant are execrated and condemned. Some of the heavenly passages will be mentioned.

In short, all the friends in America know that the founders of this sedition—namely, the violators of the Covenant—are people whose aims are known to all the friends. Yet, O glorious God, they are deceived by them!

Praise be to God, you know with perfect clearness that His Holiness Christ, was extremely kind and loving, yet there were people like Judas Iscariot who—by their own deeds—separated themselves from Christ. Therefore, what fault of Christ's could that be? Now the Nakazene say that 'Abdu'l-Bahá is despotic, drives some people out and excommunicates like the Pope. This is not so at all! Any person who has left (the Cause), did so because of his own actions, intrigues and evil plots. If this objection be raised against 'Abdu'l-Bahá, they must also object to the Blessed Beauty who, with distinct and conclusive command, forbids the friends from companionship and familiarity with the violators of the people of Bayán.

Supplication! O Lord of the Covenant! O luminous Star of the world! The persecuted 'Abdu'l-Bahá has fallen into the hands of persons who appear as sheep and in reality are ferocious wolves; they exercise every sort of oppression, endeavor to destroy the foundation of the Covenant,—and claim to be Bahá'ís. They strike at the root of the Tree of the Covenant—and count themselves persecuted—just as did the people of Bayán who broke the Covenant of His Holiness, the Báb, and from six directions shot arrows of reproach and calumny at Thy Blessed Body. Notwithstanding this great oppression, they call themselves oppressed. Now this Servant of Thy Threshold has also fallen into the hands of oppressors. Every hour they contrive new intrigues and fraud, and bring forth new calumny.

Yá-Bahá'u'l-Abhá! Protect the Stronghold of Thy Cause from these thieves, and safeguard the lamps of the Kingdom from these malevolent winds!

Yá-Bahá'u'l-Abhá! 'Abdu'l-Bahá did not rest a moment until He had raised Thy Cause and the Standard of the Kingdom of Abhá waved over the world. Now some people have arisen with intrigues and evil aspirations to trample this flag in America, but My hope is in Thy confirmations. Leave Me not single, alone and oppressed! As Thou didst promise, verbally and in writing, that Thou wouldst protect this deer of the pasture of Thy love from the attacks of the hounds of hatred and animosity, and that Thou wouldst safeguard this persecuted sheep from the claws and teeth of the ferocious wolves,—now do I await the appearance of Thy bounties and the realization of Thy definite promise. Thou art the true Protector, and Thou art the Lord of the Covenant! Therefore, protect this Lamp which Thou hast lighted, from the severe winds.

Yá-Bahá'u'l-Abhá! I have forsaken the world and its people, am heartbroken because of the unfaithful, and am weary. In the cage of this world I flutter like a frightened bird and long for the flight to Thy Kingdom.

Yá-Bahá'u'l-Abhá! Make me to drink the cup of sacrifice, and free Me! Relieve Me from these difficulties, hardships, afflictions and troubles! Thou art the assister, the helper, the protector and the supporter!

Now some of the writings, prayers and verses of the Blessed Beauty will be mentioned in which association with the violators is forbidden. In the Íránian Commune, He says:

"Protect this Servant from the doubts of the persons who have turned away from Thee and are deprived of the sea of Thy knowledge. O God! O God! Protect this Servant through Thy bounty and generosity from the evil of Thine enemies who have broken Thy Covenant and Testament."

In another place He says: "O My God and the Aim of My Life! Protect this weak one with Thy Mighty hand from the voice of the Naegh."

Also He says: "Ye have taken one whom I hate to be thy beloved, and My enemy to be thy friend."

Also He says: "The company of the wicked ones increaseth sorrow, and the association with the pious ones removeth rust from the heart. The one who desires to associate with God, let him associate with His friends; the one who wishes to hear the Words of God, let him hear the words of His chosen ones."

Also He says: "Do not associate with the wicked, because the company of the wicked changeth the light of life into the fire of remorse. If thou asketh for the bounties of the Holy Spirit, associate with the pure ones, because they have quaffed the eternal chalice from the hands of the Cupbearer of eternity."

Also He says: "The greatest of degradation is to leave the Shadow of God and enter under the shadow of Satan."

Also He says: "O ye servants! There is nothing in this heart save the effulgences of the splendor of the morn of Meeting, and it does not speak but the absolute truth from your Lord. Therefore, do not follow self; break not God's Covenant and violate not His Testament. Proceed with perfect steadfastness, and with heart, soul and tongue, turn unto Him, and be not of the thoughtless."

And still He says: "You have forgotten God's Covenant and violated His Testament."

And again He says: "If anyone comes to you with the book of the wicked, put him behind you."

"Among the people are those who have broken the Covenant, and among them are those who have followed what was ordained by the All-Knower, the All-Wise. My affliction is not from My imprisonment and persecution, or from what comes to Me from My rebellious servants,—but from the actions of those who attribute themselves to this persecuted One and commit among the people that which is degrading to the honor of God. Verily, they are of the seditious."

Likewise speaking for the violators, He says: "Thou hast made the pulpits for Thy mention, the proclamation of Thy Word and the manifestation of Thy Cause, and we have ascended them to proclaim the breaking of Thy Covenant and Testament."

Likewise, He says: "Take what has been ordained for you and follow not those who have broken God's Covenant and Testament, for lo! they are the people of error."

Again He says: "Those who have broken the Covenant of God, notwithstanding His Commands, and have turned away, they are the people of error before the most Opulent, the Exalted."

And He says: "Those who have been faithful to God's Covenant are of the highest ones in the sight of the exalted Lord. Those who have become negligent are of the people of fire in the sight of Thy Lord, the Beloved, the Independent."

Likewise He says: "Blessed is the servant or maid-servant who believes, and woe to the polytheists who have violated the Covenant of God and His Testament, and deviated from My Right Path."

Likewise He says: "I implore of Thee not to deprive me of what Thou possessest or what Thou hast ordained for Thy chosen ones who have not broken Thy Covenant and Testament. Say! Die with your hatred! Verily, He is come by Whom the pillars of the world have been shaken and because of Whom the feet have stumbled—save those who have not broken the Covenant, but have followed what God revealed in His Book."

Likewise He says: "The Supreme Concourse will pray for the one who is adorned with the garment of faithfulness between heaven and earth; but he who breaks the Covenant is cursed by heaven and earth."

Likewise He says: "Take hold of what has been revealed unto you, with a power superior to that of the hands of the unbelievers who have violated the Covenant of God and His Testament, and have turned from the Face."

Also He says: "O Yaḥyá! Verily the Book has come! Take it with a power from Us and do not follow those who have broken the Covenant of God and His Testament, and have denied what has been revealed from the Powerful, the All-Knower."

Likewise He says: "I awoke this morning, O My God, under the shadow of Thy great bounty and have taken, with Thy power, the pen to mention Thee with such mention as shall be a light unto the pure, and fire unto the wicked who have violated Thy Covenant, denied Thy Verses and put aside the Kawthar of life which appeared by Thy command and was revealed by the finger of Thy will."

Here, in a Tablet to 'Abdu'l-Bahá, He says also: "O God! This is a Branch which has sprung forth from the Tree of Oneness, the Sadrat of Thy Unity. O God! Thou seest Him looking to Thee and clinging to the rope of Thy Bounties. Protect Him in the shelter of Thy Mercy! Thou knowest, O My God, that I do not desire Him save for what Thou dost desire Him, and I do not choose Him save for what Thou dost choose Him. Assist Him with the Hosts of Thy earth and Thy heaven. Assist, O God, those who assist Him, and choose those who choose Him. Confirm those who draw nigh unto Him, and debase those who deny Him and do not want Him. O God, Thou seest that at this moment of Revelation My Pen shakes and My Being trembles. I ask Thee, By My impatience in Thy Love and My willingness to proclaim Thy Cause, to ordain for Him and His friends, what Thou hast ordained for Thy Messengers and the faithful ones of Thy Revelation. Verily, Thou art the powerful and the omnipotent! By God, O people, My eye weeps, and the eye of 'Alí weeps in the Supreme Concourse; My heart throbs, and the heart of Muḥammad throbs in the Courts of Abhá; My heart and the hearts of the Prophets lament with the people of knowledge, if you are those who are possessed of sight. My sorrow is not for

Myself, but for the One Who comes after Me in the Shadow of the Cause with a clear, undeniable reign; because these will not acknowledge His Manifestation and will deny His evidences and verses, will dispute His power, will antagonize Him and will be traitors to His Cause—as they did to His Person in those days—and ye were witnesses."

Again in a Tablet to 'Abdu'l-Bahá, He says: "O Greatest Branch! Verily, Thy illness caused Me sorrow, but God will cure Thee, and He is the most generous and best helper. Glory be upon Thee and upon those who serve Thee and encircle Thee! Woe and torment be upon him who opposes and torments Thee! Blessed is he who befriends Thee, and hell be for him who opposes Thee!"

Likewise He says: "Is it possible that after the dawning of the sun of Thy Testament from the horizon of Thy greatest Tablet, that any feet shall slip away from the right Path? We said, O My Supreme Pen, it behoves Thee to do as Thou hast been bidden by God, the exalted and the great. Do not ask about that which melts Thy heart and those of the denizens of Paradise who encompass Thy wonderful Cause. Thou shouldst not know what We have hidden from Thee. Thy Lord is the veiler and the knower. Turn Thy most luminous Face to the greatest aspect and say: O My Merciful God! Decorate the Heaven of Bayán with the stars of steadfastness, trust and truth. Verily, Thou art the Powerful over what Thou willest. There is no God save Thee, the wise and the generous."

In short, from these Holy Utterances and those of His Holiness Christ, it becomes clear, evident and proved, that man should associate with people who are firm in the Covenant and Testament, and befriend the pure ones; because bad associates bring about infection of bad qualities. It is like leprosy; it is impossible for a man to associate and befriend a leper and not be infected. This command is for the sake of protection and to safeguard.

Consider this text of the New Testament: the brothers of His Holiness Christ, came to Him and they said: "These are your brothers." He answered that His brothers were those who believed in God, and refused to associate with His own brothers.

Likewise Qurratu'l-'Ayn, who is celebrated in all the world, when she believed in God and was attracted to the Divine Breaths, she forsook her two eldest sons, although they were her two oldest children, because they did not become believers, and thereafter did not meet them. She said: "All the friends of God are my children, but these two are not. I will have nothing to do with them."

Consider! The Divine Gardener cuts off the dry or weak branch from the good tree and grafts to it, a branch from another tree. He both separates and unites. This is that which His Holiness Christ says: that from all the world they come and enter the Kingdom, and the children of the Kingdom shall be cast out. Noah's grandson, Canaan, was detested in the sight of Noah and others were accepted. The brothers of the Blessed Beauty detached themselves from Him, and the Blessed Beauty never met them. He said: "This is an eternal separation between you and Me." All this was not because the Blessed Beauty was despotic; but because these persons, through their own actions and words deprived themselves from the bounties and bestowals of the Blessed Beauty. His Holiness Christ did not exercise despotism in the case of Judas Iscariot and His own brothers,—but they separated themselves.

In short, the point is this: 'Abdu'l-Bahá is extremely kind, but when the disease is leprosy, what am I to do? Just as in bodily diseases we must prevent intermingling and infection and put into effect sanitary laws—because the infectious physical diseases uproot the foundation of humanity; likewise one must protect and safeguard the blessed souls from the breaths and fatal spiritual diseases; otherwise violation, like the plague, will become a contagion and all will perish. In the early days, after the Ascension of the Blessed Beauty, the center of violation was alone; little by little the infection spread; and this was due to companionship and association.

Excerpts from the Will and Testament of 'Abdu'l-Bahá

All-praise to Him Who, by the Shield of His Covenant, hath guarded the Temple of His Cause from the darts of doubtfulness, Who by the Hosts of His Testament hath preserved the Sanctuary of His Most Beneficent Law and protected His Straight and Luminous Path, staying thereby the onslaught of the company of Covenant-breakers, that have threatened to subvert His Divine Edifice; Who hath watched over His Mighty Stronghold and All-glorious Faith, through the aid of men whom the slander of the slanderer affects not, whom no earthly calling, glory and power can turn aside from the Covenant of God and His Testament, established firmly by His clear and manifest words, writ and revealed by His All-glorious Pen and recorded in the Preserved Tablet.

Salutation and praise, blessing and glory rest upon that primal branch of the Divine and Sacred Lote-Tree, grown out, blest, tender, verdant and flourishing from the Twin Holy Trees; the most wondrous, unique and priceless pearl that doth gleam from out the twin surging seas; upon the offshoots of the Tree of Holiness, the twigs of the Celestial Tree, they that in the Day of the Great Dividing have stood fast and firm in the Covenant; upon the Hands (pillars) of the Cause of God that have diffused widely the Divine Fragrances, declared His Proofs, proclaimed His Faith, published abroad His Law, detached themselves from all things but Him, stood for righteousness in this world, and kindled the Fire of the Love of God in the very hearts and souls of His servants; upon them that have believed, rested assured, stood steadfast in His Covenant and followed the Light that after my passing shineth from the Dayspring of Divine Guidance—for behold! he is the blest and sacred bough that hath branched out from the Twin Holy Trees. Well is it with him that seeketh the shelter of his shade that shadoweth all mankind.

O ye beloved of the Lord! The greatest of all things is the protection of the True Faith of God, the preservation of His Law, the safeguarding of His Cause and service unto His Word. Ten thousand souls have shed streams of their sacred blood in this path, their precious lives they offered in sacrifice unto Him, hastened wrapt in holy ecstasy unto the glorious field of martyrdom, upraised the Standard of God's Faith and writ with their life-blood upon the Tablet of the world the verses of His Divine Unity. The sacred breast of His Holiness, the Exalted One, (may my life be a sacrifice unto Him) was made a target to many a dart of woe, and in Mázindarán, the Blessed feet of the Abhá Beauty (may my life be offered up for His loved ones) were so grievously scourged as to bleed and be sore wounded. His neck also was put into captive chains and His feet made fast in the stocks. In every hour, for a period of fifty years, a new trial and calamity befell Him and fresh afflictions and cares beset Him. One of them: after having suffered intense vicissitudes, He was made homeless and a wanderer and fell a victim to still new vexations and troubles. In 'Iráq, the Day-Star of the world was so exposed to the wiles of the people of malice as to be eclipsed in splendor. Later on He was sent an exile to the Great City (Constantinople) and thence to the Land of Mystery (Adrianople), whence, grievously wronged, He was eventually transferred to the Most Great Prison ('Akká). He Whom the world hath wronged (may my life be offered up for His loved ones) was four times banished from city to city, till at last condemned to perpetual confinement, He was incarcerated in this Prison, the prison of highway robbers, of brigands and of manslayers. All this is but one of the trials that have afflicted the Blessed Beauty, the rest being even as grievous as this.

According to the direct and sacred command of God we are forbidden to utter slander, are commanded to show forth peace and amity, are exhorted to rectitude of conduct, straightforwardness and harmony with all the kindreds and peoples of the world. We must obey and be the well-wishers of the governments of the land, regard disloyalty unto a just king as disloyalty to God Himself and wishing evil to the government a transgression of the Cause of God.

O God, my God! Thou seest this wronged servant of Thine, held fast in the talons of ferocious lions, of ravening wolves, of bloodthirsty beasts. Graciously assist me, through my love for Thee, that I may drink deep of the chalice that brimmeth over with faithfulness to Thee and is filled with Thy bountiful Grace; so that, fallen upon the dust, I may sink prostrate and senseless whilst my vesture is dyed crimson with my blood. This is my wish, my heart's desire, my hope, my pride, my glory. Grant, O Lord my God, and my Refuge, that in my last hour, my end, may even as musk shed its fragrance of glory! Is there a bounty greater than this? Nay, by Thy Glory! I call Thee to witness that no day passeth but that I quaff my fill from this cup, so grievous are the misdeeds wrought by them that have broken the Covenant, kindled discord, showed their malice, stirred sedition in the land and dishonored Thee amidst

Thy servants. Lord! Shield Thou from these Covenant-breakers the mighty Stronghold of Thy Faith and protect Thy secret Sanctuary from the onslaught of the ungodly. Thou art in truth the Mighty, the Powerful, the Gracious, the Strong.

O God, my God! Shield Thy trusted servants from the evils of self and passion, protect them with the watchful eye of Thy loving kindness from all rancor, hate and envy, shelter them in the impregnable stronghold of Thy Cause and, safe from the darts of doubtfulness, make them the manifestations of Thy glorious Signs, illumine their faces with the effulgent rays shed from the Dayspring of Thy Divine Unity, gladden their hearts with the verses revealed from Thy Holy Kingdom, strengthen their loins by Thy all-swaying power that cometh from Thy Realm of Glory. Thou art the All-bountiful, the Protector, the Almighty, the Gracious!

O ye that stand fast in the Covenant! When the hour cometh that this wronged and broken winged bird will have taken its flight unto the celestial concourse, when it will have hastened to the Realm of the Unseen and its mortal frame will have been either lost or hidden neath the dust, it is incumbent upon the Afnán, that are steadfast in the Covenant of God, and have branched from the Tree of Holiness; the Hands, (pillars) of the Cause of God, (the glory of the Lord rest upon them), and all the friends and loved ones, one and all to bestir themselves and arise with heart and soul and in one accord, to diffuse the sweet savors of God, to teach His Cause and to promote His Faith. It behoveth them not to rest for a moment, neither to seek repose. They must disperse themselves in every land, pass by every clime and travel throughout all regions. Bestirred, without rest and steadfast to the end they must raise in every land the triumphal cry "O Thou the Glory of Glories!" (Yá-Bahá'u'l-Abhá), must achieve renown in the world wherever they go, must burn brightly even as a candle in every meeting and must kindle the flame of Divine love in every assembly; that the light of truth may rise resplendent in the midmost heart of the world, that throughout the East and throughout the West a vast concourse may gather under the shadow of the Word of God, that the sweet savors of holiness may be diffused, that faces may shine radiantly, hearts be filled with the Divine spirit and souls be made heavenly.

In these days, the most important of all things is the guidance of the nations and peoples of the world. Teaching the Cause is of utmost importance for it is the head corner-stone of the foundation itself. This wronged servant has spent his days and nights in promoting the Cause and urging the peoples to service. He rested not a moment, till the fame of the Cause of God was noised abroad in the world and the celestial strains from the Abhá Kingdom roused the East and the West. The beloved of God must also follow the same example. This is the secret of faithfulness, this is the requirement of servitude to the Threshold of Bahá!

The disciples of Christ forgot themselves and all earthly things, forsook all their cares and belongings, purged themselves of self and passion and with absolute detachment scattered far and wide and engaged in calling the peoples of the world to the Divine Guidance, till at last they made the world another world, illumined the surface of the earth and even to their last hour proved self-sacrificing in the pathway of that Beloved One of God. Finally in various lands they suffered glorious martyrdom. Let them that are men of action follow in their footsteps!

O my loving friends! After the passing away of this wronged one, it is incumbent upon the Aghsán (Branches), the Afnán (Twigs) of the Sacred Lote-Tree, the Hands (pillars) of the Cause of God and the loved ones of the Abhá Beauty to turn unto Shoghi Effendi—the youthful branch branched from the two hallowed and sacred Lote-Trees and the fruit grown from the union of the two offshoots of the Tree of Holiness,—as he is the sign of God, the chosen branch, the guardian of the Cause of God, he unto whom all the Aghsán, the Afnán, the Hands of the Cause of God and His loved ones must turn. He is the expounder of the words of God and after him will succeed the first-born of his lineal descendants.

The sacred and youthful branch, the guardian of the Cause of God, as well as the Universal House of Justice, to be universally elected and established, are both under the care and protection of the Abhá Beauty, under the shelter and unerring guidance of His Holiness, the Exalted One (may my life be offered up for them both). Whatsoever they decide is of God. Whoso obeyeth him not, neither obeyeth them, hath not obeyed God; whoso rebelleth against him and against them hath rebelled against God; whoso opposeth him hath opposed God; whoso contendeth with them hath contended with God; whoso disputeth with him hath disputed with God; whoso denieth him hath denied God; whoso disbelieveth in him hath disbelieved in God; whoso deviateth, separateth himself and turneth aside from him hath in truth deviated, separated himself and turned aside from God. May the wrath, the fierce indignation, the vengeance of God rest upon him! The mighty stronghold shall remain impregnable and safe through obedience to him who is the guardian of the Cause of God. It is incumbent upon the members of the House of Justice, upon all the Aghsán, the Afnán, the Hands of the Cause of God to show their obedience, submissiveness and subordination unto the guardian of the Cause of God, to turn unto him and be lowly before Him. He that opposeth him hath opposed the True One, will make a breach in the Cause of God, will subvert His word and will become a manifestation of the Center of Sedition. Beware, beware, lest the days after the ascension (of Bahá'u'lláh) be repeated when the Center of Sedition waxed haughty and rebellious and with Divine Unity for his excuse deprived himself and perturbed and poisoned others. No doubt every vainglorious one that purposeth dissension and discord will not openly declare his evil purposes, nay rather, even as impure gold, would he seize upon divers measures and various pretexts that he may separate the gathering of the people of Bahá. My object is to show that the Hands of the Cause of God must be ever watchful and so soon as they find anyone beginning to oppose and protest against the guardian of the Cause of God cast him out from the congregation of the people of Bahá and in no wise accept any excuse from him. How often hath grievous error been disguised in the garb of truth, that it might sow the seeds of doubt in the hearts of men!

O ye beloved of the Lord! It is incumbent upon the guardian of the Cause of God to appoint in his own life-time him that shall become his successor, that differences may not arise after his passing. He that is appointed must manifest in himself detachment from all worldly things, must be the essence of purity, must show in himself the fear of God, knowledge, wisdom and learning. Thus, should the first-born of the guardian of the Cause of God not manifest in himself the truth of the words:—"The child is the secret essence of its sire," that is, should he not inherit of the spiritual within him (the guardian of the Cause of God) and his glorious lineage not be matched with a goodly character, then must he (the guardian of the Cause of God), choose another branch to succeed him.

The Hands of the Cause of God must elect from their own number, nine persons that shall at all times be occupied in the important services in the work of the guardian of the Cause of God. The election of these nine must be carried either unanimously or by majority from the company of the Hands of the Cause of God and these whether unanimously or by a majority vote, must give their assent to the choice of the one whom the guardian of the Cause of God hath chosen as his successor. This assent must be given in such wise as the assenting and dissenting voices may not be distinguished.

O friends! The Hands of the Cause of God must be nominated and appointed by the guardian of the Cause of God. All must be under his shadow and obey his command. Should any, within or without the company of the Hands of the Cause of God disobey, and seek division, the wrath of God and His vengeance will be upon him, for he will have caused a breach in the true Faith of God.

The obligations of the Hands of the Cause of God are to diffuse the Divine Fragrances, to edify the souls of men, to promote learning, to improve the character of all men and to be, at all times and under all conditions, sanctified and detached from earthly things. They must manifest the fear of God by their conduct, their manners, their deeds and their words.

This body of the Hands of the Cause of God is under the direction of the guardian of the Cause of God. He must continually urge them to strive and endeavor to the utmost of their ability to diffuse the sweet savors of God, and to guide all the peoples of the world, for it is the light of Divine Guidance that causeth all the universe to be illumined. To disregard, though it be for a moment, this absolute command which is binding upon everyone, is in no wise permitted, that the existent world may become even as the Abhá Paradise, that the surface of the earth may become heavenly, that contention and conflict amidst peoples, kindreds, nations and governments may disappear, that all the dwellers on earth may become one people and one race, that the world may become even as one home. Should differences arise they shall be amicably and conclusively settled by the Supreme Tribunal, that shall include members from all the governments and peoples of the world.

O ye beloved of the Lord! In this sacred Dispensation, conflict and contention are in no wise permitted. Every aggressor deprives himself of God's grace. It is incumbent upon everyone to show the utmost love, rectitude of conduct, straightforwardness and sincere kindliness unto all the peoples and kindreds of the world, be they friends or strangers. So intense must be the spirit of love and loving-kindness, that the stranger may find himself a friend, the enemy a true brother, no difference whatsoever existing between them. For universality is of God and all limitations earthly. Thus man must strive that his reality may manifest virtues and perfections, the light whereof may shine upon everyone. The light of the sun shineth upon all the world and the merciful showers of Divine Providence fall upon all peoples. The vivifying breeze reviveth every living creature and all beings endued with life obtain their share and portion at His heavenly board. In like manner, the affections and loving-kindness of the servants of the One True God must be bountifully and universally extended to all mankind. Regarding this, restrictions and limitations are in no wise permitted.

Wherefore, O my loving friends! Consort with all the peoples, kindreds and religions of the world with the utmost truthfulness, uprightness, faithfulness, kindliness, good-will and friendliness; that all the world of being may be filled with the holy ecstasy of the grace of Bahá, that ignorance, enmity, hate and rancor may vanish from the world and the darkness of estrangement amidst the peoples and kindreds of the world may give way to the Light of Unity. Should other peoples and nations be unfaithful to you show your fidelity unto them, should they be unjust toward you show justice towards them, should they keep aloof from you attract them to yourself, should they show their enmity be friendly towards them, should they poison your lives sweeten their souls, should they inflict a wound upon you be a salve to their sores. Such are the attributes of the sincere! Such are the attributes of the truthful.

And now, concerning the House of Justice which God hath ordained as the source of all good and freed from all error, it must be elected by universal suffrage, that is, by the believers. Its members must be manifestations of the fear of God and daysprings of knowledge and understanding, must be steadfast in God's faith and the well-wishers of all mankind. By this House is meant the Universal House of Justice, that is, in all countries, a secondary House of Justice must be instituted, and these secondary Houses of Justice must elect the members of the Universal one. Unto this body all things must be referred. It enacteth all ordinances and regulations that are not to be found in the explicit Holy Text. By this body all the difficult problems are to be resolved and the guardian of the Cause of God is its sacred head and the distinguished member for life of that body. Should he not attend in person its deliberations, he must appoint one to represent him. Should any of the members commit a sin, injurious to the common weal, the guardian of the Cause of God hath at his own discretion the right to expel him, whereupon the people must elect another one in his stead. This House of Justice enacteth the laws and the government enforceth them. The legislative body must reinforce the executive, the executive must aid and assist the legislative body so that through the close union and harmony of these two forces, the foundation of fairness and justice may become firm and strong, that all the regions of the world may become even as Paradise itself.

O ye beloved of the Lord! It is incumbent upon you to be submissive to all monarchs that are just and show your fidelity to every righteous king. Serve ye the sovereigns of the world with utmost truthfulness and loyalty. Show obedience unto them and be their well-wishers. Without their leave and permission do not meddle with political affairs, for disloyalty to the just sovereign is disloyalty to God himself.

This is my counsel and the commandment of God unto you. Well is it with them that act accordingly.

O dearly beloved friends! I am now in very great danger and the hope of even an hour's life is lost to me. I am thus constrained to write these lines for the protection of the Cause of God, the preservation of His Law, the safeguarding of His Word, and the safety of His Teachings. By the Ancient Beauty! This wronged one hath in no wise borne nor doth he bear a grudge against any one; towards none doth he entertain any ill-feeling and uttereth no word save for the good of the world. My supreme obligation, however, of necessity, prompteth me to guard and preserve the Cause of God. Thus, with the greatest regret, I counsel you saying:—"Guard ye the Cause of God, protect His law and have the utmost fear of discord. This is the foundation of the belief of the people of Bahá (may my life be offered up for them). 'His Holiness, the Exalted One, (the Báb) is the Manifestation of the Unity and Oneness of God and the Forerunner of the Ancient Beauty. His Holiness the Abhá Beauty, (may my life be a sacrifice for His steadfast friends) is the Supreme Manifestation of God and the Dayspring of His Most Divine Essence. All others are servants unto Him and do His bidding.' " Unto the Most Holy Book every one must turn and all that is not expressly recorded therein must be referred to the Universal House of Justice. That which this body, whether unanimously or by a majority doth carry, that is verily the Truth and the Purpose of God himself. Whoso doth deviate therefrom is verily of them that love discord, hath shown forth malice and turned away from the Lord of the Covenant. By this House is meant that Universal House of Justice which is to be elected from all countries, that is, from those parts in the East and West where the loved ones are to be found, after the manner of the customary elections in Western countries such as those of England.

It is incumbent upon these members (of the Universal House of Justice) to gather in a certain place and deliberate upon all problems which have caused difference, questions that are obscure and matters that are not expressly recorded in the Book. Whatsoever they decide has the same effect as the Text itself. And inasmuch as this House of Justice hath power to enact laws that are not expressly recorded in the Book and bear upon daily transactions, so also it hath power to repeal the same. Thus for example, the House of Justice enacteth today a certain law and enforceth it, and a hundred years hence, circumstances having profoundly changed and the conditions having altered, another House of Justice will then have power, according to the exigencies of the time, to alter that law. This it can do because that law formeth no part of the Divine Explicit Text. The House of Justice is both the Initiator and the Abrogator of its own laws.

And now, one of the greatest and most fundamental principles of the Cause of God is to shun and avoid entirely the Covenant-breakers, for they will utterly destroy the Cause of God, exterminate His Law and render of no account all efforts exerted in the past. O friends! It behoveth you to call to mind with tenderness the trials of His Holiness, the Exalted One and show your fidelity to the Ever-Blest Beauty. The utmost endeavor must be exerted lest all these woes, trials and afflictions, all this pure and sacred blood that hath been shed so profusely in the Path of God, may prove to be in vain.

O ye beloved of the Lord! Strive with all your heart to shield the Cause of God from the onslaught of the insincere, for souls such as these cause the straight to become crooked and all benevolent efforts to produce contrary results.

O God, my God! I call Thee, Thy Prophets and Thy Messengers, Thy Saints and Thy Holy Ones, to witness that I have declared conclusively Thy Proofs unto Thy loved ones and set forth clearly all things unto them, that they may watch over Thy Faith, guard Thy Straight Path and protect Thy Resplendent Law. Thou art, verily, the All-knowing, the All-wise!

Whosoever and whatsoever meeting becometh a hindrance to the diffusion of the Light of Faith, let the loved ones give them counsel and say: "Of all the gifts of God the greatest is the gift of

Teaching. It draweth unto us the Grace of God and is our first obligation. Of such a gift how can we deprive ourselves? Nay, our lives, our goods, our comforts, our rest, we offer them all as a sacrifice for the Abhá Beauty and teach the Cause of God." Caution and prudence, however, must be observed even as recorded in the Book. The veil must in no wise be suddenly rent asunder. The Glory of Glories rest upon you.

O ye the faithful loved ones of 'Abdu'l-Bahá! It is incumbent upon you to take the greatest care of Shoghi Effendi, the twig that hath branched from and the fruit given forth by the two hallowed and Divine Lote-Trees, that no dust of despondency and sorrow may stain his radiant nature, that day by day he may wax greater in happiness, in joy and spirituality, and may grow to become even as a fruitful tree.

For he is, after 'Abdu'l-Bahá, the guardian of the Cause of God, the Afnán, the Hands (pillars) of the Cause and the beloved of the Lord must obey him and turn unto him. He that obeyeth him not, hath not obeyed God; he that turneth away from him, hath turned away from God and he that denieth him, hath denied the True One. Beware lest anyone falsely interpret these words, and like unto them that have broken the Covenant after the Day of Ascension (of Bahá'u'lláh) advance a pretext, raise the standard of revolt, wax stubborn and open wide the door of false interpretation. To none is given the right to put forth his own opinion or express his particular convictions. All must seek guidance and turn unto the Center of the Cause and the House of Justice. And he that turneth unto whatsoever else is indeed in grievous error.

The Glory of Glories rest upon you!

APPENDIX

Sources

CHAPTER ONE

Gleanings from the Writings of Bahá'u'lláh: pages 5, 9, 10, 11, 12, 17, 17, 46, 49, 49, 50, 56, 59, 60, 60, 88, 98, 99, 104, 136, 213, 210, 246, 250.
The Promised Day Is Come (citation): page 20.
Gleanings from the Writings of Bahá'u'lláh: page 232.
The Promised Day Is Come (citations): pages 28, 32, 34, 36, 40.
Gleanings from the Writings of Bahá'u'lláh: pages 254, 198.
The Promised Day Is Come (citations): pages 104, 30, 81.
Gleanings from the Writings of Bahá'u'lláh: page 323.

CHAPTER TWO

Prayers and Meditations By Bahá'u'lláh: pages 127, 48, 103, 179, 283, 284, 310, 35, 14, 281, 27, 275, 107, 197, 295.
Gleanings from the Writings of Bahá'u'lláh: pages 261, 167, 184, 64, 264, 279.

CHAPTER THREE

Gleanings from the Writings of Bahá'u'lláh: pages 200, 214, 214, 214, 319, 177, 316, 143, 149, 153, 158, 194, 294, 7, 330, 290, 340, 86, 200, 176, 337, 276, 289, 292, 285, 335, 315, 103, 342, 93, 175.
The Reality of Man: page 3.
Prayers and Meditations By Bahá'u'lláh: pages 5, 6, 8, 261, 13, 15, 21, 262, 31, 33, 42, 59, 86, 94, 119, 159, 170, 206, 220, 224, 248, 234, 259, 265.
The Hidden Words: From the Arabic, Nos. 1 to 71.

CHAPTER FOUR

Tablets of Bahá'u'lláh.

CHAPTER FIVE

Three Tablets of Bahá'u'lláh.
Gleanings from the Writings of Bahá'u'lláh: page 346.

CHAPTER SIX

Bahá'í Peace Program: page 27.
Promulgation of Universal Peace: pages 11, 22, 138, 135, 119, 171, 26, 449, 81, 18, 90, 185, 55, 83, 41, 355.
Some Answered Questions: page 313.
Bahá'í Peace Program: page 11.

CHAPTER SEVEN

Some Answered Questions: pages 209, 205, 215, 222, 227, 230, 233, 236, 243, 245, 247, 255, 259, 263, 267, 270, 272.
Tablets of 'Abdu'l-Bahá: page 581.
Bahá'í Peace Program: page 31.

CHAPTER EIGHT

Star of the West, XIV, 12.
Star of the West, XIV, 12.
Tablets of 'Abdu'l-Bahá, Vols. I, II, III, 641, 318, 502, 405.
Star of the West, XIV, 12.
Tablets of 'Abdu'l-Bahá, Vols. I, II, III, 36, 442.
National Bahá'í Archives, unpublished Tablets of 'Abdu'l-Bahá.
National Bahá'í Archives, unpublished Tablets of 'Abdu'l-Bahá.
National Bahá'í Archives, unpublished Tablets of 'Abdu'l-Bahá.
National Bahá'í Archives, unpublished Tablets of 'Abdu'l-Bahá.
Tablets of 'Abdu'l-Bahá, Vols. I, II, III, 145, 243, 73, 511, 162, 260, 263, 505.
National Bahá'í Archives, unpublished Tablets of 'Abdu'l-Bahá.
National Bahá'í Archives, unpublished Tablets of 'Abdu'l-Bahá.
Tablets of 'Abdu'l-Bahá, Vols. I, II, III, 22, 687, 328.
National Bahá'í Archives, unpublished Tablets of 'Abdu'l-Bahá.
Tablets of 'Abdu'l-Bahá, Vols. I, II, III, 19, 205, 683, 705, 706, 591, 115, 722, 337, 325, 326.
National Bahá'í Archives, unpublished Tablets of 'Abdu'l-Bahá.
National Bahá'í Archives, unpublished Tablets of 'Abdu'l-Bahá.

Tablets of 'Abdu'l-Bahá, Vols. I, II, III, 97.
National Bahá'í Archives, unpublished Tablets of 'Abdu'l-Bahá.
National Bahá'í Archives, unpublished Tablets of 'Abdu'l-Bahá.
Tablets of 'Abdu'l-Bahá, Vols. I, II, III, 587, 207, 448, 449.
National Bahá'í Archives, unpublished Tablets of 'Abdu'l-Bahá.
National Bahá'í Archives, unpublished Tablets of 'Abdu'l-Bahá.
National Bahá'í Archives, unpublished Tablets of 'Abdu'l-Bahá.
National Bahá'í Archives, unpublished Tablets of 'Abdu'l-Bahá.
Tablets of 'Abdu'l-Bahá, Vols. I, II, III, 537, 562, 178, 549, 87, 168, 459.
National Bahá'í Archives, unpublished Tablets of 'Abdu'l-Bahá.
Tablets of 'Abdu'l-Bahá, Vols. I, II, III, 390, 407.
National Bahá'í Archives, unpublished Tablets of 'Abdu'l-Bahá.
Tablets of 'Abdu'l-Bahá, Vols. I, II, III, 409, 453, 252, 316, 322, 327, 514, 622, 642, 164, 175, 94, 12, 592, 576.

CHAPTER NINE

Tablets of 'Abdu'l-Bahá, Vols. I, II, III, 535, 41.
Star of the West, VII, 5.
Tablets of 'Abdu'l-Bahá, Vols. I, II, III, 185.
National Bahá'í Archives, Unpublished Tablets of 'Abdu'l-Bahá.
Tablets of 'Abdu'l-Bahá, Vols. I, II, III, 690, 23, 1, 6.
'Abdu'l-Bahá in New York, 56.
National Bahá'í Archives, unpublished Tablets of 'Abdu'l-Bahá.
National Bahá'í Archives, unpublished Tablets of 'Abdu'l-Bahá.
National Bahá'í Archives, unpublished Tablets of 'Abdu'l-Bahá.
Tablets of 'Abdu'l-Bahá, Vols. I, II, III, 553, 508, 10.
National Bahá'í Archives, unpublished Tablets of 'Abdu'l-Bahá.
National Bahá'í Archives, unpublished Tablets of 'Abdu'l-Bahá.
National Bahá'í Archives, unpublished Tablets of 'Abdu'l-Bahá.
Tablets of 'Abdu'l-Bahá, Vols. I, II, III, 148, 14, 499.
National Bahá'í Archives, unpublished Tablets of 'Abdu'l-Bahá.
Tablets of 'Abdu'l-Bahá, Vols. I, II, III, 21, 124, 25, 435, 437, 17, 96, 626, 100.
National Bahá'í Archives, unpublished Tablets of 'Abdu'l-Bahá.
Tablets of 'Abdu'l-Bahá, Vols. I, II, III, 633.
America's Spiritual Mission, 17, 22.

Star of the West, XIII, 1.
Excerpts from the Will and Testament of 'Abdu'l-Bahá.

TRANSLATIONS

SHOGHI EFFENDI: Gleanings from the Writings of Bahá'u'lláh; The Promised Day Is Come (citations); Prayers and Meditations By Bahá'u'lláh; The Reality of Man (passage selected); The Hidden Words of Bahá'u'lláh; Bahá'í Peace Program (translation made with Dr. Zia M. Bagdadi, Mirza Lotfulláh Hakim and Dr. J. E. Esslemont); Will and Testament of 'Abdu'l-Bahá.
MIRZA ALI-KULI KHAN: Tablets of Bahá'u'lláh; Three Tablets of Bahá'u'lláh.
LAURA CLIFFORD BARNEY: Some Answered Questions.

The published and unpublished Tablets of 'Abdu'l-Bahá included in Chapters Seven, Eight and Nine were translated by many different Persian Bahá'ís. The Master's last Tablet to America was translated by Mrs. H. Emogene Hoagg, Ali Mohammed Baku, and Rouhi.

EDITOR'S NOTE

This volume has been compiled to replace the work published in 1923 under the title of "Bahá'í Scriptures," and contains later and more accurate translations, as well as Tablets and Prayers not then accessible in English.

INDEX

INDEX